Women, Gender and Religious Nationalism

Women, Gender and Religious Nationalism reflects the changing modalities of Hindu nationalist organizing and organizations among women and youth. It provides unique insights into how this immensely powerful political formation has been able to preside over a massive network of grassroots organizations among most segments of Indian society and capture national power. The chapters in this volume explore the techniques the Rashtriya Swayamsevak Sangh (RSS), the Vishva Hindu Parishad (VHP) and the Bharatiya Janata Party (BJP) employ and the messages they convey about masculinity, femininity and lesbian, gay, bisexual, transgender and queer (LGBTQ) communities, and analyse contrasting forms of women's activism in defending and opposing Hindu nationalism. This book contributes to the global literature on the gender dimensions of right-wing politics. By exploring why women advance the agenda of the Hindu right, despite its conservative views on gender and sexuality, the book makes an important intervention in feminist and women's studies scholarship.

Amrita Basu is the Domenic J. Paino 1955 Professor of Political Science, and Sexuality, Women's and Gender Studies at Amherst College, Massachusetts. She is the author of *Violent Conjunctures in Democratic India*, published with the Press in 2015.

Tanika Sarkar is former Professor of History at Jawaharlal Nehru University, New Delhi. Her recent research focuses on the rise of the Hindu right in India with a focus on its impact on women. Her recent book is *Hindu Nationalism in India* (2021).

METAMORPHOSES OF THE POLITICAL: MULTIDISCIPLINARY APPROACHES

The Series is a publishing collaboration of Cambridge University Press with The M. S. Merian–R. Tagore International Centre of Advanced Studies 'Metamorphoses of the Political' (ICAS:MP). It seeks to publish new books that both expand and de-centre current perspectives on politics and the 'political' in the contemporary world. It examines, from a wide array of disciplinary and methodological approaches, how the 'political' has been conceptualized, articulated and transformed in specific arenas of contestation during the 'long twentieth century'. Though primarily located in India and the Global South, the Series seeks to interrogate and contribute to wider debates about global processes and politics. It is in this sense that the Series is imagined as one that is regionally focused but globally engaged, providing a context for interrogations of universalized theories of self, society and politics.

Series Editors:

- Niraja Gopal Jayal, King's College, London
- Shail Mayaram, formerly at Centre for the Study of Developing Societies, Delhi
- Samita Sen, University of Cambridge, Cambridge
- Awadhendra Sharan, Centre for the Study of Developing Societies, Delhi
- Sanjay Srivastava, SOAS, University of London, UK
- Ravi Vasudevan, Centre for the Study of Developing Societies, Delhi
- Sebastian Vollmer, University of Göttingen, Germany

ICAS:MP is an Indo-German research collaboration of six Indian and German institutions funded by the German Federal Ministry of Education and Research (BMBF). It combines the benefits of an open, interdisciplinary forum for intellectual exchange with the advantages of a cutting-edge research centre. Located in New Delhi, ICAS:MP critically intervenes in global debates in the social sciences and humanities.

Other Titles in the Series:

- *The Secret Life of AnOther Indian Nationalism: Transitions from the Pax Britannica to the Pax Americana* • Shail Mayaram
- *Properties of Rent: Community, Capital and Politics in Globalising Delhi* • Sushmita Pati
- *Saffron Republic: Hindu Nationalism and State Power in India* • Edited by Thomas Blom Hansen and Srirupa Roy
- *Rule of the Commoner: DMK and Formations of the Political in Tamil Nadu, 1949–1967* • Rajan Krishna, Ravindran Sriramachandran, and V. M. S. Subagunarajan

Women, Gender and Religious Nationalism

Edited by

Amrita Basu
Tanika Sarkar

CAMBRIDGE
UNIVERSITY PRESS

University Printing House, Cambridge CB2 8BS, United Kingdom

One Liberty Plaza, 20th Floor, New York, NY 10006, USA

477 Williamstown Road, Port Melbourne, vic 3207, Australia

314 to 321, 3rd Floor, Plot No.3, Splendor Forum, Jasola District Centre, New Delhi 110025, India

103 Penang Road, #05–06/07, Visioncrest Commercial, Singapore 238467

Cambridge University Press is part of the University of Cambridge.

It furthers the University's mission by disseminating knowledge in the pursuit of education, learning and research at the highest international levels of excellence.

www.cambridge.org
Information on this title: www.cambridge.org/9781009123143

© Cambridge University Press 2022

This publication is in copyright. Subject to statutory exception and to the provisions of relevant collective licensing agreements, no reproduction of any part may take place without the written permission of Cambridge University Press.

First published 2022

Printed in India by Thomson Press India Ltd.

A catalogue record for this publication is available from the British Library

ISBN 978-1-009-12314-3 Hardback

Cambridge University Press has no responsibility for the persistence or accuracy of URLs for external or third-party internet websites referred to in this publication, and does not guarantee that any content on such websites is, or will remain, accurate or appropriate.

To the unforgettable women of Shaheen Bagh

Contents

List of Abbreviations ix

Introduction: Women of Hindu Rashtra 1
Tanika Sarkar

Part I. Changing Modalities of Hindu Nationalist Organizing 25

1. Right-Wing Women's Mobilization: Notes from Colonial Western India 27
Namrata Ravichandra Ganneri

2. Track Changes: Women and the BJP from the 1990s to the 2010s 52
Rina Verma Williams

Part II. Gendered Techniques of Mobilization: The Sangh and the Samiti 75

3. The *Shakha*, the Home and the World: Going beyond the *Shakha* and the RSS Family 77
Lalit Vachani

4. Spinning the Saffron Yarn: Lessons of Ideal Girlhood in Hindu Nationalist Storytelling 125
Aastha Tyagi

Part III. Cultivating Women's Militancy: The Vishva Hindu Parishad — 147

5. *Sanskaras*, Sexuality and Street Activism: VHP Women at Work — 149
   Manjari Katju

6. Conflicting Modes of Agency and Activism: Conversations with Hindutva Women — 169
   Anshu Saluja

Part IV. Refashioning Gender and Sexuality — 193

7. Tracing the Rise of Ascetic Masculinity in India — 195
   Arpita Chakraborty

8. Trans Contestations in an Era of Heightened Nationalism: The Saffronization of Transgender Identity — 224
   Jennifer Ung Loh

Part V. Alternative Activist Responses to the Hindu Right — 263

9. The Defence of *Aacharaam*, Femininity and Neo-*Savarna* Power in Kerala — 265
   J. Devika

10. The Revolution Will Come Wearing Bangles, *Bindi*s and *Hijab*s: Women's Activism for Inclusive Citizenship — 301
    Amrita Basu and Amna Pathan

Glossary — 337
About the Contributors — 346
Index — 349

Abbreviations

ABHM	Akhil Bharatiya Hindu Mahasabha
ABISY	Akhil Bharatiya Itihas Sankalan Yojana
ABVP	Akhil Bharatiya Vidyarthi Parishad
AIWC	All India Women's Conference
BBC	British Broadcasting Corporation
BJP	Bharatiya Janata Party
BJS	Bharatiya Jana Sangh
BSP	Bahujan Samaj Party
CAA	Citizenship Amendment Act
CBI	Central Bureau of Investigation
CPI(M)	Communist Party of India (Marxist)
FTII	Film and Television Institute of India
GOI	Government of India
HSS	Hindu Swayamsevak Sangh
ICHR	Indian Council of Historical Research
IIT	Indian Institute of Technology
IT	Information Technology
JKSC	Jammu Kashmir Study Circle
JNU	Jawaharlal Nehru University
LGB	lesbian, gay, bisexual
LGBT+	lesbian, gay, bisexual and transgender
LGBTQ	lesbian, gay, bisexual, transgender and queer
LGBTQIA+	lesbian, gay, bisexual, transgender, queer, intersex and asexual

MM	Mahila Morcha
MSJE	Ministry of Social Justice and Empowerment
M. Tech	Master of Technology
NALSA	National Legal Services Authority
NDA	National Democratic Alliance
NDTV	New Delhi Television
NGO	non-governmental organization
NPR	National Population Register
NRC	National Register of Citizens
NRI	non-resident Indian
NSS	Nair Service Society
OBC	Other Backward Classes
OTC	Officers' Training Corps
PA	personal assistant
PM	prime minister
PRO	public relations officer
PTI	Press Trust of India
RSS	Rashtriya Swayamsevak Sangh
RTW	#ReadyToWait
SC	Supreme Court
TG	transgender
UK	United Kingdom
UN	United Nations
UNDP	United Nations Development Programme
UP	Uttar Pradesh
US	United States
USA	United States of America
VHP	Vishva Hindu Parishad
VKA	Vanvasi Kalyan Ashram
WKKK	Women of the Ku Klux Klan
YMCA	Young Men's Christian Association

Introduction

Women of Hindu Rashtra*

Tanika Sarkar

I

The present collection of chapters explores an Indian political formation of critical importance from the vantage point of its gender ideology and practices, as well as with respect to the role of its women votaries in militant movements and organizations. Far too often, commentators either overlook these aspects of Hindutva politics or simply brand them as patriarchal and conservative. We, however, believe that we have to go much further than that in order to seize upon the distinctive elements of Hindutva's gender. Our larger purpose is to deepen and broaden our understanding of Hindutva as a political and cultural force of immense significance by employing a gendered prism. I will, therefore, try to explain some of the crucial aspects of Hindutva history in order to provide a general perspective to the chapters.

When we first planned the present volume in 2018, we were yet to grasp the full extent of Hindutva's intentions and power. The results of the 2019 national election have disabused us of several false hopes. It is now abundantly clear that no political or electoral alternative exists at this moment which can obstruct, or even challenge, the Bharatiya Janata Party's (BJP's)[1] triumphal progress at the national level. The party has won two successive elections,

---

* I am very grateful for suggestions from Amrita Basu and Amna Pathan on this chapter. Amrita and I are also grateful to Amna, Anwesha Rana and Srirupa Roy for all their help in producing and publishing this book.

considerably enlarging its vote and seat shares in 2019. Since then, relentless state repression has assumed massive proportions. Strangely, the world has not paid adequate attention to how rapidly its largest democracy is shifting its goalposts.

The tradition of Hindu majoritarianism, which is embedded in Islamophobia, goes back to the late nineteenth century.[2] This includes Hindu historical romances about supposedly fanatical Muslim conquerors, about heroic resistance by Hindu kings. The stories nested a strong gender ideology, too, with their highly coloured legends of mass self-immolations by Hindu queens to escape capture and dishonour at the hands of Muslim invaders. A tenacious popular imaginary sprang from this: the Muslim invades not just a kingdom but the royal Hindu female body as well. The images still resonate today, stronger than ever.

From the early twentieth century, Hindu extremists systematically expanded the stereotype to cover Indian Muslims in general. All – they said – are quintessentially invaders, no matter how many centuries the community has spent in the country. All of them plan to capture Hindu women and Indian territories, kill and consume the sacred cow, convert by force and try to demolish temples (Sarkar 2019). Indian Christians, on the other hand, are depicted as agents of western colonialism who have tricked and bribed Hindus into their fold. Both communities have faced everyday intimidation and sporadic attacks as well as spectacular violence: Muslims especially so. Several chapters in this collection refer to the violence.

Partition narratives added much fuel to the hate campaign: not only did Muslims divide the country in 1947 to create Pakistan but they also supposedly raped and abducted numerous Hindu women. Nothing, of course, is said about rapes of Muslim women, which were actually equal in number. Subsequent narratives of global Islamic terror have been put to effective use to paint Indian Muslims as hidden co-conspirators. An extremely vulnerable minority community has thus been branded as dangerous stooges of Pakistan and as global terrorists – therefore, fully deserving of Hindu majoritarian violence. Past, present and future are collapsed into a timeless image of evil and danger which justifies retrospective Hindu 'revenge': building a temple by demolishing a mosque, mob lynching on the merest suspicion of cow slaughter, mass killings and rapes of Muslim women in Gujarat in 2002, stigmatizing inter-community love and marriage as an insidious jihad.

As early as 1923, V. D. Savarkar, the ideological mastermind of the later Rashtriya Swayamsevak Sangh (RSS),[3] had defined India as a Hindu nation in its deepest cultural essence (Savarkar 1923). An authentic Indian, he said, is a person whose faith was born within the geographical territory of India. That, obviously, cancels the entitlement of Indian Muslims and Christians to the country in any real sense. Savarkar skilfully resolved the contradiction that caste divisions posed to Hindu unity. Even if hierarchies exist, he said, there has been a mixing of blood across castes over centuries, making Hindus part of a common family. The present-day Sangh and the BJP subscribe to the notion of a Hindu Rashtra, or Hindu nationhood, as against the constitutional definition of India as a multicultural nation where all faiths have equal rights.

Clearly, hate campaigns have paid rich political dividends. Left-secular critics of Hindu nationalism argue that behind the so-called Modi magic – Narendra Modi's charisma is all too evident[4] – lie networks of mutual dependence between the state and the multinational corporate power of Adanis, Ambanis and the like. But the political foundations of the BJP's electoral triumphs had actually been created and sustained by a century-old organizational and ideological apparatus of enormous range and depth.[5] The Sangh combine has formed cells within all possible social segments – women, workers, farmers, schools, temples, Hindu sects, Army, media, cultural and entertainment sectors, tribals/Adivasis, teachers and students, and so on – as also a political party with a formidable electoral machinery. While far-right forces and ideologies elsewhere in the world have also managed to garner massive popular support and commitment, none enjoys such a long history – so many grassroots outfits working among such a broad swathe of social groups and with such a huge, dedicated cadre base – nor have they enjoyed such political success as yet.

The RSS also enjoys a huge presence among the Indian diaspora in large parts of the world. Its votaries have embedded themselves in important positions among political parties in the United States and the United Kingdom, and several well-funded 'academic', religious and 'cultural' foundations relay its political messages and sociocultural values abroad. It is, truly, a global force of impressive dimensions.

Women's wings among different Sangh subsidiaries benefit greatly from these interconnected areas of work. A large number of them, for instance, are employed in RSS-run schools and various charitable organizations. The different streams flow into and strengthen one another.

There are several excellent individual studies of Hindutva women and their gender ideology. Practically all of them have been referenced by different chapters in this volume, so I will not mention them here. But with the exception of a much older volume of chapters published in 1995 (Sarkar and Butalia 1995), no other collection has so far offered histories of Hindutva women from different locations, organizations and functions. The present volume focuses on Hindutva's gender ideology, their women cadres and the modes of work that are allotted to different branches of this combine. Our intention is to probe areas of its strength, as well as to provide a critique of religious majoritarianism.

I will begin with a few observations of my own to provide a larger context for the book and then define the broad scope of the chapters. I will conclude with a small sequel.

II

We need a comparative framework to grasp the specific location of Hindu nationalist women. Early twentieth-century women's organizations focused on liberal social reformism and suffrage. The All India Women's Conference was closely associated with the massive anti-colonial upsurges that the Gandhian Congress led from the 1920s. The Communist Party of India, born in the same year as the RSS (according to one view), however, took a long time to develop a women's wing of its own, and the National Federation of Indian Women was formed only in 1954. Communist women, nonetheless, had been active in peasant and working-class struggles, famine relief as well as students' organizations since the 1940s. From the late 1930s, Dalit women and anti-caste feminists had emerged as a major force in movements that B. R. Ambedkar and E. V. Ramaswamy Naicker led in western and southern India. They proposed radical gender reforms as well.

The RSS resolutely stayed away from these emancipatory alternatives. But it did allow – albeit with initial reluctance – women from their families to form an organization of their own. The Rashtra Sevika Samiti was born out of the insistent demands of Lakshmibai Kelkar in 1936, and several chapters here discuss that. For a long time, Samitis were concentrated among urban, high-caste, middle-class women from conservative families. They ran daily *shakha*s, or sessions, for physical and ideological training, patterned on the lines of RSS *shakha*s.

That, however, hardly made the women separate but equals of male activists. The RSS – the apex body for the entire Sangh family – still adamantly remains a male preserve. As a consequence, their women – however active and strong a force, especially in the BJP – rarely attain positions of real authority within the complex. The Samiti, moreover, maintains a rather low profile in the public domain, although women do play a prominent vigilante role in other wings. The present BJP-led national-level government, for instance, has reserved the position of finance minister for a woman. Women have also actively participated in anti-minority violence.

Scholars, reflecting on Hindutva women, have noted their relative marginalization within the larger organizational apparatus. They have also focused on their gender conservatism. Hindutva women maintain that the primary role of women must be that of a homemaker. Domestic peace depends on them; hence, domestic abuse can only result from their own failings. Divorce is reprehensible, and so is feminism of all stripes: these are corrupting western cultural values which have no place in India. While they eloquently castigate 'triple *talaaq*'[6] and polygamy among Indian Muslims, they have nothing to say about Hindu patriarchal constraints or about gender inequality in general. When M. S. Golwalkar, the second RSS supremo and the organizational and ideological leader par excellence, addressed women of RSS families, he put it as a 'Call to Motherhood' (Golwalkar 1966). He entirely ignored the Samiti. Several chapters in this collection show how domestic conservatism is affirmed and retained even by the RSS' full-time women activists.

Since the RSS has never engaged with gender reform, it is difficult to see why women chose to be a part of their movement when there were so many gender-sensitive alternatives around them. Similar puzzles have been raised about the fundamentalist appeal of the religious right for many American women, and about Nazi women, who jettisoned their political rights to join a movement which relegated them to the nursery and the kitchen (Capps 1990; Koonz 1987). The question is raised in different forms in some of the chapters.

Even though he took women's domestication for granted, what Golwalkar did with the domestic is, nonetheless, rather interesting. 'Call to Motherhood' was a part of a larger set of eminently practical instructions for other Sangh constituencies: youth, teachers, students, volunteers. Written at a time when the Sangh's electoral wing was quite a minor actor, the book sought to promote 'man making': a patient, everyday molecular advance, directed at moulding individuals, families, neighbourhoods and localities, as well as national politics. The collection underlines the enormous importance of the small scale and the local in Hindutva politics.

Golwalkar suggested multiple strategies to transform the local, beginning with the domestic. Interestingly, he did not define the conjugal relationship at all – perhaps because he did not need to. Conservative Hindu families already had an elaborate recipe for the wife's obedience, deference and submission to the husband. It was the conventional duties of mothering that he sought to transform. He used parables, humorous and warm anecdotes from his own childhood and mythological references to drive home the lessons.

He detached mothering from nurture, which played very little part in his discourse. He insisted on two imperatives. The mother must never allow the child to fall prey to western dress habits, cultural modes or values. Instead, his attire and beliefs must be sternly *swadeshi* and emphatically Hindu: based on a polytheistic, Brahmanical ritualist variant of Hinduism. The child must never question any part of it or admire a different faith or culture – nor even know about them. The mother has to set up an example: as totally self-abnegating, unquestioning and conforming to Hindu orthodox beliefs and practices.

Above all, the mother must implant aggressive, warlike desires in the child from his infancy and teach him absolute hatred for Hindutva's adversaries as defined by the Sangh. She should not protect the child from danger but train him to confront it. His valour, rather than his life and security, must be her dominant concern. The nation, too, is defined through its enemies: it is a death-seeking, death-dealing nation; welfare and social justice are not its concerns.

Significantly, there are no separate instructions about how to bring up a daughter. Clearly, women are pre-eminently instruments for the production and reproduction of Hindu sons. But the outstanding part of the message goes beyond motherhood. Golwalkar assumed that women, by and large, would be homebound, or even if they were employed outside, the household would remain their overriding concern. He, therefore, taught women how to work from within their domestic space and, yet, to draw the world into it. A few chapters in this volume reveal how Hindutva women manipulate social barriers to recast Brahmanical purity–pollution norms and mobilize a wider social segment.

Women, said Golwalkar, should cultivate empathy for the poor and the disadvantaged and actively seek them out in their neighbourhood. Each woman must bring home at least a few illiterate children and educate them. If her domestic maid brings her baby to the workplace, and if the child wails as she works, the mistress should let the maid tend to the child's needs immediately.

She should educate disadvantaged children with songs, games and stories. Literacy is important, but, at the same time, she should impart a strong sense of Sangh-defined nationalism and proper Hindu disposition or *sanskara*s. As she entertains and educates, she must teach communalized nationalism to the subaltern child. She should help poor women neighbours in the same way: teach them, assist them materially and also make them religious and nationalist with maps and historical lessons, *à la* Sangh ideas. The home, thus, becomes a school in a doubled sense. It brings literacy and a smattering of education; it also teaches Sangh values.

In other sections of the book, Golwalkar teaches students and youth how to bend caste barriers: without, however, ever questioning caste as a system, far less seeking to overthrow it. They must always make it a point to touch the untouchable, he says, and they must bring them home for domestic festivities, dine with them and make them feel that they are a part of the family. These, obviously, require the woman's cooperation. That many RSS households did follow his message becomes clear from the autobiography of a one-time Dalit, or untouchable-caste, recruit. Bhanwar Meghwanshi found warm hospitality and respect in many RSS families. They helped to educate him and provide him with hostel space; they gave him advantages of many sorts, not the least of which was the affection that he received in RSS families. He left the Sangh when he – entirely accidentally – discovered that even though they often brought him home for meals, they had secretly thrown away the food that his mother had cooked for them (Meghwanshi 2019). Golwalkar did not ask upper-caste RSS families to forget purity–pollution taboos, but he taught them how to conceal these. The intention was to give a human face to caste hierarchy.

It was a singularly effective recipe. It gave wives and mothers a political purpose and identity. It envisaged a novel mode of ideological and political mobilization of subalterns, within the domestic space, by domesticated women: rendering housewives full-time activists, so to speak. Ironically, except for Gandhian *ashram*s – and contemporary feminists – no other political organization had, perhaps, visualized such detailed and comprehensive modes of reconfiguring the domestic. Communal nationalism began at home.

The Samiti, calibrated by full-time celibate *pracharika*s, or teachers, on the other hand, taught homebound women how to insert Sangh messages into kin groups, workplaces, neighbourhoods and casual everyday conversations. It also created an order of female ascetics – *pracharika*s and *sadhvi*s, or religious leaders – which was politicized and this-worldly.

Much has been said about the marginalization of women in Hindutva politics. However, if we look at women in other political parties, we find that it is not unique to the BJP alone. Except for the occasional women chief ministers in West Bengal, Uttar Pradesh, Tamil Nadu and Delhi, women have not been too visible in the upper echelons of other parties – nor do they hold many important legislative or ministerial positions. Both Indira Gandhi and Sonia Gandhi owed their authority to their family status: at least for their initial launch. In fact, the BJP has displayed quite a few prominent women in leading party positions and in governance in contrast to the left parties (Basu 1992, 2015).[7] By the 1980s, the Vishva Hindu Parishad (VHP), too, considerably enlarged and militarized roles of women in their organizations. Uma Bharati and Sadhvi Rithambhara emerged as national figures, promoting a plethora of violent hate campaigns.

Introduction

III

Several chapters in this volume reveal their modes of functioning: some analyse their discourses, some look at historical lineages and change and some others probe their gender-related policy decisions. Two chapters look at two very different faces of women's resistance in contemporary times. Chapter 9 by J. Devika is about a women's movement which supported discriminatory religious laws. Chapter 10, by Amrita Basu and Amna Pathan, represents, in contrast, the 'Other' of religious majoritarianism: Muslim women's protests in Delhi against a highly discriminatory Citizenship Law which grants Indian citizenship only to non-Muslims who are persecuted in Muslim-majority countries.

The chapters cover nearly a hundred years of history, from the 1930s when the Samiti was founded to the present, when the BJP has grasped practically untrammelled power. In Chapter 3, Lalit Vachani begins with the 1990s – when Hindutva first burst upon the Indian political scene as a mass movement of enormous strength and violence. His chapter has a broad sweep. He looks at how RSS *shakha*s make men out of their boys,[8] but he also goes into their homes. He begins with a children's *shakha* in a brahman-dominated neighbourhood in Nagpur in Maharashtra. Indoctrination of children, he shows, proceeds largely through the pleasure motif: daily routine and ritual practices are accompanied with games, storytelling, physical exercises and socialization networks that *shakha* boys develop among themselves. Aastha Tyagi picks up on this theme later in the context of training sessions for young girls.

Vachani then follows the boys into the world outside where they apply the techniques of mobilization they have learnt in the *shakha*. He looks at how volunteers manage their relationship with the mass media and how they try to reorient people's everyday habits: above all, how they nudge everyday inter-community relations in conflictual directions. He focuses closely on the strategies they adopt for reaching out to different social milieus. He then returns them to their home environment, where brahmanical norms are modified according to the requirements of militant Hinduism. To understand women's roles and functions in the RSS family, he explores how domestic and ideological stability is maintained by both husband and wife, and how occasional points of domestic conflict are resolved. He presents a wide and intricately interwoven canvas by bringing RSS masculinity and femininity norms together.

Namrata Ravichandra Ganneri, in Chapter 1, brings historical depth to the volume as she contrasts the divergent fortunes of Hindu Mahasabha and RSS women in the colonial period. She studies the gender perspectives of both organizations and their women's fronts through the prism of two leaders: Janakibai Joshi of Mahila Mahasabha, attached to the Hindu Mahasabha,[9] and Lakshmibai Kelkar, founder of the Samiti. She probes the points of dissonance which women's organizations stir up within the parent organizations. Lakshmibai persisted in her efforts despite several refusals from the RSS, and Janakibai had to fight hard for permission to fight assembly elections on a Mahasabha ticket.

The Mahila Mahasabha, despite its initial promise, weakened when Janakibai failed to make a mark in electoral politics. Given the exclusively electoral concerns of the Mahasabha, she carried no further importance for the party. The Samiti, on the other hand, did not enter the electoral arena at all. It maintained a steady presence in the social domain and expanded in formal and informal ways over almost eighty-odd years. The chapter recreates an almost forgotten history of women's organizations. The comparative framework illuminates hidden aspects of both.

As Ganneri shows, both the Samiti and the Mahila Mahasabha put enormous emphasis on female physical fitness and combat skills. Janakibai emphasized the need for women's self-defence training against the perceived threat posed by Muslim men. But Kelkar thought women should learn to protect themselves because men cannot do so. Ganneri suggests that Hindutva women's militarism was at first somewhat different from the agenda of their male counterparts. The RSS and the Mahasabha thought that Hindu men needed physical training to protect female honour. The Samiti and the Mahila Mahasabha, on the other hand, encouraged women to defend themselves.

In Chapter 4, Aastha Tyagi looks at the Samiti's *shakha* sessions, closely focusing on the strategy of storytelling for very young girls. The tales are from mythicized histories: they naturalize interfaith hatred, they justify caste and gender hierarchies and they provide a strong sense of an exclusivist and authoritarian Hindutva nation. But the politics of the adult world reaches children through the mediation of stories – and who does not love to listen to stories if they are cleverly crafted?

Stories incorporate child listeners into the Hindutva worldview very effectively since we suspend our critical faculties to imbibe pleasure from them. The act of listening also releases certain reflex responses in the listener which are strengthened by repetition: Hindu excellence versus Muslim and Christian perfidy and cruelty, the nation as imagined by Hindutva, the greatness of the Samiti and of its founder.

For the child listener, the reflexes are planted early and watered regularly – to the point when stories transform into personal memories and desires. Thus begins the process of her interpellation into Hindutva. But Tyagi also usefully identifies a few points of dissonance in the listener: whether they will mature into a rejection of Sangh values later is, of course, uncertain and will depend on other influences at home, at school and of the peer group.

Hindutva's electoral front, as Rina Verma Williams shows in Chapter 2, began only after Independence – when a democratic polity based on universal franchise and a Constitution whose directive principles were inimical to Hindutva's deepest convictions made electoral contests a necessity: otherwise a state based on secular–democratic principles threatened to make the project of Hindu nationalism quite redundant. Williams compares the role of BJP women in two critical temporal phases: during the BJP's emergence in the 1980s–1990s, when it became a formidable political party for the first time, and around the time of the 2014 election, when the party achieved a return to power, after the defeat of the first BJP-dominated coalition in 2004. She finds that the party shifted from drawing women into a street-based mass movement in the 1980s–1990s to incorporating them into the formal business of electoral politics and governance – a sort of routinization of charisma. Early women party leaders used to be largely ascetic figures or widows who were detached from family responsibilities. At the later phase, many more had entered multiple levels of party politics. BJP women had also formed their own organization – the Mahila Morcha. It trained a number of housewives who learnt to balance family responsibilities and political work.

Williams describes the strident militaristic asceticism of the Hindutva woman whose sacred aura was deftly utilized by the BJP to mobilize women in the 1980s and the 1990s. On one hand, their celibacy and renunciation enhanced their holiness, making their words compelling even for lay women. On the other hand, their campaigns for communal violence naturalized the aggression of ordinary BJP women. Women's presence, therefore, hardens, rather than softens, Hindutva politics.

Turning to the highly neglected domain of the BJP's policymaking in spheres of gender and sexuality in Chapter 8, Jennifer Ung Loh asks a difficult question. A lot of feminists have argued that orthodox Hindutva cannot offer any place or role to socially stigmatized people: hence, they can have no traction on their loyalty. She, however, reveals a disturbing truth. Of all the political organizations, it is Hindutva which has struck roots among sections of Hindu transgender people – and that, too, without any overt or noticeable rethinking of questions of sexuality on its part. What, then, motivated sections of the Hindu transgender community to ally with them? She tracks and analyses the national discourses on 'transgender' identity: the Supreme Court judgment, the *National Legal Services Authority (NALSA)*[10] *v. Union of India and Others* (2014) case, and subsequent parliamentary bills from 2014 to 2019.

It fell to the BJP-led National Democratic Alliance government to implement the NALSA judgment recommendations, although they were initiated in 2012, before the BJP came to power. But the subsequent Lok Sabha definition in 2016 watered down transgender self-determination and made sexual self-identification dependent on medical and bureaucratic procedure. Rejecting the more precise western classificatory terms, the groups were, moreover, absorbed within the Hindu fold as *hijra*s, who have traditionally played an accepted role in Hindu religious ceremonies. In 2016, too, the Sangh combine, displaying considerable flexibility, partly softened its earlier hard stance towards homosexuality. General Secretary Dattatreya Hosabole described the new approach as 'no criminalization, no glorification'. It however stopped short of legalizing gay marriages.

Even though the BJP diluted the possibilities of NALSA, it has managed to saffronize several trans-groups: the Kinnar Akhada, for instance, supported the Ram Temple project at Ayodhya, which culminated in the destruction of a sixteenth-century mosque and enormous violence against Muslims in different parts of the country. It has divided the queer communities politically, as well as along religious and sexual orientations. Transgender people are now more privileged than lesbian, gay, bisexual (LGB) ones, trans-women are better protected than trans-men and Hindu trans-people, obviously, have more rights than Muslim counterparts. On the anvil of pinkwashing – aligning queer people with otherwise oppressive agendas – and what Williams calls 'homonationalism', a queer Hindu nationalism has been born.

Moving away from electoral politics to female militancy, in Chapter 5, Manjari Katju describes the Durga Vahini and the Mahila Vibhag of the VHP – the most confrontational organizations among Hindutva women. The first trains young girls, and the second reaches out to mature women. Katju looks at two moments in their history – the 1990s, when these wings were founded, and the 2010s, when they had attained a large degree of success. She delineates the chief forms of their activities, then and now. In a way, they replicate the Samiti: they teach their women religious norms or *sanskara*s, which women then convey to their children. They also train them in a specific set of bodily dispositions and attitudes towards marriage, household, mothering and sexuality. Above all, they explain to their cadres why it is crucial to hate religious minorities and how best to disseminate that hatred among acquaintances. So, they create a 'new woman' and a new female mission. Thus trained, however, cadres launch themselves into larger social and public circles to bend others to their ways. Their women learn to balance two roles: to be good Hindutva homemakers, mothers and wives and to work as street-level militants.

Katju's chapter describes the VHP's shift to what she terms 'locally oriented and service activism': community and neighbourhood mobilization through constructive activities as well as through the pedagogy of hatred. Alongside intensive mobilization at local levels, they also spill out onto the streets in hate campaigns against the so-called love jihad. Vigilantism is a critical function, and they also monitor and obstruct public expressions of mutual affection or romance with anti-Romeo squads. Love – unless conjugal and blessed by parents – is anathema to Hindutva.

In Chapter 6, Anshu Saluja's case studies of VHP women in the city of Bhopal in Madhya Pradesh put flesh and blood onto the broad outline that Katju has delineated. A city ruled by progressive Muslim native rulers during the colonial era – and several rulers were highly enterprising women – it resisted communal violence even during the communal holocaust of 1946–1947. As Saluja shows, relentless efforts to suffuse intercommunity relationships with hatred bore fruit in the 1990s – with considerable help from VHP women. Violence ghettoized Muslims, already marginalized after Partition, into shrinking living spaces.

Saluja narrates two intensive encounters: one with R. S., a senior functionary, and the other with K. D., a young Durga Vahini office-bearer. The first is a mature, seasoned activist, the second is a young storm trooper rising fast within the local VHP women's unit. Both described their politics as social work: building local contacts through some degree of necessary service provision, organizing informal group activities like the *milan kendra*s after they had consolidated themselves, conducting Hindu ritual ceremonies and festivals to draw non-VHP women into their circles and then inserting communal messages into religious discourse. They try to overcome caste barriers by a symbolic violation of caste–commensality rules on certain ritual occasions, but they do not question caste. However, as we saw earlier, these occasions of shared dining provide a safe environment for propaganda among low castes. Gossip, rumours and disinformation are lifted from diverse spatial and temporal frames to craft a smooth narrative about lustful Muslims. They simultaneously police intercommunity marriages, obstruct Christian missionary initiatives and ensure that their campaigns are favourably reported in the local media. Above all, the Durga Vahini imparts ideological and combat training sessions for young girls – which, accompanied with a carefully constructed threat perception about Muslims, easily instils a will to violence.

The sessions allow them a tentative escape route from their stiflingly orthodox domestic environment. Saluja very skilfully brings out how an insidious process of transference is at work here. The young women displace their rage against their conservative social milieu into feelings of visceral hatred against Muslims: the first emotion being socially unacceptable and the second being socially valued. Helpless in their own families, Saluja shows how their combat training provides a strong and rare sense of empowerment. They worship weapons in various forms.

Coming to the Modi moment, in Chapter 7, Arpita Chakraborty traces some of the past lineages of the particular gender performance that leading

Hindutva figures enact today. She argues that while ascetic masculinity has long been a valued practice in India, there have also been shifts. Ascetic masculinity, she says, is a brahmanical ideal based on caste hierarchy: she also calls it violent masculinity, probably referring to both the overt violence that Hindutva endorses and the quiet structural violence of caste.

She explores how such masculinity operated. She begins with Vivekananda – a late nineteenth-century Hindu missionary and renowned saint, who founded educational–philanthropic projects under Ramakrishna Missions, which now have a global presence. She moves on to Gandhi, Golwalkar and thence Modi. All practised celibacy and renounced their worldly ties; all brought the moral aura derived from renunciation into cultural, social and electoral politics. None wanted the overthrow of caste – though, arguably, Vivekananda did describe its inequities and Gandhi eventually rejected it. Of course, not all were advocates of violent masculinity. Gandhi was an apostle of non-violence and Vivekanada's Hindu vision was based on transcendentalist philosophies and a form of supremacism which had no truck with communalism. They reconfigured ideal types of masculinity in different ways. Vivekananda focused on physically strengthening the Hindu male body and on filling the Hindu male mind with a moral and social purpose. His own persona offered a vigorous masculinity, while Golwalkar wore a more recognizably ascetic look. Gandhi, in Chakraborty's view, softened and modified masculinity in an androgynous direction while retaining the emphasis on celibacy.

Modi had been an RSS *pracharak* for a very long time before he moved into the BJP's electoral politics. He still practises celibacy. Chakraborty dwells on several other Hindutva figures with similar political missions. Yogi Adityanath – a monk belonging to a Hindu sect – is the current chief minister of Uttar Pradesh: in a radical break with all religious and democratic conventions and in a modified version of theocracy.

Chakraborty also reflects on how Modi displays his masculinity in front of different audiences. Though he asserts his masculine strength with yoga feats and boasts of his 56-inch chest, Chakraborty says that his present colourful and lavish sartorial makeover introduces a feminine note, pulling the erstwhile hard 'iron man' image towards elements of androgyny. We may, perhaps, also call it regal manhood. The presumed break with the older and austere self, Chakraborty says, was important for a more acceptable global image. Extremely sensitive to his global reception, Modi is now also softening his self-presentation in other ways to disavow Hindutva's closeness with Gandhi's assassin Godse.

Chapters 9 and 10 in the volume look at widely divergent forms of women's self-created resistance. J. Devika's study of the Sabarimala pilgrimage controversies between 2016 and 2019 in Kerala poses the troubling question of whether the concept of women's resistance is always and necessarily liberating. Rules at Sabarimala bar the entry of women of menstruating age from the temple and from the presence of Lord Ayyappan, the chief deity. When a Supreme Court judgment cited constitutional provisions of gender equality to annul this condition, a large number of women – educated, professional, with strong global connections, and extremely fluent in social media networking – built up an autonomous movement to uphold the discriminatory rule that keeps them out of the sight of their beloved deity. They ferociously attacked women who now tried to enter the temple as well as feminists who condemn the Hindu menstrual taboo. The campaign was called #ReadyToWait. The name said that they were ready to renounce the privilege of *darshan*, or the sighting of the deity, and wait till their menstruation stopped. They would deny themselves of religious gratification in the cause of Kerala temple rules. This signified their acceptance of purity–pollution taboos that stigmatize women's bodily functions. It also revealed their unquestioning submission to temple regulations made by men, in denial of gender equality.

The project was supported by Hindutva women, but there were also points of contradictions between the two. At the same time, it also signified their ability to form a mass movement, their stance on behalf of a particular definition of the distinctiveness of regional religious culture and ritual regime (*aachaaram*) of Kerala. Devika looks at the different reformulations in the regional religious–ritual tradition from the nineteenth century. She also looks at the formation of a 'neo-*savarna* (upper caste)' constituency of worshippers to which these women devotees belong and which modified earlier brahmanical domination to incorporate categories of dominant menial-caste Sudras within the community.

Devika confronts difficult questions about women's agency and autonomy. #RTW was, definitely, a startling example of women's self-mobilization, physical as well as virtual, at regional, national and global levels that cut across castes and cultural contexts and which deftly used cutting-edge technology to agitate. She uses the concept of an 'intimate digital public' to describe modes of mobilization and agitation. Some were quick to point out their cultural differences from Hindutva: RTW women extolled Hindu pluralism and proudly claimed the designation of paganism. Malayali Hinduism, they argued, cherished the feminine 'principle'. At the same time, in a communal vein, they compared Hindutva nationalism with monolithic Abrahamic religions, and they fiercely denounced feminism. Finally, as she follows the complicated, multiplex legal, judicial and political trajectories of their campaign, Devika concludes that rather than exclusively focusing on the subordination of women by a male brahmanical elite, we need to probe the relations between women from a larger circle of privileged castes and oppressed lower-caste women.

In a completely different vein, in Chapter 10, Amrita Basu and Amna Pathan have studied an iconic protest movement among Muslim women from Shaheen Bagh in Delhi which, for some time, had captured the attention of the world. The Modi government enacted the highly controversial Citizenship Amendment Act (CAA) in 2019. The law offered Indian citizenship rights to non-Muslims from Pakistan, Bangladesh and Afghanistan on the ground that these are persecuted minorities. Strangely, it excluded Tamil Hindus of Sri Lanka – the Sri Lankan government being close to the BJP – or Pakistani Ahmadiyyas and Rohingyas of Burma. And who can be more persecuted than these communities? In effect, for the first time in our history, citizenship is being classified and granted on religious lines.

CAA will soon be coupled with the draconian National Citizenship Register and the National Population Register to decide on citizenship entitlements according to communal and discriminatory criteria – in a manner also calculated to ensure the exclusion of the minorities and the poor who lack the reams of required documentary evidence. The chapter critically reviews the implications of these provisions.

Shaheen Bagh emerged as a response to the crisis. Basu and Pathan situate the response against a long history of Muslim predicaments in post-Partition India. Ironically, Muslims who chose to stay on in this country instead of migrating to Pakistan – befuddling the religious logic of Partition – have had to pay a huge cost for their patriotism. The chapter goes back especially to the Partition violence against women's bodies, compounded – in the case of Muslim women – by an increasing marginalization and ghettoization of Muslim existence in India.

Most Indian cities and small towns met the catastrophic law and bills with tumultuous protest rallies. They seemed unstoppable until brutal repression and the eruption of the Covid-19 pandemic eventually put a stop to them. What captivated public attention most of all was the non-stop Shaheen Bagh sit-in by local Muslim women, young and old, round the clock, in the most bitter of Delhi winters, in the face of repeated official orders to vacate the roads and despite occasional mob attacks. Beginning on 14 December 2019, the peaceful *dharna* stood resolute for 101 days. The pattern was followed by many such sit-ins by women in other Indian cities and Shaheen Bagh became something like a pilgrimage destination for secular citizens.

As Basu and Pathan describe, in the face of a desperate future, Shaheen Bagh women understood what the country and, especially, the Constitution of India actually meant to them. They discussed constitutional and legal issues at the *dharna*, they met support groups from all over the country, they made forceful and informed speeches, they sang patriotic songs and hymns from all faiths and they chanted strident slogans. They engaged in spirited dialogues with all who came to offer solidarity. There could not have been a more effective dismantling of the stereotype of the *burqa*-clad pathetic and primitive Muslim woman that Islamophobes project across the world. Basu and Pathan evoke their words and voices repeatedly as they cite from their extensive interviews with Shaheen Bagh women.

Shaheen Bagh nested a revolution within a revolution: as Muslims united with secular forces to confront the state, their women assumed the role of community guardians for the first time: as mothers and grannies they became the face of the movement. They abandoned household duties, and men from their families and neighbourhood cooked and fed them in an instantaneous inversion of entrenched gender roles. Basu and Pathan compare Shaheen Bagh with women's movements for peace and justice elsewhere in the world, especially with Argentina where mothers had sat at the Plaza, demanding information about their sons, disappeared by state repression. Basu and Pathan underline the individuated, frankly emotional, experience-based maternalism of this gendered politics. They contrast it with what they see as the masculinized Sangh politics of exclusion and aggression.

IV

Some of the chapters speak to one another in interesting ways – those on masculinity, sexuality and femininity, for instance, or those probing VHP militancy. But some also stand alone when they discuss a specific characteristic within the broad context where Hindutva operates: the chapters on Sabarimala and Shaheen Bagh, for instance. We deliberately attempted to provide a sense of diversity as well as commonality among Hindutva women and their gender agenda.

Together, the chapters give us a clear sense of how Hindutva has unified the family, the local, the national and the global in a single circuit, and how women and gender play a decisive ideological and activist role that can be simultaneously informal and homebound as well as public and aggressive. Several chapters have referred to the rhetoric of 'love jihad' and violent efforts to prohibit interfaith marriages, especially by VHP womens' vigilante groups. Unfortunately, the author who had promised to provide a chapter on the 'love jihad' movement of Hindutva was prevented from doing so by other pressing commitments. So let me add a few points on that issue briefly.

'Love jihad' campaigns draw some of their strength from the traditional Hindu insistence on endogamous marriages where consent is not really necessary from either partner. The convention puts marriage partners under the decisions of their parents, and it also blocks love between castes or communities. From its inception, the VHP had worked to ensure that such love marriages do not happen. They have watched registration courts to identify interfaith couples, they have informed their families and they have terrorized the couples with a systematic dissemination of fake news of abduction or rape by Muslim men of Hindu women and about forced conversions to Islam. This had led to court cases where, more often than not, the woman managed to extricate the man from such charges. There has also been much violence directed against such couples. Anshu Saluja has described the campaigns in her chapter. They depict all Muslim men as potential abductors or seducers who are trained to attract, marry, oppress and force helpless Hindu women to convert to Islam. Thereby, they multiply their population to overtake the Hindu numerical majority in the future. The campaigns restrict the freedom to love and to make adult decisions that may oppose familial controls as well as the freedom to convert to another faith.

The BJP has now put the stamp of official sanction on such endeavours. The Uttar Pradesh Prohibition of Unlawful Conversion of Religion Ordinance, 2020, will no doubt attain a permanent legal shape in all BJP-ruled states sooner or later: Madhya Pradesh and Karnataka are already keen to emulate it. There is a very real possibility that it may become the national template for regulating and punishing interfaith marriages and conversions in the near future.

According to the Ordinance, if a person wants to convert in order to marry someone outside their community, then the couple will have to apply for permission at the magistrate's court. Marriage is, thereby, taken away from the free will and love of adults and placed in the hands of a bureaucrat. Given the toxicity of the 'love jihad' campaigns which translates the love of a Muslim man as jihad, the magistrate may well be hostile to applications from a Hindu woman for marrying a non-Hindu: Hindutva outfits have already branded Hindu–Muslim marriages as political conspiracies to expand Muslim populations at the cost of Hindu numbers. Moreover, it will not be the would-be wife's words or consent that will matter but those of her parents'. Even an outsider can now raise objections to such a marriage at the magistrate's court. The burden of proof rests on the defendant, in disregard of basic legal norms.

On the other hand, for non-Hindus coming into the Hindu fold, conversion rules will not apply. Those cases are to be considered as 'homecoming', rather than conversion: a return to their authentic roots. Hinduism becomes the default religion for all Indians.

Civil marriages have so far been exempted from the scope of the Ordinance, but the prolonged notice that the couple is obliged to wait out before they can register their marriage already provides ample opportunity to obstructive parents to drag their daughter back and allege coercion, abduction or enticement on the part of her lover from another community. As soon as the Ordinance was enacted, the UP police swung into rapid action mode.

Within days, it had arrested several Muslim men accused of converting and marrying Hindu women. It even arrested couples who married before the Ordinance was passed, and it disregarded the consent of the wife and even that of the families. Expectedly, it did not interfere in a case where a Muslim women converted to marry a Hindu man and her family objected (Rehman 2020; Sahu 2020). In that case, the Hindu community gained a new member, along with her womb which will now bear Hindu progeny.

The Ordinance draws two most intimate and meaningful parts of human life together: love and faith. Through a state that it dominates, Hindutva now takes full charge of who can love and marry whom and who can hold which faith. Or rather, it decides who cannot do what. The Ordinance segregates religious communities as if they are from different species. Long-standing social pressures, on the other hand, keep inter-caste marriages at bay.

The new regulations – added to the reign of caste endogamy and the social opprobrium strongly associated with love marriages which strain against parental objections – effectively close down circuits of intimacy across communities of caste and religion. Reminiscent of apartheid racism in some sense, they recall an older historical precedent: the Nuremberg Laws that Germany had enacted in 1935. They had two main provisions. One was the Law for the Protection of German Blood and Honour which prohibited love and marriage between Jews and 'pure'-blooded Germans. To prevent extramarital relationships, no Jewish women under forty-five was even allowed to work in a German household. The second was the Reich Citizenship Law which restricted citizenship to people of German blood alone. Non-German minorities were designated as non-citizens, with no rights or claims in the Reich.

In the case of Indian marriage and citizenship, the distinction is not racial or blood-based but a religious one. The direction, however, is rather similar. Incidentally, this was the Nazi model that Golwalkar had warmly applauded in 1939 as one ideally suited for the minorities in India (Golwalkar 1945).

The pledge with which the Sangh had begun its career is now almost entirely redeemed. As the chapters in the volume show, women have played a significant role in the process, with a fully developed aggressive personality and a genuine commitment to majoritarian religious nationalism. This should caution us against our very understandable feminist tendency to always cast women as victims of patriarchy or as agents of emancipatory change. Profoundly disturbing though it is, we must reckon with the real presence of a female will to violence, a female right-wing commitment – even as we continue to evoke and celebrate its 'Other' in Shaheen Bagh women and in numerous Hindu, Muslim, Christian, Sikh and atheist women who stood with them.

Notes

1. The BJP is the electoral constituent of the Sangh combine. It has won two successive elections in 2014 and 2019.
2. Since the nineteenth century, colonial rulers as well as Indians have used the term 'communalism' when they referred to ethnic hatred and conflicts; though we are mindful of the limitations of this term, we sometimes use it because it is so widely employed.
3. The RSS was founded in 1925 to train Hindu upper-caste and middle-class young boys on a daily basis in combat techniques and in Hindutva ideology. Since then, it has developed a very large number of daily branches all over the country and numerous grassroots organizations. The lynchpin of Hindutva's organizational complex, it has founded its many affiliates and it trains the leaders of most of the mass fronts. Prime minister Modi is a member of the Sangh and had been a full-time activist until he became the chief minister of Gujarat
4. Narendra Modi gained in popular votes – an important segment coming from women – in the 2019 election despite a sorry record of economic decline and catastrophic policies like demonetization in his previous stint as prime minister.
5. The RSS – the parent organization – has also spawned about thirty-eight direct affiliates: the religious wing (Vishva Hindu Parishad) and the electoral wing (Bharatiya Janata Party) being the best-known.
6. A peculiar and abusive custom of oral, even posted, *talaq*s, uttered by the husband, which were held as legally valid only for Indian Muslims. Pakistan and many other Muslim-majority countries do not allow that.

In 2017, the Modi government criminalized such divorces instead of de-legalizing them.
7. If we read two works on BJP and left women concurrently, we may draw interesting contrasts and comparisons.
8. Those who are interested in pursuing notions of masculinity in these organizations may read Chandrima Chakraborty's excellent work: *Masculinity, Asceticism, Hinduism: Past and Present Imaginings of India*, Ranikhet: Permanent Black, 2011.
9. Like the RSS, the Hindu Mahasabha subscribed to the notion of Hindu nationalism, but, unlike the RSS, it was entirely an electoral party. Founded in 1915, it fought elections from 1919. Its fortunes waned after Nathuram Godse, one of its members, assassinated Gandhi in 1948.
10. The NALSA provisions allowed a measure of sexual self-identification by non-heteronormative individuals.

Bibliography

Basu, A. (1992). *Two Faces of Protest: Contrasting Modes of Women's Activism in India*. Delhi: Oxford University Press.

———. (2015). *Violent Conjunctures in Democratic India*. New York: Cambridge University Press.

Capps, W. H. (1990). *The New Religious Right: Piety, Patriotism and Politics*. Columbia: University of South Carolina Press.

Chakraborty, C. (2011). *Masculinity, Asceticism, Hinduism: Past and Present Imaginings of India*. Ranikhet: Permanent Black.

Koonz, C. (1987). *Mothers in the Fatherland: Women, the Family and Nazi Politics in Germany*. London: Jonathan Cape.

Meghwanshi, B. (2019). *I Could Not Be Hindu: The Story of a Dalit in the RSS*, translated by Nivedita Menon. Delhi: Navayana Press.

Golwalkar, M. S. (1945). *We or Our Nationhood Defined*, 3rd edition. Nagpur: Bharat Prakashan.

———. (1966). *Bunch of Thoughts*. Ahmedabad: Sahitya Sindhu Prakashan.

Sarkar, T. (2019). 'Hindutva's Historical Pedagogy'. In *Majoritarian State: How Hindu Nationalism is Changing India*, edited by A. P. Chatterjee, T. B. Hansen, and C. Jaffrelot. London: Hurst and Co.

Sarkar, T., and U. Butalia (eds.) (1995). *Women and the Hindu Right*. Delhi: Kali for Women.

Savarkar, V. D. (1923). *Essentials of Hinduism*, reprinted in 1928 as *Hindutva: Who Is a Hindu?* Nagpur: Veer Savarkar Prakashan.

Cited Dailies

Rehman, A. R. (2020). 'UP: On Way to Register Marriage, Man Held under Anti Conversion Law'. *Indian Express*, Delhi edition. 7 December, 10.

Sahu, M. (2020). 'In UP, Love Jihad Has Two Faces'. *Indian Express*, Delhi edition, 8 December, 1.

Part I

Changing Modalities of Hindu Nationalist Organizing

1

Right-Wing Women's Mobilization

Notes from Colonial Western India

Namrata Ravichandra Ganneri

In early 2019, a short video clip of Pooja Shakun Pandey, a senior woman functionary of the Akhil Bharat Hindu Mahasabha (All India Hindu Grand-Assembly, henceforth ABHM), shooting an effigy of Mahatma Gandhi went viral (*First Post* 2019). The clip flaunted the violent militancy of a party woman. The recreation of the assassination, conducted at a local party office in Aligarh, was widely reported in national dailies (Barman 2019). Controversially, overt celebrations of Gandhi's murder have become commonplace in the last few years, and the ABHM, as is well known, was actually implicated in the murder conspiracy. Pushed into insignificance since the 1950s, the ABHM has, however, dramatically resurfaced in the last decade or so alongside the political ascendancy and electoral success of the Bharatiya Janata Party (BJP). It is expanding its state-level chapters as well as front organizations among students, youth, ascetics and women. Strikingly, all its office-bearers at the central organizational level and in the working committee are upper-caste men.[1]

The 'public' presence of militant women like Pooja Shakun Pandey intrigues academics about the appeal of right-wing political movements and parties for women: a significant question because these forces are otherwise markedly conservative about gender. What is the political trajectory of women in such parties? Why do we know so little about the foremothers, as it were, of women like Pandey? Though some work has been done on women of the Sangh Parivar, the lineages of Pandey in the Mahasabha are far less familiar. Feminist scholar Andrea Peto, who has researched the lives of fascist women in countries of the former Soviet Bloc, argues that one of the main challenges for scholars working on the biographies of such women is that of reconceptualizing a key theme in feminist research: gender and power (Peto 2009).[2] Women can actually manipulate their subordinate positions to become political agents (ibid.). Scholars of fascism recognize that women craft their own agendas and gain some leverage within fascist movements and regimes, although male fascists may continue to consider their work as secondary (Passmore 2002: 130). A recognition of women as accomplices and active participants in right-wing movements leads one to think hard about their politicization and nature of participation in these movements. Indeed, prospographical research can help map 'ordinary' women participants and develop a more individualized picture (Peto 2009).

This chapter privileges women's audibility in the Hindu right-wing discourse. It seeks to fill in the relative paucity of material on lives and thoughts of right-wing women by mining organizational papers, newspaper reports and oral interviews with women sympathizers and members of women's wings affiliated to the major Hindu right-wing organizations of late colonial India. It will also contrast the divergent fortunes of the ABHM and the RSS (Rashtriya Swayamsevak Sangh) women in the colonial period. Histories of the foundation of women's wings reveal as much about the formation of women's political subjectivities as about the 'patriarchal' underpinnings of the parent organizations. In addition to adding historical depth to the literature on women and the Hindu right, this work also invites serious consideration about the challenges thrown by women's involvement to the gender ideologies of the parent organizations themselves.

Reluctant Parents? The All India Hindu Mahasabha and the Rashtriya Swayamsevak Sangh (RSS) and Their Women's Fronts

Hindu right-wing ideology or Hindutva was foregrounded in Vinayak Damodar Savarkar's tract *Hindutva: Who Is a Hindu?* written in 1923.[3] *Hindutva* argued that one's religious allegiance is paramount for establishing one's nationalist credentials and claims to citizenship. It thus called for a permanent exclusion of Muslims from the nation. The Hindu Rashtra, thus conceptualized, created 'Others' and aimed to forge a political identity for the Hindus. Two organizations with roots in the Indian political landscape accepted *Hindutva* as their avowed political ideology. The first was the Hindu Mahasabha, founded in 1915 and renamed as the All India Hindu Mahasabha (AIHM) in 1922. It entered the electoral arena under Savarkar's leadership in 1937, albeit performing dismally in the elections. The second was the ostensibly 'non-political' Rashtriya Swayamsevak Sangh (RSS, hereafter Sangh), founded by Dr Keshav Baliram Hedgewar in Nagpur in 1925. Hedgewar's successor, M. S. Golwalkar, is regarded as the main ideologue of the organization. An all-male organization till date, the *raison d'être* of the Sangh is innocuously stated as *sangathan*, or organization – to unify Hindus and to create a Hindu nation. Although Sangh activities came under a cloud after Gandhi's assassination and the organization was banned for a brief period, the Sangh adopted a formal written constitution and created a vast network of affiliates and sub-affiliates to mobilize different sections of the population.

Both the AIHM and the Sangh envisioned Hinduism as an aggressive and violent faith perpetually at war with proselytizing 'alien' religions – mainly Islam but also Christianity. Hindu men – with a few heroic exceptions – were imagined as 'weak' as they were repeatedly conquered by foreign non-Hindus in the past. Both organizations, therefore, advocated the physical regeneration of the community through programmes of military training or drilling (Jha 2013).[4] Some scholars argue that this 'masculine Hinduism' was forged through articulations of anxiety by the Hindu upper-caste male vis-á-vis perceived Muslim or even Hindu lower-caste political self-assertion (Banerjee 2007). In conjunction with the perceived need to 'masculinize' Hindu men, the figure of women played an important discursive role for Hindutva: Destitute women and widows were perceived to be particularly susceptible to proselytization and to sexual overtures from non-Hindus.[5] P. K. Datta (1999), for example, has shown that, in the middle of the 1920s – precisely when these organizations struck root – the discourse of 'abducted' Hindu women who fell prey to Muslim *goonda*s, bestowed a great sense of urgency to the programme of Hindu *sangathan* in Bengal. Women came to symbolize the victimization of the Hindu community as a whole and carried the fear of the Muslim into every Hindu home. This, too, strengthened the drive for Hindu mobilization. The women metamorphosed into a metaphor of sacredness as well as humiliation. The virility of the community came to hinge on defending her 'honour'.[6]

However, women were not merely present as objects of Hindutva discourse. They actively affiliated themselves with the Hindu Mahasabha and founded a women's wing – the All India Hindu Mahila Mahasabha. They also tried to fight elections (Williams 2013). A Brahmin woman founded the first affiliate of the Sangh – the Rashtra Sevika Samiti (hereafter Samiti) in 1936. Headquartered at Wardha, the Samiti replicates the organizational structure of the Sangh with a focus on physical training conducted in its *shakha*s, plus ideological indoctrination. It is not formally associated with electoral politics – just as the Sangh avoids it, even though the Sangh developed an electoral front after Independence.[7] Feminist scholars have written about the Samiti, but historical analyses of the origins of this organization are few.[8] In the following sections, I explain how women came to associate with and strived to achieve space within the Hindutva movement during its formative years.

Carving a Space for Women? The All India Hindu Mahila Mahasabha

Strangely, most scholars of the AIHM do not recognize the existence of a women's wing (Bapu 2013; Jones 1998). Even official histories of the Mahasabha remain silent about the presence of women in the organization.[9] S. R. Date's organizational history of the Maharashtra Hindu Sabha acknowledges the existence of a few female members and sympathizers of the Mahasabha (Date 1975: 419–420, 428). Date prominently names Sindhu Gopal Godse – Gopal Godse's wife – and Sundaratai Bhopatkar – Laxman Balwant Bhopatkar's daughter – and makes a passing reference to the Hindu Mahila Sabha.[10] Surprisingly, Date makes no mention of Jankibai Joshi, who was associated with the Hindu Mahasabha throughout the 1940s and was also a woman representative inducted in the Mahasabha Working Committee from 1942 to 1946. Her presence is amply recorded in the organizational papers I consulted, though she is absent in the Mahasabha self-narration. Joshi's own letters written to various party presidents provide the only evidence of the existence of active political campaigning by a woman member of the Hindu Mahasabha. It seems Date chose to remember women related to prominent men alone.

One first hears of Jankibai Joshi in the context of an All India Hindu Women's Conference organized in December 1935. Joshi was appointed as the first general secretary of the conference.[11] A women's conference was held alongside the annual session of the All India Hindu Mahasabha in Poona (present-day Pune) for the first time. It was presided over by the noted Marathi writer Mrs Girijabai Kelkar (*Times of India* 1935a).[12] The president recognized that it was 'necessary to *organise* Indian womanhood if they wanted to compete with women of other countries' (emphasis added) (ibid.).[13] However, she exhorted women to preserve ancient Indian cultural norms and asked them to take charge of their 'own education'. Birth control, divorce and remarriage were characterized as introducing a 'new morality' and were condemned.[14] The conference typically condemned birth control, since one of the pivots of the Hindu *sangathan* movement was the fear of 'declining Hindu numbers' (Shraddhanand 2003 [1926]).[15] A resolution was passed recommending that a proper course of physical culture be devised for all women. Women were also asked to protect the sacred cow, buy *swadeshi* goods, ban all obscene pictures and even support the ban on untouchability from all sacred places (ibid.). It was therefore a strange amalgam of conservative traditionalism and bold new initiatives in the realm of female body-building.

The veteran Sanatani leader Madan Mohan Malaviya, who officiated as the Mahasabha president, took up the question of 'untouchability' – galvanized, not least by the Dalit leader B. R. Ambedkar's threat to convert out of Hinduism. The leadership of the Mahasabha feared that the Hindu community was being hacked away by the threat of the secession of 'untouchables'. While retaining them within the Hindu fold was of paramount importance, it felt that it also had to shore up its base among yet another vulnerable group: Hindu women. One can surmise that the immediate context for the organization of the Hindu Women's Conference were the impending elections.

While the Montague–Chelmsford Reforms in 1919 had left the question of women's franchise undecided,[16] the Government of India (GOI) Act of 1935 increased the ratio of female-to-male voters to 1:5 and gave women reserved seats in provincial legislatures (Forbes 1996: 106–112). The Congress and women's organizations initially opposed reservations, yet they eventually participated in elections, and several women now began independent legislative careers.[17] Nevertheless, the secretary of the Mahila Mahasabha conference, Umabai Sahasrabudhe (*Times of India* 1935c: 16),[18] hastened to clarify that the conference harboured no hopes of rivalling the Congress-dominated All India Women's Conference (AIWC), which was perceived as the premier organization representing all Indian women (Forbes 1996: 82).[19]

After the first conference, Jankibai Joshi coordinated with the Reception Committees of Ahmedabad (1937), Nagpur (1938) and Calcutta (1939).[20] She struggled to found a permanent Hindu Women's Organization rather than hold ad hoc conferences every year.[21] Meanwhile, rival political organizations were forming fronts among Muslim and Dalit women which introduced a great sense of urgency. The Muslim League entered mass politics and started a Muslim women's sub-committee in 1938.[22] The emergence of the 'Pakistan' movement in the 1940s opened up a new space of political action for them. As the movement grew in momentum, more and more women were drawn to the League as election candidates, or even as voters. Begum Shah Nawaz, for example, became a leading force in the Muslim League's women's wing in 1938 and a successful Muslim League candidate in the 1946 elections (Everett 2001: 2073). Dalit women had also begun organizing themselves from the 1920s.[23] An All India Dalit Women's Conference was held on 20 July 1942, with representatives from all over India and a total of 25,000 women in attendance. A series of women's conferences in 1942 led to the founding of the Dalit Mahila Federation presided over by Sulochanabai Dongre (Pawar and Moon 2008: 141–156). Not only had women's politicization reached new heights, but different ideologies were competing for their affiliation as well.

The threat of rival women's organizations like the Dalit Mahila Federation and the AIWC eventually conveyed the urgency of Jankibai Joshi's pleas to the male leaders. The Kanpur session of the Hindu Mahasabha in 1942 finally endorsed the formation of a separate women's organization with the following resolution:

This conference resolves that in order to spread the Hindu Maha Sabha principles among Hindu women and to make them Hindu Mahasabha minded a Mahila Parishad should also be arranged with the A.I. Hindu Maha Sabha session in future.[24]

Jankibai Joshi seems to have had the tacit support of the new Mahasabha president V. D. Savarkar, who had assumed presidentship of the organization in 1937. Nonetheless, the Mahasabha Constitution, now suitably amended, had little effect on her efforts to found Mahila Sabhas in various parts of the country. Everywhere she had to strain against men's obduracy. This is evident from her anguished lament to a senior functionary: 'Mere pryatana ko purush varga ki sahayata milna bada kathin dekhne mein aata hai. Aur doosri baat jab se main Kanpur se aayi hoon, us din se shant nahi baithi hoon, karyasham hone ka prayatna kar rahi hoon, phal dena parameshwar ke haath mein hai.' (She indicates that she is struggling against men's opposition and that she has not rested since she returned from Kanpur. She now awaits God's grace for success.)[25] She recounts with great frustration how, despite her efforts, the Hindu Mahasabha did not pass any amendment to incorporate women more effectively.

Despite all obstacles, Joshi did become a member of the Working Committee of the All India Hindu Mahasabha, in addition to serving as the General Secretary of the All India Hindu Mahila Sabha. She constantly invoked the fear of 'half of the Hindu population going under the influence of Congress activities' unless the Mahasabha decides to mobilize women.[26] However, she had to wait for another couple of years when the Bilaspur session held on 24 and 26 December 1944, exhorted various provincial Hindu Sabhas to give 'due consideration' 'to the claims of representation of Hindu Women' (Joshi 1950). It is likely that the political leadership of the Mahasabha was finally stirred into action only because of another impending election in 1946.

Joshi contested the 1946 elections as a Hindu Mahasabha candidate in Poona against the Congress candidate Sumatibai Gore from the Poona women's constituency (*Times of India* 1946a; *Times of India* 1946b). She lost the elections. In 1946, L. B. Bhopatkar, the new Mahasabha president replaced her with the Rani of Kobra on the executive committee of the Hindu Mahasabha.[27] Joshi presided over the All India Hindu Women's Conference for another year before slipping into oblivion (*Times of India* 1946c). In all likelihood, she fell out of favour with the new Mahasabha leadership. I found no further correspondence with her in the organizational papers following her last letter to Dr N. B. Khare, the Mahasabha president in 1950 (Joshi 1950).

Joshi's disappearance from the party machinery as well as from organizational papers remains something of a mystery. She had played a fairly prominent part in the Hindu Mahasabha for nearly a decade, even though she does not seem to be related to any Mahasabha leader. It does appear that she was close to Savarkar, who had probably inspired her to 'mobilize' Hindu women. S. P. Mookerjee, who took over as president of the Hindu Mahasabha from Savarkar, commended 'steps … taken by some of our enlightened sisters from western India to consolidate Hindu women under the banner of Hindu Mahasabha', indicating his approval of women's mobilization (Mookerjee 1943: 202). Nevertheless, the party did little to honour her or her efforts. In the absence of adequate support from the broader party leadership, a fullfledged and fully functioning women's wing did not emerge. One does not see any blueprint in the party papers which would indicate plans for a separate organization for women. Perhaps Joshi's failure to win elections ruined her chances in the party.

The All India Hindu Mahila Mahasabha had no permanent office, and Joshi conducted all her correspondence from her residential address in Poona. She was frank about the patriarchy in the Mahasabha and repeatedly indicted party leaders in her correspondence. Indeed, Rina Williams (2013) blames this patriarchal oversight and the neglect of women's constituency for the overall electoral failures of the AIHM. On the other hand, Amrita Basu's analysis (Basu 1995) of the *sadhvi*s of the Sangh Parivar shows that while individual women may have advanced their personal agendas as well as that of the movement,[28] their activism created spaces for diverse gendered imagery. The contrast is striking. Was the women's wing, then, merely the product of Jankibai Joshi's own political ambitions? Was Joshi's association with Mahasabha politics driven simply by the lure of a successive legislative career?

These questions are difficult to answer though one does know that the Hindu Mahasabha itself was struggling for survival in the late 1940s. The party was in shambles with the founding of another Hindutva electoral party, the Bharatiya Jana Sangh (BJS) in 1951.[29] Meanwhile, the Mahila Mahasabha's political fortunes mirrored those of its parent political party. It was galvanized into action in the wake of elections but failed to conceptualize any innovative programmes for women.

Unlike the Mahila Mahasabha, a women's organization with a distinct ideology and practical programmes germinated and established itself on the political landscape of western India. It, too, faced initial resistance from its male leaders but managed, nonetheless, to carve out an existence. The following section recounts the story of its birth.

'A Women's Sphere'? The Founding of the Rashtra Sevika Samiti

There exists no official organizational history of the Rashtra Sevika Samiti. In the Samiti's own discourse, the founding of the organization is attributed solely to the vision of its founder Laxmibai Kelkar (1905–1978). In a lecture, Kelkar relates that the Samiti was born in a period of personal crisis for her.[30] Laxmibai Kelkar was married to a wealthy Brahmin *malguzar* in Wardha and was widowed at twenty-seven. She was left to care for six sons and two daughters from her husband's previous marriage. Kelkar also faced intense mental and ideological churning after reading reports of 'abductions of women' in newspapers; she was particularly shaken by the rape of a young Bengali woman in front of her 'educated'[31] husband by *goondas*.[32] This triggered two ideas in her mind: the fact that women are always dependent on men[33] and that such episodes could recur in her own vicinity as well. She contemplated the weakness of men and concluded: 'Ve apna sanrakshan karne mein bhi asamarth hain, phir hamara sanrakshan kya karenge?' ('If they are unable to protect themselves, how can they protect us?')[34] This 'story' was recounted in several informal and formal conversations I had with *sevikas* regarding the reasons for the founding of the Samiti, and I will dwell upon it at length in the next section.

In the same lecture, Kelkar also recounts her visit to M. K. Gandhi's *ashram* in Wardha. While she attended, merely to accompany her relatives who went to see the great man,[35] Gandhi's lecture on Sita, Ram's wife, as a role model for women, encouraged her to read the Ramayana epic. She subsequently read the epic Mahabharata as well and was inspired by Draupadi, its lead female figure who was a very powerful woman.[36] The lecture makes a few things clear: Widowhood freed her from the restraining influence of her husband, and she was alerted to the vulnerability of all women compounded by 'their' men's inability to 'protect' them. She equated the 'protection of women' with 'protection of their chastity' (*sheel*).[37] Female 'chastity' is a cardinal feature of upper-caste Hindu womanhood, and a whole range of institutions have been created to control women's sexuality: prepubertal marriages, enforced widowhood, and so on. Since patriarchy operates not through violence alone, women's internalization of these norms goes a long way in ensuring the hegemony of patriarchal structures and practices. Also, their supposed vulnerability was never explained in terms of power inequities in the family or seen as rooted in the dominant ideas of Hindu womanhood. It was portrayed as a natural and innate condition of women.

Women's mobilization was mounted on the non-threatening analogy of the family, as Kelkar described through her fateful meeting with K. B. Hedgewar, the founder of the Sangh. Her sons, who frequented the Sangh *shakha*s, told her that Hedgewar had invited guardians of all the young volunteers to the *shakha*. Kelkar insisted on meeting Hedgewar though her sons refused, pointing out strictures against women attending Sangh programmes. She persevered and argued in favour of her 'right' to be present as a 'guardian' and got special permission to attend. She returned, impressed by Hedgewar's speech, and sought a private meeting with him. Though Hedgewar rebuffed her in the first instance, she persisted in arguing that women were as important for the 'nation' as for the family.[38]

Hedgewar eventually agreed to help found a women's organization similar to that of the Sangh, provided Kelkar took full responsibility for this initiative. Over a period of two months, Hedgewar and Kelkar met several times to finalize the formation of the Samiti. The Samiti, like the Sangh, was launched on the occasion of Vijaya Dashami, or Dussehra, on 25 October 1936, in Wardha. Both organizations cultivated ideological affinity and even the same initials, and hence the name Rashtra Sevika Samiti. Bacchetta (1996: 130) comments that in the case of Samiti's *sevika*, the *swayam* (self) of *swayamsevak* is absent. Women's selves are always relational, while men are permitted individual selves. Sarkar points out that 'the sense of autonomy and self-choice that are associated with the term "volunteer" are notably missing' (Sarkar 1995: 184–185). In this story, Kelkar presents the formation of the Samiti as a result of her personal efforts.

The story recounted in *Amrit Bindu*, a collection of twenty-one lectures delivered by Kelkar from 1953 till her death in 1978, emphasizes a few things but obscures several others, perhaps so as to establish the Samiti's autonomy from the Sangh's hierarchy. Kelkar makes no mention of her prior politicization through her familiarity with the activities of other political organizations in the region. The impact of her visits to Gandhi's *ashram* is minimized. In fact, in most literature produced by the Samiti, Hedgewar's role is diminished as well.[39] Kelkar is said to have resolved all doubts on her own, and her dependence on the Sangh and its borrowings is hardly acknowledged.

Susheela Mahajan's *Deepjyotirnamohstute*, the first biography of Laxmibai Kelkar, is another valuable source for learning about the early history and organizational development of the Samiti.[40] Surprisingly, scholars writing on the origins of the Samiti have altogether ignored this source.[41] Mahajan's biography suggests that Kelkar came from a reasonably politicized household though this aspect is understated in most other biographical accounts – perhaps to underline her 'ordinariness' for the homebound potential woman recruit, as well as to underplay the possible sources of influence, other than that of the Sangh. Kelkar came from a family of Bal Gangadhar Tilak sympathizers, her mother subscribed to Tilak's newspaper *Kesari* and Appaji Dravid, a prominent member of the Servants of India Society, was her neighbour. Kelkar's brother was jailed for participation in Gandhian *satyagraha*. Even in Wardha, her husband,[42] though not interested in politics, was friendly with the prominent Congressmen Dr N. B. Khare. Congressman Jamnalal Bajaj was a family friend of the Kelkars and Bajaj's wife, Jankidevi Bajaj, was a regular visitor to the household. Another prominent Congressman C. P. Abhyankar was married to her husband's sister, and Kelkar's father-in-law was one of the earliest Congress supporters of the region. Despite these linkages to the Congress, Kelkar's stepdaughter Vatsala was married to M. R. Cholkar's son, Cholkar being a close associate of the Sangh founder

Hedgewar. At least two of her sons, who had introduced her to the Sangh, became closely involved with the formal hierarchy of the Sangh in Wardha. The overlaps between the Sangh and the Congress are interesting.

Besides relations to prominent politicians, Kelkar and her extended family were also active in the public life of the city. In 1935, her husband's brother, Yashwant Kelkar, cofounded the Maharashtra Vidyalaya in Wardha with Baburao Khare (Mahajan 2004: 33). Subsequently, Yashwant Kelkar's wife Shantabai, an educated woman, founded a school for girls in July 1936, and Kelkar served as the school's vice-president after her sister-in-law's death. Kelkar also formed a *bhagini mandal* (women's organization) at Wardha (ibid.: 18).[43] So she did have considerable experience of organizational work and was indeed experimenting with various forms of public activity in Wardha before her involvement with the Samiti began.[44]

Kelkar's political family background was coupled with her own strident interest in 'politics' (Mahajan 2004: 15) and exposure to various ongoing women's movements. In the Marathi daily *Sakaal* published from Poona, she read an editorial entitled *Mahilayen Tatha Svavlamban* (Women Should Be Self-dependent), dated 24 October 1932. The same issue contained a reference to the Vidarbha women's conference. In her presidential address at the conference, Yamunabai Hirlekar, an important woman activist, called for women to move beyond domesticity and participate in public life (ibid.: 35). Another woman, Anasuyabai Kale, had recently been elected as the president of Nagpur Congress (ibid.: 21). Given Kelkar's knowledge of these women's movements, her choice to join the right wing, as represented in the Samiti's literature, was an explicit rejection of contemporary progressive politics rather than a post-facto manufacture of dissent in response to women's mobilization in the 1980s, as Bacchetta (1996) seems to suggest. Sarkar (1995: 184) argues along similar lines: '[W]omen of the Hindu right, therefore, had a wide array of political alternatives, of models of activism to choose from. The decision to stick to the politics of the right was, therefore, not exercised in vacuum but it was an informed choice.' One may recount that the Hindu Women's Conference that began with the blessings of the Hindu Mahasabha articulated its opposition to a progressive women's movement fairly strongly.[45]

Sarkar (1995: 184) points out that women joined the right precisely at the moment that it faced a crisis in the politics of its social base and its mobilization. When challenged by powerful political adversaries like 'untouchable' groups or other left-inspired mass movements, the right simply 'accepted the demands of women of its own families for a public political space and for a non-domestic existence and organisation' (ibid.). The involvement of women is 'a totalitarian conquest of the existing base, rather than on a thinly spread out numerical expansion. An active mobilization of women was also a priority, since even among socially privileged castes and classes, women have a relatively insecure and tenuous location.' (ibid.: 187) Sarkar, nonetheless, reiterates that this departure in terms of organizational strategy did not lead to any change in the overall Sangh gender ideology (ibid.: 184). Chetan Bhatt, on the other hand, argues that the Samiti's function can be related to the development of a distinctive Hindutva gender ideology. This is because key texts of the Hindu nationalist movement, from Savarkar's *Hindutva* through Hedgewar's pronouncements and Golwalkar's tracts, celebrate Hindu masculinity alone, especially in distinctly violent forms, and ignore, virtually in their entirety, women and girls, personal and familial relationships (Bhatt 2001). But a focus on women's domestic obligations did not mean an exclusively homebound and 'constrained' role of women. I would like to dwell on the meanings and implications of women's mobilization as well as historicize it with reference to the data drawn from both Kelkar's biography and my interviews.

The Promise of Self-protection: PhysicalTraining in the *Shakhas*

It is my contention that the founding myth of the Samiti has been inadequately addressed by scholars (Bacchetta 1996: 133). The emphasis on men's perceived 'inability' to protect women was the primary self-mobilizing impulse for women. Furthermore, the cult of strong bodies has a continuous tradition in upper-caste Maharashtrian homes. In my interviews, many elderly *sevikas* recounted having received training in stave wielding in their youth. They enjoyed participating in the Samiti's *shakha*s, primarily because of the physical training programmes. By the middle of the twentieth century, Maharashtrian upper-caste culture had accommodated the notion of women cultivating strong bodies under a regimen of physical exercises.[46] Strong bodies helped to ward off unwelcome advances from the opposite sex. In fact, one of the most important triggers for the founding of the Samiti seems to have been the recognition that 'educated' men were incapable of protecting 'their' women. The theme of rape and abduction by Muslims was another important mobilizing impulse for Hindu male *sangathanist*s, but women, too, took up the task of self-defence through 'independent' organizations. Pradip Datta (1999: 150) discusses the formation of the Women's Protection League that marked the entry of women into the male preserve of physical culture. In the 1930s and the 1940s, a number of paramilitary and volunteer groups were formed and physical training became a part of training programmes even for Congress volunteer groups.[47] Many physical training institutes and physical culture clubs began to organize separate classes for women, and women were being urged to enrol in great numbers.[48] Sarkar (1995: 186) suggests that the physical training regime of the *shakha* was also propelled by contemporary eugenicist concerns. That a healthy feminine body would bear strong children was reiterated by several revivalists from the time of Swami Dayanand Saraswati onwards. Upper-caste Hindus were concerned about 'enervated' Hindu bodies and 'declining numbers' for at least three decades.[49] It was this aspect of Sangh *shakha*s that probably captured Kelkar's imagination.

I add the insufficiently acknowledged fact that the women from households sympathetic to the Sangh and imbued with the ideology of their menfolk had already begun 'organising' themselves on similar lines.[50] What inspired them was a combination of factors – from a belief in Hindutva ideas to the urge to possess strong and trained bodies. When I asked the veteran *sevika* Bakul Devkule, who had also served in the Bhonsala Military School, as to why she joined the Samiti instead of participating in Congress activities, she said that she was inspired by Savarkar: 'Hum Hinduon ke liye bhi to koi hona mangta hai' ('We Hindus, too, needed somebody').[51] Clearly, they identified themselves first as Hindus, rather than as women or as nationalists. Similarly, Veena Bodas, another veteran Mumbai-based *sevika*, said that joining the Congress was impossible while the Sangh was out of bounds for women.[52] These women had attended many different political meetings and were familiar with Congress and

Communist activities. But they 'chose' to affiliate themselves with Hindutva. Undoubtedly, their initiation was most often through a male kin who was also a part of the Sangh as it was in the case of the founder, but as Devkule's testimony reveals, it was an informed and autonomous choice. Devkule attended political meetings, listened to Savarkar's speeches and discussed the Sangh's ideology with Vinayakrao Apte, the then *sanghchalak* of Poona.[53] Devkule was introduced to the Samiti through a female friend and was close to Saraswati Apte, who became the *pramukh sanghchalika* of the Samiti after Kelkar's death.[54] Their circle of acquaintances was, therefore, an important factor in their political selection.

Members of the Samiti stepped beyond the domestic realm, organized *shakha*s and conceived their roles more broadly than merely as biological reproducers of the nation.[55] Sikata Banerjee (2006) argues that the political edge of female participation was contained through an erasure of women's sexuality that went hand in hand with the focus on strong female bodies. Bacchetta and Power argue that right-wing sex segregation ensures women's exclusion from the realms of overall larger organizational and political power. But it also enables women to forge their own discourse, practice and modes of solidarity, independent of the male wings of the movement (Bacchetta and Power 2002: 5). Women have in fact tweaked the dominant ideology, created diverse gendered imagery and transgressed models of normative femininity to enable their activism (Basu 1995).[56]

Conclusion

While the material available on the Mahila Mahasabha is sparse, this chapter seeks to reinstate the 'forgotten' women of the Mahila Mahasabha in the history of late colonial India. The women pioneers of the Samiti chose the political ideology of the Hindu right but were, nonetheless, able to create an 'independent' organization, which enabled them to thrive beyond the surveillance of its parent organization. Interestingly, the route to politicization through 'physical training' seems to be in stark contrast to the first stirrings of activism among the Islamist Jamaat-e-Islami. Its female pioneer 'Apa' Hamida Begum, a schoolteacher herself, was committed to writing and publishing tracts about the movement in the same period when right-wing women mobilized themselves (Jamal 2013: 114–117).

So how does one make sense of the larger activism of Maharashtrian Brahmin women in late colonial India? Padma Anagol (2013) has traced the articulation of a right-wing polemic among Hindu women as early as the late nineteenth century. A visible, public, militaristic role for women is advocated only in the 'service' of a Hindu nation in the Marathi treatise *Deshseva Nibandhmala* (Essays in the Service of a Nation), written by the Poona-based Laxmibai Dravid. Anagol wonders if the actions of Dravid can be incorporated within the broader realm of feminist political activism, despite its conservatism (ibid.: 106). Joane Nagel (1998) reminds us that religious nationalism, indeed all nationalism, tends to be conservative, and 'conservative' often means 'patriarchal'. At the same time, as we saw, even patriarchy may need to organize its own women.

Both Joshi and Kelkar seem to be straining and striving to practice right-wing politics within their chosen organizations. Both faced hurdles created by male conservative reluctance to visualize women as political subjects. The fact that Kelkar was able to overcome it is proof, perhaps, of her greater persistence. It could also be proof of a certain degree of flexibility in Sangh leadership which the Mahasabha lacked. Finally, the Mahasabha, being first and foremost an electoral organization, could spare little attention to organized social mobilization where women would have had a role to play. In contrast, the fact that the Sangh built itself up as a grassroots apparatus among diverse social sectors was, perhaps, the most critical factor behind the foundation and the endurance of its women's wing.

Notes

1. Akhil Bharat Hindu Mahasabha: www.abhm.org.in/.
2. Peto characterizes right-wing women as 'ugly' women. The other problem studying 'ugly' women, Peto asserts, is the difficulty in answering the question why certain women joined while others with the same social background and with the same education did not join, if political history remains the focus of inquiry (Peto 2009: 150).

3. The first edition of *Hindutva* was brought out by V. V. Kelkar, BA, LLB, advocate, Nagpur. As Savarkar was still in prison, the author's name was not published; it only said 'A Maratha' (Savarkar 1999: xviii).
4. Drilling and physical exercise is central to the Sangh routine practised in *shakha*s (neighbourhood cells).
5. The founding of 'rescue homes' for women was an important part of the overall agenda of *sangathan*. For example, one of the first programmes initiated by the Bombay Hindu Mahasabha was the founding of a home for destitute women, the Shraddhanand Anath Mahila Ashram.
6. Charu Gupta (1998: 731) makes a similar argument for 1920s northern India. Tanika Sarkar (1999: 97) argues on similar lines stating that during actual episodes of communal violence 'the figure of the Hindu woman has historically emerged as a crucial mobilizing impulse since much of the violence was also composed around allegations of abductions by Muslim criminals ... and violence became a necessary condition for Hindu male honour'.
7. The Samiti borrows its rituals and festivals from the Sangh, its members revere the *bhagwa dhwaj* (saffron flag) just like the Sangh and have accepted leadership of a (nominated) supreme leader, the *pramukh sanchalika*, under the principles of *ekchalikaanuvartitva*. For an overview of its ideology, history and organizational expansion, see Anon (2005). Also see www.rashtrasevika.org.
8. See, for example, Sarkar (1991), Bacchetta (2007) and Menon (2013).
9. Indra Prakash (1966), the official historian of the Hindu Mahasabha, does not mention the women's organization.
10. Gopal Godse was the brother of Nathuram Godse who assassinated Mahatma Gandhi. L. B. Bhopatkar was a prominent leader of the Pune Hindu Mahasabha.
11. 'Letter from Jankibai Joshi to Dr Khare, dated 5 March, 1950' in Maharashtra Provincial Hindu Mahasabha Papers, 1950, File No. P-130, 1950, All India Hindu Mahasabha Papers (AIHMP), NMML: New Delhi. This letter gives all the resolutions that founded and formalized the Hindu Mahila Sabha and traces its history from 1935 to 1949. One hears only of Jankibai Joshi and her 'struggles' in founding a women's wing in these letters.

12. Girijabai Kelkar (1886–1980) was a well-known novelist, essayist and social commentator. She wrote and lectured extensively on all aspects of women's lives and rights. Historian Padma Anagol also points out that she held complex views on the nature of women's oppression as expressed in her literary works such as *Purushance Band* (Men's Rebellion) and *Striyancha Swaraga* (Women's Paradise). Information about Girijabai Kelkar has been culled from Anagol (2005: 230).
13. It must be pointed out that the All India Women's Conference (AIWC) had endorsed its support, however 'controversial', for birth control, considering the early marriage and motherhood and its impact on health, just a year earlier (*Times of India* 1935b).
14. There were thirteen resolutions passed, some of which included education of adult women, maternity homes for middle-class women and urging the doctors and nurses to train women in maternity work (*Times of India* 1935a).
15. Swami Shraddhanand, the Arya Samajist leader, wrote a tract entitled *Hindu Sangathan: Saviour of the Dying Race*. The book was completed in late November 1924, though published only in 1926. Shraddhanand in all probability borrowed parts of the title to his book from *Hindus: A Dying Race*, a series of articles written by U. N. Mukherji and published in the newspaper *The Bengalee* during the month of June 1909. In any case, Shraddhanand acknowledged that he had met Col. Mukherji of the Indian Medical Service (IMS) in the Arya Samaj at Calcutta in February 1912. Mukherji drew Shraddhanand's attention to the fact that the 'Indo-Aryan race' would disappear in the next 420 years. For the next thirteen years, Shraddhanand himself studied statistics and, having convinced himself of the problem, began a movement for 'protection and progress of my people' in 1923 (Shraddhanand 1926: 15). For a detailed discussion on U. N. Mukherji's pamphlet, see Datta (1999: 21–63).
16. It was to be determined by provincial legislatures: Provincial legislatures between 1921 and 1930 granted voting rights to women, subject of course to the usual property and educational qualifications.
17. In the 1937 elections, approximately 41 percent of the adult males and 9 percent of the adult females were enfranchised; the female turnout ranged from 42.4 percent in Bombay to 6.6 percent in Orissa (Everett 2001, 2073).

18. In the newspaper report, Sahasrabudhe was named Secretary.
19. The AIWC had come into existence, initially as a non-political body to promote women's education in 1927. By 1945, it had 25,000 members. AIWC eventually got involved in nationalist politics and lobbied for all sorts of women's rights, from franchise to marriage reform and the rights of women labourers.
20. 'Letter from Jankibai Joshi to Dr Khare, dated 5 March, 1950' in File No. P-130.
21. Ibid.
22. Radha Kumar (1993: 92) notes cleavages among women of various communities in the 1940s.
23. In January 1928, a *mahila mandal* (women's association) was established in Bombay under Ambedkar's advice and the women were wives of his associates, Shivtarkar and Jadhav (Pawar and Moon 2008: 86). Shailaja Paik (2016) shows that Dalit women appropriated and extended the discourses of male leaders like Ambedkar and refashioned themselves and their community 'by seeking formal education, performing a body politics, and embodying a masculine womanhood'.
24. 'Letter from Jankibai Joshi to Dr Khare, dated 5 March, 1950' in File No. P-130.
25. In a handwritten note in English, she admits that she had spoken to Savarkar and he suggested that women become members of the Hindu Mahasabha first to overcome the difficulty of changes in Hindu Mahasabha constitution in any case. 'All India Hindu Mahila Sabha', File No. C-67, 1943–1945, AIHMP, NMML; 'Letter to Pandit Chandragupta' appended in the same file.
25. Ibid.
27. The reason given was that her term had expired, the term being usually four years. However, she mildly protested stating that she had been inducted only in 1942.
28. Ritambhara and Uma Bharati both belonged to low castes but became legitimate and powerful voices within the Hindutva movement.
29. The BJS was the predecessor of the BJP founded in 1980.
30. See 'Samiti ka Janam Vritant' (An Account of the Birth of the Samiti) in Anon (1991: 1–9). *Amrit Bindu* is a collection of twenty-one lectures

delivered by Kelkar from 1953 till her death in 1978. 'Samiti ka Janam Vritant' is the first lecture in this compendium.
31. Some accounts refer specifically to the fact that he was a lawyer.
32. The thugs purportedly mocked at legal provisions though we do not have any more details about the case.
33. Interestingly, she refers to the Manusmriti's famous words on the perpetual dependent status of women.
34. See 'Samiti ka Janam Vritant' in Anon (1991).
35. Christophe Jaffrelot (1996: 45–46) argues that Maharashtrian Brahmins, who formed the core constituency of the Sangh, favoured martial traditions and disliked Gandhi's emphasis on non-violence, his devotional Hinduism, and so on. The Sangh's hostility to Gandhi is in any case well known.
36. Reading the Ramayana and the Mahabharata at home was an unconventional act since traditionally these texts were neither kept nor read at home.
37. See 'Samiti ka Janam Vritant' in Anon (1991: 6).
38. She does not dwell either on the Sangh's exclusivist concept of the nation or on the exact nature of this 'nationalist project'.
39. For instance, Anon (2005) and Anon (n.d.).
40. Susheela Mahajan's *Deepjyotirnamohstute* (Worship of the Lamp that Drives Away Darkness), translated by Suneeta Paranjape, is a 1995 Hindi translation of the text in Marathi written by Susheela Mahajan with the same title. It is regarded as an authoritative biography of Laxmibai Kelkar and also contains several details about the organizational expansion of the Samiti. Other important biographies are Anon (1996) and Rai (1996) which seem to have drawn material from Mahajan's biography.
41. Bacchetta (1996) seems to have overlooked this source in her account of the founding of the Samiti.
42. Kelkar's husband, Pursushottam Rao, led a fairly anglicized personal life.
43. Women at this *mandal* would gossip or play cards. Kelkar encouraged them to read books.
44. Mahajan (2004: 61) writes that Kelkar was conscious of her lack of formal education and read widely. After the founding of the Samiti, she learnt the

skills of 'organization' from the medieval saint Ramdas Swami, Hindutva from Savarkar and Vedic Hinduism from Pandit Satavalekar's translation of the Vedas.

45. This was most evident in their opposition to birth control, as recounted previously.
46. The veteran *sevika* Bakultai Devkule recalled that boys feared her and never harassed her. Interview with Bakul Devkule (aged 82), 22 April 2003 and 30 March 2004, Thane.
47. Volunteers of Masurkar Ashram founded by Vinayak Masurkar, a Hindu religious leader, trained women in *lathi* play and these classes were extremely popular all over Maharashtra (Mahajan 2004: 67).
48. For example, the Maharashtriya Mandal of Poona (established in 1925) had evolved a separate curriculum for its women students. 'A Short History of the Origin Growth and Activities of the Maharashtriya Mandal, Poona City' appended in 'Non-Official Military Training Institutes', File No. 812. Home Department (Special), 1939, Mumbai: Maharashtra State Archives. Many of my interviewees did indulge in some form of regular physical exercise. It was a habit that they had inculcated when young, they claimed.
49. See note 15.
50. Mahajan (2004: 52) states quite clearly that women in several villages began thinking of founding organizations similar to the Sangh for themselves.
51. This observation made by Bakul Devkule during my interview with her is corroborated by Mahajan (2004: 52).
52. Interview with Veena Bodas, 80 years, 2 April 2004, Mumbai.
53. Interview with Bakul Devkule. Devkule's brother was a regular at one of the Sangh *shakha*s in Poona. Apte's wife Saraswati had founded a *samiti* shakha in Poona.
54. Many Sangh volunteers were also recruited through friends who had prior contact with the Sangh.
55. The Samiti seems to retreat into quiet, unobtrusive work as the custodian of Hindutva values immediately after moments of dramatic visibility, for example, after its public activism during the Ram Janmabhoomi movement (Sarkar 1999).

56. The Samiti foregrounds complex and multi-faceted models of womanhood, a point reiterated by Bacchetta.

Bibliography

Archival Sources

Home Department (special) Files at the Maharashtra State Archives, Mumbai.
The All India Hindu Mahasabha papers (1930–1950), Nehru Memorial Museum and Library, New Delhi.

Organizational Tracts, Pamphlets and Secondary Sources

Anagol, P. (2005). *The Emergence of Feminism in India, 1850–1920*. Hampshire and Burlington: Ashgate.
———. (2013). 'Gender, Religion and Anti-Feminism in Hindu Right Wing Writings: Notes from a Nineteenth-Century Indian Woman-Patriot's Text "Essays in the Service of a Nation"'. *Women's Studies International Forum* 37, March–April 2013: 104–113.
Anon (n.d.). *Rashtra Sevika Samiti: Ek Parichay*. Mathura: Sevika Prakashan.
——— (1991). *Amrit Bindu*. Nagpur: Sevika Prakashan.
——— (1996). *Karmayogini Vandaneeya Mausiji*. Mathura: Sevika Prakashan.
——— (2005). *Sadhana Karti Chalein*. Nagpur: Sevika Prakashan.
Bacchetta, P. (1996). 'Hindu Nationalist Women as Ideologues: The "Sangh", the "Samiti" and Their Differential Concepts of the Hindu Nation'. In *Embodied Violence Communalising Women's Sexuality in South Asia*, edited by K. Jayawardane and M. Alwis, 126–167. New Delhi: Kali for Women.
———. (2007). 'Gendered Fractures in Hindu Nationalism: On the Subject-Members of the Rashtra Sevika Samiti'. In *The Oxford India Hinduism Reader*, edited by V. Dalmia and H. von Stietencron, 373–395. New Delhi: Oxford University Press.
Bacchetta, P., and M. Power (2002). 'Introduction'. In *Right Wing Women: From Conservatives to Extremists Around the World*, edited by P. Bacchetta and M. Power, 1–15. New York: Routledge.
Banerjee, S. (2006). 'Armed Masculinity, Hindu Nationalism and Female Political Participation in India'. *International Feminist Journal of Politics* 8, no. 1: 62–83.

———. (2007). 'Gender and Nationalism: The Masculinisation of Hinduism and Female Political Participation'. In *Urban Women in Contemporary India: A Reader*, edited by R. Ghadially, 311–326. New Delhi: SAGE Publishing.

Bapu, P. (2013). *Hindu Mahasabha in Colonial North India, 1915–1930: Constructing Nation and History*. London and New York: Routledge.

Barman, S. R. (2019). 'Meet the Hindu Mahasabha Members Who "Killed the Mahatma" on January 30, 2019—in Aligarh'. *Indian Express*, 1 February. https://indianexpress.com/article/india/aligarh-killed-the-mahatma-on-january-30-2019-nathuram-godse-hindu-mahasabha-5563763.

Basu, A. (1995). 'Feminism Inverted: The Gendered Imagery and Real Women of Hindu Nationalism'. In *Women and the Hindu Right: A Collection of Essays*, edited by T. Sarkar and U. Butalia, 158–180. New Delhi: Kali for Women.

Bhatt, C. (2001). *Hindu Nationalism: Origins, Ideologies and Modern Myths*, Oxford: Berg Publishers.

Date, S. R. (1975). *Maharashtra Hindusabhecha Karyacha Itihas*. Pune: Kesari.

Datta, P. K. (1999). *Carving Blocs: Communal Ideology in Early Twentieth-century Bengal*. New Delhi: Oxford University Press.

Everett, J. (2001). "'All the Women Were Hindu and All the Muslims Were Men": State, Identity Politics and Gender, 1917–1951'. *Economic and Political Weekly* (9 June): 2071–2080.

First Post (2019). 'Hindu Mahasabha Leader "Recreates" Mahatma Gandhi's Assassination in Uttar Pradesh, Garlands Nathuram Godse's Statue'. 30 January. https://www.firstpost.com/india/hindu-mahasabha-leader-recreates-mahatma-gandhis-assassination-in-uttar-pradesh-garlands-nathuram-godses-statue-5993661.html. Accessed on 21 February 2022.

Forbes, G. (1996). *Women in Modern India*. Cambridge: Cambridge University Press.

Gupta, C. (1998). 'Articulating Hindu Masculinity and Femininity "Shuddhi" and "Sangathan" Movements in United Provinces in the 1920s'. *Economic and Political Weekly* (28 March): 727–735.

Jaffrelot, C. (1996). *The Hindu Nationalist Movement in India*. New York: Columbia University Press.

Jamal, A. (2013). *Jamaat-e-Islami Women in Pakistan: Vanguard of a New Modernity?* Syracuse: New York University Press.

Jha, B. K. (2013). 'Militarizing the Community: Hindu Mahasabha's Initiative (1915–1940)'. *Studies in History* 29, no. 1: 119–146.

Jones, K. (1998). 'Politicized Hinduism: The Ideology and Program of the Hindu Mahasabha'. In *Religion in Modern India*, edited by R. D. Baird, 240–273. New Delhi: Manohar.

Joshi, J. (1950). 'Jankibai Joshi to Dr Khare, 5 March'. In Maharashtra Provincial Hindu Sabha Papers, File No. P-130.

Kumar, R. (1993). *The History of Doing an Illustrated Account of Movements for Women's Rights and Feminism in India, 1800–1990.* New Delhi: Kali for Women.

Mahajan, S. (2004). *Deepjyotirnamohstute*, 2nd edition, translated by S. Paranjape. Nagpur: Sevika Prakashan.

Menon, K. (2013). *Everyday Nationalism Women of the Hindu Right in India.* New Delhi: Social Science Press.

Mookerjee, S. P. (1943). 'Silver Jubilee Session, Amritsar, December 26, 1943, Dr SP Mookerjee's Presidential Address'. In *Hindu Revivalism and the Indian National Movement*, edited by S. Mathur (1996), 196–205. Jodhpur: Kusumanjali Prakashan.

Nagel, J. (1998). 'Masculinity and Nationalism: Gender and Sexuality in the Making of Nations'. *Ethnic and Racial Studies* 21, no. 2: 242–269.

Paik, S. (2016). 'Forging a New Dalit Womanhood in Colonial Western India: Discourse on Modernity, Rights, Education, and Emancipation'. *Journal of Women's History* 28, no. 4: 14–40.

Passmore, K. (2002). *Fascism: A Very Short Introduction.* Oxford: Oxford University Press.

Pawar, U., and M. Moon (2008). *We Also Made History: Women in the Ambedkarite Movement*, translated by W. Sonalkar. New Delhi: Zubaan.

Peto, A. (2009). 'Who Is Afraid of the "Ugly Women"? Problems of Writing Biographies of Nazi and Fascist Women in Countries of the Former Soviet Bloc'. *Journal of Women's History* 21, no. 4: 147–151.

Prakash, I. (1966). *Hindu Mahasabha: Its Contribution to India's Politics.* Delhi: Akhil Bharat Hindu Mahasabha.

Rai, R. (1996). *Life Sketch of Vandaniya Mausiji.* Nagpur: Sevika Prakashan.

Sarkar, T. (1991). 'The Woman as a Communal Subject: Rashtra Sevika Samiti and Ram Janmabhoomi Movement'. *Economic and Political Weekly* 26, no. 35: 2057–2062.

———. (1995). 'Heroic Women, Mother Goddesses Family and Organisation in Hindutva Politics'. In *Women and the Hindu Right: A Collection of Essays*, edited by T. Sarkar and U. Butalia, 181–215. New Delhi: Kali for Women.

———. (1999). 'Woman, Community, and Nation: A Historical Trajectory for Hindu Identity Politics'. In *Resisting the Sacred and the Secular Women's Activism and Politicized Religion in South Asia*, edited by P. Jeffery and A. Basu, 89–104. New Delhi: Kali for Women.

Savarkar, V. D. (1999). *Hindutva: Who Is a Hindu?*, 7th edition. Mumbai: Swatantraveer Savarkar Rashtriya Smarak.

Shraddhanand, S. (2016 [1926]). *Hindu Sangathan: Saviour of the Dying Race*, edited by Vivek Arya. Delhi: Arsh Sahitya Prachar Trust.

Times of India (1935a). '"New Morality" Condemned: Poona Women Against Birth Control'. 30 December, 7.

———. (1935b). 'Indian Women's Demand for Economic Independence: Individual Position Freedom Wanted, Not Patronage'. 30 December, 7.

———. (1935c). 'Hindu Women's Conference'. 25 October, 16.

———. (1946a). 'Nominations for the Bombay Assembly: Thirteen Returned Unopposed in City.' 12 February, 5.

———. (1946b). 'Assembly Election in Poona: Dull Polling'. 12 March, 7.

———. (1946c). 'Resolution on Noakhali: Session Extended Mahasabha Leader'. 30 December, 7.

Williams, R. V. (2013). 'Failure to Launch: Women and Hindu Nationalist Politics in Colonial India'. *Politics, Religion and Ideology* 14, no. 4: 541–556.

2

Track Changes

Women and the BJP from the 1990s to the 2010s

Rina Verma Williams

Introduction

Women and gender issues have played a central role in the rise of Hindu nationalism to political power through its political party – the Bharatiya Janata Party (Indian People's Party, henceforth BJP). But the BJP, as a religious nationalist political party and the political wing of the Sangh Parivar,[1] faces a tension between its gender ideology – rooted in religion and nationalism, emphasizing the place of women in the home and the private sphere – and its need, as a political party in an established electoral democracy, to draw out the support of women as voters and half the electorate. How has the BJP resolved this tension over time as it evolved from a rising party striving for national presence to the predominant political formation in Indian politics?

To answer this question, I compare the role of women in the BJP in two critical time periods: its emergent phase in the 1980s and the early 1990s, and around the time of the 2014 election, as the party sought and achieved a return to power. I find that over this time period, the party moved from *mobilizing* women into street politics in the 1980s–1990s to *incorporating* them, in more routine and institutionalized ways, into its governance structures and electoral activities in the 2010s. Women leaders of the party shifted from being just a few women without significant family responsibilities (ascetic renunciants or widows) to being included at multiple levels of the party (national, state and local) in larger numbers who balanced family responsibilities and political work through the trope of 'family support'. This shift in the role of women in the party reflected the greater professionalization and institutionalization of the party in the latter period, as it evolved from a party striving for power to one that was positioning itself to recapture it.

I carry out this comparison using two interrelated and gendered lenses: my research on the BJP and my fieldwork across both time periods – first in 1993–1994, for my dissertation research, and again from 2013 to 2016 as part of the field research for my forthcoming book.[2] My primary analytical focus is on the BJP as a political party, with the understanding that the members and organizations of Hindu nationalism work hand in glove and are difficult to separate out in actual practice. Manisha Basu (2017) has argued convincingly that Hindu nationalism today is not the same movement that emerged in the northern and western parts of the country in the early 1900s, and she traces these changes through shifts in language and rhetoric. Building further on this insight, I argue that the BJP in 2014, as it returned to power, is different from what it was in its emergent phase in the 1980s and the 1990s – and those changes can be best understood through the lens of gender.

The first gendered lens I use to track changes in the role of women and gender in the BJP over time is my own research together with the well-developed secondary literature on women and gender in Hindu nationalism that evolved since the 1990s. This literature can be divided broadly into an early wave and a later one (Williams and Deo 2018). Path-breaking and field-defining analyses traced the rise to power of Hindu nationalism, since the 1980s, through a gendered lens (A. Basu 1993b; Jeffrey and A. Basu 1998; Sarkar 1993, 1998, 1999, 2001; Sarkar and Butalia 1995). Much of this early wave was sparked by the active participation of women in the lead-up to the destruction of the Ayodhya Mosque and the communal violence and rioting that followed (Jeffery and A. Basu 1998).

A second wave of literature, since about the mid-2000s, has included anthropological and ethnographic studies in which scholars seek to understand the parameters of Hindutva[3] women's participation in the movement; analyses of the role of gender and masculinity in the movement; and reflexive pieces on studying and doing fieldwork with Hindutva women (Anand 2007; Banerjee 2005; Bedi 2016; Deo 2016; K. D. Menon 2010; Sehgal 2009, 2012). One author has argued that the extent of women's participation in militant Hindu nationalist politics may be overstated (U. Menon 2003);

but the broad consensus, with which I concur, has been that the BJP rose to power by manipulating gendered discourses and issues of women's rights and with the involvement of women, from the rank and file to the leadership level, in a wide range of its activities – up to and including the instigation of violence against minority communities.

What has not been attempted is a direct comparison of the role of women in the BJP across earlier and later periods. This is the comparison I undertake in this chapter. As the party and the movement change, strategies and tactics of understanding and resistance must change accordingly. I argue that in the 1980s and the early 1990s, as a rising political party striving to gain a foothold in national politics, the BJP *mobilized* women by rallying them into the streets, deploying gendered discourses about women's rights and attacking feminism's claims to represent Indian women. At the leadership level, BJP women in this period uniformly lacked significant family responsibilities (as ascetic renunciants or widows).

As the party strove to return to national political power in 2014, after a decade in the opposition, their path back to power again turned on the role of women. But this time they had learned to *incorporate* women in more routine, institutionalized ways into the structures and activities of the party. This more routine incorporation of women can be seen in the internal governance structures of the party, as well as the party's electoral approach, including women as candidates and voters. And by the 2010s, many women BJP leaders had family responsibilities within heteronormative family structures and claimed uniformly that they had 'family support' for their political work.

The second gendered lens I use to track these changes is my own positionality – as a diasporic Indian woman working in the western academy – and fieldwork experience conducting research with the party across both these time periods. My research on the BJP takes a feminist and interpretive approach (Yanow and Schwartz-Shea 2014) as I seek to engage and understand what women's changing participation in the party has meant for women and for the party – and, ultimately, for Indian democracy. Reflexivity on the part of the researcher is a defining characteristic of both interpretive and feminist research. Both eschew a positivist 'view from nowhere' which absents the researcher from the processes and the conclusions of the research. Such reflexivity serves multiple purposes: being transparent about my research processes, excavating the possible effects of my own positionality on the research itself and shedding light on how the changing role of women in the BJP – from mobilization to incorporation – constitutes changes in the party itself over time, from a striving party in the 1980s and 1990s to a more professionalized and institutionalized one by the 2010s.

Researching the BJP over both time periods, I conducted elite interviews with political leaders, gathered and analysed archival data, party documents and visual and textual campaign materials, carried out ethnographic observation of party events and analysed quantitative election data. In this chapter, I focus on the interviews and interviewing process as the key similarity in my fieldwork and thus the best site for comparison across both periods. My fieldwork in 1993–1994 was focused on the political debates and communal violence surrounding the reform of the personal laws and a uniform civil code. In 2013 and 2015–2016 – immediately before and after the 2014 election – I again conducted interviews with party leaders, focusing this time on women leaders, along with a few prominent men.[4]

Across both periods, a key issue was access to interview subjects, which was influenced differently by changes in my own positionality, the status of the party and the Indian socio-economic context over time. Short of conducting a full autoethnographic analysis (Adams and Herrmann 2020), I reflect explicitly on how my identity mattered in both periods. My reflexive analysis reinforces the conclusions of the research: My experience conducting interviews with party leaders in the two time periods reflected the greater professionalization and institutionalization of the party that can be tracked through the changing role of women in the party.

In the next section, I consider the party's emergent phase in the 1980s and the early 1990s. My research showed that the BJP mobilized women into street politics in this period as it strove for power, and the few women leaders of the party lacked significant family responsibilities based on their social status as ascetic renunciants and widows. In this period, my fieldwork experience interviewing party leaders reflected the sense of a newer, smaller party seeking to grow into power. I then turn to consider the 2010s, when my research showed that the BJP had incorporated women into its governance structures and electoral activities in more routinized, institutionalized ways as it sought to return to power. By this time, most of the women I interviewed had significant family responsibilities and argued that they were able carry out their political work with 'family support'. My fieldwork experience conducting elite interviews with party leaders reinforced and signalled this institutionalization and professionalization of the BJP as an established party. I conclude by arguing that this professionalization and institutionalization should not be mistaken for any moderation in their radical agendas or their majoritarian, intolerant politics. My research and fieldwork experiences show how the party has accommodated women; yet the presence and participation of women in the party cannot portend, or be taken to portend, any moderation of their ideology.

Accessing the BJP in the 1990s: Mobilization without Family Responsibilities

The BJP, founded in 1980 from the remnants of the Bharatiya Jana Sangh, was a party striving to attain power and presence at the national level through much of the 1980s and the 1990s (Malik and Singh 1994). In this emergent phase, BJP leaders included a few vocal women, and the party mobilized women's participation in several campaigns and controversies. Their mobilization strategy consisted of three conceptually distinct but practically interrelated prongs: deploying gendered discourses about women's rights and protecting women; attacking feminism and feminist claims to represent the interests of Indian women; and rallying women into the streets in protests and demonstrations (Williams forthcoming: ch. 2).

In the early 1990s my research explored how political debates over the personal laws affected Hindu–Muslim relations and communal conflict over time. I interviewed the chief ideologue of the party (K. R. Malkani) as well as a prominent Muslim party leader (Sikander Bakht).[5] The elimination of the personal laws and the establishment of a uniform civil code have been an integral part of the BJP's agenda since its founding in 1980. Of the main goals of the BJP, it is the most directly gendered in terms of the implications and effects on Indian women.[6]

The establishment of a uniform civil code had historically been advocated by feminists (*The Hindu* 2003).[7] But in the 1980s the Hindu right wrested discursive control over the issue from Indian feminism. As a result, progressive and women's rights organizations no longer have a clear-cut or commonly agreed-upon position on the issue, and 'the term "uniform" has been dropped altogether as a positive value from the debates within the women's movement' (N. Menon 2014: 484); thus, feminist and progressive advocacy groups no longer speak of a 'uniform' civil code.

By the time I finished my study of the personal laws, I was left with a critically important question about how the BJP – a conservative, gender-regressive political party – was able to negotiate an inherent tension between its own ideological roots in religion and nationalism and its need, as a political party in a democracy, to involve and engage women – half or more of the electorate – in order to win elections. My research, together with the secondary literature on this period, shows that in the 1980s and the early 1990s, the BJP negotiated this tension through a strategy of gendered mobilization and the elevation of a few select women leaders who lacked significant family responsibilities.

My study of the personal laws dealt directly with the first of three major political campaigns of the 1980s and the early 1990s that displayed the BJP's strategy of gendered mobilization in this emergent phase. In the 1984–1986 Shah Bano controversy, the BJP deployed gendered discourses about women's rights and protecting women. Brewing for decades, the controversy erupted over a Supreme Court decision granting a destitute, divorced Muslim woman maintenance (alimony) under the Indian Penal Code (*Mohd. Ahmed Khan v. Shah Bano Begum*, AIR 1985 SC 945). The ruling Congress Party government initially supported the decision but quickly reversed course when faced with vocal opposition by conservative Muslim leaders who argued that it violated the tenets of Muslim personal law. The BJP supported the judgment, in opposition to the ruling Congress Party as well as conservative Muslims, and in doing so, the BJP landed on the same side of the controversy as feminist and women's rights activists as well as progressive Muslims.

Yet the BJP's position was widely seen as anti-Muslim rather than pro-women (Kishwar 1986): Their call for a uniform civil code was more accurately understood as a play to abolish Muslim personal law framed as a call to enhance Muslim women's rights. BJP leaders suggested that Muslim women were oppressed by their religion and by Muslim men and Muslim law, implying that the Hindu majority was in a position to protect and liberate them. In response to their call for a uniform civil code, feminist activists charged that the BJP did not specify any gender-progressive aspects they would implement in a uniform civil code – an interpretation Malkani effectively substantiated in an interview with me in 1994 (Williams 2006: 182).

The second major campaign of this period followed immediately on the heels of the Shah Bano controversy. In 1987, the BJP (together with local- and state-level Hindu nationalist political organizations) used a modern-day case of *sati*[8] to challenge feminist claims to represent Indian women or define their interests. As feminist and women's rights activists lobbied the state to ban celebration or 'glorification' of the practice, Hindu nationalist women responded by constructing *sati* as a right and demanding that right for women (A. Basu 1993a: 30). Such challenges included actual physical confrontations (yelling and shoving) between Hindu nationalist women and feminist activists (Kumar 1997; Butalia 2001). As in the *Shah Bano* case, a women's rights issue was conflated with religious identity: In both cases, Hindu identity was constructed as empowering for women, while in the *Shah Bano* case Muslim identity was projected as oppressive of women.[9]

Finally, in the early 1990s, the third major campaign of this period, to destroy the Babri Mosque at Ayodhya in northern India, presented a significant example of rallying women into the streets. Women participated at all phases and levels of this campaign, including the run-up to the destruction of the mosque, the actual destruction and the subsequent religious riots that spread throughout the country for two weeks. Key women leaders were critical in bringing people into the streets (through speeches and recordings that circulated widely in northern India), while at the rank-and-file level women protected rioters in their homes, blocked access to riot-torn neighbourhoods and literally cleaned up the streets after bloodletting had occurred (Banerjee 1996; Sen 2007; Sen and Jasani 2014). One observer called the Ayodhya conflict a 'turning point' in the role of women in the Hindutva movement.[10]

The defining characteristic of women BJP leaders in the 1980s and the 1990s was the absence of any significant family responsibilities. Three women were key party leaders of this era: Uma Bharati, Sadhvi Rithambara and Vijaya

Raje Scindia.[11] The first two were celibate ascetic renunciants and the third was a widow. In the prevailing Indian social context, especially for Hindus – and certainly for these three women in particular – this meant they had no significant family responsibilities in the domestic sphere.

These were the most public, well-known and identifiable faces of the movement in this period. Amrita Basu (1993a: 27) argues that for these women 'their chastity heightens their iconic status for it is deeply associated in Hinduism with notions of spirituality, purity, and otherworldliness'. The fact that these women were celibate had cultural resonance with renunciation as a moral and spiritual force in India, wherein an 'ascetic lifestyle … connotes sacrifice, martyrdom, and selflessness' (ibid.: 28).[12] Together with celibacy, Basu notes two additional key characteristics these women shared: They were all financially independent of men and relatedly 'none of their identities are defined by their roles as wives and mothers' (ibid.: 30).

For Hindu nationalist women, the nation defined as Hindu itself became their family or came to stand in as family for them. Kamlabehn, a woman leader of the RSS who was interviewed by Paola Bacchetta, 'reduced her familial responsibilities to a minimum in order to devote more time' to the cause. Kamlabehn noted that her middle-class Hindu neighbourhood is itself 'like a family' (Bacchetta 1993: 42) and that she sees herself as married to the movement and to the nation. Bacchetta (ibid.: 43) describes this as 'choosing independence through celibacy, dedication to other women … and an ideal (the Hindu nation) in place of dedication to an individual male'. Bacchetta argues that Hindu nationalism provided a space for Hindu women's participation which allowed them to escape normal social constraints and to do so not only without sanction but even with approval – 'as long as their demands are formulated not in terms of themselves, but rather in terms of self-sacrifice in the service of a higher cause, the Hindu nation' (ibid.: 46).

Women's participation in the BJP at the rank-and-file level was not necessarily marked by the absence of significant family responsibilities in the same way as it was for women at the leadership level. But these women's roles and participation were not ongoing and continual. At the rank-and-file level, women could come out for rallies or demonstrations or even participate in communal violence and then go back into their homes and carry on with their day-to-day family responsibilities. This is not to say that their support for the party or for Hindu nationalist ideology was locational or sporadic, but rather that their actual active presence and participation in the public sphere did not occur (and did not have to occur) continually.

Thus, the party's gender ideology (insofar as it had one) in this period, based on religion and nationalism, stood in some tension with the BJP's growing understanding that in order to be (or appear to be) a modern, competitive party in a competitive democracy, they needed to have the support of women. In the 1980s and the 1990s, the party resolved this tension by giving some women certain limited forms of access to the public sphere: For rank-and-file Hindu nationalist women, this access was transitory, while for women at the leadership level it was negotiated through social structures (of widowhood and ascetic renunciation) that freed women from primary responsibilities in the private spheres of home and family.

As I have argued, the BJP in this emergent phase was still striving to attain power and presence at the national level. As such, the party was smaller, with fewer formal procedures and barriers to access. Its offices in New Delhi were small and I was able to set up interviews with just a couple of phone calls. Party offices and procedures were less formalized or institutionalized at the time, and I never dealt with any personal assistants, even to interview a member of parliament in his office (Sikander Bakht). I interviewed Malkani at the party office in New Delhi. Every formal interview with subjects ended with an informal interview of me by them: Interviewees asked personal questions about my marital status, life in the United States and my family. Malkani did the same; and after our interview, he asked if I would like to peruse the party's 'library' – a small room with party pamphlets and other literature on display – and invited me to take whatever material I wanted.

Access to research subjects in this period was also mediated by my own positionality. In 1993, I went to India as a graduate student of Harvard University: a very elite institution recognized immediately by everyone I spoke with and likely to have opened doors of access. I also went as an Indian citizen. It is impossible to imagine that I would have been granted a visa, as a non-citizen, to study Hindu–Muslim communal relations; I would have had to mask my research project or change it.

In sum, the BJP in the 1980s and the early 1990s was an emergent party striving to establish itself as a viable political player at the national level.

This positioning was reflected in the mobilization of women in the party in this period: Just a few women leaders were highly visible and highly vocal, and their presence in the public sphere was mediated by a lack of significant family responsibilities. The emergent and striving nature of the BJP in this period was further evidenced in my own fieldwork experiences interviewing selected party leaders in 1993–1994. Their accessibility would change, by the 2010s, to reflect greater professionalization and institutionalization, both in the incorporation of women in the BJP itself and in the changing parameters of my access to research subjects.

Accessing BJP Women in the 2010s: Incorporation with 'Family Support'

By the time of the 2014 election, the BJP had incorporated and institutionalized the participation of women into the party's structures and activities at both the leadership and the rank-and-file levels.[13] This incorporation appears as a more routine form of women's participation, and it reflected the greater professionalization and institutionalization of the party. As in the prior period, these elements of change can be tracked both in my own fieldwork and access to research subjects, and in the findings of the research itself.

In the 2010s, I focused specifically on studying the role of women in the BJP. Between 2010 and 2016, I conducted fieldwork in India in multiple phases, travelling now as a professor and a naturalized US citizen. My visa status made each trip more precarious in terms of how to enter the country, with what specific credentials from the state and from funding institutions, and affiliations with local institutions. In this period, there was a notable lack of 'follow-up informal interviews' or interest on the part of interviewees in my personal particulars. Though the party remains suspicious of outsiders, Westerners and academics, I did find that the more senior (in terms of rank, not age) the politician I was interviewing, the more unconcerned they were about signing consent forms or speaking freely and sharing information when they had it.

By this time the BJP was a much larger, more institutionalized operation in the heart of New Delhi. The BJP's headquarters today are a large, sprawling complex, where getting in to see anyone requires signing a logbook and passing through a security screening. The party's library, which I did not visit, is now under the supervision of one particular person, and accessing it requires contacting him and setting up an appointment in advance.

In some ways, BJP leaders were more accessible in the 2010s than in the 1990s – partly because there were so many more of them at multiple levels of the party. I had no trouble obtaining cell phone numbers for various leaders; office staff handed them out readily and unhesitatingly. But in other ways they were less accessible: I quickly discovered that staffers handed the numbers out so readily because phones were invariably monitored and answered by personal assistants (PAs) who served as gatekeepers. By this time, the BJP had also established a reputation as a social-media-savvy operation. Several people noted that the best way to get an interview with high-level leaders was to tweet them! This insight – and the changing forms of communication it represented in a post-liberalization era in India – was not lost on me, and I understood that any future research along similar lines would need to involve exactly this kind of approach.

The professionalization and institutionalization of the party by the 2010s were evidenced in the incorporation of women, which I traced in two ways: within the party, in its governance structures; and in the electoral arena, in terms of women candidates and women's voting patterns.[14] Within the party, under the BJP president at the time, Rajnath Singh in 2004 actively sought to incorporate women into party governance structures through changes to the party constitution. But these changes were voluntary, and multiple informants concurred that these mandates remained unfulfilled after Amit Shah became president in July 2014.[15] Women were promoted to highly visible positions in advance of the 2014 election, especially including media spokespersons: Constantly on TV, they conveyed an impression of the importance of women within the party to the general public. After the election, Narendra Modi's cabinet in 2014 included seven women, six of whom held Cabinet rank in the Council of Ministers (which included 45 members in total). This was a new record in the Indian government (A. Basu 2016; PTI New Delhi 2014 [2017]; Soni 2014).

Electorally, the BJP did not run a notably larger number of women in 2014 than other parties or previous elections. The proportion of women as a percentage of all candidates running, across all parties, peaked at about 8 percent in 2014. But the win rate of BJP women candidates who did run skyrocketed in that year to just over 75 percent. Yet this was also true for BJP candidates, regardless of gender, across the board. In addition, a plurality of women voters in 2014 voted for the BJP, more than any other party, though the majority of voters for the BJP were men. Yet again, this was true for all parties in 2014 other than the left parties (Williams forthcoming: ch. 1). These numbers are not remarkable, but that is the point: Such trends and numbers represent not an 'extraordinary' mobilization of a few high-profile women, as in the 1980s and the early 1990s but rather a routine, perhaps unremarkable, incorporation of women into the electoral activities of the party in the 2010s.

Thus, by the time of the 2014 election, women were incorporated as important leaders in the upper echelons of party governance structures, as candidates and parliamentarians, spokespersons and in notable numbers as cabinet-level ministers. But whereas women BJP leaders in the 1980s lacked significant familial responsibilities (as widows or celibate renunciants), by 2014 most of the women BJP leaders I interviewed had active (heteronormative) family lives, including marriage and children. How did the BJP negotiate this tension between its gender ideology and the incorporation of women into its structures and activities in the 2010s? I found that 'family support' has become the trope for Hindu nationalist women's permission to enter the political sphere. This was almost universal among the women I interviewed: The assertion that for a woman in India to become active in politics, she had to have family support. I came to understand 'family support' as standing in for patriarchal (men's or familial) permission for women to engage in political activity.[16] More than one informant argued explicitly that without family support, if a woman insisted on being politically active anyway, it would 'break the family'.

Multiple aspects of my own identity were directly relevant to my fieldwork in the 2010s and shaped the forms of access I had to BJP leaders in a more professionalized and institutionalized party. In both periods, I came to the fieldwork as an Indian-born but US-raised researcher with strong emotional and cultural ties to India; but as a diasporic Indian, I work and research there as neither fully an insider nor fully an outsider

(Naples 1996; Jacobs-Huey 2002; Zinn 1979). Being cis-gender and woman-identified meant neither my research subjects nor I had to grapple with non-binary or trans constructions of sex or gender, on which the BJP, and Hindu nationalism more broadly, has a spotty record (Shah 2015). I am also an upper-caste Hindu woman. This often meant neither my informants nor I had to confront issues of upper-caste bias in the party and the movement. It did lead, in one case, to an assumption of my status as an insider: One informant felt comfortable going on and on in our interview to complain that the party, to court lower-caste votes, elevates lower-caste women and advances them ahead of (upper-caste) women who have been doing on-the-ground work for the party for much longer.[17]

During both fieldwork periods I wore traditional Indian *salwar kameez* (long tunic and loose pants), with a *dupatta* (scarf) loosely draped around my neck and partially covering my chest. This was a fairly typical – neither overly 'traditional' nor overly 'modern' – form of presentation in my research sites of New Delhi and Lucknow. I generally wore a simple gold wedding band on my left hand and a single gold bangle on my right wrist; other than these, I did not wear any of what I describe elsewhere (Williams forthcoming: ch. 5) as traditional visual markers of a married Hindu woman: I wore neither a *sari* nor a *bindi* (a dot on the forehead) nor *sindoor* (red powder in the part of the hair). Overall, I would have been easily comprehensible as what I am: a married, diasporic, upper-caste Hindu woman with some level of ties to India. Unlike other researchers' experiences (Bedi 2016; Behl 2017; Sehgal 2009), no one commented on my dress or appearance during any of my fieldwork trips in either period. Because I was conducting elite interviews, any power differential between myself and my subjects (Behl 2017) tended to favour them over me. Indeed, as is the norm in elite interviewing, I approached respondents as the experts on my topic and presented myself as seeking to learn from them (Schaffer 2014: 192). Conducting research on conservative or religious women as a feminist entails negotiating the tenuous and uncomfortable space between being taken as an ally to the movement or an enemy of it (A. Basu 2018; Blee 1993). No one tried to convince or convert me overtly, and with just one partial exception,[18] I never had a distinct sense that my research subjects understood me explicitly either as an ally or as an opponent.

In sum, the BJP by the 2010s was an established and increasingly professionalized and institutionalized national political party. This positioning was reflected in the incorporation of women in the party in this period: Women were routinely present at leadership levels within the party's internal governance structures and, electorally, as candidates and voters. BJP women in this period universally echoed the idea of 'family support' as the way they were able to balance domestic responsibilities in the private sphere with their political activism for the party in the public sphere. The more professionalized and institutionalized nature of the BJP in this period was further evidenced in my own fieldwork experiences interviewing women party leaders in 2013 and 2015–2016, wherein access was more mediated by PAs and more formalized procedures at the party headquarters itself. In the final section, however, I argue that these forms of incorporation of women into the party, and the professionalization and institutionalization of the party itself, do not signal any moderation of the party's radical agendas.

Conclusion(s): What the Changes Mean and What They Do Not

My research – buttressed by my own experiences conducting that research – demonstrates how the BJP, and the Hindu nationalist movement, has found a place for women. Much of the research on right-wing women argues that the participation of women can soften the image of a radical movement, lending it a mainstreaming or innocuous façade (Blee and Deutsch 2012; Ferber 2004). Other scholars, studying radical, religious or extremist political parties have posited – in what is called the 'inclusion-moderation' thesis – that participating in a competitive democracy can lead such parties to moderate their agendas (Brocker and Künkler 2013).

The BJP undermines both these assumptions in complex ways. Scholars have rightly noted that the party does not provide support for the inclusion–moderation thesis (A. Basu 2015; Jaffrelot 2013). And my findings on the changing role of women in the party do not suggest that the participation of women in Hindu nationalist politics in any way signals a moderation or softening of their radical agendas (even if it may help soften or mainstream their image). As the movement has found a place for women over time, it is apparent that the participation of women alone cannot be a solution to stopping the advance of its ideology.

The present moment presents a unique challenge for Indian democracy. Since its founding in 1980, the BJP has advocated three key policy goals as central to advancing its Hindutva ideology. These are (*a*) the abrogation of Article 370 of the Constitution, which grants special autonomous status and powers to the state of Jammu and Kashmir, the only Muslim-majority state in India; (*b*) building a temple to the Hindu god Ram at the contested site of Ayodhya, where the existing mosque, the Babri Masjid, was torn down by Hindu nationalist *kar sevak*s (volunteers) in December 1992; and (*c*) the abrogation of the system of religious personal laws founded by the British in the late 1700s and the establishment of a uniform civil code applicable to all Indians regardless of religion.

These three goals attack important pillars of India's unique multicultural secularism and its approach to protecting minority rights, most especially the rights of the Muslim minority since Independence (Williams and Jenkins 2015). At the time of this writing, the BJP has made significant headway on the first two goals. On 5 August 2019, the party announced in Parliament its unilateral decision to split up the state of Jammu and Kashmir and to abrogate Article 370 by rescinding many of its key provisions – such as allowing non-resident Kashmiris to purchase and own property in the state. Presented under the guise of advancing economic development in the state, its expected outcome is for the historically Muslim-majority status of the state to be swamped and ultimately diluted. At the same time, the state of Kashmir was placed under a complete lockdown – cut off from all communication with the outside world – which continues virtually unabated at the time of this writing.

The second constitutive goal of the BJP's agenda has been the construction of a Ram temple at the contested site of Ayodhya. This case was languishing in the courts for several decades; on 9 November 2019, the Indian Supreme Court rendered a decision that was widely and correctly interpreted as a significant triumph for the forces of Hindu nationalism. The judgment declared that the temple could be built on the contested site and granted an adjacent site for a Muslim mosque to be rebuilt to replace the historical structure that Hindu nationalists had destroyed on 6 December 1992.

These developments leave the third goal – the elimination of the religious personal laws and the establishment of uniform civil code – as the last unattained goal of the BJP's core agendas. It is also the most obviously gendered goal, as it directly affects the lives of Indian women across religious affiliation. The BJP has made incremental progress on chipping away at the validity of Muslim law in India: In 2017, the Supreme Court declared the practice of 'instant divorce' (triple *talaq*) unconstitutional (*Shayara Bano v. Union of India* [2017] 9 SCC 1 [SC]), and in July 2019 the Lok Sabha (the lower house of the Indian parliament) passed a bill making the practice a criminal offence (BBC News 2019). Since the establishment of the personal laws in the late 1700s, and certainly since the landmark *Shah Bano* case of 1985–1986, issues of women's legal and social rights have been inextricably bound up with the personal laws. If this third and final pillar falls, the effects for Indian women will be momentous and unprecedented; it is not at all clear what such a change would look like or what the public response might be, even having studied the issue for decades.

The participation of women can lend an air of mainstream legitimacy to radical, extremist movements, and the case of the BJP shows that such participation can also lend an air of empowerment to women. In the 1990s, Amrita Basu (1998) identified the limited spaces for activism that communalism (as opposed to fundamentalism) could create for women. In the 1990s, those limited forms of participation were mobilizational; by the 2010s they looked like routine incorporation, as the party itself changed to become more professionalized and institutionalized.

This study of mobilization and incorporation shows the limits of both these forms of participation for BJP women over time: they offer (certain) women some access to the public sphere, but that access is transitory and/or mediated by continuing to tether women to the private sphere. As such, I posit that women's participation in the BJP will not lead to dismantling patriarchal social structures that define public and private spheres. The BJP's movement over time from mobilization to incorporation of women constitutes a shift to greater descriptive or symbolic representation – with more women represented and incorporated into the party – but not a shift to the broader substantive representation of Indian women or their interests in a meaningful sense.

Notes

1. The three national organizations of the Hindu nationalist movement in India, together with local and regional counterparts, are known as, and often call themselves, the Sangh Parivar, or 'family of organizations'. In addition to the BJP, the national organizations include the Rashtriya Swayamsevak Sangh ('National Volunteer Organization', or RSS) – a domestic social movement organization founded in 1925 and the anchor organization of the movement – and the Vishva Hindu Parishad ('World Hindu Council' or VHP), founded in 1964, which is the religious and international wing of the movement. In this volume, for analogous comparisons over time of VHP women, see Chapter 5; on the RSS, see Chapter 3.
2. My dissertation and first book focused on India's religious personal laws and Hindu–Muslim conflict and included two chapters on the BJP (Williams 2006); my current book project analyses the changing role of women in the BJP over time (Williams forthcoming).
3. Hindutva is a term that encompasses the ideologies of Hindu nationalism and translates roughly to 'Hindu-ness'.
4. In both periods, interviews were conducted in the mix of Hindi and English that is characteristic of the urban, educated, upper-class and upper-caste north Indian elite.
5. I also interviewed Congress Party leaders as well as Muslim politicians, and progressive scholars and activists who were important in the debates around the personal laws – the latter of which included several women.
6. The other two goals included the establishment of a Ram temple in Ayodhya at the site of the destroyed Babri Mosque and the elimination of Article 370 of the Constitution, which grants special powers and status to Jammu and Kashmir, formerly the only Muslim-majority state in the country. I expand this point in the Conclusion.

7. It is important to note that many women's organizations do not necessarily believe the personal laws *per se* discriminate against women. Groups such as the Muslim Women's Forum and the Shariat Protection Committee, for example, hold that Muslim women need to be educated and aware of their actual rights under Muslim personal law, and that practices accrued over time that diverge from the original and true principles of Muslim law need to be eradicated. On this view, it is not the laws themselves that are discriminatory but their (mis)application that discriminates against women. It should also be noted that this has not been a mainstream feminist approach to the personal laws.
8. *Sati* is the highly contested practice of widow immolation on the funeral pyre of her husband.
9. I thank Amna Pathan for this insight.
10. Sunita Aron, Editor, *Hindustan Times*. Interview with the author, Lucknow, November 2013.
11. As noted earlier, these women were also deeply involved in other Hindu nationalist organizations, especially the VHP and the RSS. But they were also leaders of the BJP specifically: Scindia and Bharati in particular served as MPs, held multiple positions within the party and ran (and served) as BJP candidates in numerous state and national elections. At the time of writing, Bharati was the vice president of the party. The inter-movement of members between the various organizations is a defining characteristic of the movement itself.
12. For an analysis of ascetic masculinity in Hindu nationalism, see Chapter 7.
13. It is important to note that the women the BJP has incorporated by the 2010s tend overwhelmingly (though not exclusively) to be Hindu, upper-caste and upper-class, urban, educated and north Indian and Hindi-speaking. Although numbers are not readily available (despite extensive searching for them), it is evident even from the 'sample' of my interviewees that the BJP does not incorporate Indian or even Hindu women in a representative way.
14. I have omitted discussion of the BJP's women's wing, the Mahila Morcha (MM), because in my study I found it fairly irrelevant to the rise and positioning of women within the party. Some women rose to prominence without ever being involved with the MM; some were prominent in

the MM but never got significant posts in the party; and some were prominent both in the MM and in the party. The ambivalence of my interview subjects about the role of the MM supported this interpretation.
15. Interviews with the author: Pinky Anand, New Delhi, 5 January 2016; Mohua Chatterjee, New Delhi (by phone), January 2016.
16. The trope of 'family support' played a similar role in my study that the trope of 'adjustment' played in Tarini Bedi's (2016) excellent ethnographic study of women leaders of the Shiv Sena in Mumbai.
17. Reeti Singh, interview with the author (by phone). Lucknow, 20 December, 2015.
18. Vani Tripathi Tikoo (whom I interviewed in New Delhi, 12 January 2016) appeared quite enthusiastic about the research during our interview but in a subsequent phone call seemed to have cooled considerably to it.

Bibliography

Adams, T., and A. Herrmann (2020). 'Expanding Our Autoethnographic Future'. *Journal of Autoethnography* 1, no. 1: 1–8. DOI: https://doi.org/10.1525/joae.2020.1.1.1.

Anand, D. (2007). 'Anxious Sexualities: Masculinity, Nationalism and Violence'. *British Journal of Politics and International Relations* 9, no. 2: 257–269.

Bacchetta, P. (1993). 'All of Our Goddesses Are Armed: Religion, Resistance, and Revenge in the Life of a Militant in the Nationalist Woman'. *Bulletin of Concerned Asian Scholars* 25, no. 4: 38–51.

Banerjee, S. (1996). 'The Feminization of Violence in Bombay: Women in the Politics of the Shiv Sena'. *Asian Survey* 36, no. 12: 1213–1225.

———. (2005). *Make Me a Man! Masculinity, Hinduism, and Nationalism in India*. Albany: State University of New York Press.

Basu, A. (1993a). 'Feminism Inverted: The Real Women and Gendered Imagery of Hindu Nationalism'. *Bulletin of Concerned Asian Scholars* 25, no. 4: 25–37.

———. (1993b). 'Women and Religious Nationalism in India'. *Bulletin of Concerned Asian Scholars* 25, no. 4: 3–4.

———. (1998). 'Hindu Women's Activism in India and the Questions It Raises'. In *Appropriating Gender: Women's Activism and Politicized Religion in South Asia*, edited by P. Jeffrey and A. Basu, 167–184. New York: Routledge.

———. (2015). *Violent Conjunctures in Democratic India*. New York: Cambridge University Press.

———. (2016). 'Women, Dynasties and Democracy in India'. In *Democratic Dynasties: State, Party, and Family in Contemporary Indian Politics*, edited by K. Chandra, 136–172. New York: Cambridge University Press.

Basu, M. (2017). *The Rhetoric of Hindu India: Language and Urban Nationalism*. New York: Cambridge University Press.

Basu, S. (2018). 'Hiding in Plain Sight: Disclosure, Identity, and the Indian Men's Rights Movement'. *QED: A Journal in GLBTQ Worldmaking* 5, no. 3: 117–129.

BBC News (2019). 'Triple Talaq: India Criminalises Muslim "Instant Divorce"'. 30 July. https://www.bbc.com/news/world-asia-india-49160818. Accessed on 10 February 2022.

Bedi, T. (2016). *The Dashing Ladies of Shiv Sena: Political Matronage in Urbanizing India*. Albany: State University of New York Press.

Behl, N. (2017). 'Diasporic Researcher: An Autoethnographic Analysis of Race and Gender in Political Science'. *Politics, Groups, and Identities* 5, no. 4: 580–598.

Blee, K. M. (1993). 'Evidence, Empathy, and Ethics: Lessons from Oral Histories of the Klan'. *Journal of American History* 80, no. 2: 596–606.

Blee, K. M., and S. McGee Deutsch (eds.) (2012). *Women of the Right: Comparisons and Interplay across Borders*. University Park: Pennsylvania State University Press.

Brocker, M., and M. Künkler (2013). 'Revisiting the Inclusion–Moderation Hypothesis: Introduction'. *Party Politics* 19, no. 2: 171–186.

Butalia, U. (2001). 'Women and Communal Conflict'. In *Victims, Perpetrators or Actors? Gender, Armed Conflict and Political Violence*, edited by C. Moser and F. Clark, 99–114. New York: Zed.

Deo, N. (2016). *Mobilizing Gender and Religion in India: The Role of Activism*. New York: Routledge.

Ferber, A. L. (2004). *Home-grown Hate: Gender and Organized Racism*. New York: Routledge.

Jacobs-Huey, L. (2002). 'The Natives Are Gazing and Talking Back: Reviewing the Problematics of Positionality, Voice and Accountability among "Native" Anthropologists'. *American Anthropologist* 104, no. 3: 791–804.

Jaffrelot, C. (2013). 'Refining the Moderation Thesis. Two Religious Parties and Indian Democracy: The Jana Sangh and the BJP between Hindutva Radicalism and Coalition Politics'. *Democratization* 20, no. 5: 876–894.

Jeffery, P., and A. Basu (eds.) (1998). *Appropriating Gender: Women's Activism and Politicized Religion in South Asia*. New York: Routledge.

Kishwar, M. (1986). 'Pro Women or Anti Muslim? The Shahbano Controversy'. *Manushi: A Journal about Women in Society* 32, no. 4: 4–13.

Kumar, R. (1997). *The History of Doing: An Illustrated Account of Movements for Women's Rights and Feminism in India 1800–1990*, 2nd edition. New Delhi: Kali for Women.

Malik, Y. K., and V. B. Singh. (1994). *Hindu Nationalists in India: The Rise of the Bhartiya Janata Party*. Boulder, CO: Westview Press.

Menon, K. D. (2010). *Everyday Nationalism: Women of the Hindu Right in India*. University Park: University of Pennsylvania Press.

Menon, N. (2014). 'A Uniform Civil Code in India: The State of the Debate in 2014'. *Feminist Studies* 40, no. 2: 480–486.

Menon, U. (2003). 'Do Women Participate in Riots? Exploring the Notion of "Militancy" among Hindu Women'. *Nationalism and Ethnic Politics* 9, no. 1: 20–51.

Naples, N. A. (1996). 'A Feminist Revisiting of the Insider/Outsider Debate: The "Outsider Phenomenon" in Rural Iowa'. *Qualitative Sociology* 19, no. 1: 83–106.

PTI New Delhi (2017 [2014]). '7 Women Ministers in Modi Team'. *Hindu Business Line*, 26 May (updated 24 November 2017). https://www.thehindubusinessline.com/news/national/7-women-ministers-in-Modi-team/article20781751.ece. Accessed 29 May 2020.

Sarkar, T. (1993). 'Women's Agency within Authoritarian Communitarianism: The Rashtrasevika Samiti and Ram Janmabhoomi'. In *Hindus and Others: The Question of Identity in India Today*, edited by G. Pandey, 24–45. New Delhi: Viking.

———. (1998). 'Orthodoxy, Cultural Nationalism, and Hindutva Violence: An Overview of the Gender Ideology of the Hindu Right'. In *Nation, Empire, Colony: Historicizing Gender and Race*, edited by R. R. Pierson and N. Chaudhuri, 166–181. Bloomington: Indiana University Press.

———. (1999). 'The Gender Predicament of the Hindu Right'. In *The Concerned Indian's Guide to Communalism*, edited by K. N. Panikkar, 131–159. New Delhi: Penguin.

———. (2001). *Hindu Wife, Hindu Nation: Community, Religion, and Cultural Nationalism*. Bloomington: Indiana University Press.

Sarkar, T., and B. Urvashi (eds.) (1995). *Women and the Hindu Right: A Collection of Essays*. New Delhi: Kali for Women.

Schaffer, F. C. (2014). 'Ordinary Language Interviewing'. In *Interpretation and Method: Empirical Research Methods and the Interpretive Turn*, edited by D. Yanow and P. Schwartz-Shea, 183–193. Armonk (NY): M.E. Sharpe.

Sehgal, M. (2009). 'The Veiled Feminist Ethnographer: Fieldwork among Women of India's Hindu Right'. In *Women Fielding Danger: Negotiating*

Ethnographic Identities in Field Research, edited by M. K. Huggins and M. Glebbeek, 325–352. Lanham (MD): Rowman & Littlefield.

———. (2012). 'Mothering the Nation: Maternalist Frames in the Hindu Nationalist Movement in India'. In *Women of the Right: Comparisons and Interplay across Borders*, edited by K. M. Blee and S. M. Deutsch, 192–207. University Park: Pennsylvania State University Press.

Sen, A. (2007). *Shiv Sena Women: Violence and Communalism in a Bombay Slum*. Bloomington: Indiana University Press.

Sen, A., and R. Jasani (2014). 'Mumbai (1992–93) and Ahmedabad (2002), a Tale of Two Cities: Narratives of Violent and Victimized Women Enduring Urban Riots in India'. *Allegra Lab*, 4 November. https://allegralaboratory.net/mumbai-1992-93-and-ahmedabad-2002-a-tale-of-two-cities-narratives-of-violent-and-victimized-women-enduring-urban-riots-in-india. Accessed 21 March 2020.

Shah, S. P. (2015). 'Queering Critiques of Neoliberalism in India: Urbanism and Inequality in the Era of Transnational "LGBTQ" Rights'. *Antipode* 47, no. 3: 635–651.

Soni, A. (2014). 'How Well Do You Know These 7 Women Ministers in the New Indian Government?' Yourstory.com, 28 May. https://yourstory.com/2014/05/women-ministers-narendra-modi-india-government. Accessed May 29, 2020.

The Hindu (2003). 'Personal Laws Detrimental to Women's Cause'. 17 February.

Williams, R. V. (forthcoming). *Marginalized, Mobilized, Incorporated: Women and Religious Nationalism in Indian Democracy, 1915–2015*. Oxford University Press, 2022.

———. (2006). *Postcolonial Politics and Personal Laws: Colonial Legal Legacies and the Indian State*. New Delhi: Oxford University Press.

Williams, R. V., and N. Deo (2018). 'Hinduism and Democracy: Religion and Politicized Religion in India'. In *Routledge Handbook of Asian Politics*, edited by S. Hua, 546–559. New York: Routledge.

Williams, R. V., and L. D. Jenkins (2015). 'Secular Anxieties and Transnational Engagements in India'. In *Multiple Secularities beyond the West: Religion and Modernity in the Global Age*, edited by M. Burchardt, M. Wohlrab-Sahr, and M. Middell, 19–38. Boston: De Gruyter.

Yanow, D., and P. Schwartz-Shea (2014). *Interpretation and Method: Empirical Research Methods and the Interpretive Turn*. Armonk, NY: M.E. Sharpe.

Zinn, M. B. (1979). 'Field Research in Minority Communities: Ethical, Methodological and Political Observations by an Insider'. *Social Problems* 27, no. 2: 209–219.

Part II

Gendered Techniques of Mobilization

The Sangh and the Samiti

3

The *Shakha*, the Home and the World

Going beyond the *Shakha* and the RSS Family

Lalit Vachani

In this chapter, I draw upon a repository of moving images, recollections, photo fragments, notes, memories and stories from three sets of journeys that I made to Nagpur, Maharashtra, while filming the Rashtriya Swayamsevak Sangh (henceforth RSS or Sangh)[1] in 1992 when the Bhartiya Janta Party (henceforth BJP) was in the opposition; in 2000 and 2001 when the RSS–BJP came to power under the National Democratic Alliance (NDA) coalition government of Atal Bihari Vajpayee; and finally a third filming trip in 2016 when the RSS–BJP had become the force behind the state under the Narendra Modi regime. These trips have resulted in two films on the RSS[2] – *The Boy in the Branch* (1993) and *The Men in the Tree* (2002) – and in contemporary research and ongoing visual documentation about different facets of the Sangh Parivar.[3]

This chapter explores the role of the RSS *shakha* (branch) in reproducing and consolidating Hindu nationalist ideology. I argue for an extensive approach to the *shakha* that pays attention to both the daily structured activities that take place within the branch and the social connections that are forged by networks, spaces and milieus outside the *shakha* environment. I suggest that the key to the *shakha*'s effectiveness lie in these linkages that are able to extend the ideology and the form of the *shakha* from the playground, the home and the family to the world at large.

The argument is developed in three sections. In the first section of the chapter 'The Shakha Within', I explore how the RSS *shakha* structures and reproduces social relations within Maharashtrian, Brahmin-dominated neighbourhoods in Nagpur. I show how the *shakha* indoctrinates Hindu boys and young men to the worldview of the RSS through an ingenious system involving play and storytelling, somatic ritual, discipline and bodily comportment and leisure-time socialization that extends beyond the ambit of the daily *shakha* meetings. I show how the *shakha* games and stories are adapted according to the age of the volunteer, and how these gradually become more ideological and physical over time with the eventual aim of creating loyal, action-oriented and militant bodies in the service of the RSS.

In the second section 'The Shakha in the World', I move beyond the bounded time and space of the playground to analyse the practices that extend and link the *shakha* to the outside world. The *shakha* interacts with its external environment in several crucial ways in order to retain volunteers, expand its base of operations to newer areas and mobilize volunteers and disseminate information within Hindu society. The *shakha* adopts resilient but flexible practices in adapting to its new environment. RSS ideological discourse is able to transform and adapt to the needs of the contemporary moment in order to produce and embellish new stories and myths about the internal threats and external enemies that the Hindu nation must always guard against. I suggest that this adaptability is the key to Hindu *sangathan* and to the practice and the politics of RSS mobilization.

The third and final section 'The RSS Home and the World' looks at how RSS peer group pressure and professional networks play a crucial role in retaining volunteers within the organization. I discuss how the Nagpur RSS Brahmin family socializes, regulates and normalizes daily RSS-related routines for the men in the household. If the driving force behind the recruitment and territorial expansion of the RSS are the male volunteers of the *shakha*, I suggest that it is the women who are the primary drivers of stability and strength within the RSS family as they juggle competing and sometimes conflicting roles to further the interests of the RSS.

Prologue

I encountered my first RSS *shakha* in Aligarh in the winter of 1990. I was working with journalist Lindsey Hilsum on a Channel 4 radio programme on the Ram Janambhoomi (Ram's Birthplace)[4] movement. In the wake of

L. K. Advani's *rath yatra* (chariot procession), there had been orchestrated attacks on Muslims in the neighbouring districts of Aligarh, especially in the villages surrounding Atrauli. We visited a number of the riot-affected villages and the makeshift relief centres that had come up to shelter the Muslim villagers. The villagers shared identical stories of atrocity and terror. They told us that the riots had been pre-planned and caused by outsiders who came at night. The attackers were from the Lodh community, and their leader was Kalyan Singh.[5]

There was considerable consternation among the students and the faculty at Aligarh Muslim University at these riots, which were seen as being orchestrated and organized by the Sangh Parivar. An elderly Muslim professor told me about another disturbing development in his neighbourhood: a daily RSS *shakha* had begun meeting in the past month. Subsequently, I went with the professor to his local park early in the morning and saw this *shakha*. There were eight young boys performing gentle calisthenics, and I could not understand the professor's fear.

I could not forget it either. The contrast between his fear and the innocuous appearance of the *shakha* remained with me. I began to research the subject, and a few years later in 1993, I made my first documentary about the RSS *shakha*, by following its activities in the city of Nagpur where the RSS has its headquarters.

The *Shakha* Within

Established in 1925, the RSS is the chief vehicle and source of Hindutva ideology in India. Influenced by early twentieth-century European fascism, the RSS aims to remake India as a Hindu-supremacist nation[6] where other religious minorities are lesser citizens.[7] For close to a century the RSS programme and ideological vision has permeated all domains of Indian social and political life through the creation of a multitude of allied organizations[8] that together comprise the Sangh Parivar, or the RSS family, of Hindu nationalist organizations.

Central to the story of the RSS' spread and strength is the role of the *shakha*. Described as 'the life of the RSS' by senior RSS leader Mohan

Bhagwat (Vachani 1993), it is the primary mechanism by which Hindutva ideology reproduces itself both formally and spatially. *Shakha*s are organized as small, voluntary groups of boys and men who meet daily in public spaces such as neighbourhood parks, for an hour of group activities which may be led by senior or junior leaders of the organization. Using an ingenious system of play and somatic ritual, the body of the *swayamsevak* (RSS volunteer) is disciplined through these everyday activities in the *shakha*, so as to create an active and pliant resource for the RSS in the service of Hindutva ideology and the Hindu nation.

*Shakha*s offer a series of *sharirik* (physical) and *boudhik* (intellectual) activities. They are usually organized in four groups or *gana*s that cater to different age groups. The *shishu gana* is for infants and very young children between the ages of three and ten years. The *baal gana* comprises children between ten and fourteen years, while the *tarun gana* is for teenagers and young men aged between fourteen and twenty-eight years. The *proudh gana* is for older men.

Our film team focused on the residential areas of Pratapnagar and Telecomnagar in Nagpur that comprise modest, middle-class residential colonies of largely Brahmin families that provide a core of dedicated *swayamsevak*s for the RSS. To a great extent, the leadership of the RSS in Nagpur (and elsewhere in India as well) comes from this social base. Most of the volunteers we met had white-collar government jobs or else were university lecturers, lawyers, doctors, bankers, accountants and engineers. In such an environment the RSS ideology was hegemonic and self-perpetuating, and *shakha*-going activities were habitual and routinized. The *shakha*s in this Nagpur region were relatively homogeneous and mostly attended by Maharashtrian Brahmins.[9]

My research and filming in 1992 focused on the indoctrination and the socialization of young children in the RSS. We filmed two *shakha*s in diverse parts of Nagpur. The Jaripatkanagar *shakha* was a newly established *shakha* that had recently begun the process of inducting young children, mostly around six to fourteen years of age. Jaripatkanagar was also a recent area of RSS penetration, which meant that the *shakha* leaders had to work harder to get young boys to attend. For contrast, we also filmed at the Telecomnagar *shakha*, an established *shakha* steeped in RSS ideology, where we focused on the *tarun gana* – an RSS grouping of older boys who played more militant games.

Daily Routine

*Shakha*s usually meet for an hour in the early morning or evening, when it is convenient for office-going professionals and school children to attend either before or after school and work. Before and after the daily *shakha* session, it is common for *swayamsevak*s to congregate, socialize and chat. This male-bonding ritual is an informal but nevertheless central part of the RSS *shakha* routine as well, and perhaps its greatest attraction.

The formal *shakha* routine is a medley of conflicting and clashing styles and activities. The routine begins with drills involving rigid formations and military manoeuvres to harsh-sounding Sanskrit commands, in which *agresar*s (junior RSS leaders) present themselves and salute their senior functionaries – the *karyavah* (supervisor) and *mukhya shikshak* (chief instructor). This is followed by the playful excess of games in the *sharirik* (physical) programme, when self-control and rigidity are suspended in free-flowing, physical and often violent play. The games segment ends with an interregnum of *geet* (patriotic songs), *subhashit* (virtuous and moral sayings) or a *boudhik* (intellectual) session where the RSS volunteer must concentrate and attempt to absorb stories and moral lessons. At the end of a *shakha* session, the junior volunteers present themselves once again and salute their superior officers and the saffron flag. The RSS prayer is recited and sung, the *bhagwa dhwaja* (saffron flag) is carefully folded and put away, and the *shakha* routine ends in further leisure-time socialization, loitering and conversations among the volunteers.

In the following section, I take a closer look at the two formal components of the *shakha* routine – *sharirik* and *boudhik* – and the sets of physical and mental activities that work in tandem to socialize the RSS volunteer.

Sharirik (Physical Training)

A central feature of the *sharirik* (physical training) programme of the RSS *shakha* is universally played games of 'catch' and 'tag', with appropriately

Figure 3.1 The *shakha* at Reshambagh, Nagpur, 1992
Photo credit: Wide Eye Film; Lalit Vachani.

bharatiya (indigenous) names. These games were very attractive to the young boys in the *shakha* and were the primary reason for increasing attendance at the new Jaripatkanagar *shakha* in Nagpur.

The second *sarsangchalak* (supreme commander) of the RSS, Guruji Golwalkar, was candid in suggesting that children should be lured to the *shakha* in order to begin the crucial process of teaching *sanskaar* (good habits). He would repeat a story about how a rich man is able to lure a beautiful peacock to his garden by mixing opium in its food. The peacock keeps returning to the garden to partake of this opium. Eventually, the peacock is so habituated that it continues to come to the garden regularly even without the opium (Golwalkar 1966: 304).[10] The opioids at the *shakha* are the games – the primary means to entice young children to the RSS world.[11]

A central difference between the RSS *shakha* system and the Balilla[12] organizations or the Hitler *jugend* appears to be the informal recruitment of young boys. In the film *The Boy in the Branch*, the central character Kali, aka Rajesh Jodhani, joined the *shakha* because he was bored and it seemed like a fun place to play games. Alternatively, other boys like Rohit and Vicky who

The Shakha, the Home and the World

came to the Jaripatkanagar *shakha* were brought there by their friends, also in the course of casual play. Another striking difference between the RSS movement and the Nazi and fascist youth groups is the young age at which the RSS recruits its volunteers. It is not uncommon to see toddlers at the *shakha*, usually the children of full-time volunteers of the RSS. The youngest *swayamsevak* we met, Dhawal Ghai, was three years old at the time of our filming. According to senior RSS leader K. S. Sudarshan:[13]

> Young children are malleable and prone to the teaching of *sanskaar* [good habits]. We prefer to take really young children to our *shakhas*, as things that are told to them at that age tend to have a lasting impression. Of course, it is only at the age of sixteen or seventeen that a boy takes the *pratigya* [the RSS oath] and is formally initiated into the RSS, but we do prefer to take children into the branch at the stage when they are infants. (K. S. Sudarshan in Vachani 1993b)

In the *shishu* (infant) category of *shakha*s, the games played by the little children lack any overt messaging or didactic component. The main aim is for children to enjoy the *shakha* and get used to the environment. In the *baal* (child) category, the games begin to get much more physical and have underlying ideological messages. Therefore, if *shishu* games are designed to lure young children to the *shakha*, *baal* games consolidate the ranks of the new recruits, along with carefully structured ideological training designed to provoke and stimulate a sense of belonging and loyalty to the Hindu nation.

To take an example, 'Main Shivaji' (I Am Shivaji) is a universal game of catch, in which a boy is designated as the catcher while another, the runner, is designated as Shivaji[14] in the game. The catcher must pursue and tag Shivaji who shouts 'Main Shivaji!', while the other boys run around the catcher to prevent him from tagging Shivaji. In its repetitive and daily enactment in *shakha*s across the country, the universal game of 'catch' is given an ideological dimension. Mohan Bhagwat[15] told us about the origins of the game:

> This game used to be played in Christian schools and at the YMCA in Kerala and was known as 'Cross'. While this wouldn't work for the *shakha*, we adapted the game so that it was called 'Main Shivaji'. An alien concept was transformed into one that builds the mental conditioning of the young recruit. (Mohan Bhagwat in Vachani 1992)

It is tempting to interpret the adaptation of this game by the RSS as another instance that confirms Christophe Jaffrelot's insight about the 'emulation and stigmatization' with which Hindutva neutralizes a threatening 'Other' 'by borrowing the traits that endowed its instigators with strength' (Jaffrelot 1999: 20, 78).[16] However, 'Cross' had no discernible, threatening traits that needed neutralization by emulation. It was obvious to us that the game was not about religious proselytization of Hindus or about the symbolic potency of the Christian Church, which is how the RSS and Mohan Bhagwat had interpreted it. The game was called 'Cross' because the central and dramatic arc of the game involved 'crossing' the catcher. With the heightened animosity towards Christianity and alleged religious conversion practices, even a simple, universal and ideologically neutral field game was given a communal, religious interpretation by the RSS. According to Lalit,[17] the *mukhya shikshak* (chief instructor) of the Jaripatkanagar *shakha*, the repetition and the chanting of 'Main Shivaji' made the young volunteers curious and gave an opportunity to the RSS to explain to them the great deeds of Maharaja Shivaji, how he fought the Muslim rulers and how he established Hindu *swaraj* (self-rule).

Another popular game that we filmed – 'Kashmir Hamara Hai' (Kashmir Is Ours)[18] – has particular resonance today.[19] In the game, a circle is drawn out on the ground, representing Kashmir. A boy sits pinned firmly in the circle while the other boys try to pull him out. The *mukhya shikshak* shouts 'Kashmir kiska hai?' ('Who does Kashmir belong to?'), to which the jostling boys respond with 'Hamara hai, hamara hai! Kashmir hamara hai!'[20] ('Ours, ours! Kashmir is ours!'). As Mohan Bhagwat told us in *The Men in the Tree*, the main function of the games is to give the child a sense of the broader community of Hindus along with a basic political awakening about Kashmir:

> At this age we can't give them details about the Kashmir problem or about the problems that have been caused by Article 370. But through the game they learn the basics: that Kashmir belongs to India and to the Hindus. They will be taught the other details in time.... Through the games they get the sense of community: 'You are not alone, and you have many friends. Your good is in the greater common good.' And that's how we teach them the importance of community and organization. (Mohan Bhagwat in Vachani 2002)

During the filming, we observed RSS children engage in role-playing along communal lines. For example, in *The Boy in the Branch*, in one of the scenes depicting 'Kashmir Hamara Hai' at the Jaripatkanagar *shakha*, while jostling violently with his comrades a boy shouts very spontaneously, 'Hindu ki jeet, Hindu ki jeet!' ('The Hindu will win, the Hindu will win!'). Later, during a *shakha* revisit in 2016, I observed some of the older boys pushing a smaller boy roughly towards the centre of the circle while shouting, 'You be the Muslim now, we are the Hindus'. But as I will later suggest, the didactic component in the *sharirik* programme is subtle with the primary aim of tiring recruits and preparing them to be receptive for the ideological messaging that occurs in the *boudhik* (intellectual) sessions.

A third game, 'Sangathan Mein Shakti Hai' ('The Organization Has Strength') involves the children running around a makeshift circle, which gradually spreads out, increasing its diameter as well as the level of difficulty in the game. The boys must complete their run around the enlarged circle without breaking breath while chanting one of three slogans: 'Sangathan mein shakti hai', 'Bharat Mata ki jai' ('Victory to Mother India') or 'Kashmir hamara hai'. The word *sangathan* is used to refer to both the practice of organization and *the* Organization (the RSS), and the game is intentionally reflexive and self-referential in its pedagogy, as it enables the RSS to present *itself* as the key to organization for the benefit of the Hindu nation.[21] In explaining the nuances of the need for greater *sangathan* (organization), the RSS *mukhya shikshak* Lalit would explain how Hindus were once divided, how the Muslims came and conquered and caused greater weaknesses in Hindu society, how the Christians and the British colonized the nation and how the RSS was forced to intervene because the Congress party created further divisions in Hindu society by appeasing the minorities.

In the *tarun gana* (the grouping for older boys and young men aged between fourteen to twenty-eight), the physical regimen consisted of more physically strenuous games, the demonstration of physical prowess and skills in sports involving self-defence and the toughening up of Hindu bodies in service of the *rashtra* (nation). The game of *kabaddi*, a very popular game in the *tarun gana*, served all these ends. In *kabaddi*, the objective of the game is for a single player on offence, referred to as a 'raider', to run into the opposing team's section of the court, tag as many of their defenders as possible and, after evading tackles by these defenders, return to his own territory while holding his breath. While the toughening of bodies, emphasis on speed and litheness and mastery of stamina and breathing techniques are obvious benefits of the game, the RSS also takes special pride in promoting *kabaddi* as a *bharatiya* (indigenous) game that appears to have magical properties. Waxing eloquent on the subject of Hindu identity, Golwalkar professed:

> There are only two secrets of our [RSS] work: First is that there is no secret. And, second is, kabaddi…. Motherland beneath, God created skies above, and Hindu society all around us – based on these elements, kabaddi has been successful. So much power was generated by this kabaddi; power that saved lives, honour and wealth of lakhs of people during partition of Punjab…. The foundation of our unified soul in that kabaddi came to signify 'organization'. (Hari 2018)

For senior RSS leader Mohan Bhagwat, the game reinforced essential Hindu qualities of the eternal soul and reincarnation and instilled a sense of team spirit and fearlessness in the young recruit, apart from enhancing physical and mental qualities, as well as fleetness of spirit and mind. During our film shoot in 1992, he read out a poem to us, an ode to *kabaddi* from a collection of writings by RSS workers:

> Why fear, O *kabaddi* player
> Play, play the game fearlessly
> It is in the play
> That you discover life
>
> For what is death if it brings about a new life
> Your mere shadow dies here
> For you are immortal
> (an extract from 'The Kabaddi Player' by an anonymous *pracharak*)[22]

Along with *kabaddi*, the *tarun gana* played other popular games like 'Nayudh' and 'Dandyudh'. These involve the acquiring of skills and mastery in unarmed combat or with rudimentary weapons, such as sticks. 'Nayudh', an abbreviated form of *nishastra yudh* (unarmed combat), is widely touted by the RSS as one of its main *sharirik* activities for imbuing volunteers with

Figure 3.2 Mohan Bhagwat in October 1992
Photo credit: Wide Eye Film; Lalit Vachani.

techniques of defensive combat and to instil self-confidence. According to K. S. Sudarshan:

> There are 104 vital spots in the human body, and if you target these areas then it is possible to disarm and bring under control an opponent, even if he is much bigger and stronger than you. And so with 'Nayudh' after doing due research,[23] we learned to practice our attacks on these vulnerable spots of the human body. (K. S. Sudarshan in Vachani 1992)

'Dandyudh' involves a series of intricate drills for mastering the use of the *dand*, or *lathi* (stick), for purposes of self-defence and in combat situations. Arafat Valiani's work on *shakha*s in Ahmedabad, and RSS volunteers' mastery of drill 'as a time-honored and virtuous martial practice cited in the Vedas' (Valiani 2011: 7) shows how the physical regimen of the *shakha* went beyond the immediate instrumentalism of creating a pliant, disciplined cadre. Instead of circumscribing the volunteers' predilection towards violence to prescribed and limited ends, Valiani suggests that in riot situations (specifically, the Gujarat riots of 1969 and 2002), the volunteers employed their mastery of drill techniques acquired through *shakha* training in improvisatory modes to engage in brutal and prolonged violence.

An incident from our 1992 film shoot underlined the trained practices of violence at the RSS *shakha*. Our sound attendant, Vilas Raut, had begun to playfully tease and taunt the RSS boys by suggesting that their *kabaddi* play was amateurish in comparison with the skilful, professional *kabaddi* that was played in Bombay. But I sensed that Vilas' good-natured banter was getting under the skin of some of the *shakha* boys and in particular Sripad[24] was getting angry at his comments. On one occasion when we had finished filming for the day, Sripad invited Vilas to participate in the game by joining in as a raider for the opposing team. Despite our warnings to Vilas to abstain from playing, he went ahead with the game. In the ensuing melee, there was a sudden, crushing and particularly violent tackle on Vilas by Sripad that resulted in the older man having to be hospitalized with torn ligaments and a dislocated hip. While Sripad appeared contrite and later paid Vilas a visit at the hospital, I had the distinct sense that he experienced sadistic pleasure in inflicting this pain and that there was real venom and malevolence in the physical confrontation that had just taken place. Sripad had unleashed a form

The *Shakha*, the Home and the World   89

Figure 3.3   Filming the boys in the branch, 1992
Photo credit: Wide Eye Film; Lalit Vachani.

of physical assault designed to maim an opponent and illustrated how 'play' at the older boys' *shakha* could be channelled in violent acts in actual combat situations.

In his study of RSS physical regimen in Kerala, Villat (2019: 54) suggests that the development of particular games and mock drills are designed to initiate sudden violence with precision to cause maximum damage to the 'enemies of Hinduism'. In *shakha*s in Kerala, RSS volunteers practised visualization techniques targeting Muslims and Communists in simulated combat settings.

Boudhik (Intellectual Training)

In the preceding section, I have mapped a carefully planned pedagogical *sharirik* programme involving play, discipline, regimentation and release with measured forms of ideological indoctrination depending on the age of the child. Here I turn to the *boudhik* (intellectual) sessions that occur after the *sharirik* component of the *shakha* concludes. The sequence is strategic in itself.

As the *mukhya shikshak* Lalit told us:

There are games played outside the circle that are designed to tire you. We have small children, and you have to tire them to be able to control them. Once the body is tired, the mind is receptive and more amenable to receiving instruction. (Lalit Chauragrahe in Vachani 1993b)

The content and form of this 'instruction' is carefully designed. As even publications that are sympathetic to the RSS admit, the RSS *boudhik* sessions do not 'stress heavy intellectual training', with the aim being to create 'action-oriented volunteers' (Sharda 2018: 104). Further, *boudhik* sessions are 're-oriented to cover current political and economic issues' (Andersen and Damle 1987: 92). In the *baal gana* of the *shakha*, the *boudhik* takes on its most effective form in the making-up of fables and myths and refracting stories as history while discussing agendas that are in currency, thus making the story 'digestible' and also directly relevant to the contemporary moment.

Baal Bodh Kathayen (1992, 2008), an RSS publication for *boudhik* dissemination to *baal swayamsevak*s, contains several stories aimed at indoctrination. The note from the editors emphasizes that 'this compilation of RSS stories for children has been produced keeping in mind that difficult and complex issues can be deeply instilled in young minds using the medium of storytelling'.

Veer Savarkar and Muslims are the central focus of the story 'All Powerful Hindu Religion':

At the Kaalapani Prison in the Andamans, the Muslims begin to touch the food that is meant to be eaten by the Hindus. The Hindus now refuse to eat the food because they feel that they will become impure. The Muslims are able to eat 4 times their regular share, while the Hindus go hungry.

Then Veer Savarkar intervenes decisively. He begins to touch the food of the Muslims while chanting '*Om Namah Shivaya*', exhorting his fellow Hindu prisoners to do the same. 'If you chant "*Om Namah Shivaya*", the food will become pure and the Muslims won't touch the food, as they fear they will become Hindu!'

Savarkar tells the assembled Hindu prisoners: 'Brothers, our Hindu religion is all-powerful. Not only can we eat the food of the Muslim and remain intact, even if we devour the Muslim completely, we will still remain Hindu.' (Dwivedi, Bhave and Ramkumar 2008: 55)

Several elements in this story communicate Hindutva ideological tropes in indirect ways. For instance, the choice to make Savarkar the main hero-protagonist of the story introduces children to the leading icon of Hindutva. While the fear of infection of the master race by minority groups is a classic trope in fascist discourse, the suggestion in this story that Muslims eat more than their fair share at the expense of the Hindus is reflective of the distinctive Hindutva charge of Hindu majority victimization and Muslim minority appeasement that the RSS–BJP routinely levels against its political opposition – the Congress and the left parties.

In another story from the publication, 'The Boy Who Jumped Several Floors', the protagonist is ten-year-old Kutty. Set in medieval India, the story begins by telling us how Malik Kafur's rampaging Muslim army has destroyed many Hindu temples in Madurai:

> Everyone in the village of Tirupparamkundram is at their wits' end as to how they should protect the Kartikeya temple. Then Kutty, a young ten-year-old boy, goes up to a village elder and asks: What are the Muslims afraid of?
> The elder replies despairingly: The Muslims are only afraid of ghosts.
> Then Kutty asks: How does one become a ghost?
> The elder replies: Only those who commit suicide become ghosts.
> So Kutty decides to become a ghost to fight the Muslims.[25]
> He climbs to the topmost *gopuram* of the temple, jumps down, and sacrifices his life for the temple. Today, the temple honours him for this supreme sacrifice. (Ibid.: 24)[26]

The production and circulation of this fable just after L. K. Advani's *rath yatra* and the unsuccessful October 1990 assault on the Babri Mosque in which an estimated fifteen *kar sevak*s lost their lives, is not a coincidence. It sought to make topical the central campaign of the Sangh Parivar at the time – the movement to build the Ram temple. The story created narrative space to fill in basic information about how the Ram temple had been destroyed and replaced by the existing *dhancha* (the Babri Mosque's structure). In this context, the intransigence of Muslims and other traitors in not allowing *kar seva* could also be explained to the young RSS initiate as quotidian knowledge and common sense (Vachani 1993).

As these examples show, in their basic manifestation in the *boudhik* programme of the *shakha*, fable fills in for fact; storytelling substitutes for historiography; and hagiography supersedes analysis and critique. It is crucial to emphasize here that the RSS tells stories or writes history primarily for *itself* and its own rank and file of *already existing believers*. It therefore has little time for complexity or nuance, or for the historical detail[27] that it would need to convince sceptics and opponents. The function of RSS' historical writing via its *shakha* stories for believers is to hark back to a golden age of Hindutva set in the Vedic period, to show how Hindus were subsequently victimized and emasculated, and to show why Hindu *sangathan* and the righting of these historical wrongs is a necessity in order to restore Hindutva to its pristine glory.

The act of storytelling at the *shakha* is also designed to inculcate a deep sense of loyalty to Hindu nationalist leaders, while provoking outrage and hatred against secular, historical figures. For instance, two of our filmed interlocutors, the ex-RSS volunteers D. R. Goyal and Purushottam Agarwal, shared similar stories from different time periods about the RSS' vilification of secular Indian nationalist leaders like M. K. Gandhi and Jawaharlal Nehru.

Goyal recounted how in the *shakha*, stories would be told about Nehru and his excessive smoking, drinking and womanizing, while in Agarwal's Gwalior *shakha*, the boys were told about how Nehru consumed a cow's tongue daily during breakfast.

According to Goyal 'where Gandhi was concerned, the RSS said that he would tolerate all manner of abuse against Hindus, and that he allowed Hindu women to be raped in a bid to appease the Muslims' (Vachani 2002).[28] Agarwal recalled the reason the RSS offered for Gandhi's 'failure' at the Partition of India. According to this *shakha* story, Gandhi had been beaten up by a group of Muslims as a boy and hence had grown up fearing and appeasing Muslims all his life. The *shakha* instructor concluded that 'if Gandhi had to be called the Father of the Nation, he should be known as the Father of the Nation of Pakistan' (ibid.).[29]

Figure 3.4 The *shakha* for young children at Jaripatkanagar, October 1992

Phtoto credit: Wide Eye Film; Lalit Vachani.

The Shakha in the World

In the preceding section, I discussed the internal activities that take place within the *shakha* and RSS attempts to build cadres through the medium of play and storytelling and by disciplining bodies and moulding minds in the service of the Hindu nation. In this section, I show that in order to sustain and reproduce itself, the *shakha* interacts with its external environment in four principal modes of activity: retention, expansion, dissemination/mobilization and adaptation.

Retention

Once an RSS volunteer, always an RSS volunteer

RSS volunteers would occasionally admit that getting the boys to attend the daily *shakha* was a problem, especially during examination time. Absenteeism is sought to be checked by formal mechanisms with specific roles given to *shakha* functionaries to become a part of their local communities and to impress upon the families of the recruits the potential pedagogical and professional benefits of joining the RSS *shakha*.

The RSS mobilizes specific workers like the *gatanayak*[30] (group leader) to retain volunteers and to check attrition. For instance, in the Jaripatkanagar branch, two older volunteers, Lalit and Purushottam, would visit the homes of younger boys on a regular basis if they failed to show up at the *shakha* and entreat and pressurize the parents to send their sons to the *shakha*.

Lalit would also visit the Jodhani household to help Kali with his homework from time to time.[31] He told us:

> We persuade the parents that sending their boy to the *shakha* will be beneficial for his education. 'The boys are being taught discipline; they are learning to concentrate. It will help them in their studies.' We also tell them how so many of the boys who attended *shakha* got admission to the IITs [Indian Institutes of Technology] and very good marks in the engineering colleges' entrance exam. (Lalit Chauragrahe in Vachani 1992)

RSS volunteers are fond of repeating their adage 'Once an RSS volunteer, always an RSS volunteer'. This would suggest that it is exceedingly difficult for RSS volunteers to leave the crucible of the *shakha* once they have become a part of the organization. In fact, some do leave the organization and the RSS uses this aphorism to assert that even the volunteers who choose to leave remain part of the extended family because of the *amit chhaap* (indelible mark) left by the *sanskaar* (the good habits) that they imbibed at the RSS branch.

Twenty-five years later, I asked Kali (now thirty-four years old, and a father of three) why and how he left the RSS, and he responded by describing the fortuitous turn of events after our film shoot. The demolition of the Babri Mosque had been followed by the ban on the RSS for a brief period. In the interim, Lalit who was the driving force behind the Jaripatkanagar *shakha* also left the RSS,[32] and the *shakha* had stopped meeting.

> I think our group was just lucky, many others are not so fortunate. I don't miss the RSS at all. But I do miss the friends I made at the *shakha*. I remember how we all used to hang out together after the *shakha* meeting. Today we don't even see each other. No one has the time. (Kali Jodhani in Vachani 2016)

Expansion

In addition to retaining its core group of volunteers, the *shakha* performs another crucial function: to take Sangh or RSS ideology to newer areas by setting up additional RSS branches.

Central to this endeavour is the physical capture of public spaces or playgrounds.

A young *swayamsevak* Kunal described the process to us in 1992:

> We try to reach newer areas where we can get the young boys to attend *shakha*, to learn about Bharat Mata [Mother India], to work for the nation. But there are often vested political interests who oppose us.[33] Sometimes when a *shakha* moves to a new playground, they will try to stop the branch from meeting. That's when we report to our *karyavah* [supervisor], and the Sangh helps us. (Kunal in Vachani 1992)

The 'help' usually takes the form of the organization of an *ekatrikaran* (united gathering), where the strongest *shakha*s come together in the neighbourhood in a visible display of their amassed strength and numbers. Kunal explained, 'Once the show of strength happens, where our *swayamsevak*s perform "Dandyudh" and "Nayudh", the opposition usually withers away, and our new *shakha* is able to meet and resume the process of making recruits.'

Sripad, a character in *The Men in the Tree*, provided further details:

> The RSS *shakha* exerts a natural pressure on its immediate social environment. Just the fact of 25–30 able-bodied, strong RSS boys, armed with sticks walking through the neighbourhood is enough to

send a message to outsiders. Anti-national forces can never develop here, they are nipped in the bud even before they can take form. As for those who dared to stop the *shakha* from meeting, they got beaten up very badly. Till today, nobody has dared to stop the Telecomnagar *shakha* from its meetings. (Sripad Borikar in Vachani 2002)

For Sripad and Sandeep, stopping an RSS *shakha* from meeting was tantamount to insulting the saffron flag and therefore justified violence as self-defence, or a 'tit-for-tat strategy'.[34] The act of sending the strongest *shakha*s to a new neighbourhood in the form of an *ekatrikaran* was thus a method of territorial expansion of the Sangh and its Hindutva ideology.

In 2016, I asked Sripad about contemporary use of the *ekatrikaran* by the RSS in public space. He claimed that it was still employed by the RSS when necessary and compared it to a military flag march:

Just like the army uses a flag march, we will do an *ekatrikaran*. Particularly where areas are tense, or where there is a curfew, we do it to tell the people that we are on their side. They need not fear the enemy; the RSS is there to support them.

Dissemination and Mobilization

The *shakha* functions as a message dissemination centre to mobilize RSS volunteers in the service of Hindutva politics. The form of this mobilization can vary from local concerns and neighbourhood issues to creating awareness about national issues to an imagined community of *shakha*-attending volunteers.

For instance, in 1992 almost all the Nagpur *proudh* (adult) *shakha*s that we filmed would have some form of instruction or information about the Ram temple. In particular, Arun Shourie's propaganda pieces for the building of the temple were discussed, along with providing locally relevant information that he would be coming to Nagpur as the chief guest[35] during Vijayadashami, the RSS foundation day. In addition, RSS *shakha*s in Nagpur were used to mobilize volunteers to carry out the Ram *paduka*s (Lord Ram's slippers) in local neighbourhoods in order to collect donations and get volunteers to go to Ayodhya in December 1992. The

Ram *paduka poojan* (worship) programme was replicated nationally by RSS *shakha*s.

In 2001, *shakha*s nationwide participated in the Rashtra Jagran Abhiyan (National Awakening Movement), a grassroots, door-to-door propaganda campaign 'to publicize and promote the good work done by the RSS' (Sandeep Pathey in Vachani 2002). We were able to film this campaign-in-progress in both Nagpur and Delhi. Similarly, *shakha*s became important nodal centres to disseminate information about electoral campaign strategy to mobilize RSS volunteers during Narendra Modi's successful election campaigns of 2014 and 2019. The RSS replicated this strategy at the local and the national levels to mobilize cadres and influence public opinion to help the BJP win these crucial elections.

*Shakha*s are also occasional sites for rumour-mongering, with the aim of inciting violence at the local level. In a chilling scene in *The Men in the Tree*, ex-RSS volunteers D. R. Goyal and Purushottam Agarwal describe their participation in similar activities that were provoked by RSS *shakha*s during two very different time periods and in different geographical locations. The first instance involved Partition violence in 1946 in Moga, Punjab, while the second incident was set during 'peacetime' in Gwalior, Madhya Pradesh in the late 1960s. In the film, Goyal and Agarwal describe how in each instance, the *shakha* became an active site for the forging of rumours about the Muslim community. RSS volunteers attempted to execute false flag operations[36] by designing and producing posters and letters as if written by Muslims. The plan was to suggest that they (that is, the Muslims) were planning an imminent attack on Hindus, in the hope of inciting pre-emptive violence by Hindus against the Muslim community. In Moga, this led to communal violence and the killing of Muslims, while in Gwalior the area remained tense though no actual incidents of violence took place. But as Purushottam Agarwal told us on camera, 'had there been violence in the town, it would have been practically impossible for a commission of inquiry to pinpoint the blame and to attribute it to our *shakha*'.[37]

In recent years, the potential role of the *shakha* as a closed group disseminating rumour has been greatly amplified by digital technology and BJP investments in creating a robust social media platform with a massive and largely anonymous base of paid workers and volunteers. While clearly beyond the scope of this chapter, it is crucial to explore the intersections and the linkages between *shakha*s, *shakha* volunteers and their WhatsApp groups, and the corresponding role of rumour in practices of Hindutva mobilization.[38]

Adaptation

On my second set of filming trips to Nagpur in 2000–2001, I discovered that *shakha*s were not expanding exponentially and their growth rates were far below RSS goals. Neither the Jaripatkanagar nor the Telecomnagar *shakha*s were active.[39]

According to Sandeep, this was because of 'the onslaught of Western culture on our *bharatiya sanskriti* (Indian culture) via satellite television' and a cut-throat, competitive examination culture that had developed in India post-liberalization.[40] Far more plausible was Sripad's explanation that RSS volunteers neglected the basic tasks of daily *shakha* management and growth because they were ill-prepared and overwhelmed by bureaucratic and administrative responsibilities once the BJP was suddenly thrust into power as the leader of the NDA coalition government in 1998.

With the anointment of Mohan Bhagwat as the sixth *sarsangchalak* in 2009, efforts to increase *shakha* growth and penetration increased largely because of his personal initiatives. The RSS consciously tried to adapt to new environments in embracing cyber-technology nationally and globally[41] and by adopting flexible practices of *shakha* congregation. These included modifying dress codes, changing *shakha* timings to include office-goers, reducing the physical workload of the *sharirik* programme, along with a sustained effort to woo IT professionals with the organization of IT-Milans which are held once a week as opposed to daily meetings (Lulla 2010; Kumar 2014; Shukla 2015; Basu 2015). In addition, the RSS began to organize cyber-*shakha*s or e-*shakha*s as virtual meeting points for RSS volunteers globally (Khan 2009; Joshi 2010), and delegated *apartment pramukh*s to recruit like-minded volunteers with the intention of holding *shakha*s in high-rise buildings and apartment blocks in Indian cities (Verma 2018). Since 2014 in particular, the RSS has been making strategic and symbiotic use of its own BJP government at the centre to maximize the growth of *shakha*s. According to recent estimates that quote RSS sources, there are at least 60,000 daily *shakha*s around the country (Bagchi 2019).

A good site to demonstrate the adaptability of the *shakha* is its mutation within the Hindu Swayamsevak Sangh (henceforth HSS). The RSS takes the form of, and names itself, the HSS outside India. The *shakha* adapts to the needs of the local environment. For example, the *shakha* at Queens in New York City met indoors and not at a playground or a public space. The horizontal hand to chest salute to the saffron flag, which could be construed as a fascist gesture, had been replaced by a *namaskaar*, and the khaki shorts were replaced by the more casual and elegant track suits preferred by American *swayamsevak*s. Games were renamed to remove overt political references. For example, 'Kashmir Hamara Hai' was played as 'Dilli Hamari Hai'. Any direct association with Indian politics or the Hindu nationalist BJP were hidden at least during formal discourse in the few meetings that I attended, as the HSS sought to project itself as an apolitical and cultural organization.

Adaptation of Stories: Internal Threats and External Enemies

The *shakha* adapts and expands over time by constantly updating its stories and mythologies about 'internal threats and external enemies' (Golwalkar 1966).[42] In this section documenting the flexibility of *shakha* storytelling practices, I look at gendered discourses surrounding different versions of the 'love jihad'[43] story that I encountered at the different time periods of my research.

I heard my first version of the 'love jihad' story in 1999 after attending an HSS *shakha* in Queens, New York. Once he discovered that I was a fellow Sindhi, the Queens *shakha karyavah* (supervisor) Narain Kataria raged against the Indian cricketer Azharuddin and his nuptials with the Sindhi actor Sangeeta Bijlani, who had converted to Islam after their marriage. Kataria warned me that this was not just about the seduction and conversion of innocent Sindhi or Hindu women by Muslim men. He asserted that religious conversion was also rampant in the Queens area of New York. In this context, Kataria alleged that Mexican and Puerto Rican Christian and Pakistani and other Muslim women were targeting Indian Hindu men.

A few years later in 2002 in Nagpur, Sandeep told me another story about 'love jihad'.[44] Like many other RSS stories, it was set in the neighbourhood of

Mominpura, the largest Muslim-majority area of Nagpur, presented in RSS narratives as a den of vice and crime.

> The Nagpur police caught these guys from Mominpura spying on Hindu girls in our neighbourhoods. They would be fruit-sellers, *istri wallah*s [men who provide the service of ironing clothes], street vendors spying on our girls, trying to track their movements. Once they found them alone, the plan was to romance these young girls, marry them, and convert them to Islam.
>
> When the police beat them, the story came out. Fifty-five of these Muslims from Mominpura had been sent to Pakistan for training in this form of conversion. Naturally, if the girl converts to Islam, she will be estranged from her family who will disown her. And then the children will all be brought up Muslim.[45]

By 2016, a new version of the 'love jihad' story was in circulation. The modus operandi described was similar to the previous versions, but the story had been adapted to give it contemporary political salience.[46] On this occasion, Sandeep told me that 'love jihad' was happening less in Nagpur and more in the border regions of Punjab and West Bengal. The aggressors in the story were no longer the local Muslims of Mominpura but illegal Muslim immigrants from Bangladesh:

> They [illegal Bangladeshi Muslims] get jobs because they are willing to work for less money. Then they 'recce' the area thoroughly. Who are the girls from well-off families? Who are the ones who are vulnerable? It is wealthy Brahmin, Jain and Marwari girls that they covet and prey upon. They receive training in love jihad[47] at *madarsah*s; they betray the girls using love techniques.

As these variations over time about the deployment of 'love jihad' indicate, stories about internal threats and external enemies are always reworked and adapted to suit the contemporary RSS agenda and to link the local with the global.

In 2016, another story actively discussed in RSS circles contrasted and inverted the image of the lascivious, untamed, 'foreign', 'love jihadi' Muslim in its projection of the Hindu male as the 'protector' of Muslim women. The myth concerned an unnamed Muslim woman from Iran who had an abusive husband who had peremptorily divorced her. The tortured Muslim woman had fled to India from Iran. She had subsequently embraced Hinduism and found inner peace and strength. She had become well versed in Sanskrit and was now studying the Vedas and the Upanishads and translating some of the texts in Persian. In another variation of this story, she was from Saudi Arabia and not from Iran, and the translations were in Arabic and not in Persian. In yet another version, she had been given shelter by a family of RSS volunteers.

Who was this woman? Where did she live? Had anyone met her? Was there any documentary evidence of her existence? The Muslim woman who had converted to Hinduism was yet another empty signifier by which the RSS could set or circulate agendas – in this instance, by depicting Hindutva as a moral, protective force and by projecting a benevolent RSS as providing shelter for Muslim women while Hindutva groups pressed for interventions in personal law and anti-divorce legislation on their behalf. A year later, the State passed the 'triple *talaq*' bill, or the Muslim Women (Protection of Rights on Marriage) Bill, which the RSS and the BJP hailed as a victory for gender justice, while expanding possibilities for the criminalization of Muslim men.

The RSS Home and the World

In this section, I discuss how possibilities of educational mobility and peer group pressure constrain the creative desires of the RSS volunteer. Professional networks of the RSS provide business opportunities that further enhance the continuities of tradition and social control. Finally, I look at the role of women as the primary upholders of Hindutva morality and culture in extending these forms of social control within the RSS family.

Incipient Yearnings and Social Control

In 1992, one of our major filming locations was the Asha Sadan *karyalaya* (office) – an old, dilapidated bungalow rented by the RSS as a makeshift lodging for its *vidyarthi vistarak*s (student supervisors). About eight–ten RSS volunteers lived there. They were studying in the local Nagpur colleges. The RSS paid for their education, and in return the students had to run *shakha*s and participate in RSS programmes such as fund-raising and generating support and awareness about the Ram Janambhoomi movement.

There were several points of interpersonal contact and interesting exchanges between the RSS youth and the Wide Eye film team both before and after the filming. To us, the young men came across as likeable individuals who had no knowledge of international events and did not have independent opinions that differed from the worldview of the RSS. The Asha Sadan RSS volunteers were quite excited to be part of the filming process and they appeared to be quite taken in with some of the younger members of our team. Shuddha, Mohan and Satheesh[48] were only a few years older than the RSS boys, but they were film professionals and came across as worldly, cosmopolitan Hindus from the city, the likes of whom our RSS subjects had not previously met.

The filmmaking process and being filmed was of great interest to some of the volunteers. Lalit in particular began to show an interest in camerawork and was excited when Mohan and Shuddha told him about the cinematography course at the FTII (Film and Television Institute of India, the premier state institution for professional training in filmmaking). Mohan gave Lalit tutorials on camerawork and Lalit expressed interest in applying for the three-year diploma programme. The plan did not go any further. When I met Lalit over two decades later in 2016, he brought up his past interest in doing camerawork:

> For a while, it did seem I could take the FTII exams and try my hand at camerawork. But after your team left, I felt it was not possible for me despite my interest. I had some financial problems at home. I realized that it [FTII] was an impossible dream. I was really confused in those days.

When our team members suggested to Sandeep that he had his own distinctive, performative style for the camera and that he was very photogenic, he began to express an interest in doing Hindi theatre and modelling in Delhi. However, the possibility of doing theatre in Delhi and trying to make a career as a model clashed with Sandeep's prescribed role of doing Sangh work. His dreams and nascent yearnings ended abruptly when the ailing RSS *sarsangchalak* Balasaheb Deoras called for him to be part of his inner retinue and join the group of young RSS volunteers who could tend to his daily needs. Sandeep told us in 2001:

> I was very reluctant [to join] in the beginning. I thought this will be the end of my freedom. I didn't want to go. I kept making excuses to delay and to not join. But then Mohanji [Bhagwat] convinced me: He said, 'In the Sangh, we worship the *sarsangchalak*, and if he has chosen you, it is a great honour. You must do your duty to him and to the RSS.'

Sandeep then took shifts in taking care of Deoras during the RSS ban[49] and over the last days of his life which he described as 'a small contribution in terms of sacrifice' that he was very proud of. But he added:

> I do ask myself, what if I had come away with you and pursued my dreams of acting and modelling? Would I have made it? But I realize that was an impossible dream, and that would have been a very different Sandeep Pathey and not me!

The dreams were not just about alternative careers. In 2001, another *swayamsevak* Aman,[50] who lived with the boys at Asha Sadan, confided in me that he found his neighbour attractive. She was also from an RSS family. They made eye contact, would smile at each other and occasionally converse, Aman told me. He felt that the attraction was mutual. But he felt that he could not approach her as she had been promised to another *swayamsevak*. 'What would you do, *bhaisahib*?' I told Aman he should meet the young woman and talk to her to see if the feelings were mutual. But Aman never did approach her, and a year later she was married.

In contrast to Aman, another *swayamsevak* Pratap followed his desires. I looked for Pratap, a subject from our earlier period of filming and research, when I returned to Nagpur in 2016. His close friend Sandeep was initially evasive about providing information but eventually talked about the scandal that had taken place. Pratap had been in love with a girl and she reciprocated. They shared the same OBC caste background and their families also knew each other. However, the girl's parents had some financial problems and so they promised her in marriage to a wealthier *swayamsevak* family. She was married against her will but continued to meet Pratap in secret. As Sandeep told us:

> One day they eloped, and she was also with a child. We were very angry. Pratap and the girl should have forgotten that earlier phase of their lives. How could he run away with another man's wife? Why did he have to destroy the life of this other *swayamsevak*?

Sandeep told me that after these events Pratap drifted away from the RSS 'on his own', but from the reactions of a few other RSS volunteers I had the distinct sense that Pratap had been informally ostracized as someone who had broken social codes of morality and prescribed marital union.

Professional Networks

While the aspirational ideal for the young RSS volunteer is the life of a *pracharak* (an RSS preacher who will dedicate his life to RSS work), most *shakha* attendees are unable to continue with full-time RSS work and embark on a range of different professional careers. Here too, their past association with the RSS remains significant, and various RSS networks continue to assist them over the course of their careers. The following career trajectories of two of my film protagonists highlight the life-long significance of the RSS in individual lives.

In 1992, Sripad was about to join college. He was the tough, militant RSS volunteer in *The Boy in the Branch* and the martial arts expert at the Telecomnagar *shakha*. He was very active in the Ram Janambhoomi movement and one of the ten volunteers from Nagpur who were selected to do 'a particular job' in Ayodhya. Sripad did not specify what the job was at the time, but I learned later that he was on top of the dome of the Babri Mosque and had actively participated in the demolition, taking turns with other *kar sevak*s at attacking it with hand-made implements[51] (Vachani 2017). A self-described 'high-risk' volunteer, who had participated in many a battle for the RSS, Sripad's love for risk-taking extended to his professional career. When we met again in 2000, Sripad was working as a contractor on land development and construction projects. In this career, Sripad was sustained by the RSS contacts from his neighbourhood and *shakha*. He had obtained several lucrative contracts through these connections: he supervised a VHP (Vishva Hindu Parishad) temple construction project in Nagpur and the building of an RSS Ayurvedic research centre in the adjoining district of Hingna.

However, the construction business failed and Sripad set up a transport and trucking business which met with a similar fate. His next move was into the food sector, when he began to run a mobile food truck serving 'the best *pav bhaji* and *vada pav*' in Nagpur. While this family enterprise (Sripad and his wife Pranjali would cook together) was initially successful, it soon ran into financial difficulties and Sripad urgently needed to change his course yet again. Once again, the RSS connections proved invaluable. Sripad's childhood friend Devendra Fadnavis was being groomed for a political career by the RSS, and so Sripad sought an appointment with him:

> The fun of cooking and selling food had gone. I also realized I didn't want to be known as a *pav bhaji* seller all my life. So I went and met my class friend Devendraji, told him about my financial problems and he offered me a job working on his election campaign. (Vachani 2016)

Sripad has not looked back since that meeting. At the time of writing this, he has formally joined the BJP and is the *mahamantri* (chief secretary) of Fadnavis's Nagpur office. Sripad also works for another key BJP national leader Nitin Gadkari's trust, and manages ten villages[52] in the Gondia Adivasi belt. These are both prime positions within the BJP: Fadnavis was the chief minister of Maharashtra until November 2019, and Gadkari is presently a union cabinet minister. Sripad is a successful and secure professional today – a result that has entirely been produced by the workings of RSS networks and connections.

A network of RSS support was also visible in Sandeep's career trajectory. In 1992, Sandeep was completing his B. Com. degree from a local Nagpur college. He was a highly regarded *vidyarthi vistarak* (student supervisor) who was being groomed for leadership in the RSS. He was invested in running several RSS *shakha*s and programmes and was actively involved in the Ram Janambhoomi movement. Sandeep organized the Ram *paduka poojan* events

Figure 3.5 Filming Sripad in October 2016
Photo credit: Lalit Vachani.

in his neighbourhood and was involved in raising resources and enlisting *kar sevak*s (temple volunteers) to go to Ayodhya in December 1992. When the mosque was demolished, Sandeep was not in Ayodhya. He was, as he said, 'looking after the base of the Ram temple movement, while others fought at the front'.

When I met Sandeep again in 2000, his great regret was that he had not been able to dedicate his life to the RSS as a *pracharak*, a calling that he considered the pinnacle of dedication and sacrifice for the Hindu nation: 'I am proud that I gave six years to the RSS as a full-time worker and I also completed the third year of the OTC [Officers' Training Camps]. But I had my financial constraints and I could not offer more full-time work for the Sangh.'

Sandeep started his own business, a dealership for distributing Ayurvedic medicines and drugs to doctors in the Vidarbha region. He worked closely with RSS-affiliated manufacturers of Ayurvedic products and with doctors and clinics with informal RSS connections. When we next met him in 2016, Sandeep had transferred his dealership to his older brother and was now immersed in the field of Naturopathy. After doing a few state-level Naturopathic courses that earned him a diploma, 'Doctor' Sandeep Pathey started his own practice treating patients and selling Naturopathic and Ayurvedic products. Here too, the Sangh Parivar provided his clientele and support system

The RSS Family

In this section, I look at the role of women within the RSS family and suggest that it is they who are the primary upholders of Hindutva morality and culture in creating a space for male activism at home and by encouraging *shakha* activity.

In 1992, we selected Sandeep's family as the 'model' RSS family that we would follow and film. The Pathey family was quite figuratively and literally a microcosm of the Sangh Parivar: almost all family members belonged to different organizations within the Hindutva family of organizations. All the siblings of the Pathey household – Chandrakant, Deepak, Sandeep and Hemant – attended *shakha*s and had been *mukhya shikshak*s at different points in time. A cousin of the family was a member of the Durga Vahini, the women's organization of the Sangh, and a nephew coordinated the work of a few Bajrang Dal *shakha*s.

In 2016, when I visited again, the Pathey family's RSS connections had deepened. Now Sandeep's children, Shrenit (twelve years old) and Shetakshi (nine years old), regularly attended the RSS and the Rashtra Sevika Samiti (henceforth Samiti) *shakha*s. Sandeep's eighteen-year-old nephew Kartick Pathey[53] was in charge of organizing a group of the strongest *shakha*s in the Nagpur area. Sandeep himself was busy running the *proudh shakha* in Pratapnagar.

While the Pathey men and boys were the visible faces of RSS activism, the women worked behind the scenes as key drivers of activist and organizational work. Sandeep's sister-in-law Ragini kept the accounts and did organizational work for the Nagpur chapter of the Vanvasi Kalyan Ashram (VKA). Sandeep's mother Minatai Pathey and his wife Shilpa Pathey were perhaps the most prominent, active and successful Sangh workers in the Pathey family. Minatai Pathey had been active in the Ram Mandir movement, collecting donations and organizing people to go to Ayodhya in early December 1992. She was also a two-term BJP *corporator* (municipal councillor) and a senior member of the BJP Mahila Morcha (BJP Women's Wing). Very much the matriarch of the family, she along with her daughters-in-law Ragini and Shilpa ran the Pathey household on a day-to-day basis.

I met Shilpa Pathey for the first time in 2016. Shilpa is from the same Maharashtrian Chitpavin Brahmin community as Sandeep. She is a successful lawyer in Nagpur with her own practice and is active in Samiti and BJP work in Nagpur. She also organizes an annual women's scooter and moped rally around the issue of Hindu women's empowerment and is in charge of a local BJP-led Vivekananda trust. In Chandrapur, where she was born and raised, she was in charge of several Durga Vahini *shakha*s where she taught 'Niyudh', 'Dandyudh' and yoga to young women. She was also very active during the Ram Janmabhoomi movement.

I asked Shilpa about the circumstances of her marriage to Sandeep:

> We marry within Brahmin RSS families. Usually, it will be a senior *swayamsevak* known to both families who will suggest the match. Also, it helps that Mohan*ji* [Bhagwat] knows both our families very well.... Our men are good family men. They live lives of discipline and self-control and are *sanskaarit*. You could say RSS culture is in our blood.[54] My children – they have only missed attending the daily *shakha* if they have been unwell. They will always go to the *shakha* and they will always be with the Sangh. That will always be our way.

Golwalkar (1966: 283–287) devotes an entire chapter extolling the virtues of 'heroic motherhood' while underlining the significant contribution of women in instilling 'the right type of *sanskaar*' in young minds within the RSS family. As Sarkar (1995: 189) notes, these mothers are 'political creatures and agents' that are pivotal to RSS acculturation within the family, instilling 'habits of deference, of obedience and of respect for the RSS version of patriotism'.

I observed that the women whom we filmed were the primary drivers of stability and strength within the RSS family as they juggled competing and sometimes conflicting roles of the mother, housewife, cook, cleaner,

Figure 3.6 Sandeep Pathey with Shilpa Pathey and their daughter, Shetakshi, in 2016

Photo credit: Lalit Vachani.

professional breadwinner as well as activist and organizational roles in the extended RSS organization. They were responsible for creating a private, domestic space for RSS activism within the family, and were instrumental in ensuring that the RSS men and children attended the *shakha* on a daily basis.

Conclusion

This chapter[55] has looked at how the RSS *shakha* extends its presence in the world, through sites, practices and networks that intersect and converge in multiple ways to create pliant, malleable and active recruits in the service of the immediate superior officer, the supreme leader, the *bhagwa dhwaja* (the saffron flag) and the Hindu nation.

The structure of the *shakha*, the somatic rituals and regimentation, the disciplining of volunteers, a carefully structured system of rewards and punishment for insubordination commingled with unrestrained moments of play within a very clearly structured, well-researched pedagogical programme of physical exercise and storytelling socialize the young male recruit and weld him to the *shakha*, the neighbourhood, the broader Hindu community and the Hindu nation. In this milieu, with an inbuilt system of checks and balances to prevent attrition, the longer the volunteer is exposed to the *shakha* the greater the chance of life-long service in the cause of the Hindu nation. Further, RSS networks and the RSS family reinforce ties to the Sangh and fortify the act of attending *shakha*. In the absence of alternative forms of knowledge based on real experience or social contact with other religious and social groups outside of known Hindutva identities, the *shakha* becomes the primary source of knowledge and information about the neighbourhood and the outside world.

In an imaginary, hyperreal world – where the neighbourhood and the Hindu nation is always under threat from lascivious illegal immigrants, Muslim 'love jihadis' and *mullah*s, scheming Christian missionaries and girls that defile and steal your religion via financial inducement or seduction; where urban Naxals, renegade students, *tukde-tukde* gangs and Communists are constantly plotting against the Hindu nation – the RSS recruit must maintain constant vigil against multiple internal enemies and external threats.

The great tragedy for Indian secular democracy, and the great success of the RSS, has been the extension of the ideology and the form of the *shakha* from the playground, the home and the family to the world at large. In today's India, the *shakha* ideology is amplified digitally via the internet and social media and its cellular organizational form that combines decentralized flexibility with an overarching ideological core is replicated, renewed and rejuvenated by society as it begins to function semi-autonomously, cut off from its source and its material moorings in the physically contained space of the *shakha*.

The expanded social presence of the RSS also has considerable institutional support today. With the RSS–BJP in government, state institutions are formally saffronized (Anderson and Jaffrelot 2018; Kanungo 2019) and can legally and institutionally advance the Sangh programme. Then, the inexorable forward march of 'the All-Powerful Hindu Religion' that 'devours Muslims completely' and everything else in its wake as well, seems inevitable.

Notes

1. 'RSS' and 'Sangh' are used interchangeably by volunteers. Due to the frequency of their use and their interchangeability, I have used both the terms in this chapter.
2. For differences in the style and approach of the two films, on negotiating access and watching and being watched by the RSS, see the interview with Khanna (2019).
3. I use 'Sangh Parivar' to refer to the RSS-led Hindu nationalist family of organizations as distinct from the RSS family, where I refer to the nuclear or joint family unit comprising RSS volunteers.
4. The Ram Janambhoomi movement sought to build a grand temple for the Hindu god Ram at the specific site of the sixteenth-century Babri Mosque, which the Sangh Parivar claimed was his birthplace. The movement was led by the Vishva Hindu Parishad (VHP) and orchestrated by the RSS. It reached its zenith with Lal Krishna Advani's *rath yatra* (chariot procession) in creating awareness about the issue and mobilizing *kar sevak*s (temple volunteers) to go to Ayodhya. The demolition of the mosque on 6 December 1992 appears to have been minutely pre-planned by the Sangh Parivar, and several of its leaders, including Advani, were indicted by the CBI (Central Bureau of Investigation) and the Liberhan Commission on charges of criminal conspiracy (2009). With the BJP coming to power for a second term in 2019, there were renewed efforts to stall the criminal case against Sangh Parivar leaders and to expedite temple construction. On 9 November 2019, even while declaring the 1992 demolition of the mosque as against the rule of law, the Supreme Court perversely handed over the responsibility of building the Ram temple to the Hindu nationalist government. On 5 August 2020, temple construction began with the laying of the foundation stone at Ayodhya in a widely publicized ceremony attended, among others, by RSS supremo Mohan Bhagwat, prime minister Narendra Modi and the chief minister of Uttar Pradesh, Yogi Adityanath.
5. Kalyan Singh went on to become the chief minister of Uttar Pradesh and was complicit in the demolition of the Babri Mosque in December 1992. He was later appointed governor of Rajasthan in 2014 by the Narendra

Modi-led BJP government. The RSS is particularly careful and consistent in both protecting and rewarding its most aggressive *karyakarta*s (workers) over the years, as the careers of Kalyan Singh, L. K. Advani, Narendra Modi, Yogi Adityanath and, most recently, Sadhvi Pragya Singh Thakur will testify to.

6. See Savarkar [2008 (1923)] and Golwalkar (1939) on Hindutva and its genealogy; Casolari (2000) on the links and exchange between Hindu nationalist and fascist leaders; and Jaffrelot (1999: 51–64) for influences and similarities but also essential differences of RSS thought with Nazi ideology.

7. In a threatening note which has particular resonance in India today, M. S. Golwalkar (1939: 105) had railed against 'the "foreign races" in Hindusthan' who 'must either adopt the Hindu culture and language, must learn to respect and hold in reverence Hindu religion ... or, they may stay in the country wholly subordinated to the Hindu nation, claiming nothing'.

8. Andersen and Damle (2018) list thirty-six formal affiliates of the RSS, but this is a list drawn from RSS sources which often tend to suppress connections for political and pragmatic reasons. The number of allied organizations would be considerably higher when one considers informal affiliations with effective RSS control, or if one adds on organizations that are floated by the RSS on a temporary basis or for short-term agendas.

9. The extent of Brahmin dominance over the RSS can be gauged by the fact that five of the six *sarsangchalak*s (supreme commanders) have been Brahmin, with the sixth – Rajinder Singh – hailing from an upper-caste Thakur background. The first, second and third *sarsangchalak*s (Hedgewar, Golwalkar and Deoras) were Maharashtrian Brahmins, as is the current RSS supremo Mohan Bhagwat.

10. Also see Goyal (2000 [1979]: 15) and Basu et al. (1993: 34).

11. For a description and analysis of games played at the *shivir* (camp) run by the Rashtra Sevika Samiti (the women's wing of the RSS), see Menon (2010: 131–155).

12. For details on the international linkages between fascism and its influence on the RSS and Hindu Mahasabha, see Casolari (2000: 2016). Casolari also suggests that the *shakha* is a typically Indian phenomenon. While the RSS has borrowed elements from indigenous *akhada* (wrestling)

culture and adopted some Indian army rituals, there also appears to be a borrowing and modification of elements – field games, drills and salutes from the German Nazi and Italian fascist youth organizations. For essential ideological differences between the RSS *shakha* and the non-sectarian ideology of the *akhada*, see Alter (1994).

13. K. S. Sudarshan was joint general secretary of the RSS in 1992, one of our major interviewees and the person who got me permission to make *The Boy in the Branch*. He went on to become the fifth *sarsangchalak* of the RSS.

14. Shivaji Bhonsle was a seventeenth-century Maratha warrior king who is revered in RSS circles for establishing the foundations of a Hindu empire and restoring Hindu pride by famously fighting the Mughal rulers. Secular writings about Shivaji as a liberal and inclusive ruler are usually dismissed as the work of 'anti-national', Communist historians.

15. Mohan Bhagwat is the current and the sixth *sarsangchalak* of the RSS. Bhagwat was the Akhil Bharatiya Sharirik Pramukh (All India Chief of Physical Training) at the time of our filming in 1992. He was also one of our chief interlocutors in the film and was very close to the boys we filmed at the Asha Sadan RSS office.

16. Also see Christophe Jaffrelot's interview with Edward Anderson (Anderson and Jaffrelot 2018: 475–476).

17. Lalit was a gentle, atypical chief instructor who did not like the *sharirik* programme of the RSS even though he was tasked with teaching this to the young boys at the *shakha*.

18. The RSS uses flexible practices of naming games. Many RSS *shakha* primers (2016) rename this game, 'Dilli Humari Hai' (Delhi Is Ours) as references to Kashmir are left out when the RSS and the HSS (Hindu Swayamsevak Sangh) prefer to wear cultural masks for tactical reasons. However, the game is also occasionally played as 'Lahore Kiska Hai?' (Who Does Lahore Belong To?) which is useful for the RSS to explain its beliefs about the territorial footprint of 'Akhand Bharat' (Undivided India), which includes Pakistan, Nepal, Bhutan, Bangladesh, Myanmar, Sri Lanka, Thailand and Cambodia (Kumar 2014).

19. On 5 August 2019, the Narendra Modi-led BJP government revoked Article 370, which gave special status to Kashmir under the Indian

Constitution. This had been a long-standing demand of the RSS, which interpreted the provisions of Article 370 as a form of minority appeasement in Kashmir – the only Muslim-majority state in India.

20. Campaigning for Devendra Fadnavis in the Maharashtra assembly elections in September 2019, prime minister Narendra Modi referenced the game: 'We used to say "Kashmir hamara hai" ("Kashmir is ours"). This must now change to "Naya Kashmir banana hai" ("We must build a new Kashmir"). We have to once again build a paradise and hug each Kashmiri.' (Malekar 2019)

21. What is *sangathan*? The organizing and the consolidation of Hindus. What is *the* Sangathan? The RSS and its family, which consolidates Hindus for their protection and their 'greater good'.

22. Bhagwat could not tell us who the poet was, except to mention that it was by a *pracharak* (preacher) from days gone by. But other senior RSS leaders in Nagpur told us that the poem was written by Atal Bihari Vajpayee during his younger days. For RSS volunteers, this poem reinforced sentiments of sacrificing one's life for the *shakha* while dovetailing neatly with the nihilistic writings of Golwalkar about 'the Hindu race' and immortality: 'Our race is in truth, the Phoenix sprung which rises in in new youthful vigour from its very ashes. What seems to be our death merely confers upon us a fresh lease of life. We are an immortal race with perennial youth.' (Golwalkar 1939: 131)

23. K. S. Sudarshan proudly told us that he had been delegated by the second supreme commander Guruji Golwalkar to research and learn specific unarmed combat techniques from the renowned Indian army commander and martial arts expert Devi Prasad Pandey, which he (Sudarshan) subsequently wrote up and compiled in handbooks for *shakha* use. As in the case of *kabaddi*, the *bharatiya* origins of 'Nayudh' were of special significance for Sudarshan who traced its genealogy to Kalaripayattu, the martial arts tradition of Kerala.

24. Sripad was the *sharirik pramukh* (chief of physical training) at the Telecomnagar branch. He was an expert at 'Nayudh' and was the strongest and most aggressive RSS volunteer we met in Nagpur.

25. In a sleight of hand, the RSS adapted this story as we were filming the scene in the *boudhik* session of the Jaripatkanagar *shakha*. In this version,

The Shakha, the Home and the World 115

it is the *shakha* volunteers of the RSS who participate in the nationalist movement against the British. Gitti (name changed) asks the *shakha* supervisor as to what or whom the British fear. According to the supervisor, the British only fear the Devil, and you can only become the Devil if you commit suicide. Thus, Gitti sacrifices his life by committing suicide for the *shakha*, the RSS and the Hindu nation. The RSS, in this adaptation, foregrounds the work of the *shakha* and reinforces complete obeisance on the part of the volunteer to the needs of the Hindu nation. In a deft retelling of the story, the RSS reinvents itself as an organization actively fighting for Indian independence.

26. Stories of sacrificing one's life and inculcating desired values of loyalty and obedience towards the immediate officer, the RSS *shakha* and the Hindu nation are plentiful. See Goyal (2000 [1979]: 4).
27. For details on the vast canvas and the sites of historical pedagogy constructed by the RSS, and how Hindutva history is taught in schools, see Sarkar (2019).
28. This is a video interview with D. R. Goyal in August 2001.
29. This is a video interview with Purushottam Agarwal in September 2001.
30. The *gatanayak* (group leader) is also known as the twenty-four-hour *swayamsevak*. RSS texts encourage the *gatanayak* and *mukhya shikshak* to become part of the local community, to participate in festivals and social occasions, to share in their joys and sorrows and to concern themselves with the problems that the local residents face. See Andersen and Damle (1987: 84) and Hansen (1999: 113).
31. I had presumed such meetings were successful and that RSS *swayamsevaks* were universally welcomed by Hindu families, a line that the RSS is careful to promote. In 2016, I learned this was not always the case. Kali (Rajesh Jodhani) told me of his parents' discomfort when the RSS boys would drop in unannounced: 'My parents didn't like it and they found it inappropriate. I had two sisters close to marriageable age. How dare they just walk into the house?'
32. Lalit left the RSS in 1993 for 'personal reasons'. When I met him again in 2016, he had his own business distributing pharmaceutical drugs in Maharashtra. He was grateful to the RSS for the educational opportunities they had provided in Nagpur which had helped him make a

career. But he had not stayed in touch with his RSS comrades and did not seem particularly keen to renew contact with them.

33. In 1992, Lalit and Purushottam told us there were often pitched battles in Bodh *samaj* (Ambedkarite Buddhist) areas, where the BSP resisted RSS *shakha*s from gaining new territory.

34. RSS volunteers will never accept that they initiate the violence, as the code of being *sanskaarit*, or upholding good moral values, must remain intact. Violence is therefore only acceptable as a defensive reaction to a perceived wrong inflicted by the other party. Yet the Sangh has developed an entire arsenal of performative actions that are designed to provoke a response that can then justify acts of violence in the guise of self-defence. As with the *shakha* in a new neighbourhood, and the *ekatrikaran*, we can add the burgeoning processions during Ganesh Chaturthi, *maha aarti*s and *asthi kalash yatra*s in communally charged areas. L. K. Advani's *rath yatra* in 1989–1990 is another example of an event that was designed to create communal polarization by inciting violence.

35. We filmed Arun Shourie's provocative speech to the RSS faithful, in which he suggested that a Ram temple must be built and provided historical 'facts' about how mosques would be shifted as a routine exercise.

36. With its origins in naval and military warfare, a false flag operation refers to an attack or hostile action that obscures the identity of the participants carrying out the action while implicating another group, community or nation as the perpetrator.

37. The RSS' claims that commissions of inquiry never indict it in communal rioting are widely discredited (Goyal 2000 [1979]; Noorani 2019). For more details on Sangh Parivar complicity in communal riots and pogroms, see Hansen (1999), Jaffrelot (1999), Brass (2003), Valiani (2011), Ghassem-Fachandi (2012), Basu (2015), Dhanraj (1986), Vachani (2002), Sharma (2003) and Sawhney (2015).

38. See Ara (2020) for the investigation on the role of rumour and incitement to anti-Muslim violence by Hindutva groups using WhatsApp during the February 2020 Delhi riots. Other recent investigative journalism such as Scroll.in (2020), Chandra (2020) and Meghnad, Goyal and Malik (2020) also clearly establish that the violence at Jawaharlal Nehru University (JNU), where students from the left groups were brutally attacked by

masked men and women, was planned by the RSS student wing – the ABVP (Akhil Bharatiya Vidyarthi Parishad). The attacks were amplified and orchestrated by the use of multiple WhatsApp groups like 'Unity against Left' and 'Friends of RSS'. When the group communication was eventually exposed, RSS–ABVP volunteers swiftly changed their Hindu name handles and began to use 'Muslim-sounding' names. They also changed the name of the WhatsApp group to make it appear that students from the left were behind the violence at JNU. These findings suggest a similar modus operandi of rumour-mongering in the *shakha* described by D. R. Goyal and Purushottam Agarwal (Vachani 2002). The role of Indian enforcement agencies like the NIA (National Investigative Agency) and the police in working closely with Hindu nationalist groups to stifle dissent is particularly disturbing. See Jha (2020) on fake news and fabricated evidence in the Bhima–Koregaon arrests of 2019, where activists and lawyers were arrested on flimsy charges of a Maoist plot to overthrow the Indian State and assassinate prime minister Modi. Also see Mahaprashasta (2020) on how the police is attempting to frame anti-CAA and anti-communalism activists as being responsible for the Delhi riots of February 2020.

39. At Jaripatkanagar, we filmed a bunch of boys playing non-*bharatiya* games like cricket and football, while we spent the evening at Telecomnagar recording a herd of buffaloes that had taken a liking to the park as a grazing ground.

40. Also see Jaffrelot (1999: 530). For an analysis of stagnation and decline in Samiti *shakha*s in Delhi in the 1990s, see Sarkar (1999).

41. For a good account of online Hindutva growth overseas and use of cyber-*shakha*s in transnational communication practices, see Therwath (2012).

42. Golwalkar (1966) made the tenuous claim that 'the hostile elements within the country pose a far greater menace to national security than the aggressors from outside'. For Golwalkar, these internal threats were the Muslims, Christians and Communists. Since 2014, the Sangh Parivar has strategically expanded this list of internal threats to include 'Macaulayists', 'Urban Naxals', 'Tukde-tukde Gangs', 'Sickularists', 'Libtards', 'Press-titutes', 'Khan Market Gangs', and so on. Mainstream media organizations work in tandem with the Hindu nationalist press

and BJP social media networks to polarize and influence public opinion, while State institutions are enlisted to use coercive methods to remove all forms of resistance to the current RSS–BJP projects of Hindu majoritarianism.
43. 'Love jihad' is an Islamophobic conspiracy theory propagated by Hindutva ideologues insinuating that Muslim men target Hindu women for conversion to Islam by feigning love, and by means of seduction, deception, kidnapping and marriage.
44. This story was told to me even though the term 'love jihad' was not in vogue at the time. 'Love jihad' appears as a term that has public currency around 2009, with claims of widespread conversions to Islam of Christian and Hindu women in Kerala and Karnataka. Despite rulings by the courts and the police that conversion to Islam was not an organized conspiracy, the VHP and the Bajrang Dal embraced the moral panic of 'love jihad' to terrorize interreligious couples and justify violence against Muslims.
45. The source of the stories or its origins and founding myths are never revealed, apart from the information that unnamed senior leaders have 'done research on this subject' or 'the police and the VHP have evidence' of 'love jihad'.
46. Gupta (2009: 2014) shows how 'love jihad' is not a recent phenomenon and has been in public discourse at least since the Arya Samaj Hindu revivalist movement in the 1920s. Its deployment at strategic times has become part of the arsenal of the Sangh Parivar to mobilize and communalize forces on the ground, to inflict violence on the Muslim community, to restrict freedom of choice of consenting adults and to curb the independence of young Hindu women. For more details on how Hindu nationalist women's groups use discursive strategies of 'love jihad' to regulate and control the movement of young women in urban public space, see Tyagi and Sen (2019).
47. The omnipresent threat of religious conversion by 'love jihad' and its widespread dissemination on WhatsApp groups and social media leads to the dehumanization of Muslims and encourages vigilante violence against them. In December 2017, Mohamed Afrajul, a migrant worker from Malda in West Bengal, was brutally murdered in Rajsamand in Rajasthan. The culprit Shambhu Lal Regar recorded the murder and

uploaded the footage which went viral on WhatsApp. Shockingly, Regar was celebrated in subsequent Ram Navami processions and might get to contest the UP assembly election on a Navrirman Sena ticket. The extremist Hindutva party is also planning to give tickets to the killers of Mohamed Akhlaq (in Dadri, Uttar Pradesh) and fifteen-year-old Junaid Khan who was murdered on a train in Ballabhgarh, Uttar Pradesh (*Times Now* 2019). Also see Ara (2020) for reportage on the adaptation and circulation of 'love jihad' stories by a Hindutva WhatsApp group named 'Kattar Hindu Ekta' ('Unity of Staunch Hindus') formed specifically to provoke anti-Muslim violence during the February 2020 riots in Delhi.

48. Shuddhabratha Sengupta, K. U. Mohanan and P. M. Satheesh are well-known practitioners in the art and cinema worlds.
49. The RSS was banned for the third time since Indian independence for its complicity in the demolition of the Babri Mosque in December 1992. The ban was lifted soon after.
50. Some names have been changed to provide anonymity.
51. Sripad referred to the attack on the Babri Mosque as 'a well-planned war strategy' continuing the RSS fascination with armed warfare and the military.
52. Sripad's work for the Gadkari trust involved local development and providing employment opportunities, facilitating community centres for religious gatherings, supervising the running of Ekal Vidyalaya schools in the region for the local Adivasi children, and sourcing honey and herbal products from the villagers for Baba Ramdev's Patanjali corporation.
53. Kartick Pathey is the three-year-old boy in *The Men in the Tree*, whom we filmed in 2001 and who is present in the final scene of the film, laughing and saluting to the camera as he is being dressed in *ganvesh* (the RSS uniform) by his doting uncle Sandeep Pathey. When we interviewed Kartick as an eighteen-year-old in 2016, he expressed an interest in being the first person from his family to go abroad for further studies. He said he would like to do an MTech degree in Engineering and asked us to suggest some universities he could apply to. He added: 'But it will have to be with the blessings of the Sangh, and it will have to be in a city where there is the Hindu Swayamsevak Sangh. I would like

to be with like-minded people from the RSS family, and it is also for my own protection.'

54. There is a rich body of feminist work on the limits of political agency and 'emancipation' of women by the Samiti and the Durga Vahini, its complementarity with RSS aims and its complicity in strengthening Hindutva's patriarchal order and in furthering the Hindu nationalist, anti-minority agenda. See Bacchetta (1994, 1999), Sarkar (1995, 1998), Basu (1995), Sehgal (2007), Gupta (2009, 2014), Menon (2010), Pahuja (2011) and Tyagi and Sen (2019).

55. I am grateful to Amna Pathan, Amrita Basu, Tanika Sarkar, Srirupa Roy and Felix Pal for their invaluable feedback on the initial draft of this chapter.

Bibliography

Books, Articles and Documentaries

Agnes, F. (2019). 'Aggressive Hindu Nationalism: Contextualizing the Triple Talaq Controversy'. In *Majoritarian State: How Hindu Nationalism is Changing India*, edited by A. P. Chatterji, T. B. Hansen and C. Jaffrelot, 335–351. London: C. Hurst & Company.

Alter, J. S. (1994). 'Somatic Nationalism: Indian Wrestling and Militant Hinduism'. *Modern Asian Studies* 28, no. 3, 557–588. www.jstor.org/stable/313044. Accessed on 5 July 2020.

Andersen, W. K., and S. D. Damle (1987). *The Brotherhood in Saffron: The Rashtriya Swayamsevak Sangh and Hindu Revivalism*. New Delhi: Vistaar.

——— (2018). *The RSS: A View to the Inside*. Gurgaon: Penguin Random House.

Anderson, E., and C. Jaffrelot (2018). 'Hindu Nationalism and the "Saffronization of the Public Sphere": An Interview with Christophe Jaffrelot'. *Contemporary South Asia* 26, no. 4: 468–482.

Ara, I. (2020). '"Tear Them Apart": How Hindutva WhatsApp Group Demanded Murder, Rape of Muslims in Delhi Riots'. *The Wire*, 6 July. https://thewire.in/communalism/delhi-riots-hindutva-whatsapp-muslims-murder-rape. Accessed on 2 September 2021.

Bacchetta, P. (1994). 'Communal Property/Sexual Property: On Representations of Muslim Women in a Hindu Nationalist Discourse'. In *Forging Identities:*

Gender, Communities and the State, edited by Z. Hasan, 188–225. New Delhi: Kali for Women.

———. (1999). 'Militant Hindu Nationalist Women Reimagine Themselves: Notes on Mechanisms of Expansion/Adjustment'. *Journal of Women's History* 10, no. 4: 125–147.

Bagchi, S. (2019). 'Number of Shakhas Has Doubled in 10 Years: RSS Leader'. *The Hindu*, 15 August.

Basu, A. (1995). 'Feminism Inverted: The Gendered Imagery and Real Women of Hindu Nationalism'. In *Women and the Hindu Right: A Collection of Essays*, edited by T. Sarkar and U. Butalia, 158–180. New Delhi: Kali for Women.

———. (2015). *Violent Conjunctures in Democratic India* (Cambridge Studies in Contentious Politics). Cambridge: Cambridge University Press.

Basu, T., P. Datta, S. Sarkar, T. Sarkar and S. Sen (1993). *Khaki Shorts and Saffron Flags: A Critique of the Hindu Right*. New Delhi: Orient Longman.

Brass, P. (2003). *The Production of Hindu-Muslim Violence in Contemporary India*. Seattle: University of Washington Press.

Casolari, M. (2000). 'Hindutva's Foreign Tie-Up in the 1930s: Archival Evidence'. *Economic and Political Weekly* 35, no. 4: 218–228. https://www.jstor.org/stable/4408848. Accessed on 6 July 2020.

———. (2016). 'Hindutva's Fascist Heritage'. Sabrang India, 28 April. https://sabrangindia.in/article/hindutvas-fascist-heritage. Accessed on 2 September 2021.

Chandra, D. (2020). 'WhatsApp Groups Allegedly Behind JNU Violence Reveal ABVP Identity'. *The Quint*, 6 January. https://www.thequint.com/news/india/whatsapp-groups-behind-jnu-violence-reveal-abvp-identities. Accessed on 2 September 2021.

Dhanraj, D. (1986). *Kya Hua Is Shaher Ko?* (What Happened to This City?). Documentary. Hyderabad: Deccan Development Society.

Ghassem-Fachandi, P. (2012). *Pogrom in Gujarat: Hindu Nationalism and Anti-Muslim Violence in India*. Princeton: Princeton University Press.

Golwalkar, M. S. (1939). *We or Our Nationhood Defined*. Nagpur: Bharat Publications.

———. (1966). *Bunch of Thoughts*. https://www.thehinducentre.com/multimedia/archive/02486/Bunch_of_Thoughts_2486072a.pdf. Accessed on 2 September 2021.

Goyal, D. R. (2000 [1979]). *Rashtriya Swayamsevak Sangh*. Delhi: Radhakrishna Prakashan.

Gupta, C. (2009). 'Hindu Women, Muslim Men: Love Jihad and Conversions'. *Economic and Political Weekly* 44, no. 51: 13–15. https://www.jstor.org/stable/25663907. Accessed on 23 June 2020.

———. (2014). 'The Myth of Love Jihad'. *Indian Express*, 28 August. https://indianexpress.com/article/opinion/columns/the-myth-of-love-jihad/. Accessed on 2 September 2021.

Hari, R. (2018). *The Incomparable Guruji Golwalkar*. New Delhi: Prabhat Prakashan.

Hansen, T. B. (1999). *The Saffron Wave: Democracy and Hindu Nationalism in Modern India*. New Delhi: Oxford University Press.

Jaffrelot, C. (1999 [1996]). *The Hindu Nationalist Movement and Indian Politics: 1925 to the 1990s*. New Delhi: Penguin Books.

Jha, P. S. (2020). 'Why Modi and Shah Took the Bhima Koregaon Investigation Away from Maharashtra'. *The Wire*, 30 January. https://thewire.in/politics/modi-assassination-plot-letter-danger-democracy. Accessed on 2 September 2021.

Joshi, S. (2010). 'Cyber-Savvy Sangh Plans to Set Up e-Shakhas'. *Hindustan Times*, 11 January. https://www.hindustantimes.com/india/cyber-savvy-sangh-plans-to-set-up-e-*shakha*s/story-ADrsCr73SyvXw2yq3eal7K.html. Accessed on 2 September 2021.

Kanungo, P. (2019). 'Sangh and Sarkar: The RSS Power Centre Shifts from Nagpur to New Delhi'. In *Majoritarian State: How Hindu Nationalism Is Changing India*, edited by A. P. Chatterji, T. B. Hansen and C. Jaffrelot, 133–149. London: Hurst and Company.

Khan, M. I. (2009). 'RSS to Initiate "Online Shakhas" to Connect with Net-Savvy Youth'. Rediff, 24 December. https://news.rediff.com/report/2009/dec/24/rsss-new-mantra-online-shakhas.htm. Accessed on 2 September 2021.

Khanna, L. (2019). 'Interview with Lalit Vachani' *Studies in South Asian Film and Media* 9, no. 2 (January): 173–182.

Liberhan, M. S. (2009). *Report of the Liberhan Ayodhya Commission of Inquiry*. New Delhi: Ministry of Home Affairs, Government of India.

Lulla, A. B. (2010). 'Sangh's E-Sevaks'. *Open*, 25 February. https://openthemagazine.com/features/india/sanghs-e-sevaks/. Accessed on 2 September 2021.

Mahaprashasta, A. A. (2020). 'How Delhi Police Turned Anti-CAA WhatsApp Group Chats into Riots "Conspiracy"'. *The Wire*, 3 August. https://thewire.in/communalism/delhi-riots-police-activists-whatsapp-group. Accessed on 2 September 2021.

Malekar, A. (2019). 'The Man Who Defeated the Marathas: The Political Intrigues of Devendra Fadnavis'. *The Caravan*, 1 October. https://caravanmagazine.in/reportage/political-intrigues-of-devendra-fadnavis.

Meghnad S., P. Goyal and A. Malik (2020). 'JNU Violence: Inside the WhatsApp Group that "Coordinated" the Mayhem'. *Newslaundry*, 6 January. https://

www.newslaundry.com/2020/01/06/jnu-violence-whatsapp-group. Accessed on 2 September 2021.

Menon, K. D. (2010). *Everyday Nationalism: Women of the Hindu Right in India*. Philadelphia: University of Pennsylvania Press.

Noorani, A. G. (2019). *The RSS: A Menace to India*. New Delhi: LeftWord.

Pahuja, N. (2011). *The World Before Her*. Documentary. Toronto: KinoSmith.

Sarkar, T. (1995). 'Heroic Women, Mother Goddesses: Family and Organization in Hindutva Politics'. In *Women and the Hindu Right: A Collection of Essays*, edited by T. Sarkar and U. Butalia, 181–215. New Delhi: Kali for Women.

———. (1999). 'Pragmatics of the Hindu Right: Politics of Women's Organisations'. *Economic and Political Weekly* 34, no. 31: 2159–2167. www.jstor.org/stable/4408263. Accessed on 7 July 2020.

———. (2019). 'How the Sangh Parivar Writes and Teaches History'. In *Majoritarian State: How Hindu Nationalism Is Changing India*, edited by A. P. Chatterji, T. B. Hansen and C. Jaffrelot, 151–173. London: Hurst and Company.

Savarkar, V. D. (2018 [1923]). *Hindutva: Who Is a Hindu?* New Delhi: Hindi Sahitya Sadan.

Sawhney, N. S. (2015). Documentary. *Muzaffarnagar Baaqi Hai*. Muzaffarnagar: NewsClick and Chalchitra Abhiyaan.

Scroll.in (2019). 'Triple Talaq Bill Is a "Complete Charade" and Against Minorities, Say Civil Society Members'. 31 July. https://scroll.in/latest/932325/triple-talaq-bill-is-a-complete-charade-and-against-minorities-say-civil-society-members. Accessed on 2 September 2021.

———. (2020). 'JNU: WhatsApp Messages Planning Attack Traced to ABVP Activists'. 6 January. https://scroll.in/article/948899/jnu-whatsapp-messages-planning-attack-traced-to-abvp-activists. Accessed on 2 September 2021.

Sehgal, M. (2007). 'Manufacturing a Feminized Siege Mentality: Hindu Nationalist Paramilitary Camps for Women in India'. *Journal of Contemporary Ethnography* 36, no. 2: 165–183.

Shantha, S. (2020). 'How ABVP Planned Attack on JNU Students, Teachers on WhatsApp'. *The Wire*, 6 January. https://thewire.in/rights/abvp-jnu-attack-whatsapp. Accessed on 2 September 2021.

Sharda, R. (2018). *RSS 360: Demystifying Rashtriya Swayamsevak Sangh*. Delhi: Bloomsbury India.

Sharma, R. (2003). *Final Solution*. Documentary. Mumbai: Associated Cinema & Television.

Kumar, N. D. S. (2014). 'More Techies Turn Sevaks, Log into RSS IT Milans'. *Times of India*, Bengaluru, 2 December. https://timesofindia.indiatimes.

com/city/bengaluru/more-techies-turn-sevaks-log-into-rss-it-milans/articleshow/45340596.cms. Accessed on 2 September 2021.

Shukla, A. (2015). 'The Games the RSS Plays'. *The Caravan*, 1 February.

Times Now (2019). 'Uttar Pradesh Navnirman Sena Fielding Shambu Lal Regar, Men Accused in Akhlaq, Junaid Lynchings'. 27 March.

Therwath, I. (2012). 'Cyber-*Hindutva*: Hindu Nationalism, the Diaspora and the Web'. *Social Science Information* 51, no. 4: 551–577. https://journals.sagepub.com/doi/10.1177/0539018412456782. Accessed on 2 September 2021.

Tyagi, A., and A. Sen (2019). 'Love-Jihad (Muslim Sexual Seduction) and Ched-Chad (Sexual Harassment): Hindu Nationalist Discourses and the Ideal/Deviant Urban Citizen in India'. *Gender, Place and Culture* 27, no. 1: 104–125. DOI: 10.1080/0966369X.2018.1557602.

Villat, N. J. (2019). 'The Saffron Siege: Inside the Killing Fields of Kerala'. *The Caravan*, 1 April 2019.

Vachani, L. (1993). 'RSS Indoctrination of Young Minds'. *Times of India*, 20 October.

———. (1993b). *The Boy in the Branch*. Documentary. New Delhi: Wide Eye Film.

———. (2002). *The Men in the Tree*. Documentary. New Delhi: Wide Eye Film.

———. (1992, 2001, 2016). *Video Outtakes from 1992, 2001 and 2016*. Documentary. New Delhi.

———. (2017). 'The Babri Masjid Demolition Was Impossible without RSS Foot-Soldiers Like These'. *The Wire*, 8 December.

Valiani, A. A. (2011). *Militant Publics in India: Physical Culture and Violence in the Making of a Modern Polity*. London: Palgrave Macmillan.

Verma, L. (2018). 'To Expand Its Urban Reach, RSS to Send Out "Apartment Pramukhs"'. *Indian Express*, 29 April. https://indianexpress.com/article/india/to-expand-its-urban-reach-rss-to-send-out-apartment-pramukhs-5155621/h. Accessed on 2 September 2021.

RSS and HSS Publications for Use in *Shakha*s

Dwivedi R., O. Bhave and Ramkumar (2008 [1992]). *Baal Bodh Kathayein*. New Delhi: Suruchi Prakashan.

Hindu Swayamsevak Sangh (n.d.). *Khel Book*. Leicester: Keshav Pratishthan.

Kumar, V. (2014). *Aao Khelein Khel*. Lucknow: Lokhit Prakashan.

Rashtriya Swayamsevak Sangh (2016). *Shakha Pustika*. Nagpur: Shribharati Prakashan.

——— (2016). *Shakha Surabhi*. New Delhi: Suruchi Prakashan.

4

Spinning the Saffron Yarn

Lessons of Ideal Girlhood in Hindu Nationalist Storytelling

Aastha Tyagi

Introduction

Training to become a member of the Sangh Parivar (Sangh Family), India's largest and most influential Hindu nationalist collective, begins at an early age. Games, songs and stories are used to transmit Hindutva, or Hindu nationalist thought. In *shakha*s (meetings held daily, weekly or during camps) across the country, members place a special focus on storytelling and its didactic nature, an aspect that is enjoyed by listeners young and old. Pedagogic authorities everywhere have used storytelling as a mode of ideological introduction and propagation. How does the 'method' of storytelling modify itself in the service of the thought – how is it adapted, received and reproduced, and how does it become gendered? Why are many of the stories set in a historical time period, and what role does historicity play in the telling of these stories? These are the questions that would be engaged with in this chapter.

The empirical data for this chapter comes from two sources: textual (biographies of Rashtra Sevika Samiti [National Women Volunteers, henceforth Samiti] members and short stories of 'ideal women') and participant observations (from an annual summer camp of the organization in Delhi [2017] and Meerut [2013]), and *shakha*s across Delhi (March–June 2018). Stories from four books (from the Samiti's publication unit) and participant-observation data were analysed. Out of the four books, two were in Hindi and two in English. The fieldwork was conducted in Hindi. The publication materials have been divided into two: first are the stories of the influential members of the Samiti; second types of publication materials are the stories deploying historical figures (important women of the Hindu nationalist movement) that are written to highlight the important aspects of the ideology.[1] Using the stories told by Samiti members (orally and textually), I attempt to outline the stories' main themes as messages of the Hindu nationalist thought.

In this chapter, I show that these stories are important vehicles of socialization into the ideology. They are essential to the progress of the Sangh Parivar apparatus and their core project of writing a Hindutva history. There are two goals for this chapter. The first goal is to illustrate the larger objective of the Sangh Parivar to shape Hindu nationalist history. Second, the specific aim of Samiti's storytelling is to show how stories most effectively shape a gendered vision of Hindu nationalism.

Rashtra Sevika Samiti: Women of the Hindu Nationalist Movement

The Rashtra Sevika Samiti is the largest women's Hindu nationalist organization in India. Lakshmibai Kelkar, a young widow and a stepmother to Rashtriya Swayamsevak Sangh's (National Volunteers Corp; founded in 1925; henceforth RSS) *shakha*-going men, founded it in 1936. In an everyday *shakha*, a member would be introduced to anecdotes from Kelkar's life. Her life story suggests that she was impressed by the physical and intellectual aspect of the *shakha*s and desired for women to also contribute to the cause of patriotism. Another story suggests that she witnessed a sexual assault of a married woman in a crowded train and was stunned when none could defend her. She was deeply disturbed at seeing the precarious condition of women and desired for them to be physically adept at dealing with dangers.

This led to the founding of the Samiti as the first affiliate of the Sangh Parivar, the largest Hindu nationalist coalition in the world. It is sometimes referred to as the 'women's wing of the RSS'. Samiti has come a long way from its inception in 1936 to 2021 – it now reportedly has 4,00,000 members with more than 5,000 daily *shakha*s (Gandhi 2018). Local Samiti units hold district-level fifteen-day summer camps every year, and different festivals are peppered across the calendar year to ensure regular meetings and socialization, apart from the daily or weekly *shakha*s.

The Samiti provides ideological support and often hosts meetings and initiatives with women members of other women's affiliate organizations of the Sangh Parivar, like the Durga Vahini (of the Vishva Hindu Parishad, VHP), or trains female teachers of the Sangh Parivar's educational affiliate, Vidya Bharati. In the Sangh women hierarchy, Samiti women reign at the top, often looking out for and training other women's organizations like a stern, matronly figure.[2] In the larger Sangh Parivar hierarchy, the Samiti is a deeply respected but an often-neglected organization, even though it was its first affiliate. Samiti publications do not make it to Sangh Parivar bookstores. The Samiti does not have the financial and economic pull of the Sangh Parivar. It does the work of training Hindu women to be Hindu nationalist and imbibe those values for the larger good of the movement.

To uphold the core beliefs of Hindutva and the Sangh Parivar, the Samiti is RSS' most sincere ally. The Sangh Parivar's vision is to restore the glory of the '*tejaswi* Hindu *rashtra*' (glorious Hindu nation) – what that entails is to create a nation with desired 'Hindu' values derived from scriptures to the vision of the ideologues. Women should enrich the domestic sphere with patriotism and *sanskaar* (cultural values). The values of *matrutva* (motherhood), *krututva* (duty) and *netrutva* (leadership) are what Samiti women uphold. Women bear the responsibility of transmitting Hindu nationalist culture and values to the children and making the home a hospitable space for the RSS male. Women have a specific role in that vision, and the Samiti performs that role to a T – adapting the thought for women across regions and class. This also means that the Samiti adapts the Sangh Parivar's every modus operandi. These are the daily *shakha*s, camps, publications units, schools and, additionally, temple collectives, neighbourhood 'kitties', and so on.

In this chapter, I would outline three aims that Samiti storytelling hopes to achieve. First, I would show how history is invoked to create and sustain enemies of the Hindu nation to contour the Hindu nationalist historiography. Next, I would use the stories to show how storytelling encapsulates the gendered message for Hindu women. Lastly, I would describe the people who engage with these stories: the speakers and the listeners, the expectations of the former and the dissonances found within the latter.

Hindutva and History: Shaping the Hindu Nation

The Threat of the Non-Hindu: The Historically Resilient Enemy of the Hindu Nation

On a relatively cooler Sunday morning in April, a weekly *shakha* was being held. This *shakha* saw attendance from all age groups – from girls as young as five to older women who had children who were of college-going age – and was a composite of Sangh Parivar affiliates of the area. The *shakha* had members from the nearby neighbourhood. This neighbourhood was an area of socio-economically lower-class residents of Delhi. The area had witnessed the anti-Sikh riots in 1984 and, more recently, the communal riots in January 2020. The *shakha* was being conducted in an easy-to-miss Sewa Bharati building of the area.[3] All attendees sat in neat rows according to their age group. The caste demography of the attendees was mostly Other Backward Classes (OBC). The *shakha* leader was a Brahmin woman. The members had begun the *shakha* promptly at 7 a.m. It began with the morning prayers and the yoga section followed. Next was the part of the *shakha* called *baudhik* (ideology).

The *shakha* leader requested another member from the affiliate Sewa Bharati to narrate a story for the *baudhik* section of the *shakha*. The selected member spoke softly and narrated the following story:

> There was a twelve-year-old boy in Mughal king Aurangzeb's reign. Aurangzeb was known to burn 150 *janeu* [a sacred thread loosely hung around the upper body of baptized Hindu males, also a marker of caste] every day, a signifier that he either killed or converted that many Hindus. It was only then he ate breakfast. It was a time of oppressive regime against Hindus.
>
> At the time, the little boy was studying in a *madrassa* [a centre for Islamic education], because only *madrassas* existed. The boys in the *madrassa* said to the little boy that his Durga *ma* is like 'this', pointing to something less than honourable. The little boy asked the other boys calmly how they would feel if he said something like that for their Fatima *bi*. The boys complained to their *padri* just for that insinuation.

At this point in the story, the storyteller turns to P *didi* (the Samiti leader of the area; *didi*, which is Hindi for older sister, is a marker of respect) to ask what 'their' (indicating the teachers in *madrassa*s) teachers are called. P *didi* replied, 'Maulvi'. The storyteller continued:

> Yes, Maulvi. The Maulvi offered him two options: that he either converts or dies. The boy flatly refused to convert. The little boy's parents tried to reason with him to convert but he did not budge. The little boy asked his mother if he would escape death later if he converted. She said no. He then explained to her that if death is inevitable, he might as well die for the religion. He was then given a death sentence by hanging. Even today in Lahore, they have a celebratory fair on the day the boy died. (Weekly *shakha*, Delhi, April 2018)

The narrator then looked to her audience, from the young to the old. She asked them what the lesson of the story was. A hand shot up from the middle of the classroom, and the narrator asked her to tell the class. 'We should always protect our religion, even if we have to die for it,' said a little girl, not more than eight years old. The narrator nodded, smiled and looked to the class at large: 'Yes, because the Hindu religion is in danger. And we need to fight for it, just like the boy in the story.' The narrator was then congratulated by the Samiti in-charge for a moving story, and the *shakha* continued with the games portion.

The lessons of death, religion and what qualifies as something that should be fought and died for were neatly encapsulated in a story that did not last more than five minutes. There are some questions that come to mind upon hearing that story. The story is set in a historical period, during Mughal ruler Aurangzeb's reign (1658–1707). The specificities of the location are not outlined: where in the vast Mughal empire is this story set? How old were the boys in the madrassa who complained to the authorities? We are told that the day of the boy's hanging is celebrated in Lahore – but is it because the story originates in Lahore, or is it because Lahore is in present-day Pakistan and the idea is that Hindus face persecution in Pakistan, showing a historical continuity? Why are the boys in a fight in the first place, and why do a group of Muslim boys gang up on a sole Hindu boy? If there existed only *madrassa*s as centres of learning, then there must be other Hindu boys as well. Why does the Maulvi assume that the fault lies with the Hindu boy? Is it to insinuate that he is a teacher second and a Muslim preacher first and therefore his loyalties lie with his co-religionists? Is his identity as a Muslim overshadowing his identity as a teacher? The punishment given to the boy does not neatly align with the unspecified crime. Is it to show that being a Hindu made one's living condition unfair and precarious – that an insinuation could be a cause of hanging? Or could it be to add to the stereotype of the radical Muslim who is emotional and irrational? In a related example, when invoking the name of revolutionary Bhagat Singh in *shakha*s, the speaker of the story reminds the listeners that Bhagat Singh's mother's only lament at his death was that she did not have more sons to give for the cause of the nation. The pain of losing a child, the injustice of his death, her period of mourning and grief are minimized for 'the greater good'. And 'the greater good' is paramount to one's own being – 'the greater good' of working for the Hindu nation. The sacrifice is in terms of the body – with the sacrifice adding to the strength of the Hindu Rashtra.

A study on textbooks found that there was a trend of imagery of young boys sacrificing themselves for the cause of the nation-state (Bhog et al. 2010). There are images and songs, of young children (mainly boys) singing songs about sacrificing their lives for the country, especially at the site of war. Interestingly, in this context, the listeners are young girls and only boys are upheld as relevant examples. What these images underlie are those of a mind–body dichotomy – that what one does with their body is inconsequential as long it is in the service of something bigger than their corporal self. These images also insist that one's life is not important compared to the larger movement. Individual dreams, aspirations, struggles and disappointments (and even death) become secondary to the 'nation'. There is no individual; there is only the nation. Here the boy has sacrificed himself – upheld as an example for the cause of the Hindu nation under the rule of a tyrannical Muslim ruler.

In a similar vein, it was during an early morning-prayer session during the Samiti camp in 2013 that an older Samiti member waxed eloquently about a temple of mythological importance in Pakistan that has been ruined. While the 200 girls and fifty older women were barely out of their slumber, the speaker spoke of archaeologists who found a temple that contained remnants of Queen Gandhari's maternal home (a central figure from the epic Mahabharata). 'The temple was supposed to contain powerful magic and was important for local folklore,' the narrator said, 'but due to Jinnah and his followers, the Hindus lost out on the temple during Partition and it was destroyed.' In this story set within the subcontinent's trauma of the Partition in 1947, the entire country of Pakistan is subsumed as the geographical entity that possessed the temple, and mythological characters are invoked to connect with a Hindu history. The historical veracity of the context (the partition of the subcontinent) exists, but like the previous story, all other aspects remain vague. No reference is made to the identity of the culprits behind the temple demolition or when the incident occurred. Since no specific place in the country is mentioned, the narrative casts a shadow on every individual who presently lives or lived in Pakistan. The blame of the Partition is squarely placed on 'Jinnah and his followers', and the loss of the Partition has only been accrued by the Hindus. The tangibles are 'Jinnah and his followers' and Pakistan. The rest are details that cannot be fixed.

The Muslim is not just the historical plunderer of property; he is also seen as a threat to the 'soul' of the nation: the Hindu woman. To demonstrate this, I move from a figure despised in Hindutva history to a figure that has been hailed as the first Hindu king and defender of Hindu values, Shivaji. Shivaji Bhonsle (1627/1630–1680), the ruler of the Maratha Empire from 1674 to 1680, is popularly referred to by the royal title of the king or 'Chhatrapati' Shivaji. In the Samiti schema, it is his mother Jijabai Bhonsle (1598–1674) who is upheld as the epitome of an ideal Hindutva mother, the ideal of *matrutva*. Here is an illustrative story that imagines the impact of Jijabai on her son:

> One day an artist was presenting his art in the court of Shivaji. His songs spoke of queen Padmini.[4] Listening to the songs Shivba (Maratha king Shivaji) stood up suddenly and turned to leave the room. Jijabai, his mother, held his hand and asked him why he was leaving. He replied, 'Mother, this is terrible. I cannot bear it.' She replied, 'Oh! Things much terrible than this are happening. The Muslims took your aunt away. The mothers-sisters of this country are repeatedly facing such oppression and you are scared of even hearing about it! You have to avenge this! You have to release mothers-sisters from this attack. Sit and listen!' (Rashtra Sevika Samiti 2014)

The story is situated in a historical time period when both Jijabai and Shivaji were alive. We are told that the tale of 'Padmini' is being recited to Shivaji who finds it difficult to hear. From the reaction of his mother, we can infer that it is connected to the sexual violence inflicted on Hindu women by Muslims. Using the example of 'Padmini' and his aunt, Jijabai urges Shivaji to wage a war on the Muslims. Shivaji is a king who cannot bear the thought of brutal violence. His mother asks him to 'sit and listen' to invoke a justified bravery – to 'avenge' the cause of the women, to tap into a saviour masculinity (and perform his caste duty, discussed later in the chapter). His revenge is justified – because the initiator is the enemy (Sarkar 2019). A related story set three centuries later comes from the story of Nani Kolte, a Samiti member from its inception in 1936 (and a wife of an RSS member from the Bhandara district in pre-Independence India):

> Nani*ji* held a much sought after 3-day camp in her fields in winter. There they taught stick, *yogchap*, knife, and *khadag*. On the last day was a campfire. On such a day, during a programme, a tall, strongly built Muslim Pathan invaded their premises. He tried to take a girl with him. She screamed for help and everyone was in shock. Then some Sevikas built courage and ran after him. The victim was a daughter-like servant in Nani*ji*'s house. They saved the girl but could not capture the Pathan. He laughed at her face and this gave Nani*ji* determination to see if her Sevikas were strong enough. (Rashtra Sevika Samiti 2005)

In the previous example, at the outset one sees the dangers women are exposed to when they are alone as a group. The Samiti sees itself as a project that is fighting those who do not wish to see Hindu women defend themselves. What also emerges is the explicit creation of the villain as the Muslim man who is unrepentant in his acts.

The Muslims here are a homogenous category – the historical Muslim who made Padmini suffer is the same Muslim who is hurting 'mothers-sisters' of Shivaji's time. It emerges as a threat in the present to girls who go to a Samiti camp in post-Independence India. Why are we being told this story today? Does the Muslim man from the time of Shivaji commit the same crimes today? As shown, this story can be replicated – the only constant being the Muslim man who wants to conquer Hindu women. This trope is not new, and historians and anthropologists have found resonances in decades and centuries that have followed. The trope of 'love jihad' (Gupta 2009; Rao 2011; Tyagi and Sen 2019) has been invoked to limit the agency of Hindu women, while creating the image of a lascivious Muslim man as a threat to the chastity of the Hindu women and, subsequently, the Hindu nation.

While the highest disdain is reserved for the Muslim, Christian missionaries also occupy the Hindutva imagination as messengers determined to drive impressionable Hindus away from Hinduism (Sundar 2004). Christian missionaries, Christian schools and the British colonizers are subsumed under a single category of a group seeking to oppress Hindus and convert them. The following story comes from the biography of the founder. Lakshmibai (maiden name 'Kamal') began her school in a 'missionary school':

> Kamal was courageous, truthful and could stand and protest against anything that was wrong. All the girls were expected to keep their eyes shut during prayer time in school. Kamal was curious to know whether the teacher practised what she preached. She opened her eyes and found the angry eyes of the teacher staring at her. The teacher asked angrily, 'Kamal, why are your eyes open?' Kamal calmly replied, 'Madam, how did you know that my eyes are open? Aren't you expected to keep your eyes shut as well?' Kamal was slapped after. (Rai 1996: 3)

Kamal is able to challenge the school authority figure (and it would be important to reiterate that the school is a Christian convent school). According to the story's retelling, since it is a Christan school, the girl deserves to be rightfully awarded, instead of being met with a slap, for her act of rebellion against the school's authority. This act is seen as an act of courage, signifying the future of the girl who will challenge the rules laid down by the British (represented in the figure of the teacher in a Christian school). In the introduction to the stories from Kelkar's life, the translator notes that the lessons are to reiterate 'selfless sacrifices, dedication and utmost devotion' to working for the nation (Rai 1996: 1). Kamal's resistance to the non-Hindu is seen as patriotism, much like the young boy from an earlier story – to reiterate that the defence of Hinduism is the defence of the Hindu nation. The sacrifice requires an exemplary courage that must be called upon in the service of the nation. The figure of the non-Hindu authoritarian teacher is a common metaphor for a regime that is authoritarian as well. A rebellion against the diktats of the teachers is seen as a rebellion against the regime and at the same time a patriotic defence.

Fictionalizing History

History is a crucial discipline to provide a blueprint for a Hindu nationalist vision of patriotism and national identity. Many a times during fieldwork, when a speaker spoke of instances of the past to illustrate the glory of the Hindu nation, I had a tendency to 'fact check' the claims made in the stories but in vain. These unverifiable details are crucial characteristics that form the foundation of how stories are employed in indoctrination and education into an ideology. Sundar (2004) in her work among RSS schools in Chhattisgarh found that through the celebration of mythical figures on calendar dates,

> … the birth and death anniversaries of actual historical figures and those of mythical characters are thus seemingly conflated and inscribed in the child's consciousness through the regime of national holidays, celebrations, morning prayers, as well as through the context of history and cultural knowledge textbooks. (Ibid.: 1609)

She asserts that for the RSS–BJP, 'teaching of history is inevitably deeply political'. Importantly, Sarkar (2019) argues that the popular history of the Sangh Parivar has had time to gain ground because of the cadres and affiliates, and academic history, despite its rigour, has lost out due to the same. Sundar (2004), Manjrekar (2011) and Sarkar (2019) show that these stories do not remain as oral traditions in the *shakha*s or camps. They find their way in the daily functioning of public schools in the form of school assemblies, naming of classrooms, celebration of festivals and extracurricular activities. Further, they are legitimized through the educational wing, Vidya Bharati, by being taught as curriculum. Sarkar (2019: 161) shows that Vidya Bharati largely dictates the syllabi of BJP-ruled states. To illustrate its importance, a relatively unknown affiliate of the Sangh Parivar was the Jammu and Kashmir Study Centre (JKSC) that was instrumental in influencing the abrogation of Article 370 of Kashmir in 2019. Similarly, the RSS wing that deals with history, Akhil Bharatiya Itihaas Sankalan Yojana (ABISY), has now acquired key positions in the Indian Council of Historical Research (ICHR) (ibid.: 169). This progression shows us that these tales no longer remain harmless stories: These are the starting points to become legitimized for the implementation of the cultural roots of Hindutva.

Making of Gendered Hindutva: Upholding Traditions and the Duty of an Upper-Caste Hindu Woman

Lessons of ideal motherhood are extensively found in the literature and oral discourses of the Samiti and are crucial to the indoctrination in the Samiti's Hindu nationalist thought. As mentioned earlier, Samiti women look to Jijabai, the mother of Shivaji, to aspire for the highest qualities of motherhood. *Matrutva* is one of the three most important traits for Samiti women. Stories that highlight feminine kindness and compassion focus on an assumed inherently maternal nature of women. Women are expected to be more thoughtful than men, more giving and selfless. The lesson taught here is that kindness is a desired feminine virtue, and women, despite their hardships, should be able to display it. The duty of the mother is to perform the role of a selfless mentor. In stories of the members of the Samiti, the call to duty is stressed to remind members of the path laid before them, which relies heavily on its allegiance from the members and absence of disruptions, upholding the spirit of duty. In the Samiti schema, motherhood does not demand any conditions – it requires absolute commitment and performing of a role to a point of self-erasure. These stories tell women to choose their identity as a mother first and foremost. Younger women who are not yet mothers are encouraged to educate and learn skills to be better mothers in the future.

Caste in the Hindu Nation

In a book of inspirational stories of women that exemplify the three main qualities expected of Samiti women (*matrutva*: motherhood; *krututva*:

innovation; and *netrutva*: leadership), there is a story about Queen Kunti from the mythological epic Mahabharata:

> Pandavas (the group of five brothers and positive characters from the epic) were exiled to live in the forest for 13 years after the oldest brother, Yudhistir, lost the game of 'Chaupar'. Those 13 years were full of hardship and discomfort. After their period of exile ended, the Pandavas returned to Hastinapur. Their cousin and archenemy, Duryodhan declared that he would not give the Pandavas even a needlepoint's worth of land.
> On hearing this, Kunti spoke to Krishna about her son Yudhishtir's lack of retaliation. She said, 'Krishna, tell Yudhishtir that his constant recourse of "dharm" for inaction is a sign of decreasing intelligence. The "dharm" of Kshatriya is the destruction of enemy and prosperity of the kingdom. The passive nature of Yudhistir bothers me. Have I raised him for this? I feel insulted by his lack of action.' Saying this, tears began to fall from her eyes. Seeing this, the bravery that was dormant in the brothers reignited. She continued, 'This is the reason why Kshatriya sons are born. Brave men do not get discouraged when they have to face their enemy.' A battle was fought and the brothers avenged their mother with their blood. After the victory, Kunti felt satisfied with her efforts. (Rashtra Sevika Samiti 2014)

These stories highlight the struggle of two mothers: one from a historical source (Jijabai's in a story of Shivaji) and another from mythology (Kunti from the Mahabharata), who command their sons to not betray the caste script or duty that has been laid out for them (Jijabai to her son Shivaji and Kunti to her son Yudhishtir). Their duty and labour lie in the upbringing of their sons as men who would rather die than betray their caste-assigned duties. It should be pointed out here that in the telling of stories, images of Muslims and Hindus are homogenized to portray a single, unified identity. The invocation of caste duties here is interesting because it shows that caste is extremely important to the construction of the Hindu nation: when one performs their caste duties well, one becomes a good citizen of the Hindu nation. Hence, such stories also suggest for the listeners to imbibe the message of historical caste affiliation and remain within those bounds. Therefore, while there is an assumption of a single, unified Hindu identity, there is also merit granted in following one's caste identity as a Hindu.

Another aspect that I would like to draw attention to is that the castes under threat are the upper castes (Brahmins in the story about the killing of the young boy; Kshatriyas, the warrior caste, in the story about Kunti), and the commitment of these castes to the Hindu nation becomes especially important. An example in a similar vein is often hailed from the mythological epic Ramayana, in which Ram ate the fruits from the hands of a tribal woman named Shabari. Shabari tastes the fruits before giving them to Ram to make sure he eats the sweetest ones. In this narrative, Shabari is a simple-minded tribal woman who should be in grateful servitude, and she is upheld as a model because she performs her duty of serving Ram. The kindness is located in Ram, who accepts the fruits that are already tasted and his greatness lies in his ability to humour Shabari. Further, the narrative sees the kindness of Ram as reflected in the fact that he chose to see her as a mother and not someone who belonged to a caste lower than him.[5] This is the model that the Hindu nationalist organizations follow as well.

In Duty Lies Her Patriotism

Madhao Sadashiv 'Guruji' Golwalkar (1906–1973) was the second *sanghsanchalak* of the RSS. His influence on the present ideology of the RSS and the Sangh Parivar is unquestionable. In a seminal text for the Sangh Parivar titled *Bunch of Thoughts* (1966), Golwalkar has extensively written on his vision of the Sangh Parivar in unifying the larger Hindu community. He writes on 'national duty' by invoking this story:

> The martyrdom of Tanaji Malasure is a shining example in this regard. When Shivaji sent word to him and assigned him the challenging task of winning the formidable Kondana fort (later called Sinhagad), Tanaji was busy making preparations for his son's marriage. But at the word of Shivaji, Tanaji gave up the thought of the marriage saying, 'My son's marriage may well wait for some time; I will first carry out the command of my king. My first duty is towards the Swaraj.' Without a moment's hesitation Tanaji proceeded to conquer Kondana. The heroic attempt was crowned with success, but it claimed as its price the life of Tanaji himself. (Golwalkar 1966: 59)

The importance of duty, especially towards the 'nation', is an oft-invoked value to be inculcated among members of the movement. The nature of one's duty depends on their gender (a mother's duty to nurture, a father's duty to provide for the family and protect their honour, a son's duty to take care of the old parents or a daughter's duty to protect her family's honour) or their social position (the duty of the king or *rajput* as illustrated earlier). In another section of the book, Golwalkar notes, 'If he fails in that supreme duty he ruins not only himself but also others. Hence the sacred duty of preserving the Hindu Society in sound condition has devolved upon us.' (Golwalkar 1966: 17)

What is the expected 'duty' of the Hindu nationalist women? The founder of the organization Lakshmibai Kelkar directed the followers as such: 'Sewa or service is a primary duty of a woman.... It calls for self-less sacrifice, dedication, and utmost devotion. No person can do this alone ... so we have to be united under the auspices of the Samiti, follow its ideology and discipline.' (Rai 1996: 27) The reason why such a lesson becomes important is because the Hindu nationalist thought relies on the gendered division of labour and a certain idea of a status quo. The primary duty of women in the Hindu nationalist schema is to preserve traditions, serve and protect their honour. Samiti women and women of a desired Hindutva nation ought to be striving to become mothers whose children will go on to serve the Hindu nation. Keeping the amorphous idea of one's duty above everything is a theme that is recurring in Samiti literature and stories. The climax of these stories lies in the protagonist making the 'right' choice (in accordance with the societal customs) – his or her duty.

Froerer (2007) finds the idea of 'moral education', called *sadachar*, codified in the classes based on textbooks. Patriotic morality is taught in classes in RSS schools, much on the lines of stories told in the *shakha*s and camps. Similarly, Manjrekar (2011) shows us that these guidelines of ideal womanhood have been inducted into school pedagogy through Vidya Bharati's 'Balika Shikshan' (Education for Girls). The lessons of ideal girlhood are taught in classes in a curriculum format, moulded on, no doubt, lines of Hindu nationalist thought. Much like the solidifying of oral tales in Hindutva history, gendered socialization becomes legitimized through classroom education.

Who Is Listening: Dissonance and Engagement with Stories for the Hindu Nation

During an early morning camp *shakha*, the Samiti *kshetra karyavahika* (district head) started her speech with 'Today's theme is saving our Hindu heritage'. She narrated stories about various temples that are in ruin across the subcontinent. Her lesson was that the only way these temples and 'our Hindu heritage' can be saved is by uniting Hindus to become a stronger force. And thus, one needs to become a committed Hindu (a follower of the Hindu nationalist thought and a member of the Sangh Parivar) to save the temples and the 'Hindu heritage'.

After her story, she looked at the younger audience and asked them what they learnt from the story. The first girl to raise her hand attempted to be innovative with her response: 'We need to visit the temples with our families and tell the government to repair the temples.' The speaker dismissed her response. She asked again, 'What did we learn from the story?' and another hand shot up in the air. The second girl responded, repeating the speaker's words, 'We need to work harder in *shakha*s to become strong Hindus so that we can protect our temples and our Hindu heritage.' The speaker looked around her, satisfied with the response and repeating the lesson of the story once again.

Menon (2010) in her ethnography writes about a *baudhik* session that sought to portray Hindu practices like *sati* (the practice of burning widows on the pyres of their husbands; legally abolished in 1829) were products of 'Muslim invasions'. A teenage girl listened to the story and countered this claim publicly by invoking an example of the practice from the epic Mahabharata. As a reaction to this challenge to the hegemonic portrayal of the ideology, Menon (ibid.: 40) notes of the speaker: '… [U]nable or unwilling to engage in a discussion, Rukimini [the speaker] just said "yes" and continued with her lecture.' Menon tells us that the speaker and the listener later discuss their disagreement in a private setting, but it is important to note here that the speaker's position conveys her hierarchy as a storyteller as well as the position of the hegemonic ideology over the contestations that are made to it.

The *baudhik* sections in the Sangh Parivar schema deal explicitly with disseminating the ideology through sermons, stories and preaching monologues. Oral recitations of the story would start with the 'theme of the day' and at the end usually asked the audience for 'what they learned from the story' or 'what the moral is'. The lessons are shown to exhibit hope, give space to righteous seeming anger and/or provide closure. Young prospective trainees are encouraged to find a message in the stories and relate it to the nationalist cause. Many respondents, who would like to become 'better at public speaking', are encouraged or volunteer to tell the stories in their home *shakha*s. Thereafter, members suggest tangible steps to enable further internalization of the ideology: members are encouraged to recount the stories to their parents, siblings, friends and neighbours, especially those who are not familiar with the Hindu nationalist cause.

The relationship between the act of storytelling and listening encapsulates within it many simultaneous power dynamics. The goals of the Hindu nationalist thought are already set. The story format allows the storyteller to have control over the language, the content and the way the story is delivered to the audience. Credibility and hierarchies are also set through the act of storytelling that also determine how the audience then engages with it. In the stories used here, the writer or speakers are mainly middle-class Brahmin women. The listeners are girls from the ages of eight to twenty-four in the camps, from mostly upper-caste (Brahmin, Rajput, Baniya) or OBC (Jat, Gujjar) backgrounds and from lower to middle classes. Stories are usually told during *baudhik* lessons in *shakha*s or camps.

Based on the story mentioned earlier, we can note that there was an expectation from the side of the narrator, of a certain kind of answer by the person responding to her question. This is merely a tool of performance to maintain the cohesiveness of the message. The question is rhetorical (the audience is very well aware of the answers expected) because there is not a large space to manoeuvre if one wants to interpret the story. To come to one's own conclusion does not lie with the 'lesson' provided or expected by the narrator, as shown by the dismissal of the response from the first girl. By telling these stories and leaving the lesson of the story hanging in mid-air (temporarily), the narrators are asking the audience to pick their identities and a side that they identify with. If they choose 'wrong', the identity that was in flux is fixed once the lesson is announced and accepted by the group.

The younger attendees usually prefer the more active part of the *shakha*s (games, yoga, recitations, and so on), and hence it is not unusual to see them yawn, play silent games or stare blankly around, if the narrator or the content is not interesting enough. This to me is one of the ways in which listeners interact with the ideology in the form of stories. For storytelling, there is a larger, hegemonic project in place that determines the themes of the stories told. But here, there are two ways that individuals can express their agency. First, there is agency on the part of people narrating the content and nature of the story. Secondly, and more importantly, we also have to consider the agency of the young girls who are listening to the stories and interpreting them, such as the attendees of the camp.

During a *charcha* (discussion) session in the Delhi camp in 2017, an old Samiti member sat on the chair and spoke to girls aged eight to twelve. The *charcha* sessions are held in the afternoon, after a brief lunch and rest hour. The girls sat lined neatly on the carpet, looking up at the speaker. She spoke of a story about Akbar as a lascivious king. The story was as follows:

> Akbar would dress up as a woman and walk around the market Mina Bazaar. You know Mina Bazaar, the one near Jama Masjid? Yes. He would try to take advantage of the women because it was very crowded. Those times were not easy for Hindu women. If he found you beautiful, you could not say no to the king. You had to become his sixth or seventh wife.

A girl (possibly around eight years old) retorted: 'My school "ma'am" [address for teacher] said Akbar was a good king – he loved Hindus and Muslims equally.' I found this an extremely important interjection to the way stories are received. She recognized that there are two histories being taught to her: her school history and the history of the camp. She chose to uphold the history being taught to her in school, much to the chagrin of the speaker who tried to insult the ignorance of her teacher. As we see the New Education Policy (2019) being introduced in India, the value of a secular curriculum becomes even more pertinent and this example shows the value of the school being a space that does not provide a biased history. By being vocal about her experience, the girl was able to plant a seed of doubt among the rest of the girls who were sitting in her class. Yes, the stories are designed to be unidirectional, and the listeners are expected to internalize and go through the desired Hindutva transformation. But as seen from the examples here, there is pushback and an active engagement with what is taught as an undisputable fact.

Conclusion

> Raja bola raat hai
> Rani boli raat hai
> Mantri bola raat hai
> Santri bola raat hai
> Ye subah subah ki baat hai.
> —Gorakh Pandey

> [The king said it is night time
> The queen said it is night time
> The minister too claimed it is night time
> The guardsman said it is night time
> While it was morning all along.]

In this chapter, I sought to identify patterns of storytelling, in terms of protagonists, plots, problems and lessons, to understand how these patterns translate into core ideological beliefs. After analysis, there emerged a clear connection between using elements of history to suit the ideological goals of the organization. First, storytelling is a core pedagogic tool of Hindutva because it is able to smoothly incorporate its core project – to write the contours of a Hindutva history. It is the characteristics of the nature of storytelling, layout of the *shakha*s and hierarchies that enable this project to be furthered and internalized. Further, by subscribing to the larger ideology of the Sangh Parivar, the Samiti modifies its role to suit the gendered division of Hindutva-prescribed labour – to uphold tradition and culture in the home and outside. Women role models encourage their sons to maintain caste loyalties, a crucial aspect of the coherence of the Hindu nation. Second, women in the stories take on the role of preservers of the unity of the Hindu home and culture.

The construction and layout of the stories are suited for a member who juggles many responsibilities. Hence, the length of the stories does not exceed a page. In the stories analysed, the pattern of the story (whether orally told or written) is as follows: first, the theme is introduced and the protagonist of the story is established. The protagonist is made clear by highlighting their qualities and simultaneously the introduction of the villain or unsympathetic circumstances for the protagonist are usually described in the adjectives opposite to that of the protagonist. The next step in the story is a description of how the protagonist overcomes the hardships and restoration of order – usually attributing to the qualities that the organization requires or provides and something that would be essential for the larger ideology. The stories end with the repetition of the theme in the form of the qualities that were earlier attributed.

The language is simple, and the focus is not on details but the lesson. The story has a clear beginning (usually at birth) and an end (victory in a battle or a glorious death). First, in the stories told, there was more emphasis on the context of the story told (and its relation to the present). For example, if the larger theme being discussed is 'love jihad', the story might be set under Mughal rule or in a related context where it is easier to draw parallels. Second, the focus of the story is always on the reception or the lesson. The story is treated as a mere vehicle of the ideology – that is why all elements of the story can be interchanged, as long as the lesson remains intact.

In the stories of the Hindu nationalist women, women are narrating the stories and are actors of history and for the Hindu nationalist movement. It is largely through stories that women find a place in the movement – stories of their role models, in their publications and in their *shakha*s and camps – an aspect that is left wanting in the male RSS. This is also how the Hindu nationalist project gives evidence of the ways in which it is gendered and the roles that are expected of the women in the movement. Thus, the storytelling processes among the women become crucial to understand their own self-making for the Hindu nationalist movement. These stories also show us how the women contribute to making and supporting the larger Hindutva of the RSS and the Sangh Parivar. The themes might become more domesticated, but the aims of the ideology come through. For example, the villain remains the Muslim figure in many stories. For the male recipient, the story would speak about protecting the honour of the motherland. For the female, it would speak about embodying the patriarchal hierarchy and protecting her own honour for the motherland and the community.

Gorakh Pandey's poetry encapsulates the power of the narrative in ideological projects. Stories appeal to emotionality, to familiar contexts, to hidden or latent prejudice, and they create a consensus based on loosely threaded plot around a desired lesson. During my fieldwork experience, it was apparent that individuals related more to emotionality in narratives than a lecture that holds more concrete ideas of the movement. Whoever has control of the narrative has control of closure. By giving a positive range of emotions to the teller and attributing negative emotions to the villain, it distinguishes the teller and their tale as fighting for the right cause, and also decides on the mode of closure of the story. Hannah Arendt in *Men in Dark Times* (1968) says:

> It is true that storytelling reveals meaning without committing the error of defining it, that it brings about consent and reconciliation with things as they really are, and that we may even trust it to contain eventually by implication that last word which we expect from the Day of Judgment. (Arendt 1968: 105)

In my analysis, I found that stories become a powerful tool to situate the connectedness of the present Hindu nationalist movement to the scattered Hindu identity resistance incidents in the past. The story being told does not have to explicitly elaborate on the connection between Rajput kings resisting Muslim rule to claim the former as part of the larger and continuous history of Hindu versus Muslim groups. And thus, as Arendt points out, there is no complication that arises when something is not 'defined' or concrete – it is the theme and the message that the process focuses on. This method then is an ideological tool to invoke selective histories and propose a history that more suitable to the cause. It is this history that is difficult to situate and lacks tangible details. It is this very nature that enables the core project of Hindutva of writing a Hindu nationalist history. And it is this history that continues to justify the 'communal violence of the present' (Sarkar 2019: 157).

Notes

1. The larger Sangh Parivar literature is usually quiet on the women role models that are specific to the Samiti in the Hindutva thought. Therefore, such stories are important because these records are the only ones that make a mention of their significance.
2. Young women who had attended both Durga Vahini and Samiti camps preferred the former because they were 'less strict and more fun'.
3. Sewa Bharati (Service for Bharat) is an organization that is part of the Sangh Combine. It began in 1989 under the third Sangh chief Madhukar Dattatraya Deoras to work for the 'downtrodden' of the society. The Sewa Bharati primarily works among lower-caste and lower-class regions of India, with a special paternalistic focus on caste.
4. *Shakha*s consistently invoke the figure of Queen Padmini. The story details Padmini as a Rajput princess who led other women in her palace to *jauhar* (pyre), where they submitted themselves to the fire upon an attack from Muslim rulers. The legend of Padmini has been invoked to demonstrate the epitome of women upholding community honour (Datta 2017).
5. To gain further insights into how the Shabari myth has been appropriated, see Kumar (2017).

Bibliography

Arendt, H. (1968). *Men in Dark Times*. New York: Houghton Mifflin Harcourt.

Bhog, D., D. Mullick, P. Bharadwaj and J. Sharma (2010). *Textbook Regimes: A Feminist Critique of Nation and Identity*. New Delhi: Nirantar.

Datta, R. (2021). 'Rani Padmini: A Classic Case of How Lore Was Inserted into History'. *The Wire*, 1 December. https://thewire.in/books/rani-padmini-classic-case-lore-inserted-history. Accessed on 10 June 2021.

Froerer, P. (2007). 'Disciplining the Saffron Way: Moral Education and the Hindu Rashtra'. *Modern Asian Studies* 4, no. 5: 1033–1071.

Gandhi, P. (2018). 'Matrushakti and RSS: The Inspiring Saga of Rashtra Sevika Samiti'. *The Organiser*, 26 October. https://www.organiser.org/Encyc/2018/10/26/Matrushakti-and-RSS-The-Inspiring-Saga-of-Rashtra-Sevika-Samiti.html. Accessed on 6 August 2020.

Golwalkar, M. S. (1966). *A Bunch of Thoughts*. Bangalore: Vikram Prakashan.
Gupta, C. (2009). 'Hindu Women, Muslim Men: Love Jihad and Conversions'. *Economic and Political Weekly* 44, no. 51: 13–15.
Kumar, M. (2017). 'The Many Versions of Shabari: From Nandalal Bose's Paintings to Hindutva Propaganda'. *Scroll.in*, 13 August. https://scroll.in/magazine/842424/the-many-versions-of-shabari-from-nandalal-boses-paintings-to-hindutva-propaganda. Accessed on 10 June 2020.
Manjrekar, N. (2011). 'Ideals of Hindu Girlhood: Reading Vidya Bharati's Balika Shikshan'. *Childhood* 18, no. 3: 350–366.
Menon, K. (2010). *Everyday Nationalism: Women of the Hindu Right in India*. Pennsylvania: University of Pennsylvania Press.
Rai, R. (1996). *Life Sketch of Vandaniya Mausiji: Founder and Chief of Rastra Sevika Samiti, Srimati Lakshmibai Kelkar*. Nagpur: Sevika Prakashan.
Rao, M. (2011). 'Love Jihad and Demographic Fears'. *Indian Journal of Gender Studies* 18, no. 3: 425–430.
Rashtra Sevika Samiti (2005). *Smaran Tumhara, Sfuran Hamara*. Nagpur: Sevika Prakashan.
———. (2014). *Matrutva, Krututva, Netrutva*. Nagpur: Samiti Prakashan.
Sarkar, T. (2019). 'How the Sangh Parivar Writes and Teaches History'. In *Majoritarian State: How Hindu Nationalism Is Changing India*, edited by A. P. Chatterji, T. B. Hansen and C. Jaffrelot, 151–173. New Delhi: HarperCollins.
Sundar, N. (2004). 'RSS: Teaching to Hate'. *Economic and Political Weekly* 39, no. 16: 1605–1612.
Tyagi, A., and A. Sen (2019). 'Love-Jihad (Muslim Sexual Seduction) and Ched-Chad (Sexual Harassment): Hindu Nationalist Discourses and the Ideal/Deviant Urban Citizen in India'. *Gender, Place and Culture* 27, no. 1: 104–125.

Part III

Cultivating Women's Militancy

The Vishva Hindu Parishad

5

Sanskaras, Sexuality and Street Activism

VHP Women at Work*

Manjari Katju

Introduction

The Vishva Hindu Parishad (VHP), a Hindu religio-nationalist organization, came into existence in 1964 with the ostensible goals of rekindling 'Hinduness' as well as Hindu nationalism – particularly among the Hindu diaspora and among tribal communities in remote parts of India. It is a wing of the Rashtriya Swayamsevak Sangh (RSS) led Sangh Parivar that works to disseminate the beliefs of Hindu nationhood in India and abroad. As part of this goal, the VHP has worked hard to pressurize the different central governments in India to construct a Ram temple at the erstwhile Babri Mosque site in Ayodhya – which, claims the Sangh Parivar, was the birthplace of the Hindu deity Ram. It is thus central to the identity of Hindus as a religious community. The VHP has also run campaigns for *ghar wapsi*, 'love jihad' and 'cow protection'.[1] Its women members, who are part of the main VHP organization and its offshoots, the Durga Vahini (Army of Durga) and the Mahila Vibhag (Women's Wing), play an important role in the project of Hindutva-ization. They have contributed not only in building the local visibility and media presence of the VHP but also in defining and fixing meanings of social values, morality and sexuality for a large segment of Hindus.

---

* I am indebted to the editors of this volume for their suggestions and comments on the chapter, which helped immensely in revising it.

The aim of this chapter is to highlight how the women of the VHP carry forward the Sangh agenda, at a time when the Bharatiya Janata Party (BJP, also a part of the Sangh Parivar) strove to become – and, eventually, did become – the ruling party in India. The chapter is divided into two sections. The first section discusses the launch of two women's organizations by the VHP and their main aims. It also discusses how they function within the larger mould of Hindutva.[2] The second section looks at their activities in contemporary times, from around 2010. It focuses on how the organizations have moved from a national Ram Janmabhoomi-centric activism to a more locally oriented street and service activism. This section also elaborates the meanings of family, *sanskara*s and sexuality that are disseminated by these women's wings and have fed into the larger discourse of Hindu nationhood.

VHP Launches Its Women Organizations

In the early 1990s, the VHP launched its women wings – the Durga Vahini and the Mahila Vibhag – to mobilize Hindu support for a Ram temple at Ayodhya. A few vocal *sadhvi*s (women ascetics) took up the task of *sangathan*, or organization, a cardinal focus of RSS activism, and mobilized women to agitate for Ram Janmabhoomi, or the Birthplace of Ram. This was a period when Hindutva-led mass movements for a Ram temple reached fever pitch and the Sangh Parivar outfits attained a powerful presence in the Indian public sphere.

The Durga Vahini, an organization of women between the age of fifteen and thirty-five years, took up agitational activism (Katju 2003: 88). Its goals were defined as *seva* – committing oneself to community service; *suraksha* – ensuring self and community defence; and *sanskara*s – observing specific norms of cultural and moral conduct derived from Hindu traditional prescriptions, as understood by the Sangh Parivar. The goals were the same as prescribed for the Bajrang Dal, the male youth wing of the VHP. Another organization of women, called the Mahila Vibhag, was formed to bring together women above thirty-five years of age, and it was given the task of raising 'social and national consciousness in women'. Because of the members' seniority of age, the long-term task was specially entrusted to mature women (ibid.: 89). Membership of the two wings was mainly drawn from Hindu urban-middle and lower-middle classes with a professional or trading background.

While Durga Vahini members are mainly students, who mobilize through their college and neighbourhood contacts, members of the Mahila Vibhag are homemakers who are engaged in full-time household work and family care and are active locally. There are *sadhvi*s too, who play an important role in propagating the Hindutva message. Since their 'sacred' status ensures a lot of popularity for their messages, *sadhvi*s receive important positions in the organizational structure of the VHP and even in the BJP. Sadhvi Rithambhara was the first chief of the Durga Vahini, and Uma Bharati was a former chief minister of Madhya Pradesh and a minister in the union cabinet in BJP governments. Most *sadhvi*s are known for their extremist speeches and incendiary messages, targeting Muslims. With their fiery oratory, they project themselves as indefatigable Durga incarnations, intent on vanquishing the Muslim 'enemy'. With their help, the Durga Vahini could mobilize a substantial number of young women as foot soldiers for events leading up to the demolition of the Babri Mosque in 1992. Basu et al. (1993: 42) draw our attention to the massive turnout of *kar sevika*s (women workers for a religious purpose) in 1990 at Ayodhya when the first demolition attempt was carried out.

The Sangh Parivar lays considerable stress on the politicization of women for the Hindu nationalist cause. Women are seen as producers and nurturers of 'Hinduised' future generations (Katju 2003: 88). The role that the VHP has created for them is not that of a pleading docile mother or a quiet wife but of a confident and fiery woman or mother who inculcates *sanskara*s in her children and an agitator who is fiery and street-smart (Katju 2017: 114).

Sanskarsheel Women

VHP women are, therefore, expected to be assertive, but theirs is an assertiveness which is fully compatible with patriarchal norms. Women must be nurturing homemakers, good mothers and wives, obedient to rules of domesticity and family hierarchy. Any sign of defiance is sternly discouraged. The Sangh Parivar's women members are categorical that they do not stand for divorce or ask for rights against their families: in other words, they are not 'wreckers of homes' (Sarkar 1991: 2062; Basu et al 1993: 42) or breakers of families. They are clear that their work is not to build any kind of 'women's liberation movement' which is not suited to Bharatiyata, or Indian cultural values (Katju 2003: 91). At the same time, they talk about *nari shakti*, or women's power. Such power, they say, arises from following family duties as well as from commitment to the organization.

Within the household, *sanskar*-building through religiosity is the task of VHP mothers (Basu et al. 1993: 42). Children have to be taught conservative religious norms as well as Sangh versions of history and politics. Parallels have been drawn between the recruiting of housewives for the Nazi cause in Germany and the mobilizing of mothers or homemakers for the Hindutva cause in India (Mazumdar 1995: 18).

In my interviews in the 1990s, leaders of the women's wings told me that they do not believe that women should leave their home or live a life of renunciation like *sadhvi*s – even though some high-profile members of the Durga Vahini are *sadhvi*s themselves. According to them, women should work, instead, for the social good while actively being part of the community. Their public role in the service of the community and nation is seen as an extension of their roles in service of the Hindu family. One of the ways used by the Mahila Vibhag to spread its worldview is by keeping in regular touch with ordinary women as yet unconnected with the VHP. They interact with them at the local religious gatherings and at collective devotional singing sessions for women: *katha* and *kirtan*. Religious spaces are thereby converted into spaces and opportunities for mobilizing women for a political cause.

For the Mahila Vibhag, therefore, the neighbourhood is the main locale of mobilization. As religious discourses and singing go on, they start discussing their message about proper Hindu female deportment and values. The sessions are then turned into discussions of current political affairs, peppered with the Sangh Parivar's views on various issues. Elderly members who hold important organizational positions initiate the discussions. Most women who come to these religious occasions already belong to conservative middle-class families. Some have male relatives who are affiliated to the Sangh Parivar. They provide almost a ready-made constituency for VHP women. In their own meetings and workshops of the Mahila Vibhag and the Durga Vahini, young Hindu women are told that they should be responsible for self-protection. This is not a defiance of their traditional domestic role because it does not disrupt family and social hierarchies.

Thus, VHP women's organizations retain the woman's subordinate position within the family as well as an emphasis on her domestic duties while encouraging public and social duties under the Sangh guidance.

In its work, the Durga Vahini conveys the typical right-wing opposition to depictions of sexuality. It has a moral mission within society and family – that is, to inculcate discomfort with depictions of the woman's body and sexuality, which they consider a violation of 'Indian culture' and Hindu *sanskaras*. This was evident in 1996 when members came out on the streets to protest against the film *Fire* (Katju 2003: 88). A sensitive portrayal of a relationship between two women outside the boundaries of heteronormativity, the film came under severe attacks from the Durga Vahini and other Sangh Parivar affiliates. The demonstrations were so aggressive that several cinemas in Mumbai and Delhi which were screening the film had to be closed down (Phillips 2000). Any divergence from heterosexual conjugal desire, as arranged by parents, offends community honour.

The Muslim 'Other'

The ideal Hindu woman, then, is a good mother and a Hindutva activist. Hindutva is defined, above all, as antagonism against 'individualism' and the 'Muslim' – both seen as anathema to the idea of a Hindu nationhood. The first has the potential of questioning the validity of the patriarchal and paternalistic family as also monolithic and exclusivist ideas of nationhood. The second is placed outside the boundaries of the nation as an 'inimical Other' intent on violating Hindu women.

This stereotypical image of the aggressive 'Muslim' is the binding force to unite Hindus under the Sangh. The Durga Vahini disseminates ideological narratives that are woven around the myth of Muslim population growth and stereotypes of Muslim sexual aggressiveness. Muslim men are vilified as rapists of Hindu women (Khanna and Shah 2002: 5). A Durga Vahini pamphlet circulating in 1997 reads thus:

> Beware Hindus! There is an international plot using Muslim goondas to tempt and trap young college going Hindu girls with love and marriage. Prevent your ward from mixing with boys of other religions, or else you can't prevent your sister, daughter from becoming Fatima or Julia. (Ibid.)

Fears of sexual attacks are added to 'myths of population out of control' so far as Muslims are concerned (Jeffery and Jeffery 2006).

Trained in Islamophobia and taught to regard Muslims as personal threats to themselves as women, VHP women have played a dynamic role in majoritarian violence against religious minorities (Sarkar 1991: 2057; Sarkar 1995: 189–190). Whereas earlier, right-wing women did not indulge in violent action themselves even when they supported it, the rise of Hindutva has drawn them into the fold of aggression. Flavia Agnes (1995: 141) writes: 'The shakti of the modern Durga was not directed against violence within the home and community but was directed externally towards the Muslims – both men and women.'[3] Women submerge their gender identity into their community identity; they see themselves as Hindu women pitted against Muslim ones. This rules out a common struggle by women of all communities against patriarchy and blocks feelings of solidarity with other women.

Sometimes, women hit out harder and more effectively with their words than even VHP men. Saddhvi Rithambara, for instance, delivered a well-known 'lemon in milk' speech in the early 1990s. Her words incited several riots:

> Wherever I go, I say, 'Muslim, live and prosper among us. Live like milk and sugar.... Is it our fault if he seems bent upon being lemon in the milk? He wants the milk to curdle.... I say to him, come to your senses. The value of milk increases after it becomes sour. It becomes cheese. But the world knows the fate of the lemon in the milk. It is cut, squeezed dry and then thrown on the garbage heap. (Quoted in Kakar 1995: 205)

This extreme anti-Muslim stance of the Durga Vahini is often found in the speeches of its members in more recent times too.

The Durga Vahini in the 2010s

According to the VHP website, which is updated regularly, it was 'to kindle a sense of security, Sanskar and dynamism as also to solve the various problems pertaining to them, the VHP founded an independent organisation of Hindu Yuwatis [young women] in the name of Durga Vahini' (Vishva Hindu Parishad n.d.). The website also says: 'Durga Vahini is an unequalled organisation of Hindu Yuwatis, which is committed to protection of Rashtra-Dharma [national virtue] and Sanskriti [culture] through bringing about a renaissance in the Hindu society with Service, Security and Sanskaras as its motto' (ibid.).

The VHP holds its women's groups, particularly the Durga Vahini, in high esteem and takes pride in its functioning. It acknowledges that the Durga Vahini is in no way secondary to the Bajrang Dal in commitment and in strength. According to the VHP website, 'Durga Vahini is not lagging behind the Bajrang Dal in any way in accomplishing all the action-plans of Shriram Janma Mukti Andolan [Movement for the Liberation of Shriram's Birthplace] most effectively and with equal strength. They had participated in Karsewa and Satyagraha etc [*sic*] in big numbers' (ibid.). The VHP underlines the motif of equality in courage when it refers to how masses of women reached Ayodhya for *kar seva* in October–November 1990, just as did the VHP men (ibid.). Circumstances 'forced them [the Durga Vahini members] to forsake their normal female tenderness and affinity' and courageously form a wall around their brothers 'who were being assaulted by the security forces with lathis and bullets' (ibid.). The VHP showcases the 'sibling affection' between its two youth groups. At the same time, and belying their women's claims to equality, the VHP does prioritize women's primary role as a familial one in normal times. Women are encouraged to be brave and independent but under the patriarch's protective gaze. According to Mala Raval, the national convenor of the Durga Vahini, the training that it imparts to its members is 'shakti ki sadhana (worship of strength), focussing on security and service'

(Misra 2016). This training, according to her, 'helps them become good daughters-in-law, serve their mother-in-law and father-in-law, and keep the family together' (ibid.).

Street Warriors and Activists

In the decade of the 2010s, VHP women became increasingly visible as street fighters. Their public agitations made them a formidable and a highly visible force to reckon with. Though not too large in numbers, their street presence and activism gained them much publicity because of its strident nature. One study has put the total number of Durga Vahini members as 35,000 spread across twenty-nine states (Jain 2019). This is not a very impressive number, but its effectiveness lies in the clamour it creates to grab publicity and the attention of the media. Durga Vahini members portray themselves as the shouting and protesting brigade that is not opposed to agitational modes on the streets to achieve its goals (Ali 2013). The goals are part of the schema of right-wing nationalism rather than gender emancipatory projects.

The members mobilize themselves for local street action, focusing on soft targets. For instance, they have directed their collective ire and energy at youth gone 'astray' and at the young boys and girls who celebrate their affection for each other during Valentine's Day (14 February). They have worked to 'protect Hindu girls from the clutches of Jihadi Romeos' (Haindava Keralam 2009), or Muslim lovers, who are labelled as 'jihadists' in disguise. They come out to monitor internet cafes, ice-cream parlours and public parks to report any 'suspicious jihadi move to target any naïve Hindu girl' (ibid.). They warn youngsters against going to 'dance parties', as, according to them, 'the organisers of these parties do not follow Indian tradition' and allow 'vulgar activities' to take place, including consumption of alcohol (Chakravartty 2010). They are, therefore, opposed to possible relationships with Muslim men as well as to public expressions of youthful romance or of entertainments which are inspired by Western examples.

They also target art exhibitions and fashion shows that, according to them, depict Hindu women and deities 'indecently' and bring disrepute to the Hindu faith. The Hindu faith and community are always projected by them as threatened, and they must rectify the wrong. Their loud protests are often accompanied by threats that if they are not obeyed, they will return with bigger contingents made up of Bajrang Dal and VHP members (read 'men') (ibid.) and punish the 'wrongdoers'. They disseminate the impression that they possess total social power and control to fix the social codes and norms.

The Durga Vahini trains its members in *lathi* play (cudgel fight) and in the use of light arms like air rifles for 'self-defence' and for street vigilantism. This light militarization adds to the formidable image of the group. The members are also expected to become adept in martial arts like karate. They see themselves as capable of resisting sexual harassment in their everyday lives as well as cross-border terrorism in 'national life'.[4] During VHP-led demonstrations and protests, they wear saffron headbands and hold tridents and saffron flags. The effort is to showcase themselves as representing an awesome force of combat. Training in light arms – swords and air rifles – is imparted to young girls in regular camps to build their martial 'skills' (*Hindustan Times* 2019). Called 'Shourya Prashikshan Varg' (Groups for Training in Bravery), the camps involve young girls at the senior secondary or college-going levels.[5] Sometimes, the use of arms comes under the official radar, and cases have been booked by the police against VHP members in the past – for instance, at Sigra, in Varanasi (*Hindustan Times* 2016). But VHP leadership defends its use of light weapons as 'a routine exercise' and 'within the ambit of law' (ibid.). The combat role is entirely directed at Muslim 'enemies' as is clear by the worldview that informs the Durga Vahini's work. Durga Vahini dress code in camps consists of a saffron sash arranged over white traditional *kurta*-pyjamas. The VHP website says that the 'uniform of Durga Vahini would consist of a white Salwar, white Kurta, saffron Chunari, white Joota (of cloth) and socks; and a belt with inscription thereon as Durga Vahini' (Vishva Hindu Parishad). The uniform reflects the idea of regimented militarization that is common to extremist organizations. Members like to be seen as Durga or goddess incarnations, fighting for the nation to which they have devoted everything, including their personal desires related to their bodies and sexuality.

Sadhvi Prachi, a VHP and Durga Vahini leader, says: 'Hold a garland in one hand and a spear in another; because if someone shows you eyes, you would have to use your spear on them' (ABP Live 2019). Her words are directed primarily against Muslim men as they are the perpetrators of 'love jihad'. She adds: 'Those who are making *kanwars*[6] in Haridwar are Muslims, and Kanwariyas[7] should boycott them completely' (ibid.). She asks Muslim women to adopt Hinduism to protect themselves from practices like the triple *talaq* and *halala*[8] (ibid.). So, it is exclusively the Muslim man who is the primary target. While they advise Muslim women to speak against the gender practices in their community, they never call upon Hindu women to do so. The presumed concern for Muslim women – which some may see as a form of feminism – is entirely 'other-directed feminism' – a highly selective feminism which does not question 'in-house' patriarchy but is conveniently directed towards the other.

Durga Vahini members are also assigned community service among Hindus, especially in slums, which they call *seva basti*s. They are encouraged to rise above caste considerations, but no particular training is imparted on anti-caste ideology. The VHP leadership asks them to take up at least one service activity in a *seva basti*, in a city with a population of one lakh[9] (Vishva Hindu Parishad). These activities can range from starting a prayer centre to starting a *bal sanskar kendra* (centre to impart 'Hindu' values to small children), a library, tailoring centre, medical centre, and so on. They are also encouraged to arrange small camps to spread information about primary healthcare like first aid, acupressure and home remedies. They are exhorted to take up legal aid and counselling for widows, deserted women, women involved in accidents, and so on.

Durga Vahini members come together during natural calamities, like floods, cyclones and earthquakes. They help the VHP in distributing relief material among Hindus and in repairing damaged Hindu homes and businesses. For instance, in the flood affected districts of Gujarat in 2017, they ran community kitchens to prepare food and deliver them to affected families (Sharma 2017). In the words of one of the members: 'It's almost a week, we are preparing food, either at somebody's home or some society, and packing them along with pickle for distribution among the flood-affected of Jasvantpura and Khakhal villages, some 70 km from Harij' (ibid.). Mala Raval points out that 'the girls are well-trained in dealing with calamity, be it natural or man-made' along with techniques of self-defence (ibid.).

The regular gatherings of women for community and social purposes or their active public presence, however, do not challenge patriarchal sociocultural norms which perpetuate gender injustice and discrimination. It is also not geared towards any kind of larger social emancipatory efforts which afford women a chance to live and work as equal participants to men within or outside the domestic environment.

Cultural Vigilantism

According to a VHP leader, 'Our aim is to insulate young girls from cultural pollution and teach them various ancient Indian traditions.' (Khandekar 2008) Television, he feels, is destroying Indian values and affecting young girls adversely. He informs: 'The Vahini's members discuss ways to protect Indian culture from the Western onslaught' (ibid.). One of the group's Facebook posts says, 'Hi-hello chhodo, jai sri ram bolo' ('Leave hi-hello, say jai sri ram instead').[10]

The VHP's youth wings gradually moved away from agitating for the Ram temple at Ayodhya to acting as Hindu 'self-defence' or vigilante groups in neighbourhoods. The VHP looks upon them to enforce codes of conduct and discipline as prescribed by the Sangh Parivar. For instance, one of the VHP leaders in Goa declared that it does not need the government to enforce a ban on the sale and consumption of beef in Goa as its youth wings the Bajrang Dal and Durga Vahini were capable of doing this on their own (*Free Press Journal* 2017). In his words, 'Like elsewhere in the country, in Goa, too, we are awakening people against the cow slaughter and eating beef. You will have to wait for another one or two years and our Bajrang Dal and Durga Vahini workers will stop cow slaughter in the state.' (ibid.) These two organizations are thus seen as ground-level task forces to ensure that the residents of neighbourhoods follow the social instructions issued by the Sangh Parivar from time to time, whether it is to do with cow protection, 'love jihad' or religious conversions.

The members of the Durga Vahini have attacked artwork which, in their opinion, shows women 'indecently' and in a 'bad light' (Luthra 2013). For instance, during an exhibition of nude art in Delhi, a Durga Vahini activist said: 'People talk of protection of women on one hand but enjoy such perversions on the other.' (Nandi 2013) On this particular occasion, they threatened the owners of the Delhi Art gallery. They demanded its closure and said that all exhibits should be removed immediately or else face further action from them (ibid.). Outside the art gallery they shouted slogans like 'Nari shakti ka apman band karo' ('Stop insulting women's power') and 'Art gallery band karo' ('Close down the art gallery') (ibid.). The Durga Vahini felt that the art exhibition was 'an attempt to treat women as a commodity and mere sex objects' (Priyanka 2013), borrowing some feminist terms to curb freedom of expression. One of the office-bearers of the Durga Vahini said that they felt ashamed of the paintings and asked: 'How can you show nude paintings of women in the open?' (ibid.) According to her, such paintings 'would encourage criminal mentality' and did not depict 'our culture and heritage' (ibid.).

One can see a selectiveness in their approach. It targets critics of Hindutva and those who stand up for cultural pluralism and aesthetic freedom. It leaves uncriticized and unprotested the sexist and patriarchal positioning and portrayals of women in as diverse terrains as the Hindu domestic sphere and mainstream Indian (Bollywood and vernacular) cinema. Violence within the Hindu family or household is rarely mentioned by them as it is seen as possessing the potential of dividing the family and creating fissures therein. Such an approach normalizes gender violence in the family. Another sphere which is not critiqued is mainstream Indian cinema, which quite often sensationalizes sexual violence on women. Misogyny and vulgarity in this sphere are ignored. Mainstream Hindi films are attacked only when it exposes a Hindu woman's body to Muslim male gaze, in which case it becomes an issue of a Muslim man violating a Hindu woman. Then the ire of VHP women members is directed towards the film and its makers – as happened after the release of the film *Padmavati* (Kumar 2017).

In the understanding of the Durga Vahini, women are socially dependent beings, even when they may be economically independent. They must be shielded from 'bad' influences by families and kin groups that provide shelter and security. The VHP sees itself as an extended family and protector. Its self-image of an overarching patriarch is celebrated by its women members. The VHP offers direction and advice to 'aggrieved' parents of daughters who go 'astray' and indulge in 'un-Hindu acts' or get caught in the trap of 'love jihad'. Condemnation and coercion are legitimate to control errant children. On the other hand, sibling love and protection of sisters by brothers is celebrated. This is seen as building familial bonds and strengthening the foundations of the Indian family, eventually believed to lead to strong national sentiments. This comes out clearly in the *rakhi-bandhan* ceremonies – where sisters tie a thread on their brothers' wrists – which are organized regularly by VHP cadres in the course of their local work. *Rakhi bandhan* is seen to forge close bonds between Hindus, leading to political unity.

VHP women have played a marked role in communalizing popular culture. Sadhvi Prachi called for the boycott of Bollywood (the Hindi film industry) stars who are named 'Khan'. She called upon Hindutva activists to tear out the posters of their films since, according to her, they promote a culture of violence (*The Hindu* 2015). Demands are raised to boycott their films, but there is no such call against other violent films which have no Muslim actors – even though 'violence' and 'confrontation' are popular themes in cinema where both protagonist and villain unhesitatingly use violence to either overthrow or establish 'morality'. Such communal calls for violence gather huge force when religious, renunciate women issue them. In the words of Amrita Basu (1993: 27): 'Their chastity heightens their iconic status for it is deeply associated in Hinduism with notions of spirituality, purity, and otherworldliness.' *Sadhvi*s project themselves as selfless people who are not in this struggle for personal gains as they have given up everything. They see themselves as part of these (hate) campaigns solely to help people become true soldiers in the cause of the nation.

The VHP and the BJP Government

Since the Durga Vahini had been on the forefront of the Ram Janmabhoomi agitations, it was but natural for it in 2015 to exhort the BJP-led national government, which enjoyed absolute majority in the Lok Sabha, to go ahead with the construction of the Ram temple at Ayodhya and not to do a 'U-turn' on it (Chauhan 2015). Otherwise, it would betray the trust of lakhs of people, including the Vahini (ibid.). The self-confidence that such an exhortation shows is remarkable.

The Durga Vahini usually avoids direct electoral campaigning, but sometimes it does so overtly to help its co-affiliate, the BJP. Its modus operandi is to talk about the 'national cause' (Swaroop 2015) and discuss national issues with women voters. Its members organize community meetings, *prabhat pheri*s (morning processions) and *satsang*s (religious congregations), instead of raising obvious electoral issues. In the words of a member: 'We only talk about *rashtra-hit* (national cause) and support those who share the idea' (ibid.). They also warn women about proselytizing activities and 'conspiracies of alien faiths like Islam and Christianity' (Vishva Hindu Parishad).

Their indirect political work is combined well with ground-level community work, whether religious or social. Along with the VHP, members of the Durga Vahini work in neighbourhoods and localities to socialize Hindus into Hindutva viewpoints and into their notions of living a 'good' Hindu life. Like its associate Hindutva organizations, the Durga Vahini, over the years, has worked mainly as an oppositional force. But with the BJP's electoral victory of 2014 and 2019, it has now become a part of the ruling power structure. That, however, has not led to a noticeable expansion in its public presence. It still mainly involves itself in community activities and 'welfare' work among Hindus, along with occasional caustic speeches by its leaders. Its camps and training sessions are held regularly. What perhaps explains its present relative silence is that the Sangh Parivar goal of seeing a Ram temple at Ayodhya is on the way to becoming a reality.

Conclusion

A mother who takes up the responsibility of inculcating *sanskara*s, or good Hindu values, in her children, a young girl who takes up self-defence and defence of the nation (particularly from the Muslim 'other'), and a *sadhvi* who is pure, chaste and takes up the cause of leading Hindu society – these are the three icons promoted by the VHP's women's groups – namely, the Mahila Vibhag and the Durga Vahini. Together, they are seen to form a force which is looked upon by the VHP to nurture, service, discipline and defend the three entities – namely, the Hindu family, society and nation. Women members of the VHP are mothers and community activists on the one hand and 'devoted soldiers' of the nation on the other. Deeply socialized in Islamophobia, they help the VHP and the Sangh Parivar build the foundations of a strong and virile Hindu nation. For the Sangh Parivar, women's activism in the Hindu nation's cause is prioritized over their agency to fight patriarchy.

Notes

1. The VHP calls conversion or 'reconversion' to Hinduism as *ghar wapsi*, literally meaning 'returning home'. It has carried out ceremonies of 'purification' to reconvert or bring back those individuals and groups into the Hindu fold which, it feels, had moved out to other religions, mainly Islam and Christianity. Marriage by choice between Muslim men and Hindu women is termed by the VHP as 'love jihad' because, according to it, the Muslim youth indulge in it to lure Hindu girls to convert them to Islam and thus increase the number of Muslims in India. This is termed as 'jihad' because the act of marrying Hindu women by Muslim men is seen by the Sangh Parivar as a way of Muslims to vanquish the Hindu 'enemy'. The VHP also works for what it calls *gau raksha*, or 'cow protection', which is one of its organizational goals. Its message is that since the cow is considered holy by the Hindus, the VHP strives to save it from slaughter. The VHP's campaigns around cow protection directed against primarily the Muslim community have contributed to building an image of a 'violent Muslim', who is said to devour the cow to spite the Hindus. These campaigns suppress the fact that bovine meat forms the dietary habits of numerous communities in India and around the world from times immemorial.
2. Hindutva is defined by its ideologues as an idea which is larger than Hinduism (in fact, according to them, it incorporates the Hindu religion within it) and denotes a strong Hindu nationhood in India. Apart from a unified nationhood it also implies an invincible Hindu selfhood that is committed to building a Hindu nation in India.
3. Also see Sarkar and Butalia (1995), Bacchetta (2004), Patel (2005) and Setalvad (1995: 243).
4. It was reported that the BJP government of the state of Haryana was contemplating creating squads of Durga Vahini members to curb crimes against women (*The Pioneer* 2018).

5. Images of Durga Vahini members foot marching with *lathi*s and swords can be viewed at Faruqui (2006a) and Faruqui (2006b).
6. Sticks used by Kanwariyas to carry pots of Ganges water on either end.
7. Male devotees of Shiva who walk barefoot to the town of Haridwar to collect Ganges water for the Shiva shrines of their respective hometowns. For more details, see Zamin (2018).
8. Triple *talaq* and *halala* are practices within the Muslim community which the Hindu right wing often gives its opinion on. These practices might not be complementary to Muslim women and are viewed with derision by the Hindu right wing. Triple *talaq* is a form of legal divorce practised among the Muslim community. *Halala* is a practice by which remarrying one's former husband is legalized.
9. One lakh is equivalent to one hundred thousand.
10. Posted on the Durga Vahini's Facebook page in September 2015, https://www.facebook.com/Durga-Vahini-604584806653333 (accessed on 5 June 2020).

Bibliography

ABP Live (2019). 'Sadhvi Prachi Makes Another Controversial Statement; Urges Kanwariyas to Boycott Kanwars Produced by Muslims'. 25 July. https://news.abplive.com/news/india/vhp-sadhvi-prachi-kanwar-boycott-muslims-haridwar-saavan-month-1040156. Accessed on 21 February 2022.

Ali, M. (2013). 'Art Show Goes On amid Tight Security, Protest'. *The Hindu*, 7 February. http://www.thehindu.com/news/national/art-show-goes-on-amid-tight-security-protest/article4386870.ece. Accessed on 8 April 2013.

Agnes, F. (1995). 'Redefining the Agenda of the Women's Movement within a Secular Framework'. In *Women and the Hindu Right: A Collection of Essays*, edited by T. Sarkar and U. Butalia, 136–157. New Delhi: Kali for Women.

Bacchetta, P. (2004). *Gender in the Hindu Nation: RSS Women as Ideologues*. New Delhi: Women Unlimited.

Basu, A. (1993). 'Feminism Inverted: The Real Women and Gendered Imagery of Hindu Nationalism'. *Bulletin of Concerned Asian Scholars* 25, no. 4: 25–37.

Basu, T., P. Datta, S. Sarkar, T. Sarkar and S. Sen (1993). *Khaki Shorts and Saffron Flags*. Hyderabad: Orient Longman.

Business Standard (2018). 'VHP to Campaign against "Ills of Love Jihad" in WB Schools, Colleges; TMC Says "Won't Allow"'. 4 September. https://www.business-standard.com/article/pti-stories/vhp-to-launch-campaign-against-ills-of-love-jihad-in-wb-schools-colleges-tmc-says-won-t-allow-118090400876_1.html. Accessed on 20 January 2022.

Butalia, U. (1993). 'Community, State and Gender: On Women's Agency during Partition'. *Economic and Political Weekly* 28, no. 17: WS12–WS21, WS24.

Chakravartty, A. (2010). 'VHP Allows School to Host New Year Party'. *Indian Express*, 27 December. https://indianexpress.com/article/cities/ahmedabad/vhp-allows-school-to-host-new-year-party/. Accessed on 7 March 2020.

Chauhan, S. (2015). 'BJP Mustn't Backtrack on Ram Mandir: VHP Mouthpiece'. *Hindustan Times*, 4 June. https://www.hindustantimes.com/punjab/bjp-mustn-t-backtrack-on-ram-mandir-vhp-mouthpiece/story-62GuZIeSIztTXUAO58h0gM.html. Accessed on 14 February 2020.

Faruqui, A. M. (2006a). 'Durga Vahini Foot March (Path Sanchalan)'. Image ID: 7926860. *The Hindu*, 29 May. https://thehinduimages.com/details-page.php?id=7926860. Accessed on 7 March 2020.

———. (2006b). 'Durga Vahini Foot March (Path Sanchalan)'. Image ID: 7926868. *The Hindu*, 29 May. https://thehinduimages.com/details-page.php?id=7926868. Accessed on 7 March 2020.

Free Press Journal (2017). 'Vishwa Hindu Parishad Will Ban Cow Slaughter, Beef Eating in Goa in Two Years'. 17 April. https://www.freepressjournal.in/cmcm/vishwa-hindu-parishad-will-ban-cow-slaughter-beef-eating-in-goa-in-two-years. Accessed on 1 December 2019.

Haindava Keralam (2009). '"Durga Vahini" to Guard Hindu Girls from Jihadi Romeos'. 26 October. https://haindavakeralam.com/durga-vahini-gaurd-hindu-hk11219. Accessed on 4 March 2020.

Hindustan Times (2016). 'VHP Leader Booked for Arms Training to Women Cadres in Varanasid'. 31 May. https://www.hindustantimes.com/india/vhp-leader-booked-for-arms-training-to-women-cadres-in-varanasi/story-yFXYk2VP2aTDDngMagZo8I.html. Accessed on 1 March 2020.

——— (2019). "VHP Women's Wing Members Brandish Swords, Air Rifles in Rally; 25 Booked'. 4 June. https://www.hindustantimes.com/india-news/vhp-women-s-wing-members-brandish-swords-air-rifles-in-rally-250-booked/story-HjeIMcLeUHJv7UZ5nOkwGL.html. Accessed on 12 October 2020.

Jain, K. (2019). 'Good Wives, Good Soldiers: Durga Vahini Women Take Up Arms to Protect Hindu Identity'. *The World*, 14 November. https://www.pri.org/stories/2019-11-14/good-wives-good-soldiers-durga-vahini-women-take-arms-protect-hindu-identity. Accessed on 29 February 2020.

Jeffery, P., and R. Jeffery (2006). *Confronting Saffron Demography: Religion, Fertility, and Women's Status in India*. Gurgaon: Three Essays Collective.

Kakar, S. (1995). *The Colours of Violence*. New Delhi: Viking-Penguin.

Katju, M. (2003). *The Vishva Hindu Parishad and Indian Politics*. Hyderabad: Orient Blackswan.

———. (2017). *Hinduising Democracy: The Vishva Hindu Parishad in Contemporary India*. New Delhi: New Text Publications.

Khandekar, A. (2008). 'What Is the Durga Vahini?' *DNA*, 28 October. https://www.dnaindia.com/india/report-what-is-the-durga-vahini-1201682. Accessed on 10 March 2020.

Khanna, R., and T. Shah (2002). 'Women and Violence in Gujarat'. Indian Association for Women's Studies, Special Plenary Session, October. http://www.unipune.ac.in/snc/cssh/HumanRights/07%20STATE%20AND%20GENDER/27.pdf. Accessed on 27 January 2020.

Kumar, J. (2017). 'Opposition to Padmavati Grows in U'Khand'. eNewsDesk, 13 November. http://www.enewsdesk.in/2017/11/13/opposition-padmavati-grows-ukhand/. Accessed on 2 December 2019.

Luthra, P. (2013). 'More Protests by VHP Women Wing against Art Exhibition of Nudes outside Delhi Art Gallery'. IBN Live, 6 February. http://ibnlive.in.com/news/more-protests-by-vhp-women-wing-against-art-exhibition-of-nudes-outside-delhi-art-gallery/371177-3-244.html. Accessed on 8 April 2013.

Mazumdar, S. (1995). 'Women on the March: Right-Wing Mobilization in Contemporary India'. *Feminist Review* 49, no. 1: 1–28.

Misra, L. (2016). 'Fight All Demons in Society'. *Indian Express*, 28 February. https://indianexpress.com/article/india/india-news-india/nationalism-bharat-mata-durga-vahini-vishwa-hindu-parishad-sangh-parivar-fight-all-demons-in-society/. Accessed on 25 May 2021.

Nandi, J. (2013). 'VHP Cries Foul, Artists Cry Freedom'. *Times of India*, 7 February. https://timesofindia.indiatimes.com/city/delhi/VHP-cries-foul-artists-cry-freedom/articleshow/18375420.cms. Accessed on 2 December 2019.

Nath, S. (2018). 'VHP to Campaign Against "Ills of Love Jihad" in Bengal Schools and Colleges; TMC Says "Won't Allow"'. News18, 13 September. https://www.news18.com/news/india/vhp-to-campaign-against-ills-of-love-jihad-in-bengal-schools-tmc-says-wont-allow-1867583.html. Accessed on 20 January 2020.

Patel, V. (2005). 'Fundamentalism, Communalism and Gender Justice'. In *Religion, Power and Violence: Expression of Politics in Contemporary Times*, edited by R. Puniyani, 191–207. New Delhi: SAGE Publications.

Phillips, R. (2000). 'Deepa Mehta Speaks Out Against Hindu Extremist Campaign to Stop Her Film'. World Socialist Web Site, 15 February. https://www.wsws.org/en/articles/2000/02/meht-f15.html. Accessed on 14 March 2020.

Priyanka (2013). 'Why Do We Always Need the Past to Validate Our Present?' Rediff, 8 February. https://www.rediff.com/news/slide-show/slide-show-1-nude-art-exhibition-delhi-controversy/20130208.htm. Accessed on 2 March 2020.

Sarkar, T. (1991). 'The Woman as Communal Subject: Rashtra Sevika Samiti and Ram Janmabhoomi Movement'. *Economic and Political Weekly* 26, no. 35: 2057–2062.

———. (1995). 'Heroic Women, Mother Goddess: Family and Organisation in Hindutva Politics'. In *Women and the Hindu Right: A Collection of Essays*, edited by T. Sarkar and U. Butalia, 181–215. New Delhi: Kali for Women.

Sarkar, T., and U. Butalia (eds.) (1995). *Women and the Hindu Right: A Collection of Essays*. New Delhi: Kali for Women.

Setalvad, T. (1995). 'The Woman Shiv Sainik and Her Sister Swayamsevika'. In *Women and the Hindu Right: A Collection of Essays*, edited by T. Sarkar and U. Butalia, 233–244. New Delhi: Kali for Women

———. (2002). 'When Guardians Betray: The Role of the Police'. In *Gujarat: The Making of a Tragedy*, edited by S. Varadarajan, 177–213. New Delhi: Penguin Books.

Sharma, R. (2017). 'Durga Vahini Distribute Food in Flood-Hit Areas'. *Indian Express*, 31 July. https://indianexpress.com/article/india/durga-vahini-distribute-food-in-flood-hit-areas-4774877/. Accessed on 1 March 2020.

Swaroop, V. (2015). 'In Bihar, "Durga Vahini" Targets Female Voters'. *Hindustan Times*, 21 August. https://www.hindustantimes.com/patna/in-bihar-durga-vahini-targets-female-voters/story-S2KwUsmnLX50ITQVUGA4fP.html. Accessed on 2 November 2019.

The Hindu (2015). 'Sadhvi Prachi Calls for Boycott of Aamir, Shah Rukh and Salman Khan Films'. 2 March. https://www.thehindu.com/news/national/sadhvi-prachi-calls-for-boycott-of-aamir-shah-rukh-and-salman-khan-films/article6951837.ece. Accessed on 6 January 2019.

The Pioneer (2018). 'Haryana to Constitute Durga Vahini Police Squads for Women Safety'. 21 April. https://www.dailypioneer.com/2018/state-editions/haryana-to-constitute-durga-vahini-police-squads-for-women-safety.html. Accessed on 2 December 2019.

Vishva Hindu Parishad (n.d.). 'Durga Vahini'. http://vhp.org/vhp-glance/youth/durga-vahini/. Accessed on 30 November 2019.

Vrindavan Today (2018). 'Durga Vahini Offers "Bravery Seminar" for Vrindavan Girls'. 6 June. https://vrindavantoday.com/durga-vahini-offers-bravery-seminar-for-vrindavan-girls/. Accessed on 1 March 2020.

Zamin, M. (2018). 'The Kanwar Yatra: Tracing the Historical Origins and the Present Day Journey of the Kanwariyas'. *Firstpost*, 23 August. https://www.firstpost.com/india/the-kanwar-yatra-tracing-the-historical-origins-and-the-present-day-journey-of-the-kanwariyas-5005941.html. Accessed on 7 March 2020.

6

Conflicting Modes of Agency and Activism

Conversations with Hindutva Women

Anshu Saluja

In this chapter, I set out to explore certain contradictory facets of women's involvement and militancy within Hindutva.[1] The inquiry is rooted in the city of Bhopal, presenting two case studies of women functionaries[2] who are a part of the Hindutva *sangathan* (Hindu right organizational formation). A burgeoning city in central India and the capital of Madhya Pradesh, Bhopal is a major politico-cultural node of the region. It has a thriving Hindutva network, with various interlocked outfits at the ground level.

In Bhopal, Hindutva's ideological sway has been felt in a variety of ways, not just in regular electoral competition. One of the most disquieting links in this long and winding chain of events was the riot that tore through the city in December 1992, in the immediate aftermath of the demolition of the Babri Masjid, situated in the north Indian state of Uttar Pradesh. The Bhopal riot lasted for over a week and inflicted grave losses. Official sources estimated around 140 deaths, while unofficial accounts regarded the number to be much higher – at about 250 (Basu 1994: 12). Muslim residents, in particular, were hit hard, as they were largely at the receiving end of targeted attacks, led by militant Hindutva organizations and local police, often found to be acting in collaboration. The riot gave rise to hitherto unknown anxieties and vulnerabilities. In its wake, the stiffening of attitudes and hardening of socio-spatial boundaries have been keenly felt. Ironically, a city that had remained remarkably quiet for the most part in 1947 during the Partition tumult, flared up in 1992. Since then, Bhopal has come to be 'classified as a hyper-sensitive city as far as communal disturbances are concerned' (Dubey 2003: 3).

Hindutva had the most to gain from such post-riot communalization. It capitalized on growing polarization to further consolidate its influence and reap rich returns (Jaffrelot 1996). In repeated contests for power, the Sangh Parivar's political wing, the Bharatiya Janata Party (BJP), steadily improved its standing in the city. In the 2018 State Assembly elections, it gained four out of seven seats in Bhopal. Its performance had been even better in 2013, when it captured six out of seven assembly segments there. Since 1989, the Bhopal parliamentary seat has rested securely with the BJP. In the last Lok Sabha (Central Legislative Assembly) elections held in 2019, the party fielded Pragya Singh Thakur, a Hindutva hardliner and a terror accused, allegedly responsible for plotting a bomb-blast conspiracy, from this seat (Saluja 2019). Still, she won it, with a comfortable margin. Her victory bears striking testimony to the popular hold that Hindutva enjoys. In other ways too, Hindutva has sought to disfigure Bhopal's collective cultural memory and the lived experience of shared solidarities.

My aim here is to explore Hindutva women's conception and characterization of their roles at home and beyond. I seek a sense of what they think about their own agency, nature of activism, potential to challenge familial controls and their complex modes of articulating the need for some form of gender rights. I also probe the ways in which they strive to mobilize support among a larger range of non-affiliated women. Such an engagement may demystify their constitutive worldview, the social contexts from which they are drawn and the wider political appeal that prompts them to embrace the Hindutva cause.

R. S. and K. D.

I cite two narratives at length – one provided by a senior Vishva Hindu Parishad (VHP)[3] functionary, R. S.,[4] and the other by a young Durga Vahini[5] office-bearer, K. D.[6] R. S. is a seasoned VHP activist, while K. D. is a young Durga Vahini storm trooper who is rising fast within the local Hindutva cluster and enjoying important responsibilities that are increasingly delegated to her. The former has always lived in Bhopal, while the latter relocated there a few years ago from a village in the neighbouring district of Vidisha, in order to pursue higher education. She joined the Durga Vahini after she moved to Bhopal. Both come from reasonably well-to-do Brahmin families. Their familial and communal contexts are quite conservative and constraining, with traditional caste and gender hierarchies firmly in place. Their accounts testify to the continued prevalence and legitimation of entrenched power structures in their immediate social circles.

Both R. S. and K. D. described their efforts as social work and designated themselves as social workers. However, it became clear from their responses that their professed brand of social activism consisted mainly of building contacts, organizing some scattered group activities, sustaining communal propaganda, conducting Hindu ritual ceremonies and festivals, policing intercommunity marriages, obstructing Christian missionary initiatives and ensuring that their campaigns are favourably reported in the local media.

I tapped into their experiences and perceptions for two key reasons. First, they are affiliated to the wider Sangh network that commands increased ascendancy in large parts of the country, including Madhya Pradesh. This association affords them the leeway to exert at least a degree of influence on state policies. Second, the alignment of these women with a power-laden and essentially exclusivist ideological and organizational formation critically inflects their responses to the questions of women's rights, choice and agency. These complex, and often conflicting, responses call for careful consideration.[7]

Building Communication Networks

Hindutva women deploy highly creative and effective communicative strategies to disseminate their ideological stance. They forge personal relationships with their organizational member base. Even the extended families of the latter are sought to be stitched to the Hindutva ideology and network through regular visits and close interactions. Spotlighting this sphere of activity, K. D. proudly told me: 'Our work is done through building contacts in homes. We don't restrict ourselves merely to training activists, rather we establish close personal relations with them ... we treat all fellow activists as our brothers and sisters.'

They seek to foster local-level links and build associations with family members of their sympathizers, supporters and recruits in different areas. Sarkar (1991: 2060) demonstrates this through the example of the oldest Sangh affiliate, the Rashtra Sevika Samiti.[8] She discusses how Samiti members strive for 'systematic cultivation of warm personal connections.... The Samiti is then carried right into the heart of the domestic space and ceases to be an institution within the public sphere'. Thus, bit by bit, the Hindutva programme seeps in, with more and more supporters incorporated within its ambit.

'The realm of the everyday' remains a critical arena of intervention for the forces of the Hindu right (Gupta 2000: 126). Calibrated attempts are made to develop personalized day-to-day contacts by Hindutva organizations, while their actual membership record often remains purposely undisclosed. 'What is very remarkable about Sangh activities is that not all of them are institutionalized and formal. Much of the significant work happens at everyday levels, through informal conversations, interactions, relationships.... The Sangh's genius lies in suffusing quotidian activities with political intent.' (Sarkar 2015: 283)

Women members of the Sangh combine direct considerable attention towards enlarging their network and bringing in new recruits. Durga Vahini activist K. D. elaborated on the organization's programme of establishing *milan kendra*s (centres for informal get-togethers), wherein 'weekly meetings are held, with a view to foster unity among participants in different areas'. Partaking in such recurrent get-togethers and receiving combat training through the platform of the Durga Vahini allow the girls a tentative escape route from their usually stifling domestic environment as well as a semblance of agency. Simultaneously, over time, they come to absorb Hindutva's driving motivations and concerns.

Women of the Hindu right also work to 'ensure that the entire mechanism of temples, domestic ritual events, pilgrimage sites and priests is efficiently fuelled through a constant rota of scheduled activities' (Sarkar 1999a: 2163). Organizing programmes and social gatherings to mark Hindu festivals becomes especially significant for constructing a grand narrative of a glorious and inherently superior Hindu culture. This facet can be profitably deployed for uniting disparate, and often opposing, factions of a deeply fragmented and diversified religious group around certain common themes. As such, Hindutva women steadily strive to secure local-level participation in putting together ritual events and observing Hindu festivals, in the process eliciting support for their overarching agenda.

Both R. S. and K. D. plotted in detail the celebrations that the Hindutva cadres conduct to mark festivals like Makar Sankranti[9] and Gudi Padwa.[10] R. S. boasted how Hindutva organizations have exerted pressure on the management of several well-known schools in the city, controlled by different Christian missionary denominations, compelling them to shut down on the day of Gudi Padwa. K. D., on her part, described how such festivals and celebrations serve to integrate diverse sections of the Hindu community, particularly the youth, impressing upon them the richness and superiority of 'our ancient Hindu culture'. Tellingly, in these utterances, the exaltation of Hindu religious values and signifiers goes alongside the denigration of other faiths. This worldview seeps in slowly but surely through routine conversations, narrations and anecdotes. As R. S. explained, 'even during casual conversations with other women and children, I try to spread my message'.

Gossip, rumours, manufactured accounts, news snippets and misleading or exaggerated reports of selected events, lifted from diverse spatial and temporal frames, are all stitched together to craft a well-knitted and easy-flowing narrative that creates a heightened threat perception among Hindus. Vivid stories delineating Muslim aggression and oppression are accorded a special place in the communicative strategies of Hindutva women. Their propagation and circulation have striking parallels to, and remind us of, the role that women of the Ku Klux Klan played as 'poison squads', organizing 'whispering campaigns' to tarnish the reputation of their opponents in the 1920s United States.[11] Such carefully crafted and oft-repeated stories do not call for a reality check; they simply become part of an everyday common sense. Elaborating on the modes of propagation and proliferation of the Sangh's message, Bacchetta (1994: 190) writes: 'The RSS ideologues are more concerned with evoking response than with facts ... because the discourse is unclosed, constantly evolving through time, it easily accommodates contradictory statements and images.'

In multiple ways, Hindu women are warned about the dangers inherent in day-to-day association and interaction with Muslim men. For instance, R. S. regaled me with wild tales of harassment of hapless Hindu women at the hands of unscrupulous Muslims in their marital homes. She used this as an entry point to convey and expand on the rhetoric of 'love jihad'.[12] 'Hindu girls are lured away by Muslim boys, by hook or by crook. But, once they are married, they are subjected to gross exploitation and oppression. They get sexually assaulted by their affinal family members.... They have to suffer enormously after they get married into Muslim families.'

Muslim men are projected as sexually depraved and scheming aggressors who trick gullible Hindu women into marrying them, with a view to augment their population. Such actions, it is urged, can correspondingly create a situation of demographic imbalance, on account of which Hindu numbers will stand dramatically diminished over time and the existence of the community itself will be imperilled. Articulating these built-up anxieties, K. D. insisted: 'Love jihad is a means to enhance the population of Muslims. It is a way for increasing the number of Muslims at the cost of Hindus ... diverse tactics are devised to break our strength ... they [the Muslims] have hatched a conspiracy, they generally target young girls.'

Significantly, in the course of our conversation, K. D. even advised me to stock arms at home for guarding against the possibility of Muslim aggression and flagged how Muslims trap Sikh girls, as a part of the conspiracy of 'love jihad'. She cleverly inserted many such alleged examples in her narrative. It is my impression that she made a deliberate reference to Punjabi or Sikh girls, since she knew about my Sikh identity. It seems that this on-spot improvisation was intended to instil my individual fears and make me wary of Muslims. I return to the campaign of 'love jihad' later and discuss it in greater detail in a subsequent section.

Misplaced Rage, Mistaken Target

For women activists of the Hindu right, involvement in the affairs and programmes of the wider Sangh network holds special value, as it accords them a marked sense of empowerment. However, this sense emerges chiefly from their commitment to and espousal of violence for the Hindutva cause. It is no surprise then that their intentions or actions rarely challenge repressive patriarchal structures and social norms which regulate their lives. Mostly coming from conservative domestic environments, they can barely countenance the possibility of defying established familial and communal controls. Their inability to do so and negotiate a freer life for themselves often breeds frustration and dissatisfaction. These simmering resentments are astutely employed by the Hindutva umbrella, in the service of its dominant agendas. The ideological, organizational and combat training that these women receive equips them to channelize and direct their personal discontent against adversaries, as designated by the Sangh. There is a systematic 'inculcation of transgressive female roles, of female anger and defiance. But that anger is to be directed at non-Hindu Others and not against the social order within which they themselves had been disciplined' (Sarkar 2015: 288).

The case of my respondent R. S. serves as a pertinent illustration of this subtle process of transference: Her seething rage and bitterness find clear reflection in her narrative. These stem chiefly from oppressive Hindu familial and social structures, but are readily attributed by her to Muslims. The latter, in particular, are viewed as legitimate enemies and as 'dehumanized others' on whom scorn and slander can justly be poured (Basu 1999a: 183). Dwelling on the harassment to which she had been subjected by her affinal family, R. S. recalled: 'My brother-in-law broke several pairs of sunglasses that I had. I was forced to wear only *sarees* and veil my face…. My husband's home had a very conservative environment. Initially, my husband did not even allow me to step outside the home.'

This sense of being wronged and repressed was drawn upon by R. S., not to break away from her constraining social milieu but rather to revile members of the Muslim community. She asserted that her main goal is to defend Hindu religion and society (*Hindu dharm aur samaj ki raksha*), the reason for which she joined the VHP. Thereupon, she proudly told me that Hindutva ideology has been firmly ingrained in her only son who has been initiated into the Sangh network and is on his way to becoming a full-fledged trained *swayamsevak*, or volunteer. From her contentions, it can be concluded that she has performed the duty of an ideal mother, as it was defined by the Sangh's leading light, M. S. Golwalkar.

> He [Golwalkar] made motherhood a political act and a political act of a very precise kind: one that implants in impressionable, innocent mind, images of violence and revenge.... The Hindutva mother creates tales for her child not with love, not to teach love, but to train him in hatred. Through such tellings, the child is transfigured: from a child to a Sangh worker. (Sarkar 2015: 293)

Centrality of Violence

Accounts of both R. S. and K. D. are powerfully coloured by images of violations and depredations, directed against inherently peace-loving Hindus, across diverse spatial and temporal frames, by overwhelmingly aggressive and antagonistic others. The past and the present, the extraordinary and the everyday, are all fused together in Hindutva discourse which calls upon community members to defend themselves and violently counter any perceived threat to their security. This preparedness involves stocking of arms and learning how to wield them. The acquisition of arms is seen to be particularly pressing for guarding against Muslims who are assumed to be skilled at handling them.

K. D. elaborated how *shastra pujan* (weapon worship) ceremonies have significance even for women. She explained that traditionally, these ceremonies are performed by men on festivals such as Dussehra.[13] But, to her, this seems inadequate, as in her view, women too need to step in, not just to venerate weapons but to also learn the art of using them. She regarded this as a critical confidence-building measure and underscored the necessity of imparting combat training to women:

> Women need to wield weapons today for their defence.... We need to learn these things from our gods. You see their idols, they are adorned with so many weapons.... They were so strong, they were skilled in these arts. We educate women about the utility of weapons.... We train them in the use of small handy knives and daggers. We tell them that this training will instil confidence in them.

Weapon-wielding Hindu gods and goddesses are glorified, for they exemplify before their devotees the primacy of arming themselves for self-defence. Goddess Durga, in particular, is viewed as an important source of inspiration. 'Durga is explicitly upheld as an example for female activism in her own right.' She is represented 'as the Divine Mother who steps out to protect her creation and her devotees within that creation in times of need', even with violence when necessary. The requisite to revive 'Durga's power' and follow her lead to safeguard Hindus from Muslims is repeatedly stressed by Hindutva women's organizations (Kovacs 2004: 377). Their members appropriate Durga's image and meanings to justify their own militancy. They urge that the time is ripe for action, here and now, for Hindu women to defend themselves, their *dharma* (religion) and nation.

K. D.'s formulations about the need to learn the use of weapons are shot through with a great sense of urgency. She emphasizes why and how it is dangerous to be friendly with Muslim neighbours:

> If a riot breaks out and you happen to have a Muslim neighbour, with whom you share close ties, he will set no store by them.... In fact, he will look at you primarily as a Hindu and may even attack you at that moment.... In riot situations, they [Muslims] seek to target Hindus, attack their shops and homes, murder them, abduct their daughters and rape them.... They have access to weapons, so they are able to do all this. But, we [Hindus] have no weapons in our homes today.

In order to counter this alleged state of imbalance, arms-training for Hindu women seems vital to her, because of the imagined threat of Muslim weaponry:

> It is necessary to have weapons in every home from the standpoint of defence ... just conduct a random check in Muslim homes and mosques, all the mosques are storehouses of weapons.... In Muslim homes, you will find a greater number of weapons than utensils.... They are always prepared to target Hindus.

Countenancing the Caste Question

But who are Hindus? Try as they might, the fundamental reality of caste cannot be wished away by Hindutva partisans. Contrary to what the Sangh combine contends, and seeks to popularize relentlessly, Hinduism is not a monolithic entity. In fact, it is characterized by sharp internal fractures and contradictions – the most obvious being that of caste-based hierarchies and differences.

Both K. D. and R. S. failed to offer any definite programme or vision to weaken the hold of caste system on Indian society. Instead, they opted to tread carefully and played it safe for the most part, refusing to dwell on this embarrassing theme. Their narratives eschewed any need for real self-searching among upper castes. Both, however, did mention their faltering efforts at bridging these deep-rooted differences.

With considerable reformist zeal, K. D. related the Hindu right's programme of combating caste discrimination which, in effect, amounted to nothing more than sharing meals with members of lower-caste groups or calling the latter over for food on select days, such as Valmiki Jayanti.[14] 'When Valmiki Jayanti is celebrated, we call *sweepers to our homes for food* [emphasis original]. What we seek to impress upon them through such efforts is that they should not consider themselves to be different. They should not feel that they are being discriminated against. So, we work to implement these kinds of positive things in our society.' Their engagement with caste, therefore, implies a routinized, almost ritualized, inversion of purity–pollution taboos – very distant from a sustained movement and struggle against this iniquitous system as a whole.

Adopting a similar ameliorative stance, R. S. too recapitulated her attempts 'to mingle with the poor'. She proudly highlighted her participation in annual Ambedkar Jayanti[15] celebrations:

> I am a Brahmin myself. Nobody can blame me for discrimination....
> On the day of Ambedkar Jayanti, we [upper-caste Hindutva activists] go to their programmes. So, they [members of lower castes] think that there is no division, there is no distinction.

In sum, both women failed to offer any constructive critique of the *Varna* institution and the enduring division of society into various castes and sub-castes. Ambedkar, therefore, remains an empty symbol, useful for mobilizing Dalits. But his caste analysis holds no salience for the Hindutva cadre base, nor have they studied it. Critically, there is no privileging of the discourse of rights, social justice or actual equality of opportunity, either with respect to existent caste boundaries or gender roles and relations, being reproduced and played out at the level of the everyday.

Reflecting on Limits of Agency: Potential to Challenge Social Controls

Women of the Hindu right are faced with an irreconcilable dilemma. Their stance reflects a marked ambivalence: it favours harnessing women's activism for furthering the Hindutva cause and advocates their greater involvement in the public domain. But this engagement with the outside world, beyond the precincts of the home, has to be moderated, for it can in no way be allowed to supersede their primary commitment to domestic life and family. That being the case, there is obvious emphasis on the need to curtail assertions of 'excessive individual freedom' by women (Basu 1999a: 181).

Their indoctrination within the Hindutva ideology and affiliation to the Sangh network offer no scope to Hindutva women to break away from the clutches of patriarchy and conservatism. Rather, their training advocates strict conformity to familial dictates and instructs them to stay within well-established confines. They are to act as important agents for promoting the Hindutva agenda, yet the assertion of their rights as women and the related discourse of emancipation are to be kept under firm check (Katju 2005).

Still, involvement with Hindutva does undeniably grant some form of agency to these women, however fraught and fledgling. Participating in organization-building processes and ground-level mobilizations gives them the confidence to work through the public domain and wrest some space for themselves within the bounds of entrenched familial controls, without in any way defying them. For instance, R. S. noted, with obvious satisfaction, how her activism gave her strength and made it possible for her to 'overcome oppression' within her affinal home.

> My husband's family harassed me a lot. I knew I would prefer to die, rather than trouble my parents about this. I struggled against heavy

odds, with considerable patience.... Gradually, as oppression grew, I felt that I will have to fight for myself.... When I suffered a lot, I felt that I had to raise my voice.

In K. D.'s narrative too, what stood out was how her role and responsibilities, emanating from her involvement with the Hindutva organizational network, served as a source of unmistakable pride and accorded her a degree of agency within kinship and community circles, especially with respect to male relatives and elders. However, the 'rare bargaining power at home' that Hindutva women at times come to acquire, does not signal any fundamental departure from the prevalent order (Sarkar 2018: 9). R. S. told me that she could step outside the confines of home, in connection with her organizational work, mainly because she had given birth to a son which afforded her a degree of freedom and respectability within her affinal family. She admitted:

When I became pregnant, my mother-in-law started threatening me about the dire consequences that would follow if a daughter was born.... If I had given birth to a daughter, I would have had to struggle much more. I would not have been here then.... Since I gave birth to a son, I gained respectability within the family. If I had to leave a daughter back home when I was going out for work, I would have been far more tensed.

Likewise, for K. D., her affiliation to the Durga Vahini and, by extension, the Sangh network did not go so far as to give her any actual freedom to choose a life partner for herself and decide on the timing of her marriage. She stated with feeling: 'All girls have to face this dilemma in their lives. This is a critical decision in any girl's life.... The girl should only decide and zero in on her marriage partner.' Notwithstanding these plaints, K. D.'s association with Hindutva opened up a limited window of freedom.

What seems striking is that when she talked about marriage choices or their absence, and assertion of her own rights to decision-making about herself, she referred to reconstructions of an idyllic Vedic past, instead of anchoring her narration in the present: 'Our parents know about our glorious Vedic past and cultural traditions; they read about Vedic figures and worship them. Why don't they emulate those practices, while leading their lives and making everyday decisions? Women had considerable agency back then to choose a suitable marriage partner for themselves.' The supposed Vedic freedom is contrasted here with parental constraints in the present. She was painfully aware that her say in decisions relating to her own marriage will be very limited, and that these concerns will be determined chiefly by her family elders, in consultation with other influential members of the wider kinship and community circle. So, she did criticize how her will was thwarted, but she phrased it as defiance of Vedic tradition by her family.

Familial authority comes to be superimposed on all aspects of the lives of Hindutva women. K. D.'s observation that 'in any event, families have the primary claim [over their women]' becomes instructive. Explicating this, Basu writes: '... one striking feature of women's activism in ethnic and religious movements is its tendency to uphold and defend the family rather than challenging it, as feminists have' (Basu 1999b: 10). Notwithstanding the personal battles which both R. S. and K. D. had to wage within their own homes against their family members, they steadfastly defended the existing curbs on women and the corresponding entitlements of men. They decried unfettered gender equality and disparaged such talk. Both condemned the ways in which women are transgressing pre-given boundaries and the dangerous possibilities of such boldness.

'The notion of equal gender rights' came to be deplored in no uncertain terms, for it is supposed to lead to 'domestic competition, unhappiness, broken families, blighted children' (Sarkar 1999a: 2165). R. S. cautioned about how women are misusing their rights. She viewed this as a product of corrupting Western values and highlighted the need to counsel mothers for safeguarding Hindu children from their unwholesome influence. 'At times, girls misuse the rights that have been given to them.... Girls get so much freedom that they misuse it. They think whatever they are doing is right. Most children today are influenced by Western civilization. We [Hindutva activists] try to counsel mothers also. I counsel them myself.'

A warning note is sounded: if women become actively involved in the pursuit of rights and pleasures for themselves, they are bound to wreck their homes. 'Rights are pitted against the pure wife, the good mother, the Hindu woman – a very big burden of sins.... Pleasure, desire and rights are aligned together as the Other of motherhood and tradition' (Sarkar 1999b:

153–154). Taking up this thread, K. D. reiterated entrenched gender roles and boundaries:

> We [women] are competing with them [men]. But the fact is that only we can give birth to a child, not them. These are inherent natural differences.... The point is that in such a competition, girls forget their moral values and the special gift that has been bestowed on them by nature.... The responsibilities of a woman do not end simply after she gives birth to a child.... The care and service that she can give, the maternal instinct that she has, those can be found only in women, not in men. This is a natural difference and it is bound to exist.

Even so, her account did not shut out the possibilities of women partaking in remunerative productive work outside the domain of home. But this seemed acceptable mainly because of the help that their incomes can provide in managing the household. So, new roles and freedoms are validated by domestic needs and interests. By way of drawing the bottom line, she made it plain that a woman's prime focus should be familial happiness and harmony.

> Women have been the custodians of our culture.... Now, women focus too much on the need to have a career. There is too much talk of empowerment, rights and such things.... Today, women compete with men at home.... Now, there is considerable emphasis on equal sharing of household work. Such an obstinate mindset should not exist [among women]. Families are torn apart, on account of that.

Hindutva women assert that Hindu families offer the best model of domesticity. They routinely and loudly proclaim the superiority of their beliefs and traditions over other faiths, reducing Muslims and Hindus to two exclusive and contrastive collectivities, which are eternally conflicted. They deprecate all Muslim cultural and religious symbols and practices.

The Campaign of 'Love Jihad'

Hindutva proponents stoke militaristic sentiments among Hindus, exhorting them to become bold and aggressive to guard against the threatening Muslim.

The latter is portrayed as such primarily because of the seeming dangers he poses to the vulnerable Hindu woman. Crafted 'images of passive victimized Hindu women, duped at the hand of inscrutable Muslims' are frequently deployed (Gupta 2016: 297). It is urged that given their supposed gullibility and trusting nature, they face grave risk of violation and exploitation.

The campaign of 'love jihad', which refers to a conspiracy hatched by Muslim men to lure Hindu women into liaisons and marriages with them, currently forms a key plank in the agenda of the Hindu right. The obvious 'fixation on controlling women's bodies' propels this campaign (Basu 1999b: 7). It builds on community and patriarchal anxieties about misguided Hindu women being ensnared by Muslim men into loveless and debasing marriages. Religious conversion, ill-treatment and exploitation are assumed to be the natural corollaries of such marriages (Sarkar 2018). Conversely, unions of Hindu men with Muslim women are regarded as expressions of genuine love, based on willing consent. They are even branded as vehicles which ensure the latter's *ghar wapsi* (return to home) into the Hindu fold.

While spelling out the 'love jihad' rhetoric, R. S. launched into wild and deeply disturbing tales of the plight of Hindu girls who married Muslim men and 'fell into their trap'. She claimed that several Hindu girls from Bhopal, whom she knew, have suffered enormously in such marriages. The reference to her supposed – and unconfirmed – personal acquaintance with victims was cited as the ultimate proof of Muslim perfidy. R. S. seemed to derive a kind of voyeuristic pleasure and satisfaction from repeating these unsavoury details. As mentioned earlier, she was under immense pressure in the initial years of her marriage. Her husband and other marital kin mistrusted and mistreated her. Instances from her own life of oppression and harassment get seamlessly transferred to Muslim families, bent on tormenting in-marrying Hindu women.

After outlining this conspiracy, believed to be engineered by Indian and global Muslims, R. S. goes on to deplore Hindu men for their evident failure to use Muslim girls as a means of settling scores. Her disappointment on this count bears testimony to 'how communalism, operating within patriarchal structures of power, implies the advocacy of violence; often sexual violence, towards women. Communal violence frequently resorts to the violation of the Other's woman' (Jayawardena and de Alwis 1996: xiv). And it is this concern with preserving 'female modesty', shared by 'all communities, and often classes as well in South Asia', which gets manifested in the form of stringent 'sexual and moral codes' (ibid.). R. S. contends that since their community stands united, Muslim girls are safe from any external threat, while Muslim boys have a free rein to entrap and violate pliant Hindu girls.

> Their own daughters are very safe within their homes. They [Muslim men] target our children. They become friends with our daughters to lure them away.... Muslim men deliberately develop bonds with Hindu families, with a view to ensnare their daughters, sisters and even wives. They give slow poison to our women and acquire complete control over them ... they are very adept at this.

To foil such manoeuvres, vigorous calls are issued for cementing Hindu unity. As R. S. insisted, 'If all of us Hindus stand united, then our girls will not be lured away by the other.' Further, she explained the unwillingness of Hindu men to entice and ensnare Muslim women.

> Hindu boys, I would say, are very weak. Even if we ask them to lure Muslim girls, they tell us that those girls stink. We don't like them. From the beginning, we tell our children that Muslims are unclean ... they eat beef. Our children grow up hearing these things. So, they have no inclination towards Muslim girls. On the contrary, Muslim boys are taught from their childhood to secure Hindu girls.

The involvement of a foreign hand is suspected to be behind this scheme of 'love jihad'. It is designated as an 'international conspiracy', presumably masterminded by 'neighbouring Pakistan' (Sarkar 2018: 12). Notably, Pakistani authorities are believed to be working in collaboration with Muslim clerics in India. Large sums of money are evidently pumped in and made available to Indian Muslims, with the precise objective of appropriating and defiling Hindu women. The ultimate goal of this project, as deduced by the Hindutva brigade, seems to be reducing Hindu numbers and heaping dishonour upon the Indian-Hindu state as well as community.

It is to counter this purported spectre of 'love jihad' and stall impending marriages of Muslim men with Hindu women that activists of the VHP and its affiliates strategically haunt marriage registration offices. 'Lecherous behavior, skill in luring Hindu women through false promises, a high sexual appetite, a life of luxury, and religious fanaticism' count among the chief attributes that characterize the Hindu right's depictions of Muslim males (Gupta 2016: 295). This assessment readily feeds into the overstated charge of polygamy, hurled by Hindutva organizations and functionaries at Muslim families. Since the latter are routinely denounced for being polygamous, the danger for the Hindu community, particularly its women, looms large. Caste Hindu girls are seen to be the prime targets of their insidious designs. They are perceived to be the bearers of 'community identity' which they have to uphold and safeguard 'through their roles as wives and mothers' (Basu 1999b: 7).

The 'love jihad' rhetoric accords little agency to women and treats them merely as passive and misguided beings who can be easily led astray. My respondent, K. D. cannot believe that a Hindu woman may actually opt to marry a Muslim. She can do so only on account of her ignorance and naiveté, a course that inevitably leads her to abandon her family and even religion. 'I don't want our girls to go into the religion of Muslims because Muslim women are themselves facing a grim predicament…. Women don't have any freedom there … in contrast, in our religion, girls still have so much freedom to step out. They can get educated, they can do so many things.' Such claims of 'lowly status of Muslim women' are immediately contrasted with approving accounts of 'greater freedom', possible within the Hindu social order (Basu 1999a: 172–173). This comparison serves to provide a marked sense of liberation to Hindutva women.

Conclusion

In the ultimate analysis, women get constructed as repositories of culture and honour, reproducing everyday accepted patriarchal codes that govern their lives. That provides Hindutva women an empowering responsibility and self-image within an overarching acceptance of patriarchy. The other source of empowerment is their association with Sangh politics: a route outside domesticity and a sense that they are the defenders of Hindu womanhood, Hindu culture and Hindu nation.

However, the extent to which Hindutva women's militancy has to be encouraged and the distance that they can be allowed to travel in this direction are fraught issues. Left unchecked, their militancy can turn inward and pose a serious challenge to prevalent structures of control and domination. Here, the familiar 'myths of the enemy within and of Muslim lust' become especially salient for guarding against such an eventuality (Tharu and Niranjana 1994: 106).

Therefore, these women can express a degree of resentment and distress about their own constraints within their families. But processes of transference and externalization of grievances onto the Muslim enemy, learnt through their continued training within the Sangathan, invariably set safe limits to that. The Sangh acts to confirm existing controls over women, but it also allows an important window beyond it, so long as their activism remains directed towards adversaries and detractors of the Hindu Rashtra, or Hindu Nation.

Notes

1. The Hindutva organizational umbrella, led by the Sangh Parivar (Sangh Family), is the spearhead of majoritarian right-wing politics in India. The chief reservoir of Hindu right politics, the Sangh Parivar is an intricate and interlocking network of organizations, active in diverse spheres – political, social and cultural. Structurally, the Bharatiya Janata Party (BJP), which currently commands the reins of the central government in India, is one of the organs of this expansive Sangh complex. The boundaries of its interconnected affiliates and sub-affiliates remain purposely fluid, and members can shift from one to the other whenever required. Its nucleus is represented by the Rashtriya Swayamsevak Sangh (RSS), founded nearly a century ago in 1925. The Sangh combine regards itself to be the chief defender of the Hindu community and faith. Its ideological appeals and invocations have often generated a fiery response in the form of mobilization of popular support, around certain select goals, calibrated displays of Hindu solidarity and unity and perpetration of brutal violence against cultural and religious minorities. It envisions

the creation of a 'Hindu Rashtra' ('Hindu Nation'), the borders of which will presumably transcend India to devour the whole of South Asia and even beyond.

2. In order to safeguard the identity of the respondents and to ensure their privacy, their actual names have not been revealed. Instead, their initials have been used.

3. Formed in 1964, the Vishva Hindu Parishad (VHP) is the religious wing of the Sangh combine. Counting several ascetics as its members, the VHP strenuously carries on anti-Muslim and anti-Christian propaganda. It seeks to target their religious symbols and deter the influence of Western values on Indian culture and society. It counters, often violently, Christian missionary initiatives, particularly those under way in tribal belts. Its self-professed objective, as listed on its website, is 'to organise-consolidate Hindu society and to serve-protect the Hindu Dharma [Hindu Religion]'. In order to widen support for its driving agenda, the VHP network has been intricately involved in regulating the functioning of religious institutions, temples and even *gurudwara*s, and in conducting regular ritual celebrations. To gain a better understanding of how the VHP network controls and manages variegated aspects of the ritual life of Hindus, see Sarkar (2012).

4. Interview with R. S. took place on 22 December 2016 at 2 p.m., at a popular cafe in Bhopal.

5. The Durga Vahini, a sub-affiliate of the VHP, came into prominence in the early 1990s during the phase of aggressive Hindutva mobilization around the Babri Masjid and Ram Janmabhoomi dispute. The Durga Vahini holds regular training camps for girls and women between the ages of fifteen and thirty-five. It operates on three key principles: *seva* (service), *suraksha* (self-defence) and *sanskaar* (cultural values). The organization imparts physical as well as ideological training to its members. The promise of building and strengthening physical capacity, and of gaining greater confidence in the process, inspires young women to join the ranks of the Durga Vahini. It focuses on 'organising women and involving them in the task of consolidating the Hindu political community' (Katju 2005: 337). But, this commitment in no way implies that 'the patriarchal socio-cultural set-up is questioned or that a movement is built against

the various forms of gender oppression and discrimination' (Katju 2005: 339). It lays no groundwork for interrogating the conservative social and familial milieu from which the outfit's members are often drawn.

6. Interview with K. D. took place on 29 January 2017 at 11 a.m., at her rented flat in Bhopal.

7. Throughout this account, I have quoted, at length, excerpts from the interviews that I conducted with R. S. and K. D. These relevant excerpts have been translated from Hindi into English. Necessary details, including date, time and venue of the interviews, brief biographical sketches of interviewees as well as other particulars have been furnished at the outset in the text. I have refrained from spelling these out in repeated instances, in order to avoid breaking the flow of writing. Whenever I have referred to or drawn upon existing scholarship, accompanying citations have been given.

8. The Rashtra Sevika Samiti, an all-women's Hindutva organization, was founded in 1936, becoming the first affiliate of the Sangh Parivar. It holds regular *shakha*s (training sessions) for its members along the lines of the all-male parent body, the Rashtriya Swayamsevak Sangh. Identical to the Sangh *pracharak*s (proponents) who regulate its functioning, Samiti affairs are managed and coordinated by *pracharika*s (celibate teachers deeply committed to the cause of Hindutva) who impart training to the cadre base and expand support for their agenda. The Samiti, while being firmly integrated within the overarching organizational network, tries to assert relative autonomy for itself from the Sangh's supreme control. However, the latter remains indifferent to these aspirations of the Samiti and treats it simply as one among the many thriving offshoots. This tenuous relationship suggests striking parallels to the dilemmas that confronted the Women of the Ku Klux Klan (WKKK), a white supremacist front that enjoyed significant popularity in the United States in the 1920s. The Klan's women 'copied the regalia, militarism, hierarchy, and political stances of the male Ku Klux Klan' (Blee 1991: 58), but resisted the subsidiary status assigned to them.

9. A series of festivals are observed across India to mark changes in seasons which hold particular regional or local significance in a traditionally agrarian society. The festival of Makar Sankranti falls in the month of

January. It signals the end of winter and ushers in warmer and longer days. Centred around the worship of the sun, it is celebrated in different forms in different parts of the country.
10. Gudi Padwa, which marks the onset of spring, is also connected essentially to the seasonal cycle. Falling in the months of March–April, it is said to begin the new year mainly for Hindus of Maharashtra and the Konkan region.
11. Blee (1991) has discussed the recruitment strategies, organization-building activities and mobilization tactics of Women of the Ku Klux Klan, with special emphasis on the state of Indiana in the United States.
12. Writing on the 'love jihad' propaganda and its salience for Hindutva organizations, Gupta (2016: 291–316) comments: It was 'alleged to be a movement aimed at forcibly converting vulnerable Hindu women to Islam through trickery and marriage.... It was alleged by Hindu hardliners that "love jihad" was an organized conspiracy, whereby Muslim men were aggressively converting vulnerable Hindu women to Islam.' However, in effect, it turned out to be 'an emotive mythical campaign, a delicious political fantasy, a lethal mobilization strategy and a vicious crusade – a jihad against love – for political gains in elections'.
13. Observed generally in the month of October, Dussehra, or Vijaya Dashmi, brings to a close the preceding Navratri celebrations, lasting for nine days. Dussehra holds special significance for the Sangh network, for it marks the foundation day of the RSS. The festival embodies both feminine and masculine agency. The former is denoted by the triumph of Durga over demonic forces, while the latter is signified by the victory of Ram over Ravan. In the ultimate event, in both cases, evil stands defeated by good and righteous powers. For more on this, see Bacchetta (2005).
14. Several Dalit communities across India celebrate Valmiki Jayanti. It falls in the months of September–October and is said to mark the birth anniversary of Valmiki, the revered sage who is credited with authoring the Ramayana.
15. Ambedkar Jayanti, which falls on 14 April, marks the birth anniversary of Dr B. R. Ambedkar, a relentless crusader for justice, equality and dignity for lower-caste groups. Himself belonging to the Mahar caste, traditionally identified as an untouchable community, he strenuously struggled for and

demanded the elimination of the caste system, together with its built-in hierarchies and privileges. A social, political and intellectual luminary, he became the chairman of the Drafting Committee of the country's Constitution. And it is to commemorate his invaluable legacy that his birth anniversary is celebrated every year, not just in the form of an official event, observed by state actors and institutions but also through a variety of popular gatherings – big and small – held across the country.

Bibliography

Bacchetta, P. (1994). 'Communal Property/Sexual Property: On Representations of Muslim Women in a Hindu Nationalist Discourse'. In *Forging Identities: Gender, Communities and the State*, edited by Z. Hasan, 188–225. New Delhi: Kali for Women.

———. (2005). 'Hindu Nationalist Women as Ideologues: The "Sangh", the "Samiti" and Their Differential Concepts of the Hindu Nation'. In *The Sangh Parivar: A Reader*, edited by C. Jaffrelot, 188–225. New Delhi: Oxford University Press.

Basu, A. (1994). 'Bhopal Revisited: The View from Below'. *Bulletin of Concerned Asian Scholars* 26, no. 1–2: 3–14.

———. (1999a). 'Hindu Women's Activism in India and the Questions It Raises'. In *Resisting the Sacred and the Secular: Women's Activism and Politicized Religion in South Asia*, edited by P. Jeffery and A. Basu, 167–184. New Delhi: Kali for Women.

———. (1999b). 'Resisting the Sacred and the Secular'. In *Resisting the Sacred and the Secular: Women's Activism and Politicized Religion in South Asia*, edited by P. Jeffery and A. Basu, 3–14. New Delhi: Kali for Women.

Blee, K. M. (1991). 'Women in the 1920s' Ku Klux Klan Movement'. *Feminist Studies* 17, no. 1: 55–77.

Dubey, K. K. (2003). *Justice K.K. Dubey Commission Report: Inquiry Commission on Bhopal and Ujjain Riots*. Bhopal: Government Central Press.

Gupta, C. (2000). 'Hindu Women, Muslim Men: Cleavages in Shared Spaces of Everyday Life, United Provinces, c. 1890–1930'. *Indian Economic and Social History Review* 37, no. 2: 121–149.

———. (2016). 'Allegories of "Love Jihad" and Ghar Vāpasī: Interlocking the Socio-Religious with the Political'. *Archiv Orientální* 84, no. 2: 291–316.

Jaffrelot, C. (1996). 'Setback to BJP'. *Economic and Political Weekly* 31, no. 2–3: 129–137.

Jayawardena, K., and M. de Alwis (eds.) (1996). *Embodied Violence: Communalising Women's Sexuality in South Asia*. New Delhi: Kali for Women.

Katju, M. (2005). 'The Bajrang Dal and Durga Vahini'. In *The Sangh Parivar: A Reader*, edited by C. Jaffrelot, 335–341. New Delhi: Oxford University Press.

Kovacs, A. (2004). 'You Don't Understand, We Are at War! Refashioning Durga in the Service of Hindu Nationalism'. *Contemporary South Asia* 13, no. 4: 373–388.

Saluja, A. (2019). 'Lok Sabha Polls: BJP's Choice of Sadhvi Pragya to Contest from Bhopal Indicates Party's Polarising Strategy in Crucial Seat'. *Firstpost*, 19 April. www.firstpost.com/politics/lok-sabha-polls-bjps-choice-of-sadhvi-pragya-to-contest-from-bhopal-indicates-partys-polarising-strategy-in-crucial-seat-6479401.html. Accessed on 29 September 2020.

Sarkar, T. (1991). 'The Woman as Communal Subject: Rashtrasevika Samiti and Ram Janmabhoomi Movement'. *Economic and Political Weekly* 26, no. 35: 2057–2062.

———. (1999a). 'Pragmatics of the Hindu Right: Politics of Women's Organisations'. *Economic and Political Weekly* 34, no. 31: 2159–2167.

———. (1999b). 'The Gender Predicament of the Hindu Right'. In *The Concerned Indian's Guide to Communalism*, edited by K. N. Panikkar, 131–159. Delhi: Penguin Random House India.

———. (2012). 'Hindutva's Hinduism'. In *Public Hinduisms*, edited by J. Zavos, P. Kanungo, D. S. Reddy, M. Warrier and R. B. Williams, 264–282. Delhi: SAGE Publishing.

———. (2015). 'Violent and Violated Women in Hindu Extremist Politics'. In *Pluralism and Democracy in India: Debating the Hindu Right*, edited by W. Doniger and M. C. Nussbaum, 280–295. New York: Oxford University Press.

———. (2018). 'Is Love without Borders Possible?' *Feminist Review* 119, no. 1: 7–19.

Tharu, S., and T. Niranjana (1994). 'Problems for a Contemporary Theory of Gender'. *Social Scientist* 22, no. 3–4: 93–117.

Part IV

Refashioning Gender and Sexuality

7
Tracing the Rise of Ascetic Masculinity in India

Arpita Chakraborty

Introduction

Religious ideas have played – and as this chapter will show, continue to play – a central role in Indian politics, and these ideas are gendered in nature. Some of these take a particular masculine form – violent, heterosexual and upper caste – and it finds expression in the political sphere through physical as well as symbolic forms of violence. One such form of masculinity gaining political capital is ascetic masculinity. I demonstrate in this chapter that the manifestation of ascetic masculinity traced in the works of Vivekananda,[1] Golwalkar[2] and Gandhi continue to be present and influence politics in India. A politics of appropriation in the contemporary Indian politics has seen right-wing Hindutva organizations applauding Gandhi and Vivekananda often. There is a growing trend within the Bharatiya Janata Party (BJP) to celebrate both Gandhi and his assassin, Nathuram Godse (Mukherjee 2019). This chapter will look at how ascetic aspects of the works of Vivekananda and Gandhi are taken out of context and appropriated by the RSS–BJP that helps them correlate their ideas of asceticism with that of Golwalkar, and how that appropriation is serving their violent masculinist tendencies.

The practices of violent masculinism in Indian politics in the early twentieth century bear resemblance to the political masculinity in contemporary India. This violent masculinism derives its strength from other structural hierarchies such as casteism. The need of the hour is to understand gender relations in their totality – the whole spectrum of manhood, womanhood, sexes, sexualities and their interconnections with our social spheres of culture, politics and religion. In fact, in either responding to a sociopolitical moment or attempting to re-enact a particular sociopolitical situation, the formation of hegemonic masculinity can be of use to bring back historical memories and past imaginings into present use. As Anand (2009) observes:

> The sexual dimension of the Hindutva discourse, as revealed in the jokes, slogans, gossip, and conversations of young male activists, is relevant ... it assures the Hindu nationalist self of its moral superiority and yet instils an anxiety about the threatening masculine Other.

In the performance of Hindu masculinity, the spheres of politics and religion continually intersect. The self-identity manifested by the state is that of a father figure – heterosexual, Hindu and patriarchal. This chapter will interrogate this Hindu masculine identity and how violent ascetic masculinity plays a role in its creation based on Islamophobia since the nineteenth century. Ascetic masculinity is indivisible from communalized anxiety about emasculation.

In the first section, I briefly discuss the writings of Vivekananda and Gandhi in relation to celibacy and ascetic masculinity. The second section will then look at Golwalkar's idea of celibacy and how the *pracharak*s of the RSS have put it into practice. The resurgence of ascetic masculinity in the wake of the BJP's hegemonization of state structure at both national and state levels since 2014 is discussed in the third section. This section will thus build on the previous discussions of ascetic masculinity and show its praxis in contemporary times. Through these sections, I argue that ascetic masculinity is becoming a dominant articulation of masculinity in Indian politics. It is propagated as ahistorical, or perennially present in the Hindu culture. With the rise of Hindu supremacists into prominence in Indian politics, ascetic masculinity is claimed as a true representation of ideal masculinity in India.

Tension between the Celibate and the Mother

Evidence of religiously motivated violent assertions of masculinity is a lived reality in India. The beef lynchings by vigilant right-wing Hindu nationalist or Gau Raksha committees (Ayyub 2018; *The Wire* 2017), the growing political capital ascribed to celibacy as seen, for example, in prime minister Narendra Modi's election campaign, which focused on his image as a celibate (Srivastava 2015), increasing violence against women and Muslims (Ellis-Peterson 2020; Reuters 2019) and the rising nationalist othering of minority communities (Subramanian 2020) all bear testimony of it. As contemporary globalized Indian society continues to be saturated with violent communal imaginations of masculinity, Vivekananda's ideas are also regaining popularity. His focus on virile masculinity and Vedantic philosophy has attracted the Hindu right wing. Beckerlegge (2004) shows how Vivekananda continues to directly inspire organizations such as the Vivekananda Kendra, which is also influenced by the RSS. On the topic of the Somnath Temple, for example, Vivekananda commented: 'We took this and others over and re-Hinduized them. We shall have to do many things like that yet' (ibid.: xiii). This 'othering' of non-Hindu religious communities is attractive to the Hindutva ideology. However, Vivekananda rejected the notion of violence celebrated by both the Christian and the Kshatriya model of masculinity (Vivekananda 1900a):[3]

> [F]rom the point of view of the Englishman, the brave, the heroic, the Kshatriya – conquest is the greatest glory that one man can have over another. That is true from his point of view, but from ours it is quite the opposite. If I ask myself what has been the cause of India's greatness, I answer, because we have never conquered. That is our glory.

Selective, out-of-context appropriation of quotes such as the earlier one have led to his popularization among Hindutva organizations, even though he had never justified the use of violence against other communities.

Hindu leaders have often employed religious ideas about celibacy to achieve political ends. Celibacy was variously understood as *brahmacharya*, or sexual constraint or the act of renunciation. Vivekananda, Golwalkar, Gandhi – all three use celibacy as a prominent feature in their ideological teachings. Gandhi defined a *brahmachari* as 'one who never has any lustful intention, who by constant attendance upon God has become proof against conscious or unconscious emissions, who is capable of lying naked with naked women, however beautiful they may be, without being in any manner whatsoever sexually excited' (Lal 2000: 123). In his lecture on the Vedas and the Upanishads, delivered in San Francisco on 26 May 1900, Vivekananda also upheld renouncement as the highest ideal[4] for men (Vivekananda 1900d).

He considered spirituality and intellect to constitute two separate spheres of social and political lives. While the spiritual nature of women contributes to the moral fabric of society, it is the intellect that drives political aspirations. Hence, we see him promote education among women, but repeatedly stress its use by women as mothers[5] rather than politically active members of the society. Renunciation of marital and familial life is thus never an ideal for Indian women,[6] unlike his male disciples. Celibacy was a symbolic capital unavailable to women. Making renunciation a necessary aspect of masculinity denies the role of reproduction to men. Dissociation of masculinity from reproduction was one of the central elements of Vivekananda's mission of recuperating Hindu glory – and this Hindu glory was for all practical purposes the glory of Hindu masculinity. The myth of lost masculinity is, contrary to established expectations, not countered by a claim to hyper-fertility. In Vivekananda's work, the highest form of masculinity is bestowed to those who refrain from sexuality in all forms. This loftiest spiritually ideal state of being was not a possibility for women in Vivekananda's imagination. Thus, ideal femininity and ideal masculinity seem to be always in tension with each other. The achievement of ideal femininity and masculinity together was a spiritual impossibility since motherhood and celibacy were in contradiction.

But why was *brahmacharya* so crucial to Gandhi and Vivekananda? According to Gandhi (M. K. Gandhi 1925: 316), without *brahmacharya*, men will be unable to conduct their duty towards the family and duty towards the greater good of the community together. The importance of the concept of *seva* emerges here:

> I clearly saw that one aspiring to serve humanity with his whole soul could not do without it. It was borne in upon me that I should have more and more occasions for service of the kind I was rendering, and that I should find myself unequal to the task if I were engaged in the pleasures of family life and in the propagation and rearing of children.... Without the observance of brahmacharya service of the family would be inconsistent with service of the community. With brahmacharya they would be perfectly consistent.

Gandhi firmly believed that sex, even marital sex, leads to the loss of the vital bodily fluid, or semen, which is the cause of masculine effeminacy among Indians. Celibacy played a central part in his politics of non-violence. Sex was merely a tool of reproduction, and *brahmacharya* is to be followed even by a married couple. This is a distinctive difference from Vivekananda's ideology, who clearly envisioned a more sexual reproductive role of motherhood for women. In his obsession with *brahmacharya*, Gandhi had imagined masculinity not only as bodily strength but also self-control through semen retention. There was a mystification of the semen and its extraordinary power, which was based on hardly any scientific evidence. He could link any bodily ailment with the imperfect practice of celibacy, be it constipation (M. K. Gandhi 1913: 103), pleurisy, dysentery or appendicitis (M. K. Gandhi 1924: 117).

Somatic conceptualization of sexuality also played a central role in his sexual experimentation; he was firmly of the belief that retention of semen in the male body was related to increased strength and masculinity.[7] Joseph Alter (1994: 45) writes about how Gandhi succeeded in amalgamating politics, religion and morality through this sexual self-control:

Affecting the persona of a world-renouncer, Gandhi was able to mix political, religious, and moral power, thus translating personal self-control into radical social criticism and nationalist goals. Gandhi's mass appeal was partly effected on a visceral level at which many Hindu men were able to fully appreciate the logic of celibacy as a means to psychological security, self-improvement, and national reform.

His advocacy of androgyny (Lal 2000: 119) would perhaps have been revolutionary, but for the fact that it was limited to a re-imagination of solely masculinity. Androgyny became the other of Christian masculinity, but it was also the other to a liberated femininity that he had been critical of all his life. It was Gandhi's position that in order to make Indian masculinity stronger, it had to induct the virtues of suffering and restraint from Indian femininity. However, the induction of such qualities was not intended to uplift Indian women to an equal status.

The idea of celibacy in married relationships was only tenable if initiated by the husband. This is a social reality Gandhi left unaddressed. While he formulated this *brahmacharya* for both men and women, denial of a sexual relationship by a married woman would have been an impossibility in conjugal relations in India in the twentieth century. In other words, *brahmacharya* as a spiritual or political choice was present only for married men like himself, while women like Kasturbai could only have been the passive recipient of such a decision. In these women's inability to take this decision lies the greatest gendered manifestation of Gandhi's political philosophy. While thinking of *seva*, he ignored a man's sexual responsibility towards their partner. And this led to another tension in his conceptualization, pointed at by Palshikar (2016: 420):

> ... its practice was supposed to make the practitioner more maternal, but it was also supposed to give him access to extraordinary potency. Gandhi ascribed asexual nature to women and 'lust' to men. If women were naturally less driven by sexual urge, if they were naturally maternal, if they had natural capacity for enduring suffering, then there was no 'overcoming'; where there is no 'overcoming', there could be no extraordinary potency.

This ideation of women being their finest as 'domestic goddesses' continues to this day, as verified by the lowering of percentage of women in Indian workforce from 42.7% in 2004–2005 to 23.3 per cent in 2017–2018 (Government of India 2019). Three out of four Indian women are neither working nor seeking paid work, putting India among the bottom ten countries in the world in terms of women's workforce participation. This brings us to the concept of work, or *karma*,[8] and how work is imagined in the ideation of ascetic masculinity. In the next section, I will look at the conceptualization of ascetic masculinity and how it is integrally connected to the religious imagination of *karma* in the works of Vivekananda, Gandhi and Golwalkar.

Celibacy and the *Swayamsevak*s

The idea of *seva* (organized service to humanity) (Beckerlegge 2004) is the conceptual connector between *karma* and *dharma*[9] for Vivekananda,

Golwalkar and Gandhi. Vivekananda stressed the role of the *sanyasi* as not spiritual renunciation but social activism through service of humanity. Influenced by the Western ideas of Christian masculinity, as well as the traditional ideas of sperm retention or 'spermatic economy' (Bramen 2001) as a way towards garnering masculine prowess (*kshatra-virya*), Vivekananda's central aim was to create a generation of young men who would dedicate their lives to service of the community and their spiritual upliftment through a focus on the teachings of the Upanishads and the Gita. In the formation and daily rituals of the RSS, we find reflection of the same aspiration in a more violent, communal form.

Currently estimated to have more than six million members spread among 74,622 *shakha*s (branches) and more than a hundred affiliated bodies (P. Gandhi 2014; Sagar 2020a), apart from thousands of other shadow organizations, the RSS is one of the principal forces of Hindu religion-centred politics in India. Its political thought envisages a future for India where Hindus will be able to retrieve their prominence in society, lost allegedly during the Mughal and British periods of domination. A theory broadly contested by historians like Thapar (2016), it has been enjoying growing popularity. According to the Constitution of the RSS (Chitkara 2004: 318), members have different roles based on their level of participation in the activities of the Sangh. The initiation role is that of a *swayamsevak*: 'Any male Hindu of 18 years or above, who subscribes to the Aims and Objects of the Sangh and conforms generally to its discipline and associates himself with the activities of the Shakha will be considered as a Swayamsevak.' In this conceptualization of general discipline, celibacy plays a crucial role.

Just like in the ideology of Swami Vivekananda, the idea of the celibate *sannyasi*s of Hinduism and Christian missionaries amalgamated in Golwalkar's imagination (Golwalkar 1966: ch. 35) to create the imagined rescuer of the Hindu nation (Golwalkar 1939: 88, quoted in Jaffrelot 1996):

> It is always the selfless, self-confident and devoted band of missionaries, intensely proud of their national ethos, who have roused the sleeping manliness in our nation in times of adversity and made our nation rise gloriously from a heap of shambles. Verily such men have been the true salt of this soil.

Religion played a significant role in such a reinvigoration, as is amply shown by the speeches of Golwalkar: 'Today, more than anything else, Mother needs such men – young, intelligent, dedicated and more than all virile and masculine. When Narayana – eternal knowledge – and Nara – eternal manliness – combine, victory is ensured. And such are the men who make history – men with capital "M"' (Golwalkar 1966: ch. 35).

However, there is a decisive shift of importance from the Mahabharata (of which the Bhagavad Gita is a part) to the Ramayana when one compares Golwalkar's teachings with that of Vivekananda. While the warrior image of Krishna repeatedly finds mention in the works of Vivekananda, the RSS shifts its focus to the warrior Rama, starting from the times of Golwalkar. Physical training, exercises and drills were introduced from the very first day of the RSS (Rashtriya Swayamsevak Sangh n.d.). The inspiration behind the formation of muscular, virile Hindu men was not the spiritual conquest of the world as Vivekananda envisaged but the political conquest of the Indian subcontinent from foreign rulers – the Muslims. The creation of Ramrajya – a political utopia with Hindu cultural, religious and political identity – is the ultimate goal of the organization, as is evident from the focus on building the Ram temple in Ayodhya. This indicates a decisive shift from the field of religion of Vivekananda to the field of communal politics by Golwalkar, despite the oft-repeated disavowal from the RSS.

Another crucial similarity between Vivekananda and Golwalkar is the idea of 'man-making religion' – religion coming to the use of masculinization. Golwalkar's interpretation of *dharma* and *karma*, decisively shaped by the protective duty one has towards the country as the mother figure, was imagined as the assertion of protectionist, virulent heteronormative masculinity. Golwalkar appropriated Vivekananda's conception of *seva* and conceptualized the idea of 'Positive Hinduism' (Beckerlegge 2004: 49). For Golwalkar, the *karma* of every Hindu was the service of the Hindu nation, and the *dharma* was to protect the Hindu nation from outsiders.[10] The humanity in Vivekananda's vision is narrowed to 'Hindus' in Golwalkar's definition of *karma*, thus religiously coding the subjects of such service. Andersen (1972) discusses at length the daily practice of physical exercises at every RSS *shakha* during Golwalkar's leadership, a practice which continues to this day. The use of weapons was also a common practice, especially in the *shakha*s in Punjab in the 1940s. He envisioned the 'work' of an individual as realizing his manhood while strengthening his Hindu community:

> The ultimate vision of our work ... is a perfectly organised state of society wherein each individual has been moulded into a model of ideal Hindu manhood and made into a living limb of the corporate personality of society.

I argue that for both Vivekananda and Golwalkar the conscious use of religion as a tool worked towards masculinizing not only individual men but the entire political habitus. Their belief in the 'spermatic economy' (Bramen 2001) excluded those unable to reinforce virile masculinity in a visible, physical way. The concept of 'spermatic economy' for personal as well as collective regeneration desexualized individual masculinity on the one hand while on the other it made this desexualized masculinity a central element of Indian politics. Thus, during the 2014 election campaign, we see Modi being projected as a *brahmachari*, *lauha purush* (iron man), whose unceremonious discarding of marital life was seen as proof of his virile masculinity necessary to be a national leader. By desexualizing himself and distancing himself from the marital responsibilities, he was seen as able to masculinize and dedicate himself towards the entire society rather than merely his family.

Distrust in the role of women as political agents is a recurring feature of the writings of Vivekananda and Golwalkar. Irrespective of their political positions in relation to caste, communal politics or violence, Vivekananda, Golwalkar and Gandhi all subscribe to the symbolic capital associated with ascetic masculinity. This symbolic capital (Bourdieu 1989) in the field of Indian politics can be capitalized to influence political practice: a vicious cycle exists that rewards masculinist practices ensuring its continued existence. The aim of Golwalkar's teaching is thus to create a habitus that will ensure the sustenance of this Hindu symbolic capital and its dominance over all others. In this he differed from the vision of Vivekananda, which was based upon a spiritual reawakening of the Hindu religion and Hindu men. Vivekananda did not provide a hierarchy in terms of citizenship in his teachings. In the light of this observation, let us remember one of Golwalkar's most quoted lines about the position of non-Hindu populations in his vision of 'Akhand Bharat' (Undivided India)[11] (Golwalkar 1939: 55–56):

> [They] must either adopt Hindu culture and language, must learn to respect and hold in reverence Hindu religion ... and give up their attitude of intolerance and ungratefulness towards this land and its age long traditions ... or may stay in this country, wholly subordinated to the Hindu nation, claiming nothing, deserving no privileges ... not even citizen's rights.

This exclusivist view of nationality, as Smyth (1972) called it, has been brought into practice by the post-2014 BJP government in India. The *seva vibhag* is one of the 'six pillars' of the RSS, and according to Shankar Das, the *bauddhik pramukh* or intellectual head of the RSS in Assam, works cohesively in the form of social work to achieve the ultimate aim of Hindu Rashtra (Sagar 2020b).

The field of communal politics and Hindu religion are located sartorially in the body of the Hindu man, in contradiction to the nineteenth-century focus on the body of the Hindu woman by theorists like Chatterjee (1989). The shift of anxiety from the female body in the home to the male body in the field of politics shows that the resolution of the women's question was negotiated in complex social and political re-imaginations. By moving our focus from social reform to the broader political field, it becomes clear that masculinity as both political agency and symbolic capital came into crucial focus in the last century. The culmination of this masculinization occurred in the Hindu supremacist politics of communalization after 2014. The last six years have seen a communalized masculinism in Indian politics – with the state structure in the hands of the BJP, all three pillars of the state have been communalized and masculinized. The next section will therefore focus specifically on this period.

Ascetic Masculinity and Violence in Post-2014 Indian Politics

Ascetic masculinity is on the rise in the political sphere in India. Despite their decreed renunciation of worldly affairs, ironically more and more ascetic figures are occupying political positions. There is a calculated promotion of religious ascetic figures in the public and political sphere in India. Sri Sri Ravi Shankar, Yogi Adityanath and Sakshi Maharaj are only the more well-known of such figures. RSS chief Mohan Bhagwat's annual address to the organization was broadcast live on the state television channel Doordarshan. Doordarshan till date had been reserved as a communication medium for the state – allowing only democratically elected leaders such as the prime minister or the president to address the entire nation. The three most important and symbolic political positions in the Indian federal system of government are the posts of prime minister, president and vice-president. The current president has close ties with the RSS, while the other two are former RSS *pracharak*s themselves. These are definite markers of the rising importance of non-elected ascetic masculine figures in the Indian political landscape. They reaffirm the intersection of religion and politics in Indian society and are embodiments of ascetic masculinity in praxis in Indian politics. The political appeal of such figures lies in their lack of personal attachments, since their proclaimed celibacy is proof of their ability to serve the country without any partiality. There is a connection made between celibacy, patriotic duty and masculinism that makes ascetic male figures the ideal political subjects and agents. Both the prime ministers of India from the BJP – former prime minister Atal Bihari Vajpayee and current prime minister Narendra Modi – have been projected as *brahmacharis*.[12]

The current prime minister of India is the biggest promoter of this brand of political asceticism. In the 2014 election campaigns, Modi was pictured as a national 'strongman' with a hypermasculine image. This is in sync with his tactical navigation of symbolic masculinity, which has also manifested in his dress, as described by Visvanathan (2013): 'Originally Modi appeared in the drabness of white kurtas, which conveyed a swadeshi asceticism.... Modi realized that ascetic white was an archaic language. His PROs forged a more colourful Modi, a Brand Modi more cheerful in blue and peach, more ethnic in gorgeous turbans.' He reformulates and publicizes ascetic masculinity in a more palatable garb even while the essence of his communalized politics continues to remain the same.

While Muslim masculinity expressed through violence is commonly associated with Islamic terrorism, violence by Hindu masculine organizations has achieved acceptance from a large group of Indians as a necessity to save Hindu cultural heritage. This symbolic approval also leads to and promotes a gender and caste hierarchy. The recent state policies taken up by the Modi government – planting trees to collect dowry for daughters thus reconfirming the dowry system,[13] banning of beef, silence on communal lynchings across the country – are manifestations of the same Hindu upper-caste masculinity, which gains legitimacy and religious sanctions through repeated quotes from the Gita and images of Vivekananda by Modi and other leaders. The popularization of Vivekananda in current times is particularly ironic, given his professed preference for beef eating. In a traditionally leftist stronghold like Bengal, using the imagery of Vivekananda has given the BJP an initial level of acceptance and opening into mass politics. The RSS and its various umbrella organizations have also strategically used Vivekananda to give the current government's policies a more acceptable face among its Hindu middle-class followers across India.

The reverence to Vivekananda is itself shown as evidence against reported conservatism – by using the beef-eater Vivekananda as their front face, they deflect the criticism against beef lynchings from within Hindus. This dissociation of masculinity from culinary restrictions, I argue, has made Vivekananda more acceptable to the middle classes in contemporary India.[14] Vivekananda and Gandhi have been appropriated as the faces of various governmental campaigns launched by the BJP government to increase its acceptability to a wider section of the population (Sen 2016). Vivekananda has been extensively used as an acceptable front for Hindu nationalist ideas to the middle class in India, associating his name with youth-related schemes such as the Yuva Vichar Vikas Rath (Menon 2014).

In contrast, Modi's silence on Golwalkar, whom he had professed earlier as one of the seminal influences in his life, also demonstrates his strategic use of all three leaders (Patel 2014). Though he has been a *pracharak* of the RSS, Golwalkar's imprisonment in Gandhi's murder case has made it imperative for Modi to distance himself publicly from his Guru. Publicly acknowledging Golwalkar as his Guru will affirm the xenophobic, Islamophobic ideas of the RSS and the BJP which Modi follows. However, the influence of Golwalkar's violent communal masculinism is clearly evident from the recent Citizenship Act and the Babri Masjid verdict, among others. Instead of directly professing to follow Golwalkar's path, Modi has instead appropriated a distorted, militarized version of the teachings of Vivekananda and Gandhi to promote sectarian, violent masculinity. It is a cultivated tactic that helps the party navigate a thin line between their ideology and realpolitik. Swami Vivekananda appeals to the middle class and youth in India and gives the BJP a more palatable face to these other Hindu sects, while Golwalkar is used to cater to the RSS's core following and its affiliate organizations. The cultural hegemony within the RSS following is important because it translates into votes for the BJP in electoral politics. The ironical co-optation of Vivekananda and Gandhi has made the violence acceptable, giving it a more bearable, internationally recognized face. Even while Gandhi and Vivekananda had promoted an ascetic masculinity which was not sensitive to the goals of gender equality, they would not have subscribed to the state-sponsored violent Hindu masculinism that the BJP has unleashed against minorities and any dissident voices.

Consider the occurrence of 'love jihad'[15] cases in the political sphere in recent times, the most famous of which was the case of a medical student Hadiya. In seeking to convert to Islam and marry a Muslim, Hadiya came to the centre of a controversy around Islamophobia, conversion and the freedom of Indian women to take decisions on their personal life. Hadiya, a twenty-four-year-old woman previously known as Akhila, was reported missing by her father in early 2016. In 2017, the Kerala High Court annulled her marriage with Shafin Jehan, on the grounds that Hadiya was a victim of 'indoctrination and psychological kidnapping' (Indian Express 2017). She was handed over to her father by the High Court, in one of the most blatant examples of patriarchal and masculinist essence of the Indian judiciary, with the remark: 'As per Indian tradition, the custody of an unmarried daughter is with the parents, until she is properly married' (Krishnan 2017). The Supreme Court finally restored their marriage in March 2018 (Mahapatra 2018). However, the prevalent masculinism in judiciary continues to affect judgments in cases that clearly define the lives and choices of many. Hadiya's experience is one among many incidents which have been termed 'love jihad'.

Anti-Romeo squads have now been created by shadow armies of the RSS such as the Bajrang Dal and the Hindu Yuva Vahini led by another violent ascetic politician Yogi Adityanath to stop such interreligious relationships.

With the tacit approval of the state and inaction of the police forces, these squads resort to a violent show of masculine force on such couples, terrorizing them, separating them and, in some instances, killing the Muslim men involved in such relationships (Jha 2017) in an extra-judicial show of violent Hindu masculinity. These squads are primarily made of young, unemployed, lower-middle class, upper- and middle-caste Hindu men trained in arms and committed to the ideology of Hindutva through involvement with one of its many organizations (Chacko 2020). The rise of the Hindu Yuva Vahini has catapulted Yogi Adityanath into the national political scenario. They use social media such as WhatsApp and Facebook to campaign against 'love jihad' and share information about suspected interreligious couples. The political hegemony of the Hindu right has been concurrent with the increase in the number of such groups all over the country.

According to Golwalkar, the only ground for Indian unity and harmony was a common respect for the cow (A. Sarkar and R. Sarkar 2016a: 334; Golwalkar 1966). Thus, it is no surprise that in keeping with the RSS position on cow slaughter, the BJP has encouraged the state-level ban of cow slaughter in BJP-ruled states, thus creating the horror of beef lynchings across the country. As of now, twenty-four out of twenty-nine states in the country have laws against cow slaughter (Indian Express 2015).[16] Cows have been a source of not only protein but also livelihood for many Dalits who used cowhide for leather, handicrafts and other forms of income generation.[17] The performance of such ascetic masculinity is also related to another form – culinary masculinity, which focuses on dietary habits as an expression of masculine performance.

Thousands of *gau-rakshak dal*s (cow-protection vigilante groups) have been created by Hindutva activists at local levels to prevent cow slaughter. Violent shows of masculine force are the signature mark of these groups inspired by Golwalkar's active participation in the *goraksha* (cow protection) movement in the 1960s. There are reports of lynchings by these groups from across the country. Accused of having beef in his refrigerator, Mohammad Akhlaq was lynched by a mob in Dadri, Uttar Pradesh, in 2015 (Kumar 2017). Other cow-related lynchings have been reported from the states of Gujarat (Chaturvedi 2016), Rajasthan (*Huffington Post* 2018) and Jharkhand (Dasgupta 2018), among others. Muslims and Dalits have been forced to eat cow dung (Dayal and Verma 2016), stripped and beaten, and incidences of harassment in the hands of these vigilante groups have become a common occurrence in various parts of India in the last few years. Apart from causing death, grievous bodily harm and psychological trauma, these groups are also successfully establishing cultural and symbolic hegemony of the masculinist Brahmanical Hindutva ideology. The violence of these groups in the name of cow protection supported by ascetic politicians like Uma Bharati and Yogi Adityanath[18] is meant as a show of virile Hindu masculinity. Rising ascetic masculinity in Indian politics and the reclamation of ascetic political figures like Swami Vivekananda as masculine ideals signify the growing popularity of right-wing politics.[19] The integral characteristics of this ascetic masculinity is misogyny, homophobia, anti-conversion and Islamophobia – gender equality, LGBTQ rights, Islam are all seen as foreign imports detrimental to the Hindu religion. Vivekananda and Gandhi are regularly mentioned in RSS rhetoric against conversion to other religions (Ghatwai 2014). The Ayodhya judgment of November 2019 has also brought to the fore the concerns about not only the secular framework of the state but also the judiciary. The violent ascetic masculinity championed in the name of saving Hindu religion is gaining traction.

The writings of Vivekananda, Golwalkar and Gandhi had symbolic power precisely because they act as repositories of such symbolic capital which can be easily manoeuvred and manipulated to influence public opinion and shape social positions on issues. The image of the violent Muslim prevalent in popular media has a much more complex and ambivalent history. This is the antithesis on which the idea of the violent Hindu masculinity has been created and propagated. Hindu nationalist masculinity thus works towards the consolidation of the boundaries between the two communities of Hindus and Muslims, and nowhere is this more evident than on the bodies of women. In the performance of Hindu nationalist masculinity, a significant characteristic is the violent claim on women's bodies made by the Anti-Romeo squads.

Even while hegemonic masculinity is transitioning, there are certain culturally significant events or metaphors that can be brought forth in order to stress on an eternal essence that remains unchanged. For example, in attempting to remind people of the communal tensions during pre-Independence and Partition times under the influence of which Golwalkar formed his ideology, forms of hegemonic masculinity practised at that time are brought into use by the RSS and its sister organizations in the name of *seva*. In this process, religious capital is efficiently utilized due to its permanence across political and temporal spaces.

The idea of *seva*, discussed earlier in this chapter, continues to be effective in the daily RSS activities. Bhattacharjee (2019) has shown how disasters like earthquakes are used to promote the ideology of masculinity using the idea of *seva*. In a speech delivered on 26 April 2020, RSS chief Mohan Bhagwat urged RSS workers to focus on *seva* in the context of Covid-19 as in a way 'part of an ongoing exercise of rebuilding the nation' (Bhagwat 2020). During the Covid-19 pandemic, evidence from investigative journalism has shown that the state administrations have been collaborating with 736 RSS-affiliated non-governmental organizations (NGOs) (Sagar 2020c) to distribute relief, control migrant crowds and issue special passes to RSS cadres. Government funds were reported to have been siphoned to RSS organizations in order to be distributed as relief (ibid.). These state resources were then distributed among BJP families by RSS workers as *seva*, thus helping to consolidate its organizational network among beneficiaries and donors. Questions arise as to who ensures that these state resources were distributed according to need and not according to religious and caste identities. There is little evidence of this *seva* benefiting non-Hindu faiths, particularly Muslims during the Odisha super cyclone, the Gujarat carnage in 2002 as well as the Delhi riot in 2020 (Rehman 2020). This majoritarian *seva* advances the image of Hindu masculine prowess in the figure of the masculine *sevak* at the expense of state resources.

Through an analysis of masculinism in the written works of Vivekananda, Golwalkar and Gandhi and ascetic masculinity practised in the contemporary Indian political sphere, I argue that even while hegemonic masculinity changes in form as it responds to cultural, social and political moments, this process does not take place in historical amnesia. The formation of hegemonic masculinity attempts to bring back historical memory and past imaginings of masculinity into present use. Mining through the archives of their written works is a method that proves rewarding in two ways: it shows the role of prominent individuals in building regional masculinity, and it points towards the historical continuity of notions around masculinity that plays a critical role in masculinism.

The violent masculine practices in contemporary India are both an attempt to practise hegemonic anti-Muslim masculinity of the kind propagated by Golwalkar and an attempt to convince people that the sociopolitical reality of contemporary society is the same as the perceived Muslim threat from pre-Partition times. Riots at Mujaffarnagar, the beef lynchings, the surgical operations against Pakistan are all examples of such a vicious cycle of masculinism and masculinist habitus reinforcing each other. Hindu religious concepts upholding such violence, especially in the form of the caste system, is shaping the violent nature of hegemonic masculinity in India. However, it is an ideal that very few Indian men actually embody in its totality. To understand contemporary Indian politics, the comprehension of this cycle remains crucial and as yet partially explored.

In this context, it is also vital to address the existence of concurrent regional hegemonic masculinities globally. As Ratele (2014) mentions, often political masculinities occupying a hegemonic role in the region might be marginal in the global political context. The rise of the alt-right globally and its relations with the rise of Hindu masculinity in India will make for a very necessary study. In fact, the understanding of political masculinism needs to address both cross-temporal and cross-geographical spaces.

The place of such heteronormative, virile masculinity in the times of technology-based capitalism remains unquestioned. In fact, gendered violence and violent masculinity are taking on newer forms in the virtual space. The performance of masculinity in Indian society can be seen live on social media today. Feminists, activists and politicians are all visibly and often violently interacting with each other on social media. Narendra Modi is now the second most followed politician on Twitter (Paul 2015). The role social media played in the last general election showed abundantly the promise of online platforms in an age when India has more mobile phones than toilets. This also means the politics of violent masculinity has become more visible and traceable in these spaces. Paid Twitter handles, paid media houses (*Al Jazeera* 2018) and trolls have emerged as the new violent masculine Hindu nationalists, defining the Indian political discourse. While I have mostly focused on incidents of violence manifested physically in this chapter,

I have discussed this elsewhere (Chakraborty 2019). The role of social media companies like Facebook and Twitter in giving space to hate speech and dissemination of the image of a politician (for example, Modi as a modern iron-man) and the impact these have on perpetuation of the gender hierarchy need detailed research.

Modi has been recast as a 'modern, development hero' through his Facebook page, Twitter handle @narendramodi, Pinterest board, YouTube channel, profiles on Google+, LinkedIn, Tumblr, Instagram and online products like laptop bags featuring him (Paul 2015: 380). Even in this recast Modi, however, nascent ideas of hegemonic masculinity are clearly present. The capitalist mode of economy that Modi has come to usher in since 2014 – opening the market for foreign investments, divestment from public sector undertakings and privatization of public sector enterprises – has been leading to increasing inequality and poverty for more than 80 per cent of the population. It is thus understandable why the current government has renewed initiatives to popularize the Gita (Nanda 2016). The Bhagavad Gita has already rationalized and justified inequality in society and in the production systems through its acceptance of one's position in the society according to *guna* and *karma* (Nayak 2018).

Conclusion

As Pandey (1993: 240) pointed out long before the BJP came to political power and formed the national government, 'What we sometimes have is the remarkable proposition that all social and political activities of the nineteenth and twentieth centuries in which Hindus took part were geared to the task of re-establishing the Hindu nation in its superior and glorious splendour.' This seems to be valid even today – and so does the masculine nature of such a 're-established Hindu nation'. The threat it poses is not only to minorities or the women but it can subsume the Hindu men themselves and restrain them from achieving their potential as human beings. In the same way, violent Hindu nationalist masculinity can restrain India from achieving its potential to become a nurturing and peaceful space for people of all beliefs, genders and sexualities.

Hegemonic masculinity can and is reconstructed continuously. But even while it is transitioning, there are certain culturally significant events or metaphors that it can go back to in order to stress on an eternal form of masculinity. Religion is one of the many discursive networks that shape up the definition of masculinity in India – sexual, economic, political and legal. This hegemonic masculinity, even while marginalized in the global scale of masculinities (Ratele 2014), continues to influence the shaping of bodies and bodily practices physically, socially and psychologically. These bodies are not only biologically male ones but all those who aspire to be a part of the masculinist power structure. It is clear that all men have been victims of this idea of violent masculinity. Constricted within the expectations of confirming to this idea of masculinity, unable to find any other form of expression of their identity, normative masculinity often impedes the right to freedom of expression.

On the other hand, the masculinism prevalent in state structures has meant that at the legislative and executive levels, mitigation of violence against women has been addressed primarily by aiming reformative policies at women, rather than addressing the pervasive presence of masculinism in society. The state has been trying to treat the symptoms without treating the disease, which lies at the heart of the issue of violence. Locating this research in the context of the work already done in terms of masculinity and colonization, one can see that the myth of manliness is not a static concept handed over across generations. Manliness, as an idea, as an ideal concept of gender performativity for those who want to be seen as 'men' in the society, go through repeated processes of adaptation. This adaptation takes place through accommodation of new information, changing social realities and discursive shifts in the society. Myth does not adhere to historical accuracy by definition, and the changing nature of myth only serves to show its dependence on a host of historical factors (Barthes 1972). Thus, the myth of manliness and the myth of the Hindu nation worked hand in hand in times of colonial struggle and are still working in tandem to continue the project of Bharat Mata (Banerjee 2006; Blansett 2012; Thapar-Björkert and Ryan 2002). The questions around gender roles in India, and continuing gender discrimination in all walks of life despite rising education and income, cannot therefore be addressed if we do not look at how the myths that are the foundation of the idea of the 'nation' perpetuate it. Their invisibilization is only the last step of their normalization: once made commonsensical, these ideological components are assured societal acceptance at large. In Indian society, the diversity of societal, communal and geographical richness makes the workings of ideologies localized to a large extent. The concurrent myths surrounding masculinity continue to prop up masculine domination as a natural phenomenon.

Notes

1. Swami Vivekananda was born as Narendra Nath Dutta on 12 January 1863, in Kolkata, West Bengal. Vivekananda was first recognized internationally when he represented Hinduism at the World Parliament of Religions in Chicago in 1893, and stories about the effect of his speech at the convention reached mythical dimensions in India. His speech also fuelled interest in Hinduism in the West, and for the next few years, Vivekananda travelled across North America and Europe, giving lectures and collecting disciples in various parts of the continents. This was deemed by him to be of crucial value for the reinstatement of Hinduism to its previous glory, and 'over time, several prominent Western intellectuals such as Leo Tolstoy, Romain Rolland, William James, J. D. Salinger, Christopher Isherwood, Henry Miller, Sarah Bernhardt, and Aldous Huxley, to name a few, were influenced by Vivekananda's teachings about Vedanta philosophy' (Roy and Hammers 2014). He returned to India in 1897 and, on 1 May of the same year, founded the Ramakrishna Mission. The last few years of his life were spent in nurturing the mission, giving lectures on Vedanta across the world – in cities as diverse as New York, Vienna, Paris, Constantinople, Cairo, San Francisco, Los Angeles and London. He died on 4 July 1902, at Belur Math in Calcutta.
2. The Rashtriya Swayamsevak Sangh, or RSS, is the largest voluntary organization of Hindu men created in the pre-Independence days to serve the nation. Madhavrao Sadashivrao Golwalkar, the second chief of the RSS, played a crucial role in the propagation and popularization of this theory. With almost three decades of being *sarsanghchalak* (1940–1973),

it was under his leadership that the RSS built up its organizational framework to 10,000 *shakha*s and more than a million members (Hoda 2006). Golwalkar's vision has become the vision of the RSS; and hence, his works have considerable social influence in contemporary Indian society with regard to not just matters communal and political but also gender and sexualization. Golwalkar in turn was influenced by Swami Vivekananda and even lived in the Sargacchi Ashram of Ramakrishna Mission under the guidance of Swami Akhandananda.

3. Also see Vivekananda (1900b), Vivekananda (1896a) and Vivekananda (1900c).
4. He quotes the Upanishad: 'The Upanishads say, renounce. That is the test of everything. Renounce everything. It is the creative faculty that brings us into all this entanglement'. Also see Vivekananda (1896b), Vivekananda (1898) and Vivekananda (1899).
5. Vivekananda often addressed his female disciples as 'Mother' or 'Sister', even while Bramen (2001) points out to the sexual appeal of the monk to his Western female audiences. For more on his vision for Indian women, see Vivekananda (1896b) and Vivekananda (1894).
6. Most of his female disciples who took up celibacy during his lifetime were Western.
7. In a letter to Harilal, his eldest son, he advocated celibacy since it 'increases your power' (Reddy 2007).
8. *Karma* can be roughly translated as 'the ethics of work'. In the Hindu philosophy of multiple lives, *karma*, or the fruits of one's work, can affect the person either in this life or their consequent next lives.
9. *Dharma* in Sanskrit means sacred duty, the moral order that sustains the cosmos, society and the individual (Miller 1986: 2–3).
10. Jaffrelot (1993: 41) has pointed out: 'In the RSS, one of the usual ways of honouring *pracharak*s when they die has been to designate them as Karma Yogis.'
11. Golwalkar (2000: 178) also places the blame for Partition on Muslims:

> The Muslim desire, growing ever since they stepped on this land some twelve hundreds years ago, to convert and enslave the entire country could not bear fruit, in spite of their political domination

for several centuries. In the coming of the British they found an opportunity to fulfil their desire. Naked fact remains that an aggressive Muslim state has been carved out of our Motherland.

12. Though Modi was married as a child, he left his family to live as a *pracharak*, and his followers claim he is celibate.
13. Recent studies have shown links between dowry system, rise of gold prices and increase in female foeticide in India, contributing to gender imbalance (Ratcliffe 2018).
14. The Ramakrishna Mission disciples still follow this tradition, and joining the organization does not include vegetarianism as a requirement, unlike most other prominent Hindu religious organizations like the Arya Samaj or Vaishnavite sects like the Gaudiya Mission.
15. 'Love Jihad refers to love between a Hindu woman and a Muslim man which, as a transgression of communal boundaries, is alleged to be a conspiracy to convert Hindu women.' (T. Sarkar 2018: 119)
16. For a more detailed discussion on the differences between cow-protection laws across various states and its effects on Indian secularism, see A. Sarkar and R. Sarkar (2016b).
17. Muslims are primarily engaged in the USD 10 billion leather and meat production business in India, and thus have been hit the hardest by the Prevention of Cruelty to Animals (Regulation of Livestock Market) Rules, 2017, which banned the sale and purchase of cattle at livestock markets (Hull 2017).
18. The BJP government in Uttar Pradesh introduced a 0.5 per cent '*gau raksha* cess' in the state to protect stray cattle.
19. Ironically, Vivekananda's dreams of global conquest have also come to partial fruition with diasporic nationalism – also known as long-distance nationalism (Jaffrelot and Therwath 2007).

Bibliography

Al Jazeera (2018). 'Cobrapost Sting: Indian Media Outlets and Paid News'. 2 June. https://www.aljazeera.com/program/the-listening-post/2018/6/

2/cobrapost-sting-indian-media-outlets-and-paid-news. Accessed on 10 September 2018.
Alter, J. (1994). 'Celibacy, Sexuality, and the Transformation of Gender into Nationalism in North India'. *Journal of Asian Studies* 53, no. 1: 45–63.
Anand, D. (2009). 'Hindutva: A Schizophrenic Nationalism'. *Seminar* 601, September. http://www.india-seminar.com/2009/601/601_dibyesh_anand.htm. Accessed on 2 February 2022.
Andersen, W. (1972). 'The Rashtriya Swayamsevak Sangh: I: Early Concerns'. *Economic and Political Weekly* 7, no. 11: 589: 591–597.
Ayyub, R. (2018). 'Mobs Are Killing Muslims in India. Why Is No One Stopping Them?' *The Guardian*, 20 July. https://www.theguardian.com/commentisfree/2018/jul/20/mobs-killing-muslims-india-narendra-modi-bjp. Accessed on 13 July 2020.
Banerjee, S. (2006). 'Armed Masculinity, Hindu Nationalism and Female Political Participation in India'. *International Feminist Journal of Politics* 8, no. 1: 62–83. DOI: 10.1080/14616740500415482.
Barthes, R. (1972 [1957]). *Mythologies*. New York: The Noonday Press.
Beckerlegge, G. (2004). 'Iconographic Representations of Renunciation and Activism in the Ramakrishna Math and Mission and the Rashtriya Swayamsevak Sangh'. *Journal of Contemporary Religion* 19, no. 1: 47–66.
Bhagwat, M. (2020). 'Corona Se Ladhai Ghar Mein Rehkar Ladhni Hai: Mohan Bhagwat'. ABP News Hindi, YouTube video. https://www.youtube.com/watch?v=IppRGS4Vkqs&feature=youtu.be. Accessed on 2 February 2022.
Bhattacharjee, M. (2019). *Disaster Relief and the RSS: Resurrecting 'Religion' through Humanitarianism*. New Delhi: SAGE Publications.
Blansett, L. (2012). 'Review of "The Goddess and the Nation: Mapping Mother India" by Sumathi Ramaswamy'. *Imago Mundi* 64, no. 1: 125–126. DOI: 10.1080/03085694.2012.621603.
Bourdieu, P. (1989). 'Social Space and Symbolic Power'. *Sociological Theory* 7, no. 1: 14–25. http://www.soc.ucsb.edu/ct/pages/JWM/Syllabi/Bourdieu/SocSpaceSPowr.pdf. Accessed on 10 September 2018.
Bramen, C. T. (2001). 'Christian Maidens and Heathen Monks: Oratorical Seduction at the 1893 World's Parliament of Religions'. In *The Puritan Origins of American Sex: Religion, Sexuality, and National Identity in American Literature*, edited by T. Fessenden, N. F. Radel and M. J. Zaborowska, 191–212. London and New York: Routledge.
Chacko, P. (2020). 'Gender and Authoritarian Populism: Empowerment, Protection, and the Politics of Resentful Aspiration in India'. *Critical Asian Studies* 52, no. 2: 204–225. DOI: 10.1080/14672715.2020.1711789.

Chakraborty, A. (2019). 'Politics of #LoSha: Using Naming and Shaming as a Feminist Tool on Facebook'. In *Gender Hate Online: Understanding the New Anti-Feminism*, edited by D. Ging and E. Siapera, 191–212. London: Palgrave Macmillan.

Chatterjee, P. (1989). 'The Nationalist Resolution of the Women's Question'. In *Recasting Women: Essays in Colonial History*, edited by K. Sangari and S. Vaid, 233–253. New Delhi: Kali for Women.

Chaturvedi, N. (2016). 'Four Men Stripped and Beaten in Gujarat for Allegedly Trading in Cow Skin'. *Huffington Post*, 15 July. https://www.huffingtonpost.in/2016/07/12/watch-four-men-stripped-and-beaten-in-gujarat-for-allegedly-tra_a_21430450/. Accessed on 10 September 2018. Chitkara, M. G. (2004). *Rashtriya Swayamsevak Sangh: National Upsurge*. New Delhi: A.P.H. Publishing Corporation.

Dasgupta, P. (2018). 'Killers Out on Bail, Ramgarh Lynching Victim's Family to Move to SC to Have Them Jailed'. *Huffington Post*, 12 August. https://www.huffingtonpost.in/2018/08/10/killers-out-on-bail-ramgarh-lynching-victims-family-to-moves-sc-to-have-them-jailed_a_23499640/?utm_hp_ref=in-gau-rakshak. Accessed on 10 September 2018.

Dayal, S., and S. Verma (2016). 'Two "Beef Transporters" Forced to Eat Cow Dung by Gau Rakshaks'. *Indian Express*, 29 June. https://indianexpress.com/article/india/india-news-india/two-beef-transporters-forced-to-eat-cow-dung-by-gau-rakshaks-2880282/. Accessed on 10 September 2018.

Ellis-Peterson, H. (2020). '"We Are Not Safe": Indian Muslims Tell of Wave of Police Brutality'. *The Guardian*, 3 January. https://www.theguardian.com/world/2020/jan/03/we-are-not-safe-indias-muslims-tell-of-wave-of-police-brutality. Accessed on 13 July 2020.

Indian Express (2015). 'The States Where Cow Slaughter Is Legal in India'. 8 October. https://indianexpress.com/article/explained/explained-no-beef-nation/. Accessed on 10 September 2018.

——— (2017). 'Hadiya Case: Critical Findings Demolish Petitioner's Case, Says NIA in Court'. 28 November. https://indianexpress.com/article/india/kerala-love-jihad-hadiya-case-critical-findings-demolish-petitioners-case-says-nia-in-court-4957814/. Accessed on 10 September 2018.

Gandhi, M. K. (1913) 'General Knowledge about Health: Constipation, Sprue, Dysentery, Piles'. In *The Collected Works of Mahatma Gandhi*, vol. 12. New Delhi: Publications Division (Ministry of Information and Broadcasting, Government of India).

———. (1924) 'Brahmacharya'. In *The Collected Works of Mahatma Gandhi*, vol. 24. New Delhi: Publications Division (Ministry of Information and Broadcasting, Government of India).

———. (1925). *An Autobiography: The Story of My Experiments with Truth.* http://www.columbia.edu/itc/mealac/pritchett/00litlinks/gandhi. Accessed on 9 January 2017.

Gandhi, P. (2014). 'Rashtriya Swayamsewak Sangh: How the World's Largest NGO Has Changed the Face of Indian Democracy'. DNA, 15 May. http://www.dnaindia.com/analysis/standpoint-rashtriya-swayamsewak-sangh-how-the-world-s-largest-ngo-has-changed-the-face-of-indian-democracy-1988636. Accessed on 22 October 2016.

Ghatwai, M. (2014). 'Want to Protect Hindus Today and 1,000 Years from Now: Pravin Togadia'. *Indian Express*, 22 December. https://indianexpress.com/article/india/india-others/will-raise-hindu-population-of-country-to-100-says-togadia/. Accessed on 10 September 2018.

Golwalkar, M. S. (1939). *We, or Our Nationhood Defined.* Pune: Bharat Prakashan.

———. (1966). *Bunch of Thoughts.* Archives of RSS. http://www.archivesofrss.org/Encyc/2014/1/20/23_07_20_06_thoughts.pdf. Accessed on 19 February 2018.

———. (2000). *Samadhan.* New Delhi: Suruchi Prakashan.

Government of India (2019). 'Periodic Labour Force Survey Annual Report (June 2017–June 2018)'. National Statistical Office. https://cse.azimpremjiuniversity.edu.in/wp-content/uploads/2019/02/Annual-Report-PLFS-2017-18_31052019.pdf. Accessed on 2 February 2022.

Hoda, K. (2006). 'Golwalkar: The Brain of RSS'. *Milli Gazette*, 26 February. http://www.milligazette.com/dailyupdate/2006/20060226_Golwalkar_RSS.htm. Accessed on 22 October 2016.

Huffington Post (2018). 'Alwar Lynching: Give Cow Smugglers a Couple of Slaps, Tie Them to Tree before Calling Cops, Says BJP MLA Gyan Dev Ahuja'. 31 July. https://www.huffingtonpost.in/2018/07/31/alwar-lynching-give-cow-smugglers-a-couple-of-slaps-tie-them-to-tree-before-calling-cops-says-bjp-mla-gyan-dev-ahuja_a_23492729/?utm_hp_ref=in-cow. Accessed on 10 September 2018.

Hull, P. (2017). 'Sale of Cattle for Slaughter Banned in Animal Markets'. *The Tribune*, 26 May. http://www.tribuneindia.com/news/nation/sale-of-cattle-for-slaughter-banned-in-animal-markets/413088.html. Accessed on 11 July 2018.

Jaffrelot, C. (1993). *The Hindu Nationalist Movement and Indian Politics: 1925 to the 1990s.* London: Hurst & Co.

———. (1996). *The Hindu Nationalist Movement in India*, 53–64. New York: Columbia University Press.

Jaffrelot, C., and I. Therwath (2017). 'The Sangh Parivar and the Hindu Diaspora in the West: What Kind of "Long-Distance Nationalism"?' *International Political Sociology* 1, no. 3: 278–295.

Jha, D. K. (2017). *Shadow Armies: Fringe Organizations and Foot Soldiers of Hindutva*. New Delhi: Juggernaut.
Krishnan, K. (2017). 'Hadiya's Choices'. *Indian Express*, 30 November. https://indianexpress.com/article/opinion/columns/hadiyas-choices-kerala-conversion-case-islam-hindu-marriage-4960951/. Accessed on 10 September 2018.
Kumar, A. (2017). 'The Lynching That Changed India'. *Al Jazeera*, 5 October. https://www.aljazeera.com/indepth/features/2017/09/lynching-changed-india-170927084018325.html. Accessed on 10 September 2018.
Lal, V. (2000). 'Nakedness, Non-violence and Brahmacharya: Gandhi's Experiments in Celibate Sexuality'. *Journal of the History of Sexuality* 9, no. 1–2: 105–136.
Mahapatra, D. (2018). "Hadiya's Marriage Valid, Can Live with Husband: SC'. *Times of India*, 9 March. https://timesofindia.indiatimes.com/india/hadiyas-marriage-valid-can-live-with-husband-sc/articleshow/63225015.cms. Accessed on 10 September 2018.
Menon, R. (2014). *Modi Demystified*. New Delhi: Harper Collins.
Miller, B. S. (1986). *The Bhagavad-Gita: Krishna's Counsel in Time of War*. New York: Bantam Classics.
Misra, M. (2014). 'Sergeant-Major Gandhi: Indian Nationalism and "Non-Violent" Martiality'. *Journal of Asian Studies* 73, no. 3: 689–709.
Mukherjee, M. (2019). 'RSS Claiming the Legacy of Both Gandhi and His Assassin, Is Amusing as well as Outrageous'. *National Herald*, 12 October. https://www.nationalheraldindia.com/opinion/rss-claiming-the-legacy-of-both-gandhi-and-his-assassin-is-amusing-and-outrageous. Accessed on 30 July 2020.
Nanda, M. (2016). 'Ambedkar's Gita'. *Economic and Political Weekly* 51, no. 49: 38–45.
Nayak, B. S. (2018). 'Bhagavad Gita and the Hindu Modes of Capitalist Accumulation in India'. *Society and Business Review* 13, no. 2: 151–164.
Palshikar, S. (2016). 'The Androgynous Warrior: Gandhi's Search for Strength' *European Journal of Political Theory* 15, no. 4: 404–423.
Pandey, G. (1993). 'Which of Us Are Hindus?' In *Hindus and Others: The Question of Identity in India Today*, edited by G. Pandey, 238–271. New Delhi: Viking.
Patel, A. (2014). 'Narendra Modi on MS Golwalkar, Translated by Aakar Patel: Part I'. *The Caravan*, 31 May. http://www.caravanmagazine.in/vantage/modi-golwalkar-part-1. Accessed on 8 September 2018.
Paul, J. (2015). 'Banalities Turned Viral: Narendra Modi and the Political Tweet'. *Television and New Media* 16, no. 4: 378–387.

Rashtriya Swayamsevak Sangh (n.d.). 'Timelimc'. Rashtriya Swayamsevak Sangh. https://www.rss.org/Timeline.html. Accessed on 20 August 2021.

Ratcliffe, R. (2018). 'Dowries a major contributor to India's gender imbalance, researchers find'. *The Guardian*, 28 September. https://www.theguardian.com/global-development/2018/sep/28/dowries-india-gender-imbalance-inflated-gold-price-survival-rates-baby-girls?CMP=share_btn_fb. Accessed on 29 September 2018.

Ratele, K. (2014). 'Currents Against Gender Transformation of South African Men: Relocating Marginality to the Centre of Research and Theory of Masculinities'. *NORMA: International Journal for Masculinity Studies* 9, no. 1: 30–44.

Reddy, S. (2007). 'The Prodigal Who Didn't Return.' *Outlook*, 27 August. http://www.outlookindia.com/magazine/story/the-prodigal-who-didnt-return/235415. Accessed on 22 January 2017.

Rehman, S. M. (2020). 'Selective Kindness: RSS Philanthropy'. *The Telegraph*, 15 May. https://www.telegraphindia.com/culture/books/review-disaster-relief-and-the-rss-resurrecting-religion-through-humanitarianism-by-malini-bhattacharjee/cid/1773168. Accessed on 14 August 2020.

Reuters (2019). 'Statistics on Rape in India and Some Well-known Cases'. 6 December. https://www.reuters.com/article/us-india-rape-factbox-idUSKBN1YA0UV. Accessed on 13 July 2020.

Roy, A., and M. L. Hammers (2014). 'Swami Vivekananda's Rhetoric of Spiritual Masculinity: Transforming Effeminate Bengalis into Virile Men'. *Western Journal of Communication* 78, no. 4: 545–562.

Sagar (2020a). '736 Sangh Parivar NGOs Qualified for Government Funds, Subsidised Rations During the COVID-19 Lockdown'. *The Caravan*, 10 July. https://caravanmagazine.in/politics/rss-coronavirus-lockdown-sewa-bharti-ngos-government-funds. Accessed on 13 August 2020.

——— (2020b). 'How the RSS Co-opted Local Administrations for Its Relief Interventions During the COVID-19 Lockdown'. *The Caravan*, 10 July. https://caravanmagazine.in/politics/rss-coronavirus-lockdown-ngos-relief-work-sewa-hindu-rashtra. Accessed on 13 August 2020.

——— (2020c). 'For the RSS, "Sewa" Is a Means to Achieve the Hindu Rashtra'. *The Caravan*, 15 July. https://caravanmagazine.in/politics/rss-sewa-coronavirus-lockdown-brahmanical-hindu-rashtra. Accessed on 13 August 2020.

Sarkar, R., and A. Sarkar (2016a). 'Dalit Politics in India'. *Economic and Political Weekly* 51, no. 20: 14–16. http://www.epw.in/journal/2016/20/commentary/dalit-politics-india.html. Accessed on 13 September 2018.

———. (2016b). 'Sacred Slaughter: An Analysis of Historical, Communal, and Constitutional Aspects of Beef Ban in India'. *Politics, Religion and Ideology* 17, no. 4: 329–351.

Sarkar, T. (2018). 'Special Guest Contribution: "Is Love Without Borders Possible?"' *Feminist Review* 119, no. 1: 7–19.

Sen, R. (2016). 'Narendra Modi's Makeover and the Politics of Symbolism'. *Journal of Asian Public Policy* 9, no. 2: 98–111.

Smyth, D. (1972). 'The Social Basis of Militant Hindu Nationalism'. *Journal of Developing Areas* 6, no. 3: 323–344.

Srivastava, S. (2015). 'Modi-Masculinity: Media, Manhood, and "Traditions" in a Time of Consumerism'. *Television and New Media* 16, no. 4: 331–338.

Subramanian, S. (2020). 'How Hindu Supremacists Are Tearing India Apart'. *The Guardian*, 20 February. https://www.theguardian.com/world/2020/feb/20/hindu-supremacists-nationalism-tearing-india-apart-modi-bjp-rss-jnu-attacks. Accessed on 13 July 2020.

Thapar, R. (2016). 'Reflections on Nationalism and History'. In *On Nationalism*, edited by R Thapar, A. G. Noorani and S. Menon, 13–67. New Delhi: Aleph Book Company.

Thapar-Bjokert, S., and L. Ryan (2002). 'Mother India/Mother Ireland: Comparative Gendered Dialogues of Colonialism and Nationalism in the Early 20th Century'. *Women's Studies International Forum* 25, no. 3: 301–313.

The Wire (2017). 'Story Map: Documenting Lynchings in India'. 13 July. https://thewire.in/caste/storymap-lynchings-india-cow-slaughter-beef-ban-gau-rakshak. Accessed on 13 July 2020.

Visvanathan, S. (2013). 'The Remaking of Narendra Modi'. *Seminar* 641. http://www.india-seminar.com/2013/641/641_shiv_visvanathan.htm. Accessed on 14 September 2018.

Vivekananda, S. (1894). 'Letter to Mr. Manmatha Nath Bhattacharya, 5 September'. In *Complete Works of Swami Vivekananda*, vol. 7. Belur: Advaita Ashrama.

———. (1896a). *Complete Works of Swami Vivekananda*, vol. 7. Belur: Advaita Ashrama.

———. (1896b). 'Notes of Class Talks'. In *Complete Works of Swami Vivekananda*, vol. 8. Belur: Advaita Ashrama.

———. (1898). 'Conversations and Dialogues: VII'. In *Complete Works of Swami Vivekananda*, vol. 7. Belur: Advaita Ashrama.

———. (1899). 'Conversations and Dialogues: XIII'. In *Complete Works of Swami Vivekananda*, vol. 7. Belur: Advaita Ashrama.

———. (1900a). 'The Work Before Us'. In *Complete Works of Swami Vivekananda*, vol. 3. Belur: Advaita Ashrama.

———. (1900b). 'At the Parliament of Religions'. In *Complete Works of Swami Vivekananda*, vol. 3. Belur: Advaita Ashrama.

———. (1900c). 'Bhakti Yoga: Chapter X'. In *Complete Works of Swami Vivekananda*, vol. 3. Belur: Advaita Ashrama.

———. (1900d). 'The Gita: I'. In *Complete Works of Swami Vivekananda*, vol. 1. Belur: Advaita Ashrama.

8

Trans Contestations in an Era of Heightened Nationalism

The Saffronization of Transgender Identity

Jennifer Ung Loh

Introduction*

In November 2018, the Kinnar Akhada, a religious order established by members of the *kinnar* and *hijra* communities,[1] declared that they supported the demand for the construction of a Ram temple on the site of the destroyed Babri Masjid in Ayodhya.[2] At a meeting organized by the Akhil Bharatiya Sant Samiti, an umbrella body of Hindu monks and ascetics, to which the Kinnar Akhada had been invited, Acharya Mahamandleshwar[3] Laxmi Narayan Tripathi declared, 'whether anybody is gay, lesbian, transgender, whatever is anybody [*sic*] sexuality ... the biggest thing is the Hindu sanatan dharma [duty]. And the sanatan vedic practice has never questioned anyone's sexuality. Our religion has space for everyone ... it takes every one along' (Verma 2018).

---

* I am most grateful to Professors Amrita Basu and Tanika Sarkar for their generous invitation to contribute this chapter and for their engaged comments on earlier drafts, alongside those of Amna Pathan. Sincere thanks to Kyoung Kim and the 2020 *Feminist Review* writing workshop participants for their suggestions and encouragement and to J. Daniel Luther for ongoing conversations and constant support. I do not intend to speak on behalf of transgender movements or activists in India; I offer this analysis of state discourses in constructing LGBTQ+ and specifically trans identities as a queer feminist academic who is invested in examining how the state is involved in shaping contemporary gender and sexual identities. All errors and inaccuracies remain mine.

Is there a place in the nation for 'queer' communities? LGBT+[4] groups have gained significant rights in the last decade, with two Supreme Court judgment declaring equal rights and protections for transgender communities and decriminalizing same-sex sexual practices.[5] The right-wing Bharatiya Janata Party (hereafter BJP) has drafted and passed Parliament bills, enshrining in law protections of transgender rights. The Indian state has acted as the paternalistic giver of rights. But it does not consider all LGBT+ citizens equal: transgender communities appear to benefit over LGB ones, trans women over trans men, Hindu trans communities over Muslim ones.

How – and why – might the Hindu right foreground some forms of transgender identity at the expense of others? Considering the Supreme Court judgment on transgender rights, *National Legal Services Authority (NALSA) v. Union of India and Others* (2014), and Parliament bills subsequent to this judgment, this chapter considers how and why the Hindu right favours Hindu trans (feminine) identities above other less visible, non-homonormative trans identities and Muslim trans people. Although the NALSA judgment was delivered in April 2014, preceding the BJP election in May of the same year, the incoming government was mandated to adopt the judgment's recommendations. The Indian state has treated trans rights as something to be undertaken in a procedural manner rather than an ethical one, with certain trans communities benefitting from unequal representation (notably Hindu, trans feminine identities), demonstrating a lack of care with which the government has attended to this task. Though support for trans rights represents a departure from the Hindu right's previous stance on non-heteronormative identities (more later), I argue that it might benefit from endorsing rights for trans feminine, Hindu communities, which align with its broader goals of promoting Hindu ideologies, through the reinforcement of existing gender and religious norms. Resultantly, it has marginalized a variety of other trans communities, including Muslim transgender ones: an exclusion that should be read within wider contemporary contexts, wherein a rise in conservative right-wing sentiments and the nationalist BJP's ascendance to political power has created an increasingly hostile environment for a wide cross-section of society, including religious minorities and lower-caste and *adivasi* communities.[6] Thus, a broader trend of communal violence and exclusion form a backdrop to interpret this shoring-up of rights for certain 'Hindu' communities.

Promises of rights and protections in the NALSA judgment and parliamentary legislation appear to pertain to any individuals identifying as 'transgender'. Yet the wording of these documents foregrounds particular (visible) forms of transgender identity, notably trans women, narrowly identified and commonly conflating transgender and *hijra* identity. Furthermore, the texts emphasize the validity of specifically identified 'Hindu' trans identities because of the legitimacy granted through the historical and mythological canon, emphasizing a Hinduized version of history.[7] This narrow representation is both a product of the inclusion of 'transgender' into national debates (via state policy on sexual health) and the visibility of *kinnar* or *hijra* subjects. *Kinnar*s and *hijra*s hold a specific place in the cultural subconscious, through their performance of 'cultural authenticity' stemming from their established (albeit marginalized) place in the nation. By contrast, wider LGBT+ communities experience unequal visibility (particularly invisibilized trans identities including trans men and lower-caste and religious minorities and 'non-visible' sexuality-based identities, in light of prominent views which regard same-sex sexual orientation as a 'western', modern import). An emphasis on *kinnar*s and *hijra*s, in conjunction with 'Hinduized' versions of history that reiterate their place in the Hindu canon – with elision of the significance and role of Islam to this form of trans identity – creates these trans identities as 'homonormative' trans subjects and leads to exclusions of Muslim and Dalit trans communities.

Trans communities have been divided in their response. Some Hindu trans communities, as exemplified by the Kinnar Akhada's support for the campaign to construct a Ram temple, have accepted right-wing narratives in order to create spaces for themselves and establish their place in the modern nation. Other trans and LGBT+ groups have called for solidarity in resisting 'right-wing politics of communal hatred' that they argue will only deepen existing hierarchies within trans communities (Trans, Gender Nonconforming and Intersex Collectives 2018). While certain communities appear to support or oppose right-wing narratives, these actions are determined by existing matrices of power, so 'support' may function as a tool to gain space in an otherwise hostile context that would maintain their marginalization. Many communities cannot afford to turn their backs on the state when it finally recognizes them. The intent of this chapter is not to find blame with specific communities but rather to explicate wider contemporary operations of power within which trans communities find themselves, which play out in the apparent conflict between different activist and trans communities.

This chapter begins with questions surrounding the intention of the Hindu right in advocating rights for certain trans communities. Next, I offer a genealogy of the term 'transgender' in the Indian context, from including gender variance in sexual health discourses to a marker of gender identity itself and as an established state category. Understanding how state and legal discourses frame – and limit – the category 'transgender' over time allows us to examine how specific trans forms are rendered as normative, at the expense of other less visible identities. I then proceed to examine three primary thematic concerns around which the chapter is organized: (*a*) the conflation of transgender with *hijra* identity (with *hijra* interpreted as trans feminine and normatively Hindu), (*b*) the contemporary saffronization of trans identity and (*c*) trans 'adaptations' of the right-wing agenda. Throughout the chapter I draw upon the NALSA judgment and Parliament bills; while the bills bound the transgender subject in law, it is the NALSA judgment that establishes who the imagined subject for rights is. I investigate how specific forms of transgender identity, namely Hindu trans (feminine) identities, benefit at the expense of other trans identities, and how this supports the wider agenda of the Hindu right.

Why Support Trans Rights?

Establishing the Hindu right's[8] conscious or deliberate intentions behind granting rights for 'Hindu' trans communities is complicated. However, the impact of the Hindu right's (and specifically the BJP's) treatment of trans communities is clear, which is important to consider, given a consistent rise in nationalist sentiment and the consolidation of right-wing political power in the last few decades. Conservative ideas of morality, family and sexual norms usually do not align with LGBT+ rights. Yet the relationship between right-wing movements and rights struggles based on gender and sexuality is complex globally (Graff, Kapur and Walters 2019), with the rise of the global right leading to anti-feminist, anti-minority positions in some contexts, but collusion through 'pinkwashing' and 'homonationalism' in others, where nationalist ideologies and 'queer' assimilationist politics collude to the exclusion of cultural others.[9] In India, recent governmental advancement (or at least acceptance) of decriminalization of homosexuality and trans 'rights' appears at odds with extensive communitarian homophobia – sometimes encouraged by state institutions themselves[10] – based on conservative policing of gender norms and practices. The Hindu right historically has maintained a (hetero)normative moral code based on majority consensus, such as in its 1998 election manifesto which celebrated the integrity of the family unit and kinship networks (Tan 2018: 148). 'Support' of trans rights contradicts this conservative position unless we interpret such actions through a lens of serving existing gender norms and perpetuating racist and exclusionary agendas and religious hierarchies, supporting a larger nationalist project.[11] Through configuration of the tools and language of gender equality, the Hindu right can define trans (*hijra*) subjects as Hindu- and gender (female)- normative, posited as homonormative subjects in a specific cultural setting that aids to shore up right-wing dominance and ideologies. This Trojan horse allows the Hindu right to showcase a progressive stance on trans rights – nationally and internationally – and simultaneously bolster essentialist gender norms and performances that do not challenge binary gender frameworks and dominant religious traditions. For the Hindu right, *hijra*s might be posited as model trans identities through configuration as principally Hindu and as trans women (that is, not as non-binary nor 'gender-queer'):[12] identities which do not challenge the mainstream heterosexual imperative and social order, according to Hindu logics.[13] Thus, certain trans identities might provide symbolic value, similar to the deployment of Hindu women in defence of the nationalist project regarding visions of morality, family and home. Establishing norms, however, demands adherence, and thus the question of the extent to which trans subjects also comply with these norms is significant.

It is unclear how intentional the Hindu right's (particularly the BJP's) support of trans rights is. The Indian state itself, historically and now – currently guided by the BJP and right-wing nationalist organizations – cannot be viewed as an individual actor committed to a single pathway. The BJP has not pursued rights for transgender subjects, rather it has been mandated to deliver them. Any change of national government must deal with the consequences of past policy instigated by another political party. In this case, the BJP-led NDA (National Democratic Alliance) was required to deliver the NALSA judgment recommendations, despite the petition's initiation by a governmental body (NALSA) in 2012 and delivered in April 2014 under Congress-led rule. Thus, despite a historically lacklustre – and often regressive approach – to wider support for LGBTQ+ rights,[14] the BJP has produced legislation to ensure transgender rights. Simultaneously though, the BJP's actions can be interpreted as seeking to limit beneficiaries under the NALSA judgment, such as the filing of the 2014 clarification petition by the Ministry of Social Justice and Empowerment (MSJE)[15] and in its procedural approach to granting rights through the Parliament bills. Thus, the BJP's support of trans rights appears bureaucratic and reactionary, developing according to context.[16]

Additionally, the BJP's 'support' of trans rights has been informed by demands from different social actors. Initially, the NALSA judgment was responding to varying trans communities as petitioners in the case.[17] Following the judgment, divergent political parties, individual politicians, activists and protesters have sought to influence the bills as they have moved through Parliament (more later). Thus, there is no solitary force behind envisioning and implementing (or curtailing) rights and protections for trans communities, due to multiple demands and motivations.[18]

While pinpointing the intentionality of this project is complex, what can be analysed are the effects on trans communities with respect to who is included and excluded by shifting boundaries of the category 'transgender'. The state's actions foreground specific forms of trans identity that sustain existing gender and religious norms: this is a worrying trend that advances an exclusionary far-right agenda. While gains of rights are positive, I offer a careful consideration of this trajectory towards transgender rights, which simultaneously marginalizes communities posited as outside of normative 'transgender' subjectivity.[19] Turning to look at the historical utilization of the term 'transgender' through state policy, I examine how the state has imagined and thus bounded the term itself.

State Definitions of 'Transgender'

Tracing 'Transgender' in State Policy

The term 'transgender' refers to a variety of communities in India, including trans women, trans men or 'third' gender individuals, who may identify and present themselves according to binary gender categories or as gender non-conforming. Individuals cross a variety of caste, class, regional and religious backgrounds. Some variously identify with Anglicized terms or vernacular terms, some as transgender, some as not transgender, some as male or female; identifications may change according to time, place and space (reflecting company and context). Individuals may identify with a number of sexual orientations. Thus, definitions of what 'transgender' is remain contested: the only demarcation being its opposition to cisgender, denoting the correspondence between a person's personal identity and gender and the sex assigned at birth. Yet categorization is crucial to establishing a framework for identification, a named subject to whom rights can be given (Seckinelgin 2009). Although this is a process of selection and inclusion, one significant consequence is that populations themselves come to identify in particular ways, usually adhering to a fairly limited understanding of what counts as a specific identity or even conforming to fit legally recognized identities.

Alternative lived realities may not fit easily into recognized categories for identification. However, subjects can only make claims to rights if they can identify themselves with existing, politically intelligible identity categories (ibid.: 109). As 'transgender' as an identity became integrated into the language of the state, it became a dominant marker for identification. Historically, 'transgender' groups became a focus for the state through sexual health interventions. Since late 2000s, state policy has utilized the term 'transgender' (also commonly 'TG') as an umbrella term for numerous communities (Dutta 2012), although primarily with reference to 'male-to-female' trans people (often conflated with *hijra* identity).[20]

Transgender is seen as a gender identity, living 'in the gender role opposite to the one in which they are born' (SAATHII 2009: 16), although 'opposite' presumes a binary framework and transition from one gender to the other. A UNDP Issue Brief on the '*Hijras*/Transgender' notes that 'transgender' describes those who 'transgress' and defy 'rigid, binary gender constructions', who 'break' or 'blur' prevalent gender roles; yet it acknowledges people may live part or full time in the gender role 'opposite' to their biological sex (Chakrapani 2010: 3). *Hijra*s are classified alongside TG populations or contained under the umbrella term 'transgender' (SAATHII 2009: 14–17; Chakrapani 2010: 3), conflating these identities as similar or part of the same group (UNDP 2008: 17, 24). *Hijra* is seen as a 'traditional culture' for trans people and a 'historical cult' (SAATHII 2009: 17). The UNDP Brief additionally acknowledges the limits of the (western) term 'transgender' in this context, which may erase the 'long history, culture, and tradition' of local trans communities, acknowledging that certain *hijra*s may prefer this term and not 'transgender', although they might use the latter on a global platform (Chakrapani 2010: 3). These extracts demonstrate that context can influence self-identification and that the umbrella term 'transgender' fails to recognize the complexity of Indian trans identities.

Consolidating a range of gender non-conforming people under a 'stable and bounded' identity ('transgender'), Dutta (2014: 228) argues, produces 'biopolitical subjects for care and management by the state'. Additionally, naming *hijra* identity as a subsection or group linked to transgender identity, and sometimes synonymously ('*Hijras*/Transgender'; Chakrapani 2010), establishes a bounded category where specifically *hijra* identity is transgender. Classifying 'transgender' as primarily referencing 'male-to-female' trans identities – specifically *hijra*/third gender identities – elides other less visible 'trans' and gender non-conforming identities.

Bounding 'Transgender' through the State

Building upon sexual health policy definitions, the state continues to define 'transgender' through judicial and legislative frameworks, such as the 2014 Supreme Court judgment and the subsequent Parliament bills. Activist Gee Imaan Semmalar (2014) notes that 'any interaction with legal structures is tricky and can go both ways', where trans subjects are made legible to the state and are thus subject, violently, to their logics. The history of the NALSA judgment and Parliament bills outlines the state's role in constructing the bounded category 'transgender', building successively on earlier policy definitions.

The Supreme Court's judgment in April 2014, *NALSA v Union of India*, affirms constitutional rights for transgender people[21] and provides diverse recommendations for national and state governments regarding legal reform and advocating social and cultural change. Notable recommendations uphold self-determination of gender; include communities within socially and educationally backward classes of citizens; provide reservations[22] in education and public appointments; and establish health, social welfare and public awareness schemes (*NALSA*: 110–111). To implement practical application of the judgment, both houses of Parliament have passed legislative bills: the Rajya Sabha's Rights of Transgender Persons Bill, 2014 (April 2015)[23] and the Lok Sabha's Transgender Persons (Protection of Rights) Act, 2019 (August 2019).[24] Following drafts in the Lok Sabha in 2016 and 2018,[25] minister of social justice and empowerment, Thawar Chand Gehlot, reintroduced a draft bill at the start of the NDA government's second term.[26] The Rajya Sabha then passed the 2019 act on globally recognized Transgender Day of Remembrance (20 November), rejecting motions from members – and calls from activists – to refer it to a select committee to actualize anti-discrimination legislation.[27] In September 2020, the government published the 'Transgender Persons (Protection of Rights) Rules, 2020', enacting measures proscribed in the 2019 Act.[28]

The state's attitude to trans rights can be critiqued for a trend of passing 'bill after bill' (Bose 2019); little substantial debate in the Lok Sabha (Mudraboyina, Jagirdar and Philip 2019); lack of engagement with activists, including trans masculine activists (for example, Round Table India 2014; Amitava et al. 2014) and general apathy towards communities' concerns (Masih 2019).[29] Its approach, exemplified by the 2014 MSJE clarification petition to the Supreme Court to limit NALSA beneficiaries (through exclusion and delay; Ung Loh 2018: 50, 52)[30] and the MSJE's disregard of the Parliamentary Standing Committee recommendations in redrafting the 2018 bill, reveals the state's motivations in limiting meaningful interventions and serving procedural ends rather than ethical ones.

Activists have responded vocally in opposition to the state's procedural mindset, despite the state largely ignoring them. Activist voices have shaped debates around the content of the bills and kept them in the public realm. Rachana Mudraboyina, a founding member of Telangana Hijra

Intersex Transgender Samiti, writes with Sammera Jagirdar and Philip C. Philip:

> ... the sole purpose of a social welfare legislation should be to protect the rights of the marginalised. In instances where discourse by the marginalised is not allowed, purely because of a very real threat to their lives and systemic obstructions in place to not just dissuade, but to disallow members from the community from occupying and participating in political spaces, it is incumbent then on the state to actively engage with such communities to create such a discourse. (Mudraboyina, Jagirdar and Philip 2019)

Calling for active engagement with trans communities in developing legislation and arguing against 'unnecessary policing of our existence by the state', they write that 'we need protection mechanisms from those bent on violating our identities, bodies and lives' (ibid.). Yet it is the state itself that activists and protestors argue is failing: each draft has been met with strong criticism and protests[31] due to regressive provisions (Mogli et al. 2016; Guest Writer 2017); policing and gatekeeping of identity (Mogli et al. 2016); and failure to practically benefit trans communities, for example, through the establishment of reservations.[32] Activists such as Grace Banu, Founder of Trans Rights Now Collective, contend that reservations (recommended by the NALSA judgment) remain crucial for addressing anti-trans structural discrimination.[33] As a Dalit transwoman, Banu argues the 2019 bill provides no protection of minorities, including Adivasi, Dalit or Muslim trans persons who face extreme discrimination, given their lack of social and financial security (Bose 2019). Further, Gee Imaan Semmalar, trans activist and member of Sampoorna Working Group, maintains that 'the bill goes against the right to dignity and bodily autonomy of trans people', flouting NALSA recommendations regarding self-determination (Pathak 2019). Forcing through bills and wilfully ignoring activists' own demands exposes a paternalistic state, invested in granting 'rights' on their own terms. This is demonstrated by the passing of the 2019 Act, despite criticism, in both houses and among activists.

The NALSA judgment and Parliament bills are critical in further constructing the imagined trans subject for rights, building successively on sexual health interventions. Through examination of these texts in the next two sections, I focus on how the state and law frame – and simultaneously limit – the boundaries of the category 'transgender'. One example of how state logics frame trans identity is found in the question of self-determination versus the requirement of external testing (based in biological essentialism): a subject of activist critiques. The Parliament bills designate individuals as 'transgender' without allowing individuals to self-identify, contravening the self-determination advocated by the NALSA judgment (*NALSA*: 109–110).[34] The question of self versus external identification is thus a fallacy because the state, through the Parliament bills, governs what people are ('transgender') and what self-determination is. This example demonstrates how the state and law construct 'transgender' identity; this is further strengthened by the ways certain presentations and expressions are envisioned as central to transgender identity. This is the focus of the next section in which I investigate the prominence of *hijra* identity within the NALSA judgment and how this further elision of *hijra* and transgender identity reimagines 'transgender' as normatively trans feminine. This framing is fundamental in unpacking how Hindu trans feminine identities have been foregrounded as normative, at the expense of less visible, non-homonormative trans identities and Muslim trans people.

Conjoining Terms: Hijra/Transgender

Supplementing the term 'transgender' with the term *hijra* serves to bind the specificity of *hijra* identity to a 'general' transgender category. This is further supported through the role of authenticity that *hijra*s perform culturally. In this section, I examine the conjoining of these terms to argue that in the eyes of the state, transgender cannot be read with the exclusion of *hijra* identity.

'*Hijra*/Transgender': The NALSA Judgment and Restrictive Meanings

The NALSA judgment[35] utilizes both encompassing terms like 'transgender' or 'third gender' and culturally comprehensible vernacular terms (Ung Loh

2018: 46). While its focus is on trans feminine communities – generally ignoring wider definitions of gender expressions – the judgment is confusing in its scope and ultimate directives by establishing that 'transgender' relates to trans communities who identify as female and male, as well as *hijra*s, described as a 'third gender'.[36] It further mentions 'eunuchs' (a derogatory term), people who dress in clothing of the 'opposite' gender (*NALSA*: 9–10), people with intersex variations (*NALSA*: 28, 48), and notes that the 'TG Community' is said to comprise a range of 'vernacular' identities: *hijra*s, eunuchs, *kothi*s, *aravani*s, *jogappa*s, *shiv-shakti*s (*NALSA*: 10), *thirunangi* and *jogta*s or *jogappa*s (*NALSA*: 48–49).[37] 'Gay, lesbian, and bisexual' individuals are mentioned, but the text states explicitly that their inclusion within a wider meaning of 'transgender' is not the focus here (*NALSA*: 93). While the judgment includes numerous trans identities, there is a notable lone reference to 'female-to-male trans-sexual persons' that describes their invisibility (unlike publicly visible '*hijra*/transgender persons') and notes their concerns are often ignored (*NALSA*: 53).[38] Trans masculine communities need additional support as a 'minority within that minority' (Round Table India 2014) but receive a lack of recognition in the judgment.

In contrast, the collated term '*hijra*/transgender' appears prominently, mirroring the focus on trans feminine communities in wider debates and the historical genealogy of the association between trans and *hijra* identity. The term *hijra* appears on around a third of 111 pages.[39] *Hijra*s are described as a 'third gender', not identifying as male or female, and including emasculated and non-emasculated individuals and 'inter-sexed' persons (*NALSA*: 9). As a notably visible, trans feminine(-presenting) social identity, plentiful references in the judgment support conceptions of *hijra* identity as a normative trans identity.[40] In India, Justice Sikri writes, 'transgender are referred [to] as Hizra [*sic*] or third gendered people', such that the Justices 'are restrictive in our meaning which has to be given to [the] TG community i.e. hijra etc.' (*NALSA*: 94–95). The establishment of Indian 'trans' identity as synonymous with *hijra* identity thus determines trans feminine identity as the imagined subject for rights, with the effect of further marginalizing other unnamed and invisible trans communities.

'"Transgender Person" Means a Person Who Is – ':[41]
Parliament's Definitions

The Parliament bills mirror the range of terms used in the NALSA judgment but move away from an emphasis on trans feminine communities. The bills' definition of 'transgender' is crucial as the 'fulcrum' of who benefits from inclusion in the 'transgender' category: the 'whole law' depends 'on the scope of this definition'.[42] The bills contain divergent definitions and are a key ground for contestation between state and activists. While they may appear inclusive in scope, they also shut down avenues for potential identification by bounding 'transgender' within certain parameters. The definitions appear at the start of each bill; the term then used throughout is simply 'transgender'.

The more 'progressive' Rajya Sabha Bill describes transgender as:

> ... (*t*) 'transgender person' means a person, whose gender does not match with the gender assigned to that person at birth and includes trans-men and trans-women (whether or not they have undergone sex reassignment surgery or hormone therapy or laser therapy etc.), gender-queers and a number of socio-cultural identities such as – *kinnar*s, *hijra*s, *aravani*s, *jogta*s etc.[43]

It might be notable that 'trans-men' are named first and that among sociocultural identities *kinnar*s are named before *hijra*s.[44] This definition states that surgical or medical intervention is not essential, but intersex and non-binary communities are not mentioned. In stark contrast, the MSJE's 2016 Lok Sabha Bill, despite consultations with numerous communities (Sampoorna 2019), contained negative stereotypes:

> (i) ... means a person who is –
> (A) neither wholly female nor wholly male; or
> (B) a combination of female or male; or
> (C) neither female nor male; and
> whose sense of gender does not match with the gender assigned to that person at the time of birth, and includes trans-men and trans-women, persons with intersex variations and gender-queers.[45]

This 'pathologising' definition (Mogli et al. 2016) views trans as 'neither wholly', 'a combination' or 'neither' female nor male, premised on binary gender logic. No 'socio-cultural' identities are named, which is striking given the NALSA judgment's inclusion of *hijra* and vernacular identities, but it includes 'persons with intersex variations and gender-queers'. Activists vehemently protested this definition, condemning its 'dehumanising', unscientific and regressive language, framed in addition to its violation of the principle of self-determination (through the inclusion of District Screening Committees, argued to gate-keep and police trans identity; Mogli et al. 2016; Dutta 2016; Guest Writer 2017). The redrafted (but lapsed) 2018 Bill and passed 2019 Act carried the following definition:[46]

> ... (*k*) 'transgender person' means a person whose gender does not match with the gender assigned to that person at birth and includes trans-man or trans-woman [*sic*] (whether or not such person has undergone Sex Reassignment Surgery or hormone therapy or laser therapy or such other therapy), person with intersex variations, gender- queer and person having such socio-cultural identities as kinner, hijra, aravani and jogta.[47]

The inclusion of intersex variations[48] and socio-cultural identities is important. However, all these definitions frame trans identity through a binary gender system, where biologically essentialist logic suggests that transgender is when one's gender 'does not match' that 'assigned' at birth. The inclusion that surgery or medial intervention is not essential is encouraging, denoting that medical intervention is not a criterion in determining identity. Yet emphasis on the term 'transgender' (over other self-definition) ignores the NALSA judgment's self-determination principle.

The range of identities referred to previously, I would argue, are not powerful enough to override the etymological trajectory of the term 'transgender' as used within state policy and the NALSA judgment. With its focus on *hijra* and trans feminine identities, the judgment establishes who the imagined 'transgender' subject is. This is supplemented through its emphasis on 'Hinduized' histories of trans subjects to which I turn next.

Saffronizing Trans

Selective Histories

Narratives focusing on 'transgender + Hindu' frame Indian trans identities within a long-standing ('Hinduized') tradition of historical non-normative expressions of gender and sexuality. Textual emphasis on particular versions of history constructs *hijra* (and other vernacular) identities primarily as Hindu, 'saffonizing' *hijra* identity and producing a 'Hindu-ized' historicization of transgender existence. Furthermore, this divides wider sexuality-based identities from trans ones, especially in framing the former as 'western' imports and therefore non-authentic (but ignoring that trans people may be same-sex desiring).

The NALSA judgment section entitled 'Historical Background of Transgenders in India' begins:

> TG Community comprises of *Hijras*, eunuchs, *Kothis*, *Aravanis*, *Jogappas*, *Shiv-Shakthis* etc. and they, as a group, have got a strong historical presence in our country in the Hindu mythology and other religious texts. The Concept of *tritiya prakrti* or *napunsaka* has also been an integral part of vedic and puranic literatures. (*NALSA*: 10)

'Hindu' history is immediately invoked as providing legitimacy ('strong historical presence') for 'trans communities', in mythology and religious texts.[49] The relationships drawn between heroes of classical Hindu mythology and *hijra* communities thus provide one 'genealogy' for modern trans communities. By contrast, reference to Muslim history is given a single sentence:

> Hijras also played a prominent role in the royal courts of the Islamic world, especially in the Ottaman [*sic*] empires and the Mughal rule in the Medieval India. (*NALSA*: 11)

This sentence – where 'medieval' encompasses over ten centuries – undermines deeply the significance of Islam to *hijra* communities.[50] An opposing example stressing that *hijra* identity is not solely 'Hindu' historically can be found in the Intervenor's Written Submission filed with the NALSA judgment (submitted on behalf of Tripathi):

> Hijras played a prominent role in the royal courts of the Islamic world, especially in the Ottoman empires and the Mughal rule in the Medieval India. They rose to eminent positions as political advisors, administrators, generals as well as guardians of the harems. Hijras were considered clever, trustworthy and fiercely loyal ... playing a crucial role in the politics of empire building.... Hijras also occupied high positions in the Islamic religious institutions, especially in guarding the holy places of Mecca and Medina. (Grover 2013: 7)

Emphasis on prominent past roles demonstrates that this period of history is crucial to *hijra* identity, both historically and now: as equally important to Hinduized aspects.[51] The NALSA judgment's brevity regarding Islamic history and religion is problematic when juxtaposed next to the extensive discussion of Hindu history, especially since the significance of Islam to *hijra* communities[52] – and the existence of Muslim *hijra* communities themselves – are both well documented in ethnographic literature.[53] Therefore, this is not only an erasure of Muslim aspects of *hijra* identity but also of Muslim *hijra* and trans identities themselves.

The sole NALSA sentence regarding Muslim history – however (un)intentional – performs a particular function. It reveals a misleading historicization of trans – specifically *hijra* – identity, which cements social understandings of trans identity as normatively *hijra*, with *hijra* understood as trans feminine and as Hindu normative. While various trans groups are subsumed under 'transgender', the ultimate frame of reference rests on the *hijra* ('female') Hindu subject and it is this particular abstraction that can be weaponized in the service of right-wing logics.

Envisioning Trans for the 'Nation'

Nuance is needed to theorize this trend of saffronization. Support for minority gender or sexual rights is possible, if one does not draw a false opposition between religion and LGBT+ gender and sexuality: LGBT+ or 'queer' people can be right-wing and equally the right can be 'queer' (Sircar

2017: 21). Additionally, there is little consensus among the Hindu right, with right-wing voices historically demonstrating a range of attitudes on non-heteronormativity, namely homosexuality (Sircar 2017: 21; Yadav and Kirk 2018: 679). In the face of historical conservatism, prior to the 2014 election, BJP president Rajnath Singh said the party unambiguously endorsed support for Section 377 following the 2013 Supreme Court judgment (Ramaseshan 2013). However, prominent leader Arun Jaitley criticized the ruling, arguing the court should have favoured reading down the section to address the concerns of sexual minorities (Tiwari 2016).[54] In 2016, the RSS softened its stance towards homosexuality, when general secretary Dattatreya Hosabole declared that their approach was 'no criminalization, no glorification', but called gay marriage an 'institutionalisation of homosexuality' (Munshi 2018).

Legal and parliamentary developments add further layers: the NALSA judgment preceded the 2014 BJP election and the BJP's 2014 MSJE clarification petition served to quash progress (delaying implementation of recommendations for two years). The BJP government has attempted to push through its own version of trans rights, despite protests demanding trans inclusion and consultation. This reveals a paternalistic state intent on providing rights on its own terms, exhibiting apathy to community concerns (Mudraboyina, Jagirdar and Philip 2019). However, the BJP's focus on endowing trans rights could be interpreted as adding value to a larger nationalist project. To borrow Sircar's (2017: 22) portentous claim, once the immense possibilities have been worked through for 'Hinduizing the neoliberal queer as a means to forward their agenda of establishing a Hindu *rashtra*', multiple ends are possible.

The first historic mention of 'transgender' issues emerges in the 2019 BJP election manifesto, aiming to 'empower' transgender people through socioeconomic means, policy and employment and skill-based initiatives.[55] Yet two months after the BJP won their second term, in July 2019 (the same month that Gehlot reintroduced the Transgender Persons [Protection of Rights] Bill, 2019, in the Lok Sabha), India abstained from voting on the renewal of the UN Human Rights Council mandate for a special rapporteur for protection against violence and discrimination against LGBTQ+ persons (Mitra 2019).[56] This inconsistent action reveals a separation of populations, limiting who is worthy of protections and rights, where trans subjects are included but wider LGBQ+ individuals are not. The distinction drawn between non-heteronormative sexuality and gender, where the former has no place in the nation while the latter is allowed – based upon a re-characterization of trans communities as the subjects of 'welfare and uplift' – avoids provocation of 'moral panic, or the ire of the sex-phobic Hindu Right' (Sircar 2017: 18). Thus, trans subjects are emancipated insofar as they perform roles deemed respectable and non-threatening,[57] abiding by expectations of what is permissible within the nation.

Trans (read 'specifically *hijra*') rights that simultaneously endorse a fashioned version of Hindu history thus feed into right-wing claims about the nation. 'Queer gender' can be acceptable and even revered in Hindu nationalist discourses (Bacchetta 1999), with trans (*hijra*) subjects posited as Hindu- and gender-normative, in ways that sustain conservative ideologies and more so that serve to limit acceptable ways of being for other trans identities. The Hindu right can thus promote themselves as progressive regarding (trans)gender rights and simultaneously reinforce essentialized gender norms and normative religious practices.

Queerness that aligns with wider right-wing ideologies is thus welcomed into the (Hindu) fold. References to precolonial, non-heteronormative identities in classical 'Hindu' literature produce a Hinduized version of gender ambiguity and particularly transgender existence. Any narrative that 'Hinduizes' Indian history is compatible with the project of the Hindu right, especially in its erasure of LGBT+ (specifically trans here) Muslim subjects. Claims to historical authenticity for *hijra* subjects shore up visions of the ideal nation, particularly when these claims function as 'nostalgic idealisation of a libertarian Hindu antiquity' framed as 'classical' culture and as Hindu-normative (Dutta 2012: 120). Semmalar (2014) argues that by proving that trans communities are not 'western imports' and instead presenting 'a golden Hindu period' without discrimination, the Hindu right wilfully ignores the demonstrated significance of Islam within transgender communities. The additional inclusion of 'authentic' vernacular expressions as 'transgender' (*jogta*s or *jogappa*s and *shiv-shakti*s) further establishes Hindu-centric narratives: as Semmalar (ibid.) writes, 'there is a co-option of such alternate expressions and cultures which might not be identities in the modern sense of the term'. Reframing these vernacular expressions as trans identities and as 'Hindu' aids in the project of saffronization.

Re-signifying trans identity through association with *hijra* identity promotes a specific Hindu history and world vision. Due to their 'history', visibility and 'traditional' – but still practised – socioreligious roles, *hijra*s perform a labour of cultural authenticity due to their established (albeit marginalized) place in the Indian (read 'Hindu') nation in a way that other 'LGBT' subjectivities, posited as modern and imported (read 'Western'), do not. It is expedient for the Hindu right to incorporate *hijra*s within their vision of the state, not only given the size and visibility of communities, but because cultural narratives framed to include these transgender subjects add symbolic value to the Hindu right's project of assimilation and exclusion. Thus, the Hindu right can saffronize trans subjects to serve an essentialist, Hindu normative vision of the nation. Yet the consequent exclusions – of other trans and gender-diverse communities, non-Hindu trans identities and identifications based on sexual practices – may also be espoused by certain trans individuals in carving out their place within the Hindu nation.

The Guise of Belonging and In/Exclusion

Tripathi's claim that started this chapter, that 'our religion has a space for everyone', implies that Hinduism can encompass LGBT+ communities within its fold. The Kinnar Akhada has sought to establish itself as a faith-based space for *kinnar*s and *hijra*s practising Hinduism (Goel 2020).[58] Employing religious imagery and performing culturally symbolic ritual acts, including bathing in the confluence of the Ganges, Yamuna and mythical Saraswati Rivers and constructing a *kinnar* village under the banner of their *akhada* during the Prayagraj (Allahabad) Kumbh Mela in 2019, the Kinnar Akhada has adopted discourses that have long marginalized trans communities. It has commandeered them to access power and resources, carving out a place within existing religious spaces.

Tripathi argues that the Akhada does not support any political organization – although in November 2018 it did urge people to vote the BJP back into power (Verma 2018) – but they support temple construction since

'Ram Temple is an issue of faith also for *kinnar*s as we too are followers of Sanatan dharma' (Dixit 2019).[59] Equally, they appear to support militaristic actions, including the ongoing antagonism between India and Pakistan. Responding to a media question on an alleged strike by Pakistan, Tripathi proclaimed that there should be a '*kinnar* battalion' to wipe Pakistan off the face of the planet (Bhattacharya 2019: 4). The imagery of *kinnar*s as serving as part of military action against Pakistan is informative as it sustains narratives constructing the supposed Muslim 'enemy', severing any association between *kinnar* or *hijra* identity and Islam. Rather than *kinnar*s and *hijra*s being read as subjects simply for state welfare and uplift, here they are actively transforming negative stereotypes about themselves within frameworks of respectability and responsibility (although these are mediated within right-wing discourses; Sircar 2017).

This re-signification of identity in relation to right-wing discourses is complex. Goel (2020) raises concerns regarding the burden of political correctness resting heavily on those from marginal spaces, where 'institutionalised structural degradation' has affected both identity formation and the othering of that identity. Access to power and resources is appealing for historically marginalized groups, as is inclusion into mainstream religious traditions.[60] The Kinnar Akhada's adoption or adaptation of existing religious and right-wing discourses should be framed within larger operations of power in which they are located. The ascendance of the Hindu right, alongside legal developments regarding trans rights, determines the context in which trans communities make these claims. This context also determines the limits of what is possible in terms of creating new social identities. If *hijra* behaviour (indeed all behaviour?) is enacted according to 'circumscribed contexts, rather than universal rules governing all conduct' (Reddy 2005: 113),[61] no autonomous decisions are made devoid of social context: in this case, the dominance of right-wing discourses. It is important to recognize the agency of communities in demanding acknowledgment of their existence, alongside understanding that any extraction of space itself is determined within and by a system that maintains the marginalization of other identities (even as it serves, at least rhetorically, to distribute rights). Yet legitimation of *kinnar*s and *hijra*s' own status through these discourses violently excludes non-Hindus, non-*kinnar*s and non-*hijra*s and other trans communities.

This combination of Hindu right rhetoric and '*hijra*/transgender' visibility has dangerous consequences, with other trans and LGBT+ activists denouncing this collusion. A joint statement by Indian Trans, Intersex and Gender Nonconforming individuals and groups (signed by 183 individuals, 146 allies and twenty-eight LGBTQIA+ groups and ally organizations) condemned the Akhada's support for the Ram Temple. They argued that such communal statements were 'appalling and dangerous' and that, as members of trans and gender-diverse communities, they strongly condemned them.[62] The statement asserts that Tripathi's position:

> ... negates the politics of communal harmony that is espoused by Hijras and Kinnars, who have historically maintained a syncretic faith of belonging to both Hinduism and Islam. Laxmi Narayan Tripathi's position idealises a mythical past of the Sanatan Dharam and supports the right-wing politics of communal hatred in the guise of 'we were always accepted'. (Trans, Gender Nonconforming and Intersex Collectives 2018)

The statement posits that Tripathi's stance (informed as a 'dominant-caste brahmin trans woman') will 'likely deepen existing hierarchies of trans persons in dangerous ways, especially alienating minority-religious and atheist, gender expressions and identities', increase oppression for many transgender persons and damage the 'secular fabric of Hijra and transgender communities'. The signatories contest that Tripathi and other trans persons representing religious bodies do not represent all trans and gender-diverse communities and that as a collective they 'resist the saffronisation of trans and intersex spaces' (ibid.). Other trans people have raised criticisms about Tripathi's emphasis on religion as essential to identity and her influential position in 'representing' trans communities, which further marginalizes other groups (Sitlhou 2019). Living Smile Vidya, Dalit trans feminist writer and theatre artist, argues, 'if you are connecting identity with religion, then you're getting distracted from the core issues ... it doesn't really help us if they only see us as mythological beings'. Santa Khurai, Founder of All Manipur Nubi Manbi Association, posits that equating trans identity with Hinduism excludes those from indigenous cultures and puts them at risk. Further, consultation of 'prominent' figures like Tripathi ignores other senior community leaders, who have less access to platforms from which they can speak, trans activist Gauri Sawant contends (ibid.). By exposing these logics of assimilation, where certain trans communities are co-opted in the guise they always 'belonged', these collective voices draw attention to the saffronization of trans identity where Hinduized *hijra*s are constructed as legitimate subjects for the nation.

This raises a significant question concerning the representation of trans identity: who gets to represent it? While the NALSA judgment affords self-determination of identity, 'irrespective of religious or physiological factors' as the collective asserts (Trans, Gender Nonconforming and Intersex Collectives 2018), the judgment might also be read alternatively as re-signifying a normative trans feminine, Hindu identity as synonymous with 'transgender'. Furthermore, the protests over the Parliament bills reveal a lack of consensus – between state and activists – over what is meant by 'transgender'. The collective statement demonstrates this, referencing 'minority-religious and atheist, gender expressions and identities' and the 'secular fabric of Hijra and transgender communities' (ibid.), strongly opposing the position taken by Tripathi and the Akhada. There is a clear contestation over the ways in which different activists approach and define trans identity, as aligned with, or different from, dominant state narratives.[63]

Conclusion

Who counts as transgender (even as its boundaries are constantly defined) and who represents – or is represented by – 'transgender'? I have considered how, and to some extent why, specific forms of transgender identity – namely that associated with *hijra* identity, configured as trans feminine and normatively Hindu – have been foregrounded at the expense of other identities and the relationship of this phenomenon to the Hindu right. The progressive steps taken to discursively and physically produce the transgender subject have been part of a fraught endeavour, demonstrating tension between state and different social actors. Tracing the rise of the term 'transgender' in state policy from health interventions to the NALSA judgment and Parliament bills designed to implement the practical grant of 'rights', I have argued that normatively conceived 'transgender' identity by the state has drawn strongly on conceptions of *hijra* identity as trans, leading to a conflation of *hijra* identity and 'transgender'. In the NALSA judgment, a focus on 'vernacular' trans identities, namely *hijra* identity, alongside emphasis on 'Hinduized' histories, might further construct trans subjects as trans feminine and Hindu normative. Although the intentionality behind this project is questionable, the Hindu right has been able to saffronize trans identity and thus affirm essentialized norms concerning gender and religion. These norms bolster a vision of the nation as Hindu normative in its erasure of 'queer' non-Hindu subjects.

The developing contestations around transgender rights in contemporary India, against a backdrop of dominant right-wing political and socio-cultural movements, necessitates careful examination of the ways in which certain trans communities gain rights at the expense of others. Different communities are played off against one another, whereby the process of granting citizenship to some necessarily excludes others. In the act of claiming citizenship, more 'privileged' actors frame the boundaries of that identity and define who within it is deserving of recognition. As the framework also changes – how the state itself develops definitions of 'transgender' – identities will also shift. As long as rights are premised on bounded identities, fractures will occur between communities. Presently some trans communities continue to protest, while others benefit from embracing the state's narratives: trans communities are pitted against one another in ways that serve the nationalist project and have little do to with recognizing real beneficiaries for rights.

The saffronization of trans by trans communities themselves is noteworthy. Yet these actions must be interpreted within a framework that accounts for long-standing marginality and the difficulty of resisting established normative discourses that yield benefits. It is evident that some trans communities are welcomed within the nation at the same time that others are further ostracized, within a context of enduring communal violence and the exclusion of non-Hindu communities. Continuing calls within LGBTQ+ movements demand an articulation of intersectional politics that include those on the 'wrong' side of caste, religion and ethnicity. The question is whether or not communities, side-lined for so long, will resist inclusion within a nationalist project that rejects some of their own.

Notes

1. Forms of 'transgender' identity with distinct sociocultural roles and community regulations (including a formalized process for joining communities), amalgamating variations of sex, gender and sexual orientations that challenge western understandings of 'trans' as primarily a gender identity. The term *kinnar* may be a more respectful term, whereas *hijra* can be read as derogatory. Additionally, numerous regional, historical and westernized terms exist with regional and linguistic specificity.
2. This narrative has been an expedient tool in the nationalist agenda to mobilize votes and incite anti-Muslim violence.
3. Hindu monastic title, depicting the holder as elevated by peers to the highest level of spiritual guardianship.
4. The terms 'LGBT+' (lesbian, gay, bisexual, trans, 'plus' referring to alternative expressions or identifications) and 'queer' (an Anglophone slur reclaimed to encapsulate a range of alternative sexualities and gender identities) may be used to self-identify. I use 'LGBT+' here except when drawing on language used by individuals themselves. Both terms may be inadequate in a non-western context (based on a sexual ontology linked with western experience [Seckinelgin 2009: 104]). Some writers note that 'queer' retains a mode of inclusivity around dissident gender and same-sex sexuality (Bacchetta 1999: 144) but it is not commonly used. 'Queer' in the South Asian context has the (troubling) potential to subsume non-elite and indigenous sexualities 'that resist neat identification', replicating class dynamics surrounding the movement (Sircar 2017: 11, n. 58; also see Gupta 2005).
5. *National Legal Services Authority (NALSA) v. Union of India and Others* (2014). 5 SCC 438 (Supreme Court of India, 15 April 2014); and *Navtej Singh Johar & Others v. Union of India* (2018). 10 SCC 1 (Supreme Court of India, 6 September 2018).
6. For example, the Citizenship Amendment Act (December 2019) and the National Register of Citizens have severe consequences for transgender persons (alongside trans Muslims). In Assam, activists have argued trans people will be left off the citizenship list due to mismatching gender markers and lack of documentation (Narsee 2020).

7. I note that the term 'Hindutva', the predominant form of Hindu nationalism and an ideology seeking to establish Hindu hegemony and culture, could describe the re-signification of trans identity in ways that can be weaponized by the Hindu right through a focus on 'Hindu-ized' histories and narratives. I acknowledge the distinction between Hindu and Hindutva but choose not to use the latter because the objectives of the actors involved are not always evident. However, many of the actions described, particularly in the last two sections regarding saffronization of trans identity and trans adaptations of the right-wing agenda, do indicate that debates around and trans identity itself (particularly reinscribed as legitimate through 'Hindutva' logics) do sustain a nationalist project, especially in their exclusion of 'non-Hindu' communities.
8. I define the term 'Hindu right' as the RSS and its affiliates when alluding to overall nationalist ideologies, but I focus on the BJP as the purpose of this chapter is to examine the central government's role, particularly since 2014, in the construction of the category 'transgender'.
9. The term 'homonationalism' is used with care. The term's intellectual trajectory in Jasbir Puar's work and in Maya Mikdashi's, Schotten (2016: 361) posits, refocuses from homonationalism as dual movement (collusion between American nationalism and queer subjects, generated diametrically) to a marker of general imperial sexual exceptionalism globally, transcending an American context and severing the notion of gay complicity with the state. Here I utilize the possibility for accountability offered in Puar's earlier theorization, allowing analysis of the complicity of saffronized trans subjects with the state.
10. See Sircar (2017: 17) for examples of right-wing violence and censorship.
11. Graff, Kapur and Walters (2019: 549) argue that the global 'right' utilizes various tools to reinstate 'dominant essentialised gender and sexual norms', with efforts 'often coupled with assertions of racial, ethnic, or religious majoritarianism'.
12. Used in the Parliament bill definitions; it is not an accessible term (referencing class and language privilege; see Gupta 2005) and separately has been critiqued for allowing LGB individuals to claim rights as 'transgender' (Dutta 2016; also for analysis of complex experiences of class, caste, gender, sexuality expressions in lived reality and in claiming identity).

13. That *hijra* identity is produced as feminine – rather than as masculine, as 'third' or as a subversion of norms – adheres to heterosexual, patriarchal norms that view gender as binary and privilege 'male' identity (for example, mythological examples where men transformed into women are often explained as a 'curse' or punishment). Within logics of masculine Hinduism, transition from 'male to female' is less threatening than 'female to male' (a 'loss' rather than 'gain' of power). Androcentric societies depict women who 'transgress' their sexuality as threats to be controlled and produce homophobic and heteronormative expectations of 'masculine' behaviour.

14. While individual politicians across different parties have shown support or opposition, the Congress remains the only political party with a 'stance' on decriminalizing homosexuality (since 2013; Yadav and Kirk 2018: 679). BJP politicians have offered a range of regressive and progressive stances, with no clear official guidance from the centre (more later).

15. Ministry of Social Justice and Empowerment (MSJE) (2014), 'Application for clarification/modification of judgment and order dated 15.04.2014 (2014) in *National Legal Services Authority (NALSA) v. Union of India and Others (2014) 5 SCC 438*' (Filed 30 July), creating delays of two years in implementation. Also see Shukla (2016).

16. Furthermore, a lack of consistent vision from India's judicial system has failed to provide guidance; for example, the Supreme Court issued rulings within four months that contrastingly overturned the reading down of Section 377 which re-criminalized homosexuality: *Suresh Kumar Koushal and Another v. Naz Foundation and Others* (2014). 1 SCC 1, 2014, 3 SCC 220 (Supreme Court of India, 11 December 2013); and the 2014 NALSA judgment, granting extensive trans rights and protections.

17. These were (*a*) the NALSA (a governmental body): *National Legal Services Authority (NALSA) v. Union of India and Others* (2012), Writ Petition WP(C) 400/2012; (*b*) an organization working with *kinnar*s: *Poojaya Mata Nasib Kaur Ji Women's Welfare Society*, Writ Petition WP(C) 604 of 2013; (*c*) Laxmi Narayan Tripathi, seeking recognition of gender self-identification as male, female or 'third gender': Grover, A. (2013) *Written submissions by Anand Grover, Sr. Advocate for the Intervenor, Laxmi Narayan Tripathy in Writ Petition WP(C) 400/2012* (Redding 2018: 203–204).

18. Additionally, the international dimension complicates matters. The influence (or lack thereof) of international bodies may affect national policy. For example, India has adopted contradictory stances regarding LGBT+ rights at the United Nations, opposing or abstaining from votes, producing a disjointed policy approach without clear orientation and reflecting contradictory pressures at national and global levels (Yadav and Kirk 2018; Mitra 2019).
19. See Tan (2018: 152) regarding how conventional narratives of LGBT+ progress fail to capture the othering of Muslim LGBT+ identities.
20. The term entered policy discourse following calls to accommodate gender within HIV/AIDS funding policy, mirroring National AIDS Control Organisation interventions (influenced by international funding bodies). Originally covering gender variance, it became instituted as a separate identity category to achieve policy aims (for example, see UNDP 2008: 16–17). The separation of trans communities from communities identified according to sexual practices marks a shift in perceptions from seeing homosexuality and gender variance as closely related or the same thing (Dutta 2012).
21. Articles 14, 15, 16, 19 (1)(A), and 21.
22. Thereby extending reservations mandated for historically marginalized communities in education and government employment. This extension remains unfulfilled (Shukla 2016; Bose 2019); it remains unmentioned in the 2020 Rules (Transgender Persons [Protections of Rights] Rules, 2020).
23. Rights of Transgender Persons Bill, 2014 (2014) Bill No. 49 of 2014 (New Delhi: Rajya Sabha, Government of India). Introduced by Tiruchi Siva, leader of DMK (Dravida Munnetra Kaazhagam), a Dravidian political party committed to social justice and reform. Tamil Nadu was the first state to produce a trans welfare policy and maintains a progressive stance towards LGBTQ+ rights. Initially, BJP MPs insisted on the bill's withdrawal, including then BJP finance minister, Arun Jaitley, and minister of social justice and empowerment, Thawar Chand Gehlot. Gehlot promised the government would produce its own bill, but the bill was passed after Jaitley noted a divided house would be 'improper'.

24. Transgender Persons (Protection of Rights) Act, 2019 (2019) Act No. 40 of 2019 (New Delhi: Lok Sabha, Government of India).
25. In December 2015, the MSJE released a draft bill. Despite feedback from trans, intersex and gender non-binary communities (Sampoorna 2019), in August 2016 they produced a more regressive draft for Lok Sabha debate: Transgender Persons [Protection of Rights] Bill, 2016 (2016) Bill No. 210 of 2016 (New Delhi: Lok Sabha, Government of India) (Mogli et al. 2016). A Parliamentary Standing Committee report was released in July 2017 based on written recommendations and personal depositions from trans communities and activists (Ministry of Social Justice and Empowerment [MSJE] [2017], 'Standing Committee on Social Justice and Empowerment Report on Transgender Persons [Protection of Rights] Bill 2016' [July 2017]). The MSJE largely disregarded this report (Guest Writer 2017; Sampoorna 2019) for its draft bill passed in December 2018 (Transgender Persons [Protection of Rights] Bill, 2018 [2018] Bill No. 210-C of 2016 [New Delhi: Lok Sabha, Government of India]). Neglect of the report's recommendations (regards to civil rights of marriage, divorce and adoption) provoked activists to demand its overhaul. Before reaching the Rajya Sabha, Parliament was dissolved and the bill lapsed (Mudraboyina, Jagirdar and Philip 2019).
26. The 2019 draft bill removed two criticized provisions of the 2018 bill, regarding District Screening Committees and that criminalized begging (problematically failing to acknowledge structural discrimination creating such conditions; Mogli et al. 2016; Dutta 2016). However, this draft failed to address gender self-determination and mandatory reservations (the NALSA judgment). The 2019 Act passed in Lok Sabha on 5 August (the same day as the Rajya Sabha's abrogation of Article 370), despite protest from members of the Congress, the DMK and the All India Trinamool Congress.
27. Calling it 'Gender Justice Murder Day', activists demanded comprehensive anti-discrimination legislation to guarantee civil rights (Pathak 2019). At time of writing, three challenges have been raised with the Supreme Court against the 2019 Act: *Swati Bidhan Baruah v. Union of India*, Writ Petition WP(C) 51/2020; *Rachana Mudraboyina & Ors. v Union of India*,

Writ Petition WP(C) 281/2020; *Grace Banu Ganesan & Ors. v. Union of India & anr.*, Writ Petition WP(C) 406/2020.
28. The Rules attempt to integrate certain critiques of the 2019 Act and bridge gaps between the Act and the NALSA judgment. The Rules describe the application process for identity certificates, but they leave to each 'appropriate government' the provision of welfare, education, social security, health; non-discrimination mechanisms (left undefined); and grievance redressal mechanisms. It remains to be seen how differing criteria between the 2019 Act and the 2020 Rules will be implemented in practice and how District Magistrates, instructed to handle applications, will proceed.
29. For example, the 2019 draft text was unavailable to communities until it was tabled (Mudraboyina, Jagirdar and Philip 2019).
30. MSJE, 'Application for clarification/modification'. The petition queried excluding LGB persons under the category 'transgender', advised against classification of transgender groups under the 'other backwards classes' category and required the court to 'properly define' transgender.
31. For example, protest rallies in December 2017 and December 2018.
32. Each bill contains problematic inclusions beyond scope for discussion here. For issues relating to trans healthcare (including separate HIV centres), intersex variations, reservations, emphasis on 'family relations', ongoing discrimination and violence (in education, biological families, healthcare, police, employment) and unequal punishments for anti-trans crimes, see Mogli et al. (2016), Guest Writer (2017), Sampoorna (2019), Mudraboyina, Jagirdar and Philip (2019), Masih (2019) and Pathak (2019).
33. Additionally, Dalit trans feminist writer and theatre artist, Living Smile Vidya, keenly argues that reservation must account for gender and caste privilege, so that both Dalit women and Dalit transgenders will benefit (Round Table India 2013).
34. The NALSA judgment is generally read as advocating self-determination, alongside the Rajya Sabha bill (Ung Loh 2018: 48–49), but the 2016 and 2018 Lok Sabha draft bills, including a 'District Screening Committee' to certify applications, stress external identification. This imposes an externally granted, medicalized understanding of gender through a

bureaucratized approach that limits beneficiaries (disproportionately affecting poor and Dalit trans people; Dutta 2016). While the 2019 Act removes the committee, 'transgender' identity certificate applications are approved by a District Magistrate (also mandated in the 2020 Rules). The Act states amending one's gender to 'female' or 'male' is allowed after 'surgery' and provision of medical certification (Transgender Persons [Protection of Rights] Act, 2019: 4). This premises female/male gender identity on surgical intervention in contradiction to the NALSA recommendation (*NALSA*: 110; Dutta 2016). Bridging the NALSA judgment and the 2019 Act, the 2020 Rules permit a revised certificate of identity (as male or female) to applicants who have undergone 'any gender affirming' medical intervention (with evidence of medical certification): this more inclusive definition may be closer to the NALSA judgment's self-determination principle (Transgender Persons Rules, 2020: 16).

35. Two individual persuasive statements (*obiter dicta*) by Justices K. S. Radhakrishnan and A. K. Sikri, with a jointly written, final recommendation section (*ratio decidendi*, reason or rationale).

36. This is because the judgment stems from three separate petitions representing different communities (trans, *kinnar*s and *hijra*s) (Redding 2018: 203–204; see note 17 in this chapter). Justice Radhakrishnan's *obiter* defines 'transgender' as people whose gender identity, gender expression or behaviour does not conform to 'their biological sex', and those who intend to or have undergone sex reassignment surgery (SRS, also known as gender affirmation or confirmation surgery). This *obiter* includes 'Hijras/Eunuchs' who describe themselves as 'third gender', described as 'neither men nor women' (based on essentialist logic of lacking reproductive capacities; *NALSA*: 9–10). Justice Sikri's *obiter* argues that the core issue is whether one has the right to self-identify with the other binary gender and if those who 'are neither' can identify as 'third' (*NALSA*: 75). Confusion that allows for identification as male or female or as third (or something else altogether) stems from encompassing different trans subjects under the judgment's remit.

37. Although these terms may not have a Hindu connotation, they are described as part of Indian history through the co-option of these expressions and subcultures as 'transgender' and due to the neglect

of other aspects of their history (for example, lack of attention paid to 'eunuchs' under Mughal rule). See the section on saffronization.
38. Recommendations to the MSJE in early 2014 from trans masculine activists document government consultations with trans feminine communities since 2009, but none with trans masculine communities. Government policy therefore focuses on '*Hijras, Aravanis* and other trans feminine communities' (Nagpaul and Suleiman 2014).
39. The *ratio's* (joint recommendations) first directive is that 'Hijras, Eunuchs, apart from binary gender, be treated as "third gender" for the purpose of safeguarding their rights'. Of nine recommendations, three reference 'Transgenders' or 'TGs', three contain non-specific 'they' or 'them' and three mention '*Hijras*/Eunuchs' or '*Hijras*/Transgenders'. Significantly, *hijra* (and 'eunuch') is the only specific term mentioned apart from 'transgender' in the recommendations (*NALSA*: 109–111).
40. *Hijra*s appear under the section named 'Historical Background of Transgenders in India (*NALSA*: 10ff); as part of a 'wide range of transgender related identities, cultures, or experiences' found in the 'Indian Scenario' (ibid.: 47ff); and as part of a 'distinct and separate class/category' of Indian trans persons (ibid.: 93–94).
41. This phrasing begins each definition in the Parliament bills.
42. MSJE, Standing Committee Report, 34.
43. Rights of Transgender Persons Bill, 2014, 3.
44. *Kinnar* appears three times in the NALSA judgment: twice regarding the 2012 petition filed on their behalf (*NALSA*: 3, 6) and once as a regionally specific ('Delhi') term (ibid.: 47–48).
45. Transgender Persons (Protection of Rights) Bill, 2016, 2.
46. Drawn from the Standing Committee Report definition (MSJE, Standing Committee Report, 41).
47. Transgender Persons (Protection of Rights) Bill, 2018, 2; Transgender Persons (Protection of Rights) Act, 2019, 2.
48. However, the 2019 Act does not contain explicit protections for intersex communities, including specific documentation for gender, consultation for related law and policy and consent for non-emergency medical procedures.
49. Two paragraphs consider mythology associated with Lord Rama and Aravan, where *hijra*s are described as sanctioned by Rama to confer

blessings (referencing contemporary sociocultural performances) and that *hijra*s of Tamil Nadu consider Aravan their 'progenitor', hence self-identification as 'Aravanis' (*NALSA*: 10–11).

50. The text references academic work regarding the significance of Islam to *hijra* communities (Reddy 2005) but provides no detail.

51. While Reddy (2005: 22ff) references 'eunuchs' rather than individuals of a 'third nature' during this period ('third' denoting non-cisgender communities), gender non-conforming individuals rose to prominent positions, even if such identities are not synonymous with *hijra* identity.

52. Syncretic religiosity – amalgamating practices categorized as 'Muslim' or 'Hindu' – can be read as affirmations of community (rather than of faith, which are context and individual driven; Nair 2000 in Ung Loh 2014) or performed from positions of liminality, allowing for heterodox and subaltern practices (Reddy 2005: 113–114, 117). Reddy (ibid.: 113) writes: '… for hijras, contexts are clearly specified, and behaviour is enacted and interpreted according to these circumscribed contexts, rather than according to universal rules governing all conduct.' Thus, religious practices from divergent traditions are possible in differently demarcated contexts (if 'religion' is understood as exclusionary practices rather than as dynamic and contested; Kalra and Purewal 2019). No autonomous decisions are made devoid of social context: a logic extending to *hijra* adoption of right-wing discourses.

53. For instance, see discussion in Ung Loh (2014) (specifically works by Gayatri Reddy and Adnan Hossain). Identification and enumeration of what proportion of *hijra*s identify as (or practise traditions that might be identified as) 'Muslim' is complex for various reasons. 'Muslim' trans communities' existence in general is not contested – and thus the impact of state policy or actions and who is affected negatively can be considered – but making concrete statements about specific groups may be problematic. Criticism regarding counting trans populations as 'other' during the 2011 census (regarding who was included and how the information was subsequently used) demonstrate that empirical studies that enumerate trans communities must be undertaken cautiously, if at all. Enumerating communities does not equate to representation or determine group rights: instead, people are hemmed in within existing categories (even if they do

not fit lived realities) and are demarcated according to the state's logics. Naming particular groups (whether trans and Muslim or any other trans group) carries ethical considerations: it might be overstating the case regarding their social or political organization or influence (or lack thereof), create (perhaps unwanted) visibility for already marginalized communities or potentially enact harms. Lastly, identification can be context-based and strategic which problematizes set enumeration. Thus, I maintain that the existence of communities is reason enough for their erasure to be named, without identification or enumeration.

54. Sircar (2017: 26) argues that ex-finance minister Jaitley's support of decriminalization from 2015 onwards could be read contextually with a 2014 World Bank report on the economic cost of homophobia and LGBT exclusion in India, pointing to the need for the BJP to rethink support of LGBTQ+ rights as part of its neoliberal and developmentalist agenda.

55. No mention in earlier manifestos; no other mention of other LGBT+ rights in the 2019 version.

56. India first abstained in 2016, revealing reluctance to support LGBT+ rights internationally: sources stated there was no change in vote because as yet no legislation had been put in place by Parliament, despite the 2018 Johar judgment decriminalizing homosexuality (Mitra 2019).

57. The containment of subversive gender performance and behaviours viewed as 'disruptive' or 'deviant' mirrors the self-policing of 'queer' communities (including of middle-class LGBT+ communities against *hijra* modes of visibility) in recreating (hetero-)normative culture (Dutta 2012: 130–131).

58. The Akhada has determined itself as a Hindu organization, despite biased treatment as a self-proclaimed order by mainstream practitioners, including from the thirteen established *akhada*s (Goel 2020).

59. Tripathi argued that the Akhada would launch a peaceful *satyagraha* if temple construction is not undertaken (Dixit 2019). Referencing nonviolent resistance in the face of the Babri Masjid's demolition (and ensuing anti-Muslim violence) is noteworthy.

60. The Kinnar Akhada have in turn used increased popularity as a means to offer a range of public services, including employment opportunities such as through Kineer Services and making donations of food and goods

during Covid-19. Similar resource-sharing initiatives from *hijra* and trans communities have been reported in different states.
61. See note 52.
62. The statement's cover note describes threats against individuals who wanted to support it and those who initiated it: a silencing of dissent that reveals violent consequences in speaking against right-wing ideologies.
63. Any exclusionary stance regards a particular identity might itself slide into essentialist and problematic stereotyping. This occurred in relation to an exclusion of *hijra* identity from 'transgender' identity in the 2016 'I am not a *hijra*' campaign by 'Transgender India' (a platform to 'emancipate' and 'empower' transgender people). This photo project was a series of images of people holding signs over their faces, including ones that read 'I am trans* & I am a daughter, sister, wife & mother. I am not a hijra' and 'I am trans* but I'm not a sex maniac, I am not a hijra'. While differentiations exist between trans identities, the demarcation of identity undertaken in this series (which was eventually withdrawn), exploited long-standing, discriminatory stereotypes associated with *hijra*s.

Bibliography

Amitava, B. D'Mello, Chandini, E. Kumar, G. A. Suleiman, K. Karthik, Living Smile Vidya, Dr Payoshni, A. Revathi, Shyam and Satya (2014). 'Recommendations to Ministry of Social Justice and Empowerment (MSJE) for India's Emerging Trans Policy'. 27 January. http://orinam.net/recommendations-trans-inclusion-india/. Accessed on 5 July 2020.

Bacchetta, P. (1999). 'When the (Hindu) Nation Exiles Its Queers'. *Social Text* 61 (Winter): 141–166.

Bhattacharya, S. (2019). 'The Transgender Nation and Its Margins: The Many Lives of the Law'. *South Asia Multidisciplinary Academic Journal* 20 (2019): 1–19.

Bose, R. (2019). '"Murder of Gender Justice": Activists Call Out "Trans(Phobic) Bill" for Violating Fundamental Rights'. News18, 27 November. www.news18.com/news/buzz/transgender-bill-2019-rajya-sabha-thawar-chand-gehlot-trans-activists-unconstitutional-gender-justice-2402293.html. Accessed on 3 July 2020.

Chakrapani, V. (2010). 'Hijras/Transgender in India: HIV, Human Rights, and Social Exclusion'. United Nations Development Programme (UNDP), India,

December. www.undp.org/content/dam/india/docs/hijras_transgender_in_india_hiv_human_rights_and_social_exclusion.pdf. Accessed on 5 July 2020.

Dixit, K. (2019). 'Kinnar Akhara Committed to Ram Temple: Tripathi'. *Times of India*, 2 February. https://timesofindia.indiatimes.com/city/allahabad/kinnar-akhara-committed-to-ram-temple-tripathi/articleshow/67800287.cms. Accessed on 3 July 2020.

Dutta, A. (2012). 'Claiming Citizenship, Contesting Civility: The Institutional LGBT Movement and the Regulation of Gender/Sexual Dissidence in West Bengal, India'. *Jindal Global Law Review* 4, no. 1: 110–141.

———. (2014). 'Contradictory Tendencies: The Supreme Court's NALSA Judgment on Transgender Recognition and Rights'. *Journal of Indian Law and Society* 5 (Monsoon): 225–236.

———. (2016). 'Gatekeeping Transgender'. Raiot, 3 October. www.raiot.in/gatekeeping-transgender/. Accessed on 5 July 2020.

Goel, I. (2020). 'Queer Politics of Representation: Ram Mandir and Kinnar Akhada Controversy'. *Economic and Political Weekly* 55, no. 4 (25 January).

Graff, A., R. Kapur and S. D. Walters. (2019). 'Introduction: Gender and the Rise of the Global Right'. *Signs: Journal of Women in Culture and Society* 44, no. 3: 541–560.

Guest Writer (2017). 'Joint Statement by Trans Community Against the Transgender Bill'. 11 December. https://feminisminindia.com/2017/12/11/transgender-bill-statement/. Accessed on 1 July 2020.

Gupta, A. (2005). 'Englishpur Ki Kothi: Class Dynamics in the Queer Movement in India'. In *Because I Have a Voice: Queer Politics in India*, edited by A. Narrain and G. Bhan, 123–143. New Delhi: Yoda Press.

Kalra, V. S., and N. K. Purewal (2019). *Beyond Religion in India and Pakistan: Gender and Caste, Borders and Boundaries*. London: Bloomsbury.

Masih, N. (2019). 'A Bill Meant to Protect India's Transgender Community Instead Leaves Them Angry and Aggrieved'. *Washington Post*, 30 November. www.washingtonpost.com/world/asia-pacific/a-bill-meant-to-protect-indias-transgender-community-instead-leaves-them-angry-and-aggrieved/2019/11/29/6c2c7b7e-116b-11ea-924c-b34d09bbc948_story.html. Accessed on 3 July 2020.

Mitra, D. (2019) 'Despite SC Ruling, India Abstains Again on Vote on LGBT Rights at UN'. *The Wire*, 13 July. https://thewire.in/diplomacy/india-abstains-again-on-vote-expert-lgbt-rights-at-un. Accessed on 5 July 2020.

Mogli, V. V., Nirangal, Orinam, Sampoorna Working Group, and Telangana Hijra Intersex Transgender Samiti (2016). 'Response From Trans and Intersex Communities on the Transgender Bill 2016'. Feminism in India,

9 August. https://feminisminindia.com/2016/08/09/trans-community-response-transgender-rights-bill-2016/. Accessed on 1 July 2020.

Mudraboyina, R., S. Jagirdar and P. C. Philip (2019). 'A Critique of the Transgender Persons (Protection of Rights) Bill, 2019'. Feminism in India, 5 August. https://feminisminindia.com/2019/08/05/critique-transgender-persons-protection-of-rights-bill-2019/. Accessed on 3 July 2020.

Munshi, S. (2018). 'From "Immoral" to "Not a Crime": How RSS Stand on Section 377 Has Changed Over the Years'. News18, 8 September. www.news18.com/news/politics/from-immoral-to-not-a-crime-how-rss-stand-on-section-377-lgbtq-has-changed-over-the-years-1871345.html. Accessed on 3 July 2020.

Nagpaul, S. R., and G. A. Suleiman (2014). 'Towards the Annihilation of Imposed Genders: Recommendations to the Indian Ministry of Social Justice and Empowerment'. Round Table India, 7 February. https://roundtableindia.co.in/index.php?option=com_content&view=article&id=7216:towards-the-annihilation-of-imposed-genders&catid=129&Itemid=195. Accessed on 30 June 2020.

Narsee, A. J. (2020). 'India's Citizenship Law Hurts Transgender People'. NewsClick, 1 March. www.newsclick.in/India-Citizenship-Law-Hurts-Transgender-People. Accessed on 6 July 2020.

Pathak, S. (2019). 'India Just Passed a Trans Rights Bill. Why Are Trans Activists Protesting It?' National Public Radio, 4 December. https://text.npr.org/s.php?sId=784398783. Accessed on 5 July 2020.

Ramaseshan, R. (2013). 'BJP Comes Out, Vows to Oppose Homosexuality'. *Telegraph India*, 14 December. www.telegraphindia.com/india/bjp-comes-out-vows-to-oppose-homosexuality/cid/231442. Accessed 3 July 2020.

Reddy, G. (2005). *With Respect to Sex: Negotiating Hijra Identity in South India*. Chicago: University of Chicago Press.

Redding, J. A. (2018). 'The Rule of Disgust? Contemporary Transgender Rights Discourse in India'. In *The Empire of Disgust: Prejudice, Discrimination, and Policy in India and the US*, edited by Z. Hasan, A. Z. Huq, M. C. Nussbaum and V. Verma, 195–219. Oxford: Oxford University Press.

Round Table India (2013). '(Trans)Gender and Caste Lived Experience – Transphobia as a Form of Brahminism: An Interview of Living Smile Vidya'. 2 March. https://roundtableindia.co.in/index.php?option=com_content&view=article&id=6254:transgender-and-caste-lived-experience-transphobia-as-a-form-of-brahminism-an-interview-of-living-smile-vidya&catid=-120&Itemid=133. Accessed on 6 July 2020.

——— (2014). 'Letter by Trans Men to Ministry of Social Justice and Empowerment'. 24 January. https://roundtableindia.co.in/index.php?option

=com_content&view=article&id=7185:open-letter-by-trans-men-to-ministry-of-social-justice-and-empowerment&catid=129&Itemid=195. Accessed on 30 June 2020.

SAATHII (Solidarity and Action Against the HIV Infection in India) (2009). 'Report of the Regional Transgender/Hijra Consultation in Eastern India'. SAATHII Kolkata and United Nations Development Programme. http://saathii.org/calcuttapages/undp-tg-hijra-cnslttn-report-final.pdf. Accessed on 5 July 2020.

Sampoorna (2019). 'SPWG Statement on Transgender Persons (Protection of Rights) Bill 2019'. 19 July. https://sampoornaindiablog.wordpress.com/2019/07/19/spwg-statement-on-transgender-persons-protection-of-rights-bill-2019/. Accessed on 5 July 2020.

Schotten, C. H. (2016). 'Homonationalism: From Critique to Diagnosis, or, We Are All Homonational Now'. *International Feminist Journal of Politics* 18, no. 3: 351–370.

Seckinelgin, H. (2009). 'Global Activism and Sexualities in the Time of HIV/AIDS'. *Contemporary Politics* 15, no. 1: 103–118.

Semmalar, G. I. (2014). 'Gender Outlawed: The Supreme Court Judgment on Third Gender and Its Implications'. Round Table India, 19 April. https://roundtableindia.co.in/index.php?option=com_content&view=article&id=7377:because-we-have-a-voice-too-the-supreme-court-judgment-on-third-gender-and-its-implications&catid=120&Itemid=133. Accessed on 5 July 2020.

Shukla, S. (2016). 'Why the Clarification Petition Filed by the Union of India in the Transgender Case Is Incorrect in Law and in Bad Faith on the Question of Reservation'. *William and Mary Journal of Women and the Law* 22, no. 3: 585–607.

Sitlhou, M. (2019) 'Ram Mandir and Trans Rights: Is Communalism Dividing the Movement?' *The Quint*, 11 January. www.thequint.com/voices/opinion/transgender-rights-bill-bjp-govt-laxmi-narayan-tripathi-communal-politics. Accessed on 5 July 2020.

Sircar, O. (2017). 'New Queer Politics in the New India: Notes on Failure and Stuckness in a Negative Moment'. *Unbound* 11, no. 1: 1–36.

Tan, N. (2018). 'Was 1992 a Turning Point for Homosexuals in Contemporary India?' *Sexuality and Culture* 23, no. 4: 142–153.

Tiwari, R. (2016). 'Section 377: Unlike RSS, BJP Shies Away from Taking a Stance on Homosexuality'. *Economic Times*, 19 March. https://economictimes.indiatimes.com/news/politics-and-nation/section-377-unlike-rss-bjp-shies-away-from-taking-a-stand-on-homosexuality/articleshow/51464248.cms. Accessed on 3 July 2020.

Trans, Gender Nonconforming and Intersex Collectives (2018). 'Trans, Gender Nonconforming and Intersex Collectives Strongly Condemn Kinnar Akhara's Support for Ram Temple at Ayodhya, India'. Sampoorna, 24 November. https://sampoornaindiablog.wordpress.com/2018/11/24/trans-gender-nonconforming-intersex-collectives-strongly-condemn-kinnar-akharas-support-for-ram-temple-at-ayodhya-india/. Accessed on 3 July 2020.

Ung Loh, J. (2014). '"Why Vote for a Fake Kinnar When You Can Vote for a Real One?": Representation and Political Identity among Kinnars in Madhya Pradesh, India'. PhD Thesis. London: SOAS University of London.

———. (2018). 'Transgender Identity, Sexual Versus Gender "Rights" and the Tools of the Indian State'. *Feminist Review* 119, no. 1: 39–55.

United Nations Development Programme (UNDP) (2008). 'Missing Pieces: HIV Related Needs of Sexual Minorities in India, National Stakeholder Consultation Report October 24–25, 2008'. United Nations Development Programme (UNDP), India. http://www.ph.undp.org/content/dam/india/docs/msm_publications.pdf. Accessed on 5 July 2020.

Verma, L. (2018). 'Kinnar Akhara Bats for Ram Temple in Ayodhya, Second Term for PM Modi'. *Indian Express*, 6 November. https://indianexpress.com/article/india/kinnar-akhara-bats-for-ram-temple-in-ayodhya-second-term-for-pm-narendra-modi-5435495/. Accessed on 5 July 2020.

Yadav, V., and J. A. Kirk (2018). 'State Homophobia? India's Shifting UN Positions on LGBTQ Issues'. *Globalizations* 15, no. 5: 670–684.

Bills, Judgments, Orders, Petitions

Grover, A. (2013). 'Written Submissions by Anand Grover, Sr. Advocate for the Intervenor, Laxmi Narayan Tripathy'. Writ Petition WP(C) 400/2012 (Filed 12 November). http://www.lawyerscollective.org/wp-content/uploads/2014/04/NALSA-Written-Submissions.pdf. Accessed on 8 March 2018.

Ministry of Social Justice and Empowerment (MSJE) (2014). 'Application for Clarification/Modification of Judgment and Order Dated 15.04.2014'. *National Legal Services Authority (NALSA) v. Union of India and Others*, 5 SCC 438 (Filed 30 July). http://orinam.net/content/wp-content/uploads/2014/09/NALSA_UOI.pdf. Accessed on 5 July 2020.

——— (2017). 'Standing Committee on Social Justice and Empowerment Report on Transgender Persons (Protection of Rights) Bill 2016'. Department of Social Justice and Empowerment, 21 July. http://orinam.net/content/wp-content/uploads/2016/08/StandingCommitteeReport2017.pdf. Accessed on 5 July 2020.

National Legal Services Authority (NALSA) v. Union of India and Others (2014). 5 SCC 438 (Supreme Court of India, 15 April). http://orinam.net/377/wp-content/uploads/2014/04/Judgement_Nalsa_Transgenderrights.pdf. Accessed on 5 July 2020.

Rights of Transgender Persons Bill, 2014 (2014). Bill No. 49 of 2014. New Delhi: Rajya Sabha, Government of India. http://orinam.net/content/wp-content/uploads/2015/04/Rights-of-Trangenders-Bill.pdf. Accessed on 5 July 2020.

Transgender Persons (Protection of Rights) Bill, 2016 (2016). Bill No. 210 of 2016. New Delhi: Lok Sabha, Government of India. http://www.prsindia.org/uploads/media/Transgender/Transgender%20Persons%20Bill,%202016.pdf. Accessed on 5 July 2020.

Transgender Persons (Protection of Rights) Bill, 2018 (2018). Bill No. 210-C of 2016. New Delhi: Lok Sabha, Government of India. http://orinam.net/content/wp-content/uploads/2018/12/2018_LS_Eng.pdf. Accessed on 5 July 2020.

Transgender Persons (Protection of Rights) Act, 2019 (2019). Act No. 40 of 2019. New Delhi: Lok Sabha, Government of India. http://orinam.net/content/wp-content/uploads/2019/12/TransgenderRightsAct2019.pdf. Accessed on 5 July 2020.

Transgender Persons (Protections of Rights) Rules, 2020 (2020). *Gazette of India*, 29 September. https://translaw.clpr.org.in/wp-content/uploads/2020/10/222096-1.pdf. Accessed on 10 June 2021.

Part V

Alternative Activist Responses to the Hindu Right

9

The Defence of *Aacharaam*, Femininity and Neo-*Savarna* Power in Kerala

J. Devika

Introduction

On 28 September 2018, the Supreme Court (SC) of India struck down the prohibition of women of menstruating ages in the forest-shrine of Sabarimala in Kerala as gender discrimination and a variant of untouchability (*Indian Express* 2018a). Subsequently, brahmin and *kshatriya* temple authorities, the *sudra* community organization known as the Nair Service Society (NSS) and the Sangh Parivar organizations organized protests against the judgment.[1] However, much before the SC verdict even as the matter was in court, in 2016, a group of Malayali women had already created a high-decibel campaign on social media called #ReadyToWait (RTW), which announced their determination to preserve the custom at Sabarimala that disallowed women of menstruating ages as pilgrims (IndiaFacts 2016). Their campaign proved so successful that this prohibition of women of menstruating ages in Sabarimala began to stand for Hinduism in general; soon, the denial of the former was perceived as tantamount to the rejection of the latter. The campaign grew even more powerful in the days following the verdict and was important in bringing many educated and upper- or middle-class women with no direct exposure to Hindutva ideology closer to politics focused on 'Hindu interests'. The confrontation between the Kerala government led by the Communist Party of India (Marxist) (CPM) and the forces of caste privilege and Hindutva in Kerala deeply polarized civil society; the confrontation was marked by several incidents of violence (Roopesh 2018).[2]

Through this examination of the RTW discourse, I hope to address the relative absence of Malayali women in the burgeoning literature on women in conservative Hindutva formations. There are a few studies on the growing public religiosity and piety of Hindu women in Kerala (Jennet 1999; Warrier 2005; Sreedhar 2016; Thomas 2018; Dempsey 2001). But for the most, Malayali women are viewed within the frame of social development in social science and historical literature in twentieth-century Kerala.[3] In the debate about the achievement of remarkable social development in Kerala despite the state's poor economic growth in the twentieth century (commonly referred to as the 'Kerala Model' debate; R. Jeffrey 2003), women figured mainly as positive, rational, domestic agents of change who benefited unequivocally from the social transformation of the twentieth century. Questions about gender were mainly about how they came to be so (see, for example, ibid.). Also, we tend to associate the twentieth-century calls for the reform of the Malayali family and communities with 'progressive forces'. The feminist critique of the Kerala Model debates contested these framings (see, for example, Mukhopadhyay 2007) but did not examine women's conservatism or participation in explicitly right-wing ideological formations or violent public protests.[4] How such an examination would impact our historical knowledge of twentieth-century Malayali society in general is a crucial question in the present.

It is also important to examine the RTW articulations in the light of the themes and insights that emerge from the more plentiful literature on women in Hindu right-wing nationalism in other Indian contexts. To understand 'Hindu nationalism' for the purposes of this chapter, I rely upon Paola Bacchetta's formulation: 'an extremist religious nationalism of elites, in which elites make strategic political use of elements drawn from one religion to construct an exclusive, homogenized, Other-repressive, "cultural" nationalist ideology and practice to retain and increase elite power' (Bacchetta 1999: 141). I hope to enrich this understanding further by indicating that specific regional interests can well ride on or use such religious nationalism to extend the power of regional elites and that the latter may exist in tension with the Hindu majoritarian national mainstream even as they help further national Hindutva politics and social agendas in regions.

The Sabarimala controversy does confirm several insights from this literature: the alliance of elite women and men in the name of saving the (whole) religious community or nation (Phalkey 1999); the complexity and flexibility of women's agency in Hindutva and the fact that agentive spaces do arise in it even if intermittently (Sarkar and Butalia 1995; Hansen 1995; P. Jeffrey and Basu 1999; Sarkar 2001; Phalkey 1999; Sethi 2002; Bacchetta 2004; Banerjee 2005; Bhatia 2009; Menon 2010); the development of new spaces and political conjectures in which new Hindutva feminine subjectivities are shaped (Bedi 2006; Sen 2007; Menon 2010); the problematization of the difference between times of everyday peace and the riot (Sethi 2002; Gupta 2002; Menon 2010; Mehta 2015); the ambivalence of Hindutva women's discourses that simultaneously excoriate feminists while sharing many of their goals (Bacchetta 2004; Bedi 2006; Phalkey 1999).

Thinking of the Kerala case within the national context, there are important specificities. Historically, unlike in Bengal (Sarkar 2001), militant Hindu nationalism was never a strong presence in Malayali society. State intervention to change social institutions through law-making was welcomed, and social and community reformism was more often than not perceived as unambiguously 'progressive' even as it served to brahminize social institutions and cultural mores – an observation often made in critical feminist and Dalit history of twentieth-century Malayali society. I suggest that we deepen this insight to obtain a more precise view of twentieth-century Malayali community reformism as also involving, to a very significant extent, the reconsolidation of traditional caste privilege. Later in the chapter, I offer a brief history of the shaping of the 'neo-*savarna*' social formation which now lays claim to being the 'purified, true' Hindu. This history is important when we consider the fact that while the subjectivity of the neo-*savarna* woman clearly lends itself easily to the call of majoritarian Hindu politics, its shaping within the matrix of regional caste power seems to have left a strong imprint.

The materials that I chiefly rely upon for this study are from the public debate around women's entry into Sabarimala and from Facebook – over seventy conversations or posts by Malayali women in or drawn to Hindutva and some by male supporters mostly written in the wake of the Sabarimala controversy. The BJP is a relatively less successful political formation in Kerala. The main founts and spaces of explicitly Hindu majoritarian ideologies here have often been cultural and spiritual, like guru-worship and educational and cultural institutions controlled by Sangh supporters – in such a context, the importance of social media and other digital spaces in furthering these ideologies can hardly be understated. The Facebook posts I use are part of a 'digital intimate public' shaped by the RTW that drew women devotees from the region, nation and abroad. I draw here from Lauren Berlant's concept of the 'intimate public' in which women who are strangers to each other form communities through affective ties (Berlant 1997).[5] As Berlant remarks, such publics are not always political; they may refer to structural and historical injustice or subordination but without forming a politics around them. But in times of crisis, this may change, and they may take on the 'logics of intimate ones, deploying sentimental models of affective recognition to establish political grounds for imagining survival according to their own interest' (Berlant and Prosser 2011: 184). The digital intimate publics of women supporters ('devotees') of the Hindutva organizations' position on the Supreme Court judgment was often rich in personal accounts of conversations about belief and ritual practices in homes and domestic circles. However, the very public BJP–Sangh circles on Facebook did not always use 'public' language – they often relied on familial tropes to bind together disparate individuals who partook of Hindutva ideology to different degrees and in different ways, suggesting intimate kin connection, thus creating the semblance of intimacy. Unlike statements in public-political discussions which are often offered up as fixed and final, the exchanges in intimate discussions in Hindutva Facebook circles are often relaxed and willing to reveal dilemmas, confusions and contradictions.

This chapter comprises four sections and a conclusion. The first section provides a historical background to the rise of the neo-*savarna* social formation in which the RTW is rooted. It outlines the reconsolidation of privileged-caste power in early twentieth-century Malayali society and after. The second section dwells on the key aspects of the RTW's understanding of *aachaaram*, which was different in significant ways from the RSS' national Hindutva project. The third section focuses on the nature of agency the RTW women claim. The fourth discusses the manner in which patriarchy is both denied and gestured at in the RTW discussions of gender power. A concluding section reflects on the implications of the RTW campaign for our understanding of the history of women, development and Hindu-centric politics in Kerala and for our understanding of the workings of brahmanical patriarchy in India.

The Decline and Rebirth of *Aachaaram* in the Twentieth-Century Malayali Society

Though understood presently as *religious* custom and practice authorized by brahmin priesthood, *aachaaram* once embraced all activities (including everyday bathing or cleaning one's teeth) in all social spaces in Malayali society. It was part of a socioeconomic order known as *janma-bhedam* – literally, 'difference-by-birth' – in and through which caste difference and deference reproduced themselves. Malayali brahmins and the *sudra* groups (Nairs and Ambalavasis mainly) in alliance with them dominated this order.[6] The commonplace present-day understanding of it as religious rituals or practices undertaken for spiritual benefit (Sunandan 2015) or even the definition preferred by Hindutva groups – that of observance and practice of daily life open to all but which orients the self towards spiritual and material wellbeing as understood in brahmanical terms – does not help us understand the nature of traditional *aachaaram* (for example, Aathmavichaaram 2018).[7] It was validated with reference to the *Keralolppathy*, the founding myth centred upon the brahmin warrior Parasurama. Sixty-four special rules of social conduct were purportedly laid down by him for the Malayali society (Bhaskaranunny 2012). Political authority in traditional Kerala was committed to the reproduction of the *janma-bhedam* order (Bhaskaranunny 2012: 91–156). *Aachaaram* underpinned and justified brahmins' appropriation of labour of all other castes, as K. N. Sunandan (2015) argues. Furthermore, it differed for different caste groups, and the ideas, institutions and practices it sanctioned often deviated from Victorian and north Indian high-Hindu notions of individual dignity, gender, marriage, domesticity, sexuality, inheritance, and so on.

However, with rising challenges from the *avarna* groups (of those excluded from and oppressed by the privileged *varna* order of brahmins, *kshatriya*s and *sudra*s) in the late nineteenth to early twentieth centuries, the integration of Malayalam-speaking areas to the colonial-capitalist economy, and the widening and deepening presence of colonial knowledge, *aachaaram* had to be radically revised. Besides explicit attack on it by the *avarna* (R. Jeffrey 2003), the brahmin–*sudra* alliance on which high-caste power rested was threatened when educated *sudra*s – the Nairs – began to demand a revision of *aachaaram* quite vociferously (Sreekumar 2019).

The elite defenders of *aachaaram* now had to take on three challenges. First, the missionary criticism had to be countered and *aachaaram* adequately modernized. Second, the brahmin–*sudra* alliance would have to be redone eliminating practices demeaning to *sudra*s. Third, the damage done by the rejection of *aachaaram* by the oppressed castes would have to be minimized. The early attempts to meet the first challenge – by trying to add new practices like modern schooling into *aachaaram*-dictated rhythms of everyday life or by creating 'scientific' justifications for specific *aachaaram*-dictated practices (Sunandan 2015: 188) – failed. A third attempt, however, proved successful. Malayali brahmin and *sudra* reformisms initiated a selection process in which *aachaaram* practices were subjected to scrutiny with north Indian-centred high-Hindu social reformist ideals and Victorian domestic values and sexual mores as the implicit standards. This was projected as 'Hindu self-purification'. Those aspects of *aachaaram* which did not conform to the preferred standards were rejected as the undesirable by-products of the history of the 'decay of Hinduism' – for example, marital, sexual and family arrangements like those of *sudra* matriliny and hypergamy. The revisionist Hindu theology advanced by such early twentieth-century reformers as Chattampi Swamikal was hugely influential in this effort (Sreekumar 2019).

The second challenge was met in two ways – through assertions of *sudra* worth and a reimagining of the hierarchy between the privileged *varna* castes. *Sudra* power was asserted, for instance, in the novels of C. V. Raman Pillai which were granted near-historical status in Travancore, in which the Nairs were projected as the backbone of the monarchical order. The reimagining of the relationship of the *varna* communities happened, for example, through caste-histories in which the *varna* castes were presented as the repositories of specific knowledges. Indeed, in public discourse, the term *savarna* became more common now, and it referred to a transformed connection, largely cultural, between the *varna* castes (Sundandan 2015: 191). The third challenge was met by privileged-caste members' participation and leadership in ongoing political struggles around nationalism and communism, their century-long effort to thwart the conversion of oppressed castes and the 'neutralised' deployment of their considerable cultural capital in Malayali sub-nationalism (Devika forthcoming).

By the mid-twentieth century, then, some part of *aachaaram* was salvaged through drastic transformation even as the most dehumanizing aspects such as unseeability and untouchability were abandoned for the most. Much of it was 'secularized' – reinserted into modern, secular contexts with explanations that referred to such concerns as hygiene. The privileged-caste home was now divided into secular and non-secular spaces, the latter being the kitchen and the prayer-room. *Aaacharaam* was observed strictly only in the latter spaces, and this was a huge change from the earlier times when most domestic arrangements were dictated by it. However, the domination of public spaces of the Hindu faith such as temples by the brahmins and *sudra*s continued, and in the growing Hindu nationalist discourse, Nairs were recognized as the leading Malayali Hindu community; for example, Savarkar in 1923 (quoted in Katju 2011: 5) seems to affirm this. Now, the transformed *aachaaram* marked the purified Hindu.

In the subsequent decades, the wealthier members of Ezhava and other underprivileged groups like Araya began to make a bid for a place in the Hindu fold (Roopesh 2017). It is here that we may speak of the transformation of the *savarna* – which comprised only members of the *varna* castes, which largely monopolized privilege – into the 'neo-*savarna*' which is no longer restricted culturally to the *varna* castes.[8] The shriller assertion of Hindu majoritarian politics in Kerala since the 1980s has also created an atmosphere conducive for the redeployment of *aachaaram*. Very crucial, too, has been the burgeoning of 'spiritual capitalism' in which particular temples and deities are commoditized and certain rituals and forms of worship foregrounded as indispensable and timeless (Sreedhar 2016). Also, aspects and elements of *aachaaram* transformed and extended in the present – fasts, *puja*s, ceremonies, and so on – are now prescribed and marketed widely as cures for various individual and social ills.

In the above brahmin–*sudra* reform and reconsolidation, women too were reimagined as active domestic subjects. Chattampi Swamikal's championing of women's equal worth and equal ritual and social agency was furthered by the work of early *sudra* women reformers who were active in the sifting of 'true Hindu' practices from the decadent ones in *aachaaram* and engaged in public polemics with men who lamented the decline of traditional practices.[9] And besides, in nearly all Malayali community reformisms, women were projected as moral guardians and protectors of faith and virtue in the home.

Several distinct developments in the twentieth century ensured further that Hindu women's worth within community and family settings would rest not just on education and other modern achievements but also on their observance of (the reformed) *aachaaram*. Important among these was complacency that arose from the communist faith that 'superstitions' would die automatically with economic change and the reluctance of communist leaders to question acutely enough the *savarna* foundations of the emergent Malayali sub-national discourse. This has often led to the projection of the reformed *savarna* woman as the embodiment of Malayali culture. Second, family and gender were at the heart of the attempts by *avarna*s to enter the *savarna* fold in the 1980s and after (Roopesh 2017). As Sharika Thiranagama (2019: 16) notes in her recent ethnography of poor neighbourhoods in contemporary Kerala, OBC (Other Backward Classes which includes the Ezhava and Thiyya) women are no less laden with the responsibility of protecting caste purity and symbolic privilege. Third, *guru*-worship, like that around the well-known female *guru* Matha Amrithanandamayi, often redeploys *aachaaram* as essentially to do with family and domestic rituals and practices (Warrier 2003).[10]

The reach of these ideas has increased manifold in the present with information technology and a numerous and vocal neo-*savarna* non-resident Malayali population engaging in long-distance nationalism. Research on technically qualified middle-class women from privileged-caste backgrounds in Kerala indicates that they aspire for a balance between 'tradition' and 'modernity' through education, employment, an independent income and other such modern achievements and the performance of domestic norms and practices that communities and families expect of them (Arun 2017) – these include the refined *aachaaram* that women were expected to be custodians and agents of. These processes form the background in which the RTW became the leading voice in the agitation against the SC judgment.

#ReadyToWait Women and the Defence of *Aachaaram*

The first noteworthy public appearance of the RTW campaigners was in 2016, when the new CPM government came to power and readied to file a fresh affidavit in the SC in support of the entry of women of all age groups into Sabarimala.[11] A group of younger, highly educated women started the #ReadytoWait hashtag campaign against it, describing themselves in universal terms such as 'women devotees' who wished to protect Hindu *dharma*. Their remarkable use of social and visual media between 2016 and 2018 brought together thousands of women, including many non-Malayali Hindu and Malayali NRI women, especially those already in circles of *guru*-worship. They also attracted national media attention (*Newscafe* 2018; George 2019). The group's contribution to garnering the support of the neo-*savarna* middle class to the conservative cause was widely acknowledged by BJP politicians and others.

Like many Hindutva groups who saw *aachaaram* as a neutral path of practice towards individual spiritual and material wellbeing, for the RTW campaigners too it was a caste-neutral, gender-neutral faith practice. But they insisted that the benefits of *aachaaram* and its rationale may be evident to believers but not others. However, they themselves did apply some standards tacitly – for example, many RTW voices clarified that Hindu reformers had already retrieved the 'purity' of Hindu culture by discarding 'social evils' such as *sati* and child marriage – without mentioning the standards used to discard those aspects of *aachaaram*.[12] However, they were adamant that no external evaluation of temple *aachaaram* was permissible.

Further, according to them, *aachaaram* links the deity and the worshipper in a web of vulnerability such that the observance of *aachaaram* is necessary for the well-being of both – unlike commonplace Hindutva understandings of *aachaaram* as essentially benefitting the devotee. Such is this faith that *aachaaram* is demanded as a 'right'. In their social media posts, it appears as harmless consumables or rights – in fact, so harmless that underage girl children demand it as their right to Hindu culture in RTW Facebook videos under the hashtag 'KidsForSabarimala'.[13] And this also enables RTW propagandists to speak of the ascetic divinity of Ayyappan as though he were just a young mortal. A female *aachaaram* supporter remarked in her 'RTW story' video : 'Say you have a friend and he says I really want to study, I don't want to be disturbed, but what you do is get a million other people and come to his house to party! ... Why is it not moral? Because it is a matter of his privacy.... We consider Ayyappan to be a real person, right?' (Shruthi 2019)[14] God appears as vulnerable as mortals. Another RTW voice quoted her *guru* Matha Amrithanandamayi: 'God is like a fish in the ocean that does not need to be taken care of. But the deity is like a fish in an aquarium and it needs to be cleaned.'[15] Besides, many define 'purification' not as caste practice but related to maintaining 'divine energies'.[16] The uniqueness of the RTW was in its success in mobilizing sentiment around the 'crisis' into which devotee and deity are equally thrown by the SC judgment, projecting it as an attack on the sentimental and sacred bond between the two – making the devotee–deity connection and the *aachaaram* regulating it a strictly private affair. In the process, *aachaaram* looks as though it has nothing to do with public power of any kind, of caste or gender.

Third, the RTW campaigners insist on the uniqueness of Hinduism in Kerala. In this frame, *aachaaram* is precisely an aspect of the uniqueness of Malayali Hinduism which cannot be sacrificed at any cost. This generated much ire among the RSS supporters in Kerala. Indeed, the differences were not trivial, and there were sharp exchanges between RTW leaders and RSS supporters around them.[17] R. Hari, a leading intellectual of the RSS, openly supported the SC judgment, and the RSS too had initially welcomed it. However, sensing the outrage among the neo-*savarna*, the Sangh changed its stance, saying that local sentiments should be respected (Mathew and Verma 2018). RTW leaders accused the BJP of using the RTW campaign as a tool to merely topple the government and gain power. Following this, they were attacked sharply on Facebook. RTW followers responded that the RSS did not understand Malayali Hinduism,[18] ridiculing RSS supporters of the SC judgment as 'ultra-progressive Sangh intellectual [pretenders]' (*atipurogamana sangh bu-ji-kal*)[19] and rejecting their argument that any such practice can be changed through the convening of a Hindu *aachaaryasabha*, or national ritual authority.[20]

But interestingly enough, this local Hindu practice is defended with an active effort to draw upon the global discourse of paganism which allows the RTW commentators to simultaneously argue on the pluralistic nature of Hinduism and place it in a relation of antagonism vis-á-vis Abrahamic religions. They also argue that when it trivializes regional faith practices, like in Sabarimala, Hindu nationalism often resembles the Abrahamic religions. Countering the attacks from RSS supporters on Facebook, some RTW publicists shared hashtags like 'ProudPagan' along with 'ProudHindu', claiming for Hinduism the victim status of paganism.[21] 'Pagan' is also understood as catering to infinite diversity of 'tastes' in faith. Sanatana Dharma is equated with 'pagan' Hinduism, diverse enough to suit an infinite range of spiritual consumption tastes.[22] This apparent desire for a decentralized *dharma* did not go down well with Hindutva nationalists accustomed to centralized order.

Nevertheless, this is no egalitarian and democratized vision of Hinduism, nor are these arguments new. The Hindu-as-pagan argument in the RTW discourse is often explicitly drawn from the work of European conservative scholars such as Koenraad Elst – for instance, the arguments he advances in *Who Is Hindu?* (2001) to claim that caste was impermanent in India until colonial rule, and originally, it represented 'the full flowering of diversity and its harmonious integration within a functioning whole' (Elst 2002). As scholars of the pagan revival in Europe have noted, early twentieth-century anti-Semitic strands of paganism are still alive (von Schnurbein 2016). The celebration of 'Aryan religion' as 'diverse (polytheistic), rational, immanent, modern, and formed by god-men or avatars' (ibid.: 152–153) goes back to Ernest Renan and other Orientalists, and the Hindutva assimilation of the work of even a-racist paganists like Jan Assmann is noted (ibid.: 166). *Aachaaram*, then, is projected by the RTW supporters, as merely functional to this 'pagan diversity', which serves three very convenient purposes: first, it provides a handy guise within which injustice and inequalities of caste and gender can be rendered invisible. Second, it enables the defence of *aachaaram* as belonging to a regional, more pristine, Hinduism, which the RSS with its Abrahamic ambitions cannot understand. Third, it was also useful to project the Hindu as a victim of colonization by Semitic religions, which helps to render invisible Hindutva aggression against others.

Not surprisingly then, many RTW voices declared that their interest was not just in the *aachaaram* of the rituals at Sabarimala alone but of all *aachaaram* in general. Many RTW supporters called for the restoration of *aachaaram* in worship and faith practices. Respecting 'pagan diversity' meant that they concede that brahmanical and non-brahmanical deities were of equal worth, only separated from each other physically, not hierarchically ordered. In the Facebook conversations among the RTW supporters, there were discussions on how to recover older forms of worship made impossible by the dismantling of joint families and other structural changes in Malayali society or discredited as brutal and violent by reformers – that is, such practices as bringing back the spirits of family elders by conducting astrological inquiry, animal sacrifice, non-vegetarian offerings and toddy.[23] Even lower-caste practices such as that of *odi*, a potent form of *avarna* magic, were assigned a place.[24] Arguments that this 'diversity' also implies gender equality abound in their Facebook writings and videos, and the evidence for this is sought in the existence of Hindu temples where only women are allowed (Shruthi 2019).[25] All these were red herrings in the debate as to whether the exclusion of women devotees of menstruating ages into Sabarimala is discriminatory and a form of untouchability or not.

Fourth, along with stressing the status of *aachaaram* as 'wisdom' – its incommensurability with other national conceptions of Hinduism and imperviousness to all discourses indebted, however, remotely to Abrahamic monotheism – much effort is also devoted to depicting *aachaaram* as knowledge. This knowledge claim rests on the authenticity of empirical experience verifying it. For example, the RTW campaign was enthusiastically endorsed by a menstrual-education NGO, Mythri, which offers advice supposedly vetted by 'experts' and proclaims commitment to girls' education and the dispelling of superstitions around menstruation that affects their mobility. This organization is led by a pro-Sangh 'menstruation educator' who claimed that 'actual' experiences of women confirm that menstrual taboos exist not out of blind faith but from knowledge accrued through experience – for example, that some foods may exacerbate bleeding. That is, the menstrual taboo is rooted in 'wisdom' that accrues from the accumulated 'experience' of women (Joseph 2018). The argument about the deity's divine energies being susceptible to the presence of women of menstruating ages or the reverse – the presence of celibate gods or men affecting women's menstrual cycles – is projected as a phenomenon not yet visible to modern science but sanctioned by the accumulated experience of women that has coalesced into unfalsifiable wisdom. This was shared by RTW supporters, highly placed professional women ranging from chartered accountants to cardiologists during the neo-*savarna* agitation (Daily Hunt 2018).[26]

In short, the conception of *aachaaram* developed by the RTW campaigners was no simple assertion of the conception of Hinduism advocated by the Hindutva nationalist mainstream. It drew upon European neopaganism to mask *aachaaram*'s implication in the caste order and brahmanical patriarchy, at the same time setting it up as a victim of the Semitic religions that deserved sympathy and protection. It implied that 'Malayali Hinduism' was a more unspoiled – pre-Abrahamic – form of Hinduism that deserved preservation. Much effort was thus made to insulate it from critical thinking of all sorts – scientific, historical and social scientific – and elevate it into a practice that mediated a sacred, sentimental and ostensibly deeply private bond between divinity and devotee, the violation of which would make both vulnerable. In other words, this was a perfect focal point around which sentimental outrage could be generated in intimate publics online.

Women's Agency and the RTW Campaign

From the earliest days of the RTW, its spokespersons took over, almost aggressively, the space and voice of 'the true Hindu woman', claiming that 'Hindu women's voices were absent' in the debate on faith practices. This instantly portrayed the Hindu female supporters of the SC judgment as 'false' (Manu 2016). Their defence of *aachaaram* was almost entirely in the language of rights, agency and voice – in and to private acts. As an RTW leader remarked: 'If it was man-made and wrong, I will fight against the tradition. But if it's in the shastras, it's my right to fight to obey.' (Koshy 2016) Nevertheless, the assertion of women's agency by the RTW campaign stayed well within terms set by the historical gendering of agency in Malayali society. Women were to change society through 'gentle power' (Devika 2007).

Not surprisingly, this view of feminine agency has been the subject of much feminist critique in Kerala and especially so with the increasing presence of queer politics in Kerala. Against this critique, the RTW spokespersons deployed a series of false equations to create space for their voice: they equated the feminist critique of the reformist conception of women's agency with the dismissal of women who preferred it; 'the feminist' was made out to be always and already a non-believer and a temple-wrecker; and women who stayed with reformist conceptions of agency were equated with women believers. In this way, the RTW women claimed for themselves agency that could be presented as 'feminine' but was not feminist; importantly, it allowed them to be believers – women who willingly put faith above inclusion, choice and freedom.

But this maternalist and self-professedly apolitical agency could be militant and public – the outraged mother protesting in the streets. The leaders described themselves in the media as 'ordinary housewives' and commentators did not question this self-description, though the connections that some of them had with Hindutva organizations were public knowledge.[27] The RTW campaigners called their demonstrations 'prayer processions' or *namajapa ghoshayatra*s, despite their aggressive, militant nature, and this naming was unquestioned in media reportage. The easy shifting between the self-images of heartbroken and confused mother and the indignant protestor defending *aachaaram* against execrable leftists and lower-caste upstarts was keenly visible in an incident during one such 'prayer procession' in which a senior Nair woman protestor hurled an unquotable casteist abuse publicly at Kerala's *avarna* chief minister in a clear display of caste power. When it turned serious with a police complaint filed against her for caste abuse, she apologized, asking those she offended to 'forgive this mother' (*Indian Express* 2018b).

Sentimentalizing maternal agency (which, according to an RTW campaigner, made the RTW supporters 'sob heart-brokenly in front of the TV' over the SC verdict[28]) is hailed as a force that connected total strangers, erasing class, caste and all other differences. RTW leaders repeatedly testified that the mobilization happened on its own, with 'mothers' reaching out to the RTW campaigners in tears at the 'destruction' of Sabarimala (Dhanya 2018). The elite backgrounds of the protestors escape notice and somehow endow them with purity of purpose; therefore, they proudly say that these are not people amassed by political parties with promises of bribes. And almost inevitably, it brought into view other exemplary qualities that ostensibly inhered in them alike, like *bhakti*. On the RTW Facebook page, many

The Defence of *Aacharaam*, Femininity and Neo-*Savarna* Power in Kerala

women retold their 'stories', and the claim about *bhakti* being the sentimental glue that held them together emerges many times.[29] The patience required for the wait is celebrated as a truly feminine virtue characteristic of the family woman. Waiting till menopause is an act of sentimental commitment – a woman's dedication to her family that makes her patient and adjusting.[30] Evocative images in which Ayyappan bows down to the aged mother, were created.

This emphasizes the fragility of the deity who then would need protection – and women's 'natural instincts' of care and nurture are called upon. Thus, participating in the RTW would be the exercise of feminine, specifically maternal, agency: maternal devotees protecting a deity under assault by unbelievers.

The sentimentalization of the deity–devotee bond is generalized in the RTW discourse, extending to other gods and not just Ayyappan. These include even fierce deities such as the goddesses in their forceful aspect, like Kali or the Bhagavathy, now projected as intimate and domestic, often reduced to otherworldly counterparts of close kin, 'mothers' and 'grandmothers'.[31]

It is also evident that the sentimental agency claimed by the RTW campaigners gestures towards a notion of citizenship which, as Lauren Berlant puts it, is not directed towards the public. In short, the agency claimed by the RTW women did not promise to open up new political space at all; rather, their politics is, borrowing Berlant's words again, sentimental 'because it is a politics that abjures politics, made on behalf of a private life protected from the harsh realities of power' and essentially 'about using power only to create the conditions of true intimacy' (Berlant 1997: 11). *Savarna* elite power is reasserted precisely through such non-politics. Further, the maternal and sentimental agency claimed by the RTW women rests on the general gender conservatism in Kerala which recommends strict segregation of the sexes. The idea that female bodies tempt and arouse male sexuality which leads to rape – essentially the rapist's defence in patriarchy the world over – is frequently reiterated by them. While most of them seem to agree that even the male deity, Ayappan, is susceptible to this, some RTW women claim that the prohibition is aimed not at the deity but the male devotees and is analogous to women's non-entry into bachelors' hostels.[32]

Put another way, the RTW remains heavily indebted to the modern heteropatriarchy of early twentieth-century Malayali modernity. Indeed, and for all their embrace of neo-paganism[33] and celebration of the diversity of 'Malayali Hinduism' which includes the worship of the vagina, the *yoni*, they react with Victorian horror when faced with the feminist celebration of the vagina. Padma Pillai, an RTW leader, condemned a public event organized by a group of rationalist-progressives in which the main gateway to the venue was shaped like a vagina as reducing the female body to a mere machine that menstruated, gave birth and had sex. The word she uses for 'sex' is not the direct translation – *laingikabandham* – but the almost-never-used *garbhadaanam*, which literally means 'the gift or donation of pregnancy'.[34] Like many other RTW voices, Pillai interprets the SC's striking down of Section 497 as a license for sexual profligacy.[35]

But despite these efforts to keep agential claims strictly within the boundaries of community acceptability, the RTW was viewed as a strong assertion by women in the Sangh Parivar circles. Not only was it unprecedented, but it also challenged directly the views of the senior male leadership in the RSS (*Times of India* 2019).[36] An RSS worker recounted in a Facebook post:

> Though there were a lot of issues in Kerala after the SC verdict, I was determined to go to Sabarimala this year. I thought of taking the children, and as someone who agreed with allowing the entry of young women there, I thought, after all, the verdict has come, I will also take my wife, she'll be happy. I called her and said, make the kids take the forty-one-day *vratam* [vow], and since you can't take it that long, keep it for 14 days. But she startled me by saying 'Ready to Wait'!... The next day we saw, a huge rally at Pandalam. Most of the demonstrators, women. All of them saying, ready to wait.[37]

Frenemies with Feminism? RTW and Female Individuation

The leadership of the Sangh Parivar in Kerala acknowledged the role conservative neo-*savarna* were playing in the Sabarimala agitation by celebrating them on International Women's Day, 2019.[38] This recognition of the public role they played has been very valuable to many RTW women who reflect on and value their individuation – in ways that remind one of a group that they take pains to distance themselves from: the feminists. Though the RTW leadership insists that their collective agency is maternal, sentimental and apolitical, many RTW women also take pride in representing a woman's voice within the Sangh Parivar and becoming full members of the Hindutva community. By early 2019, many pro-Hindutva women activists were recalling the Sabarimala conflict and the RTW as a crucial event in their journey towards becoming a fulfilled Hindu subject with voice.[39] Indeed, some of the newer Hindutva voices which participated in the debate on Sabarimala are of highly individuated women who take explicit pride in their unique life-trajectories.[40]

This is perhaps one of the main aspects in which many leading RTW women differed from the women leaders of the Sangh organizations in Kerala – they asserted their individuality and right to think individually. They also differed quite strikingly from the familiar female faces of the BJP in Kerala in many other aspects, including location and leadership. For example, the contrast they make with familiar fiery Hindutva spokeswomen like K. P. Sasikala is worth noticing. In contrast, the most visible faces of the RTW are elite upper-class women who fit the popular imagination of the well-groomed, sophisticated, articulate, mobile, 'liberated' woman who is comfortable with English and fits well into corporate backgrounds – someone who may resemble the feminist in education and confidence but actually claims to be living evidence for the irrelevance of feminism as a politics.

The open hatred of feminism is a powerful link that connects RTW women.[41] However some RTW women and their supporters do call themselves by that name – for example, the one who titled her video on YouTube 'I am a Feminist and I don't want to enter Sabarimala' or the US-based pro-Hindutva author Sankrant Sanu, who explicitly calls the RTW the 'indigenous feminist movement' (Sanu 2016). Such subjects praise and acknowledge women achievers among themselves but rely upon a language and idiom that makes no reference to the patriarchal challenge these achievers probably overcame to attain success. For example, they use comparisons with goddesses and heroines from Hindu mythology to praise women achievers.[42]

And when RTW women do recognize women's subordination as an existing social reality, they reduce it to an individual–psychological issue or an unfortunate result of cultural decline due to materialism. Their individual descriptions and explanations vary, sometimes offering communalized–culturalist explanations, sometimes simply individual–psychological – for instance, one of them explained the recent series of violent incidents against women and children in Kerala as stemming from the preference for non-vegetarian diets here;[43] another claimed that some Malayali women may suffer from the lack of rest, mood swings, and so on but not any serious structural discrimination or disadvantage because of menstruation.[44] The avoidance of places of worship is voluntary and therefore not patriarchal.[45] An RTW supporter seeks to prevent sexual violence, making recommendations that are essentially individualistic and reinforcing male 'sexual need' and female sexual vulnerability arguments: the legalization of prostitution and training girls in self-defence.[46] This acknowledgement of women's subordination but not patriarchy is also common in the broader discourses they partake in, such as Matha Amrithanandamayi's advice to her devotees, widely shared by them on social media which often calls upon men to soften their presence at home through greater interaction among family members and a more flexible division of labour.[47] When RTW supporters agree that patriarchy does exist, they immediately attribute it to the influence of the Abrahamic religions. These arguments resemble those put forward by proponents of the so-called matriarchal studies which blame Abrahamic religions (and sometimes Brahminism) for the spread of patriarchy worldwide and, by implication, claim that women are not oppressed in matriarchies (Goettner-Abendroth 2013).

But when it comes to assessing present-day empirical realities of women's existence, it may appear initially that there is a great deal of agreement between the RTW women and feminists – except about the origins of women's subordination, as mentioned earlier. Even when they demand that the state keep its hand off *aachaaram*, these women demand state protection against almost every single form of patriarchal oppression named by the feminists – domestic violence, workplace harassment, unequal employment opportunities, unsafe and unequal public spaces, and so on. Indeed, they frequently claim that feminists need to focus on these instead of *aachaaram*, which they claim, has nothing to do with patriarchy. Some of the RTW videos directly address women's empowerment: 'Having the right to visit a deity in a temple is not empowerment.... There are issues to be addressed urgently – sexual harassment, workplace discrimination, misogyny, domestic violence, *hazaar* issues harming thousands of women.'[48]

However, there are clear limits to even this sharing. First, when it comes to misogyny and physical attacks on women within Hindutva circles, there is much denial, and when accepted, it is always partial. The limits of their social media articulations are set by the echo chamber of the Hindu right-wing. Thus, silence, dismissal through ad hominem or whataboutery is deployed to fend off accusations about Hindu right-wing attacks on women. For example, some RTW voices claimed that the polemics between them and the RSS men who were in favour of women's entry into Sabarimala were a sign of 'healthy internal debate', offering no evidence and instead alleging that the left women who criticized them could not possibly perceive of it, given the total lack of freedom and voice among women in left political organizations.[49] Second, when they do not indulge in these, self-criticism is always partial and conservative. For example, in what appears to be a rare exception, an ardent RTW supporter condemned the violent and uncouth behaviour of the crowds of 'devotees' at Sabarimala towards young women who tried to assert their right to worship: 'It is not possible to accept on whatever grounds, even of the defence of the faith, the behaviour of the men and women who crowded on the roadside to boo and jeer when Rehana Fatima was arrested and led away. I am certain that no devotee who believes that gaining sight of Ayyappan is possible only though observing a vow and adopting stringent self-control would behave this way.'[50] However, it is also apparent that the author is concerned more about the breach of *aachaaram* – which devotees are bound to observe – than about the mockery and destruction of gender justice there. Third, RTW women refer to patriarchy and privilege directly most often when the issue they discuss has to do with the alleged attack of leftists on poor and underprivileged women or negligence of the CPM-led government.[51] Fourth, women's agency can only be imagined within the space of the Hindu community – a Hindu woman who embraces Islam on her own accord cannot be viewed as exercising agency.[52] Finally, the RTW discourse uses casteist language in describing women who, according to them, threaten the sanctity of Sabarimala; many of them shared the racist and casteist abuse heaped on the Dalit women who entered or tried to enter Sabarimala; they also ignore Dalit women's voices in the debate. Women who attempted the pilgrimage are called 'Mahishikal' – daughters of Mahishi, the *asura* woman who Ayyappan was born to annihilate according to the brahmin version of the myth of the temple – and their supporters, the 'Marava' army, or the lower-caste army that Ayyappan allegedly defeated.[53]

But in the end, despite their pains to distance themselves from feminists, RTW women proved equally vulnerable to the charge of being 'not real' women but 'elite socialites' who claim more credit than they deserve, which feminists in Kerala have been accustomed to since long.[54] RSS men made this claim in their public polemics with the RTW after the national election in May 2019. In response to Padma Pillai's statement that the BJP was interested only in power and not *aacharam*, RSS men accused her of being an elitist who did not participate in struggles 'on the ground' and claimed too much credit for 'putting on make-up and yakking away in TV studios' while the RSS workers were facing the police.[55] Yet compared to feminists, it was easier for the RTW woman to escape the charges of elitism. The accusation of Padma Pillai being a non-activist was countered by her male supporters by using its flipside – by pointing out that she is a 'housewife' and so was doing more than what was expected of her.[56] 'Housewife' appears to be the identity that clears the woman of the charges of elite class affiliations, high levels of education and modern lifestyle instantly. It is also one that is taken locally as almost the opposite of 'feminist' – which, therefore, cannot be used to rescue the feminist from similar charges. But the RTW campaigners' claim that they are a homogeneous group united by *bhakti* is also dismissed by irate male RSS supporters – the prominent RTW campaigner Anjali George, particularly vulnerable because of her Christian-sounding name, was accused widely of participating in a Christian–evangelist conspiracy against Sabarimala and Hindu culture.[57]

Conclusions

It may well be the case that the RTW campaign and its success suggest a shift in Hindutva politics in Kerala. In the early years of the new millennium, mass agitations that gave visibility to Hindutva were by the coastal Araya community traditionally lower than the *sudra*s. There are similarities between the Sabarimala agitation of 2018–2019 and the earlier mobilization of the women of the coastal Hindu Araya community following the communal (Hindu–Muslim) violence at the coastal village of Marad in 2004, especially in the way violence was sentimentalized in both instances. But it has been argued that Araya women's public violence against Muslim neighbours needs to be understood in the light of the longer history of the 'failed community-building' endeavours of the Arayas in the twentieth century (Zacharias and Devika 2006). That is clearly not the case in the present instance – the anti-SC judgment agitation was spearheaded by the powerful neo-*savarna*. Neo-*savarna* women are clearly invested in securing their power within this cultural formation even as they continue to hold on to the gains resulting from Kerala's twentieth-century social development. Given the combination of their dismissal of the caste question and distrust of the Savarkarite Hinduism, the RTW position ultimately benefits the caste elites in the neo-*savarna* formation – the brahmin and *sudra* communities that control temples and rituals in Kerala. This is similar to the very first right-wing mass agitation in Kerala that mobilized elite and non-elite women protestors in large numbers in the streets, the anti-communist 'Liberation Struggle' led by the Nairs and Syrian Christians of 1958–1959 against Kerala's first elected communist government. One of its slogans was 'Christianity in danger' – and it ended up benefitting mainly the Christian caste-elite, the Syrian Christian (Gopalakrishnan 1994; Thomas 2018). It was no accident then that the RTW campaign was embraced by the Nair Service Society and the traditional ritual authority at Sabarimala consisting of the brahmin priestly family (the *tantris*) and the Pandalam palace, because it helped protect their direct material gains, institutional control and symbolic privilege (Thiranagama 2019: 16).

It is all the more important to note when we consider the fact that the endorsement of regressive *aachaaram* by women who participate in brahminized worship in Kerala is not new – the only new aspect is that it became the focal point for neo-*savarna* mobilization in the name of protecting Hindu culture. For instance, Sonja Thomas recounts a similar dispute arose around temple practice in the famous Vishnu temple of Guruvayur in 2007, in which the Devaswom managing committee decided to permit women, who were earlier allowed to worship only in saris or skirts, to wear *salwar*s or *churidar*s. In the days immediately after, women worshippers seemed to be moving to the more convenient *salwar* suits, but soon writ petitions were filed against the move in the Kerala High Court. These were dismissed, but women worshippers apparently stopped wearing *salwar* suits, and this was portrayed as a voluntary decision (Thomas 2011: 121–123; DNA 2013).[58] Here too, it appears that the objectors were worried about the challenge to the *tantri*'s authority (Das 2007). The significance of the RTW campaign was that it was able to mobilize all these arguments and place them within the discourse of the 'Hindu in peril'. Even though male RSS leadership identified RTW women as 'dissonant subjects' (Menon 2010) early on, the campaign proved to be a most efficacious vehicle for mobilization of popular support for the BJP's assault on the ruling Left Democratic Front government and the cultural legacy it claimed in Kerala.

And the RTW challenge was no simple affirmation of reigning local conservatisms. As a politics, the RTW campaign relied upon a notion of citizenship that rested on private acts and built an intimate public around the 'right to pray' that directly challenged both political society and the oppositional civil social politics in Kerala. As a gender politics, the RTW campaign rested solidly on twentieth-century gender common sense of community reformism that is twenty-first-century conservatism. This was an important reason why their discourse could be brought into articulation with the gendered vision of Hindu nationalism, even when they clearly defended regional privileged-caste interests and drew upon other, more global, right-wing imagination of the Hindu. Yet the RTW leaders proved no less vulnerable to misogynist attacks than feminists for their differences and criticism of the leadership of the Sabarimala agitation.

The RTW campaign also calls for more critical research on better-off neo-*savarna* women in Kerala who may be poorly researched but are hugely influential today, as the Sabarimala agitation showed. Their struggle, as Shoba Arun's work (2017) on the educated women from matrilineal families in post-matriliny Kerala shows, appears to be between 'female' and 'feminine' capitals. Arun finds these women devoting a great deal of energy to achieving balance between the two. However, she is unable to explain why exactly this struggle is necessary. Perhaps there is indeed a reason: neo-*savarna* women *not only protect but actually maximize* their caste power through preserving their 'feminine capital', and they often prioritize caste power over labour market presence.

Perhaps this gives us an opportunity to expand and strengthen our understandings of brahmanical patriarchy in India. Two observations may be made here. Uma Chakravati's influential essay (1993) associated it with the tightening of male control over women's sexuality – their exclusion from ritual and sacrificial roles and confinement within reproductive roles. She notes that stratification between the Aryan women and the conquered *dasi*s was evident as early as the Rig Veda and that privileged-caste women's compliance was secured 'through their investment in a structure that rewarded them even as it subordinated them at the same time' (Chakravarti 1993: 585). Second, Chakravarti's historical analysis mentions but does not foreground the historical vicissitudes of the power relations that bind privileged-caste women and the women of the oppressed castes within domestic spaces. It may be important to theorize more carefully and closely the power relations between *savarna* and *avarna* women given in the caste order – and make sure that it informs our understandings of the politics of transactions between them, such as in domestic labour. In the *janma-bhedam* order of the nineteenth century, Malayali brahmin women performed a large number of ritual tasks within domestic spaces, and aspects of domestic labour that involved pollution were carried out by *sudra* women servants – including childcare. Chattampi Swamikal's championing of women's right to performance of rituals and Vedic studies did not reverse brahmanical patriarchy; it merely allowed domestic rituals to become part of the ideal *savarna* woman's domestic labour. As the neo-*savarna* formation began to take shape, it became part of the labour of 'family status production' (Papanek 1979). The increasing importance of ritual tasks in neo-*savarna* woman's daily labour at home may mean that the symbolic capital harvested by neo-*savarna* women through the performance of *aachaaram* probably rests on the stigmatized domestic labour performed by *avarna* women. This is a hypothesis that needs further exploration.

The dominant left in Kerala has much to learn from this long, drawn-out battle. For many decades now, feminists have been critical of the left's tendency to be politically progressive and socially regressive, warning them that this will undermine the humanistic civil society on which their politics rests. Hindutva nationalism today offers women a vital if subordinate space in their imagination of the future. But the left parties in Kerala which once offered women such space through reservations in the *panchayati raj* institutions and the state-wide network of government-supported women's self-help groups, the emancipatory potential of which seems exhausted now, needs to now renew its own imagination of women's place in left politics.[59] Given that the dominant left in Kerala seems to be moving away from a vision of development focused on the state-centric civil society in the *panchayat*s, and women seem peripheral to the left's current infrastructure-obsessed vision of the future, there is a real void opening up. Also, the success of the so-called Women's Wall (Thomas 2019) organized by the CPM-led government in Kerala merely shows that women welfare beneficiaries and party supporters will assent to male-designed shows of female support for the left and will not challenge the male leadership. But neo-*savarna* women's assertion within the space of the SSangh indicates just the opposite. They mobilized on their own and built a large base separate from the entrenched Sangh Parivar organizations and also contested the very terms on which fundamental categories such as the Hindu are understood by the RSS leadership.[60] All that, sadly enough, was in the service of conservative anti-politics and against democracy.

Notes

1. These included the organization of Ayyappa devotees, the Akhila Bharatha Ayappa Seva Sangham, the Vishva Hindu Parishad, the Bharatiya Janata Yuva Morcha, the BJP Mahila Morcha, the Hindu Aikya Vedi and the Bharatiya Janata Party's adversary, the Hindu outfit led by Pravin Togadia, Antarrashtriya Hindu Parishad. The Indian National Congress criticized the Sangh organizations on agitation but joined in the condemnation of the SC judgment (Nair 2018).
2. The confrontation began with the public interest litigation filed in the SC praying for women's entry into the temple by the Young Indian Lawyers' Association in 2006 and peaked in 2018–2019 after the SC verdict and with the commencement of the annual pilgrim season at Sabarimala.

Given the extremely hostile, misogynist atmosphere created at Sabarimala for women pilgrims, few women ventured to go. The few who tried were hounded by Hindutva extremists and not adequately protected by the Kerala government. It soon became a matter of prestige for chief minister Pinarayi Vijayan but the government vacillated in its determination to facilitate women's entry into Sabarimala. Finally, two women pilgrims managed to sneak into the temple with help from the government on 1 January 2019, but that made the conservatives' complaints even shriller. The controversy was raging even as this chapter was being written, in May 2019.

3. However, this is not to say that studying women in Kerala's Sangh politics will not require a critical examination of the history of development.

4. Indeed, early feminist neglect of this aspect in Kerala may also be related to the lingering idea of false consciousness among women, something problematized today widely in feminist research. This was not because of the dearth of such presence. Indeed, women workers were very prominent in the militant working-class protests of the 1950s, right up to the 1970s, and they were also very active in violent right-wing public protests such as the huge anti-communist struggle in the late 1950s (Lindberg 2001; Gopalakrishnan 1994). Also, the ideas advanced by women commentators in the early twentieth-century Malayali public cannot be characterized as neatly 'progressive', even though their very act of intervening in public debate was radical (Devika 2005).

5. This is of course quite different from other theorizations of the digital intimate public, such as Berlant (1997).

6. *Kshatriya*s were a very small minority and so the Hindu *varna* castes in nineteenth-century Kerala were largely *sudra* and brahmin. The trading communities – Syrian Christian, Muslim and Jewish – were placed among the *varna* groups, treated as the equivalent of *vaishya*. For details, see Bhaskaranunny (2012).

7. As K. N. Sunandan points out, the practised *aachaaram* of nineteenth-century Malayali society was far from Eurocentric ideological scholarship, which often understood it as 'a spiritual activity practiced with an objective of attaining salvation and a better afterlife' (Sunandan 2015: 177, note 8).

8. The social hierarchy between the brahmin and the *sudra*, or between the *varna* caste members and those from aspiring *avarna* castes, was not, however, set aside. It was merely softened through cultural inclusion, and strict endogamy is still practiced by groups that share the space of the neo-*savarna*.
9. See, for example, the essay by C. P. Kalyani Amma in Devika (2005: 37–39).
10. Also see Mahesh Tharammel, 'Amrithavachanam', Facebook post, 13 May 2019, 6:06 hrs, https://www.facebook.com/photo.php?fbid=1330077573814935&set=a.132418996914138&type=3&theater (accessed on 13 May 2019).
11. The Kerala government's stance changed with change of leadership as power passed between the political fronts led by the CPM and the Indian National Congress (*The Wire* 2019).
12. Amritha Krishna, Facebook status update, 3 April 2019, 19:23 hrs, https://www.facebook.com/photo.php?fbid=1981262712182314&set=a.1413085225666735&type=3&theater (accessed on 11 May 2019). Also see IndiaFacts (2016).
13. Video on 'Ready To Wait' Facebook page, 13 February 2019, 13:12 hrs, under #KidsForSabarimala, https://www.facebook.com/WeAreReadyToWait/videos/389456298285691/ (accessed on 14 June 2019).
14. Also see VidyalakshmiIyer Iyer, video story on 'Ready to Wait' Facebook page, 3 February 2019, 19:05 hrs, https://www.facebook.com/vidyalakshmi.iyer.79/videos/338017533722948/ (accessed on 12 May 2019).
15. Mythili Vinod, video story on 'Ready to Wait' Facebook page, 10 January 2019, 17:50 hrs, https://www.facebook.com/mythili.vinod.5/videos/367421287387355/ (accessed on 12 May 2019). The Matha was an active supporter of the RTW and a frontline campaigner in the protests for the retention of the prohibition of women of menstruating ages at Sabarimala.
16. Divya Bharadwaj, video story on 'Ready to Wait' Facebook page, 21 January 2019, 17:04 hrs, https://www.facebook.com/divya.bharadwaj.3956/videos/521294451693056/ (accessed on 12 May 2019).

The Defence of *Aacharaam*, Femininity and Neo-*Savarna* Power in Kerala   291

17. Though a prominent section of the RSS leadership disagreed with the RTW right from the beginning, after their campaign helped to raise the 'Hindu in peril' slogan in Kerala powerfully for the very first time, the Sangh parivar leadership in Kerala and elsewhere offered strong support to the RTW and the mobilizations it enabled. The BJP manifesto for the national election of May 2019 assured that they 'will endeavour to secure constitutional protection on issues related to faith and to belief'. However, the rumblings and personal attacks continued well into May 2019. The RTW leaders were careful not to antagonize the RSS in toto (Narayan 2018; Viswanath 2019).

18. Girish Bin Kunhoottan, Facebook status update, 10 May 2019, 19:51 hrs, https://www.facebook.com/girish.mannil/posts/10216582777300172 (accessed on 13 May 2019).

19. Vinay Mynagappally, Facebook status update, 6 May 2019, 16:24 hrs, https://www.facebook.com/vinay.spillai.1/posts/2730371543656180 (accessed on 11 May 2019).

20. Padma Pillai, Facebook status update, 5 May 2019, 20:06 hrs, https://www.facebook.com/photo.php?fbid=10157192421177760&set=a.10152188256397760&type=3&theater (accessed on 13 May 2019).

21. Amritha Krishna, Facebook status update, 29 March 2019, 17:33 hrs, https://www.facebook.com/durgalakshmi.lakshmi/posts/1978508909124361 (accessed on 11 May 2019).

22. Lakshika, video story on 'Ready To Wait' Facebook page, 16 January 2019, 7:34 hrs, https://www.facebook.com/lakshika.sugavanam/videos/2071694332896685/ (accessed on 12 May 2019).

23. Padma Pillai, Facebook status update, 29 March 2019, 19:21 hrs, https://www.facebook.com/photo.php?fbid=10157105452312760&set=a.164901532759&type=3&theater (accessed on 13 May 2019).

24. Padma Pillai, Facebook status update, 12 December 2018, 9:03 hrs, https://www.facebook.com/PadmaRadha/posts/10156860365152760 (accessed on 14 June 2019).

25. Mythili Vinod, video story on 'Ready To Wait' Facebook page, 10 January 2019, 17:50 hrs, https://www.facebook.com/mythili.vinod.5/videos/367421287387355/ (accessed on 12 May 2019); Lakshika, video story on 'Ready To Wait' Facebook page, 16 January 2019, 7:34 hrs, https://

www.facebook.com/lakshika.sugavanam/videos/2071694332896685/ (accessed on 12 May 2019). The portrayal of Hindu goddesses as feminist has been problematized in the feminist literature on Hinduism and early positions, such as those of Madhu Kishwar, and has been critiqued thoroughly, for example, by Rajan (1998) and Govinda (2013).

26. Sreejitha Manu Vasudevan, Facebook status update, 5 January 2019, 11:51 hrs, https://www.facebook.com/sreejitha88/posts/2724518750891937 (accessed on 12 May 2019).
27. See *Newscafe* (2018); George (2019).
28. Padma Pillai, Facebook status update, 10 May 2019, 14:17 hrs, https://www.facebook.com/PadmaRadha/posts/10157204044047760 (accessed on 11 May 2019). Also see comments on this post.
29. Mekha S. Gopi, video story shared on 'Ready To Wait' Facebook page, 28 January 2019, 16:12 hrs, https://www.facebook.com/megha.sgopi/videos/2047571935332428/ (accessed on 12 May 2019).
30. Amritha Jayan, video story shared on 'Ready To Wait' Facebook page, 13 January 2019, 16:24 hrs, https://www.facebook.com/honey.jayan.3/videos/2550096115032969/ (accessed on 13 June 2019).
31. Padma Pillai, Status Update, March 29, 2019, 19:21 hrs, https://www.facebook.com/photo.php?fbid=10157085437422760&set=a.10152188256397760&type=3&theater (accessed on 13 May 2019).
32. Aswathy Varma, video story on 'Ready To Wait' Facebook page, 26 January 2019, 23:11 hrs, https://www.facebook.com/aswathy.varma.7359/videos/2173276272889388/ (accessed on 12 May 2019).
33. As the proponents of feminist spirituality note, while the neo-pagan turn towards the worship of nature and immanentism is welcome, it still stereotypes female deities and relies upon conservative conceptions of the male–female binary (Straffron 1994, cited in Raphael 1996: 9, note 2). But pagan cults like the Wicca do celebrate sexual expression and sexuality as an affirmation of the body (Kraemer 2012). Clearly, the RTW campaign refers to the conservative, nationalist, homophobic versions of neopaganism which resemble their own social vision, not to the more feminist ones.
34. Padma Pillai, Facebook status update, 13 January 2019, 17:38 hrs, https://www.facebook.com/photo.php?fbid=10156932734632760&set=a.10152188256397760&type=3&theater (accessed on 13 June 2019).

The Defence of *Aacharaam*, Femininity and Neo-*Savarna* Power in Kerala 293

35. Padma Pillai, Facebook Status Update, 16 January 2019, 22:11 hrs, https://www.facebook.com/PadmaRadha/posts/10156939998322760?__tn__=-R (accessed on 13 May 2019).
36. Also, the RTW's stance threatens the moral claims that RSS senior leaders silently advance through the practice of celibacy (Bacchetta 1999: 149). The RTW argues that young women's presence at Sabarimala could disturb the deity's vow of celibacy – implicitly underlining the fragility of the celibate life. So it was no surprise that many RSS intellectuals were uncomfortable with the RTW campaigners.
37. Girish Bin Kunhoottan, Facebook status update, 10 May 2019, 19:51 hrs, https://www.facebook.com/girish.mannil/posts/10216582777300172 (accessed on 13 May 2019).
38. Mekha S. Gopi, video story shared on 'Ready To Wait' Facebook page, 28 January 2019, 16:12 hrs, https://www.facebook.com/megha.sgopi/videos/2047571935332428/ (accessed on 12 May 2019).
39. Krishna Priya, Facebook status update, 6 May 2019, 16:09 hrs, https://www.facebook.com/photo.php?fbid=1998558620272540&set=a.298874276907658&type=3&theater (accessed on 13 June 2019).
40. Ambika J. K., Facebook status update, 28 May 2019, 20:19 hrs, https://www.facebook.com/photo.php?fbid=2222797214472213&set=a.727657077319575&type=3&theater (accessed on 29 May 2019).
41. For example, Padma Pillai's response to Sunitha Devadas. Facebook status update, 28 December 2018, 22:52 hrs, https://www.facebook.com/photo.php?fbid=10156897670097760&set=a.164901532759&type=3 (accessed on 13 May 2019); Sri Bala, Facebook status update, 8 May 2019, 20:13 hrs: https://www.facebook.com/ranilechu/posts/446311305942579 (accessed on 29 May 2019. Also see Padma Pillai, Facebook status update, 7 May 2019, 12:58 hrs, https://www.facebook.com/PadmaRadha/posts/10157196673992760 (accessed on 13 June 2019).
42. BJP Keralam, Facebook page video, 16 April 2019, 21:39 hrs, https://www.facebook.com/BJP4keralam/videos/2405024459519285/?__xts__[0]=68.ARA01bWKGUAp0RxA_5UwrvNd1u0g7rd8dXT (accessed on 13 May 2019); Bodhi Datta, Facebook status update, 26 December 2018, 13:11 hrs, https://www.facebook.com/photo.php?fbid=656274358148146&set=pcb.656263568149225&type=3&theater (accessed on 12 May 2019).

43. Sreelakshmi Satheesh, Facebook status update, 19 January 2019, 00:13 hrs, https://www.facebook.com/photo.php?fbid=10213846456742695&set=a.3696878867664&type=3&theater (accessed on 12 May 2019).
44. Lakshmi Priya, Facebook status update, 25 December 2018, 23:32 hrs, https://www.facebook.com/permalink.php?story_fbid=1125172367654231&id=100004844348944 (accessed on 11 May 2019).
45. Mini Unnithan, Facebook status update, 7 April 2019, 9:30 hrs, https://www.facebook.com/photo.php?fbid=2733412910011525&set=a.1416412638378232&type=3&theater (accessed on 16 June 2019). However, this is not to say that all RTW supporters or Hindutva women take this attitude. Indeed, an equal or greater number adhere to extreme conservatism. For instance, Supriya K. P. Marar, Facebook status update, 13 May 2019, 9:59 hrs, https://www.facebook.com/photo.php?fbid=684699581965581&set=a.105579046544307&type=3&theater (accessed on 16 June 2019).
46. Anaswara Rahul, Facebook status update, 21 March 2019, 7:22 hrs, https://www.facebook.com/rana.niha.1/posts/768318796886320 (accessed on 19 May 2019).
47. Mahesh Tharammel, 'Amrithavachanam', 13 May 2019, 6:06 hrs, https://www.facebook.com/photo.php?fbid=13300775573814935&set=a.132418996914138&type=3&theater (accessed on 13 May 2019).
48. Mukta Sukumar, video uploaded on 'Ready To Wait' Facebook page, 27 January 2019, 20:25 hrs, https://www.facebook.com/muktha.sukumar/videos/1671769496301647/ (accessed on 12 May 2019).
49. Sri Bala, Facebook status update, 8 May 2019, 13: 45 hrs, https://www.facebook.com/ranilechu/posts/446176985956011 (accessed on 11 May 2019).
50. Girija Navaneeth, Facebook status update, 27 November 2018, 21:14 hrs, https://www.facebook.com/search/top/?q=Girija%20Navaneeth%20&epa=SEARCH_BOX (accessed on 12 May 2019).
51. Uma Krishnakumar, Facebook status update, 21 March 2019, 11:58 hrs, https://www.facebook.com/sheeba.krishnakumar/posts/10158511734722501 (accessed on 14 May 2019).
52. Krishna Kumari, Facebook status update, 11 May 2019, 16:26 hrs, https://www.facebook.com/photo.php?fbid=2657313194284481&set=a.289329927749498&type=3&theater (accessed on 12 May 2019).

53. Padma Pillai, Facebook status update, 16 October 2019, 13:11 hrs, https://www.facebook.com/photo.php?fbid=10156721246267760&set=a.10152188256397760&type=3 (accessed on 13 May 2019).
54. Feminists in Kerala have long dealt with this accusation (Devika and Kodoth 2001).
55. Comments on Padma Pillai, Facebook status update, 10 May 2019, 17:17 hrs, https://www.facebook.com/PadmaRadha/posts/10157204044047760 (accessed on 11 May 2019).
56. Anil Menon, Facebook status update, 8 May 2019, 8:05 hrs, https://www.facebook.com/photo.php?fbid=1156401581187108&set=a.578095575684381&type=3&theater (accessed on 13 May 2019).
57. Rajeev U., Facebook status update, 8 May 2019, 10:13 hrs, https://www.facebook.com/photo.php?fbid=1201375130030198&set=a.115797741921281&type=3&theater (accessed on 12 May 2019).
58. However, more than ten years after, women are entering the temple in *churidar*s.
59. Kerala's much-lauded excellent containment of the Covid-19 pandemic of 2020 and women's role in mitigating it, is evidence that they now play a vital role in governance. But the absence of women in politics and power is definitely unresolved.
60. Interestingly enough, the BJP and Sangh organizations organized a state-long 'Ayyappa Jyothi' on 26 December 2018, and the Women's Wall was the CPM's answer to it. RTW members participated actively in the Ayyappa Jyothi, but the big difference between them and the CPM women supporters who formed the Women's Wall was that they had their own discourse unlike the latter, who did not question the chief minister's total side-lining of women in decision-making regarding the Women's Wall.

Bibliography

Aathmavichaaram (2018). 'More Vicharam'. 11 October. https://aathmavichaaram.home.blog/. Accessed on 8 June 2019.

Arun, S. (2017). *Development and Gender Capital in India: Change, Continuity, and Conflict in Kerala*. London and New York: Routledge.

Bacchetta, P. (1999). 'When the (Hindu) Nation Exiles Its Queers'. *Social Text* 17, no. 4: 141–66.

———. (2004). *Gender in the Hindu Nation: RSS Women as Ideologues*. New Delhi: Women Unlimited.

Banerjee, S. (2005). *Make Me A Man! Masculinity, Hinduism, and Nationalism in India*. Albany: State University of New York.

Bhaskaranunny, P. (2012). *Pathonpathaam Noottandile Keralam* Kerala of the Nineteenth Century). Thrissur: Kerala Sahitya Akademi.

Bedi, T. (2006). 'Feminist Theory and the Right-Wing: Shiv Sena Women Mobilize Mumbai'. *Journal of International Women's Studies* 7, no. 4: 51–68.

Berlant, L. (1997). *The Queen of America Goes to Washington City*. Durham: Duke University Press.

Berlant, L., and J. Prosser (2011). 'Life Writing and Intimate Public: A Conversation with Laurent Berlant'. *Biography* 34, no. 1: 180–187.

Bhatia, M. (2009). 'Women's Mobilization in the Jammu Agitation: Religion, Caste, Community, and Gender'. *Economic and Political Weekly* 44, no. 26–27: 447–452.

Chakravarti, U. (1993). 'Conceptualizing Brahmanical Patriarchy in Early India: Gender, Caste, Class and State'. *Economic and Political Weekly* 28, no. 14 (April 3): 579–585.

Daily Hunt (2018). 'Lady Doctor's Video about Women's Entry to Sabarimala Goes Viral'. 1 October. https://dailyhunt.in/news/india/english/kaumudi global-epaper-kglobal/lady+doctor+s+video+about+women+s+entry+to+sab arimala+goes+viral-newsid-98278858. Accessed on 17 June 2019.

Das, N. (2007). 'Guruvayoor Devaprasnam Completed on 7 Nov... (The Final Details)'. Haindava Keralam, 8 November. Accessed on 14 June 2019.

Dempsey, C. G. (2001). *Kerala Christian Sainthood: Collisions of Culture and Worldview in South India*. London: Oxford University Press.

Devika J. (2005). *Her-Self: Early Writings on Gender by Malayali Women*. Kolkata: Stree–Samya.

———. (2007). *En-Gendering Individuals: The Language of Re-forming in Early 20th Century Keralam*. Hyderabad: Orient Longman.

———. (forthcoming). 'Women and the Defence of Aachaaram in Kerala: A Historical Account in the Wake of the Neo-Savarna Disturbances around Sabarimala'. In *Saffron in the South: Violence, Gender, Media and Hindutva in Kerala*, edited by Y. Arafat and N. Mannathukaren. New Delhi: Routledge India.

Devika J., and P. Kodoth (2001). 'Sexual Violence and the Predicament of Feminist Politics in Kerala'. *Economic and Political Weekly* 36, no. 33: 3170–3177.

Dhanya, K. R. (2018). 'Who Organized the Sabarimala Agitation, and When and How? Inquiry' (Malayalam). Azhimukayam, 22 October. https://azhimukham.com/archive/kerala-who-has-organised-sabarimala-protest-against-women/cid3362454.htm. Accessed on 11 June 2019.

DNA (2013). 'Drop in churidar-clad women devotees at Guruvayur temple'. DNA, 19 November 2013. https://www.dnaindia.com/india/report-drop-in-churidar-clad-women-devotees-at-guruvayur-temple-1134099. Accessed on 14 June 2019.

Dobson, A. S., B. Robards and N. Carah (eds.) (2018). *Digital Intimate Publics and Social Media*. Palgrave Macmillan Studies in Communication for Social Change. Cham: Springer International Publishing.

Elst, K. (2002). 'Semitization of Hinduism'. In *Who Is a Hindu? Hindu Revivalist Views of Animism, Buddhism, Sikhism, and Other Offshoots of Hinduism*. https://web.bookstruck.in/book/chapter/20129. Accessed on 12 June 2019.

George, A. (2019). 'How Can NRIs Help the 'Ready-to-Wait' Movement?' YouTube video, 11 February. https://www.youtube.com/watch?v=zEgXjzuKzVc. Accessed on 3 April 2020.

Goettner-Abendroth, H. (2013). *Matriarchal Societies: Studies on Indigenous Cultures across the Globe*. Bern: Peter Lang.

Gopalakrishnan, K. G. (1994). *Vimochana Samaram: Oru Padhanam* (The Liberation Struggle: A Study). Thiruvananthapuram. Attingal: Nakshathram Books.

Govinda, R. (2013). 'Didi, Are You Hindu?' Politics of Secularism in Women's Activism in India. *Modern Asian Studies* 47, no. 2: 612–651.

Gupta, C. (2002). 'Anxieties of Hindu Right in Everyday Realm'. *Economic and Political Weekly* 37, no. 3 (19 January): 198–199.

Guru, G. (1991). 'Appropriating Ambedkar'. *Economic and Political Weekly* 26, no. 27–28: 1697–1699.

Hansen, T. B. (1995). 'Controlled Emancipation: Women and Hindu Nationalism'. In *Gender and the Subversion of Nationalism*, edited by F. Wilkison and B. F. Frederiksen, 82–94. London: Frank Cass and Co. Ltd.

IndiaFacts (2016). '#ReadyToWait: A Campaign to Reclaim Hindu Temples and Traditions'. 31 August. http://indiafacts.org/readytowait-campaign-reclaim-hindu-temples-traditions. Accessed on 5 June 2019.

Indian Express (2018a). 'Full Text: Supreme Court Sabarimala Temple Judgment'. 28 September. https://indianexpress.com/article/india/full-text-supreme-court-sabarimala-temple-judgment-5378255. Accessed on 5 June 2019.

――― (2018b). '"Please Forgive This Mother": Woman Who Used Casteist Slur on CM Pinarayi Vijayan Apologises'. 12 October. https://indianexpress.com/article/india/please-forgive-this-mother-woman-who-used-casteist

-slur-on-cm-pinarayi-vijayan-apologises-5399507/. Accessed on 11 June 2019.

Jeffrey, P., and A. Basu (1999). *Resisting the Sacred and the Secular: Women's Activism and Politicized Religion in South Asia*. New Delhi: Kali for Women.

Jeffrey, R. (2003). *Politics, Women and Well-Being: How Kerala Became a Model*. New Delhi: Oxford University Press.

Jennet, D. (1999). 'Red Rice for Bhagavathy/Cooking for Kannagi: An Ethnographic Organic Enquiry of the Pongala Ritual at Attukal Temple, Kerala, South India'. PhD thesis. School of Consciousness and Transformation, California Institute of Integral Studies, San Francisco.

Joseph, S. (2018). 'Sabarimala Verdict: Fabricated Rights Over Real Experiences of Women'. Mythri Speaks, 23 October. https://mythrispeaks.wordpress.com/2018/10/23/sabarimala-verdict-fabricated-rights-over-real-experiences-of-women/. Accessed on 16 June 2019.

Katju, M. (2011). 'The Understanding of Freedom in Hindutva'. *Social Scientist* 39, no. 3–4: 3–22.

Koshy, S. M. (2016). '#ReadyToWait: Keep Women Out of Sabarimala, Says New Campaign by Women'. NDTV, 29 August. https://www.ndtv.com/kerala-news/readytowait-lets-not-change-sabarimala-traditions-say-some-women-1451711. Accessed on 11 June 2019.

Kraemer, C. H. (2012). 'Gender and Sexuality in Contemporary Paganism'. *Religion Compass* 6, no. 8: 390–401.

Lindberg, A. (2001). *Experience and Identity: A Historical Account of Class, Caste, and Gender Among the Cashew Workers of Kerala, India*. Lund: University of Lund.

Manu, M. (2016). 'Waiting for God Or?' *Deccan Chronicle*, 30 August. https://www.deccanchronicle.com/lifestyle/viral-and-trending/300816/waiting-for-god-or.html. Accessed on 17 June 2019.

Mathew, L., and L. Verma (2018). 'Sentiments of Devotees Cannot Be Ignored: RSS Leader on Sabarimala Verdict'. *Indian Express*, 4 October. Accessed on 2 April 2020.

Mehta, A. (2015). 'The Aesthetics of "Everyday Violence": Narratives of Violence and Hindu Right-Wing Women'. *Critical Studies on Terrorism* 8, no. 3: 416–438. DOI: 10.1080/17539153.2015.1091656.

Menon, K. D. (2010). *Everyday Nationalism: Women of the Hindu Right in India*. Philadelphia: University of Pennsylvania Press.

Mukhopadhyay, S. (ed.) (2007). *The Enigma of the Kerala Woman: A Failed Promise of Literacy*. New Delhi: Social Science Press.

Nair, N. J. (2018). 'Sabarimala: Parties Set to Step Up Campaign'. *The Hindu*, 23 October. https://www.thehindu.com/news/national/kerala/

sabarimala-parties-set-to-step-up-campaign/article25302452.ece. Accessed on 17 April 2020.
Narayan, A. (2018). 'Opinion: As RSS Grapples with Its Biggest Crisis in Kerala, Pinarayi Vijayan Gives away the Solution'. News18, 8 October. https://www.news18.com/news/opinion/as-rss-grapples-with-its-biggest-crisis-in-kerala-pinarayi-vijayan-gives-away-the-solution-1901447.html. Accessed on 17 April 2020.
Newscafe (2018). 'To Who Does the Paternity of the RTW Go?' 8 August. https://newscafe.live/08/08/2018/keralam/21858/. Accessed on 11 June 2019.
Papanek, H. (1979). 'Family Status Production: The "Work" and "Non-Work" of Women'. *Signs* 4, no. 4: 775–781.
Phalkey, J. (1999). 'Right-Wing Mobilization of Women in India: Hindutva's Willing Performers'. In *Women, Globalization, and Fragmentation in the Developing World*, edited by H. Afshar and S. Barrientos, 38–53. London: Palgrave Macmillan.
Rajan, R. S. (1998). 'Is the Hindu Goddess a Feminist?' *Economic and Political Weekly* 33, no. 44: WS34–38.
Raphael, M. (1996). *Thealogy and Embodiment: The Post-Patriarchal Reconstruction of Female Sacrality*. Sheffield: Sheffield Academic Press.
Roopesh, O. B. (2017). 'Temple as the Political Arena in Kerala'. *Economic and Political Weekly* 52, no. 16: 12–16.
———. (2018). 'Sabarimala Protest: Politics of Standarising Religious Pluralism'. *Economic and Political Weekly* 53, no. 49: 12–16.
Sanu, S. (2016). 'Sacred Sabarimala: "Right to Destroy a Tradition" versus "Ready to Wait"'. *Swarajya*, 31 August 2016. https://swarajyamag.com/culture/sacred-sabarimala-right-to-pray-versus-right-to-destroy-a-tradition. Accessed on 8 April 2020.
Sarkar, T. (2001). *Hindu Wife, Hindu Nation: Community, Religion and Cultural Nationalism*. New Delhi: Permanent Black.
Sarkar, T., and U. Butalia (eds.) (1995). *Women and the Hindu Right*. New Delhi: Kali for Women.
Sen, A. (2007). *Shiva Sena Women: Violence and Communalism in a Bombay Slum*. Bloomington: Indiana University Press.
Sethi, M. (2002). 'Avenging Angels and Nurturing Mothers: Women in Hindu Nationalism'. *Economic and Political Weekly* 37, no. 16 (April): 20–26, 1545–1552.
Shruthi. (2019). 'I Am a Feminist and I Don't Want Entry into Sabarimala'. YouTube video, 9 January. https://www.youtube.com/watch?v=u44-Ug-lNc8. Accessed on 13 June 2019.
Sreedhar, D. M. (2016). 'Attukal "Pongala": The "Everydayness" in a Religious Space'. *Journal of Ritual Studies* 30, no. 1: 63–73.

Sreekumar, T. T. (2019). 'Chattampi Swamikal and the Deconstruction of the Sudra: Contradictions of Hindu Revisionist Theology in Nineteenth Century Kerala'. Paper presented at the Ninth Backwaters Collective Conference, Kochi, 25–28 July.

Straffron, C. (1994). 'Pagan Philosophy and Women'. *From the Flames* 13: 26–27.

Sudhi, K. S. (2019). 'New Quota Norm to Come into Being in TDB Posting'. *The Hindu*, 9 January. https://www.thehindu.com/news/national/kerala/new-quota-norm-to-come-into-being-in-tdb-posting/article25950759.ece. Accessed on 15 June 2019.

Sunandan, K. N. (2015). 'From Acharam to Knowledge: Claims of Caste Dominance in Twentieth Century Malabar'. *History and Sociology of South Asia* 9, no. 2: 172–194.

The Wire (2019). 'Sabarimala Verdict: A Timeline of Temple Entry Issue'. 14 November. https://thewire.in/law/sabarimala-review-petition-verdict. Accessed on 31 March 2020.

Thiranagama, S. (2019). 'Rural Civilities: Caste, Gender and Public Life in Kerala'. *South Asia: Journal of South Asian Studies* 42, no. 2: 1–18.

Thomas, S. (2011). 'From Chattas to Churidars: Syrian Christian Religious Minorities in a Secular Indian State'. Dissertation submitted to the Graduate School. New Brunswick, Rutgers, State University of New Jersey.

———. (2018). *Privileged Minorities: Syrian Christianity, Gender, and Minority Rights in Postcolonial India*. Seattle: University of Washington Press.

———. (2019). 'The Women's Wall in Kerala, India, and Brahmanical Patriarchy'. *Feminist Studies* 45, no. 1: 253–261.

Times of India (2019). 'Questions Raised Over RSS Leader's Stand'. 8 May. https://timesofindia.indiatimes.com/city/kozhikode/questions-raised-over-rss-leaders-stand/articleshow/69224658.cms. Accessed on 12 June 2019.

Viswanath, C. (2019). 'Sangh Followers Stand Divided on Sabarimala Women Entry Over Vested Interests'. News18, 8 May. https://www.news18.com/news/india/sangh-followers-stand-divided-on-sabarimala-women-entry-over-vested-interests-2133655.html. Accessed on 17 April 2020.

Von Schnurbein, S. (2016). *Norse Revival: Transformation of Germanic Neopaganism*. Leiden: Brill.

Warrier, M. (2003). 'Processes of Secularization in Contemporary India: Guru Faith in the Mata Amritanandamayi Mission'. *Modern Asian Studies* 37, no. 1: 213–253.

Zacharias, U., and J. Devika (2006). 'Powers of the Weak: Spaces of Fear and Violation in the Discourse of Communalism'. In *Violence, Communalism and the State in India*, edited by A. Basu and S. Ray, 123–147. New York and London: Seagull.

10

The Revolution Will Come Wearing Bangles, *Bindi*s and *Hijab*s

Women's Activism for Inclusive Citizenship*

Amrita Basu and Amna Pathan

When about a dozen women organized a sit-in by blockading the Kalindi Kunj Road, which borders Shaheen Bagh in southeast Delhi, on 14 December 2019, no one predicted that they would launch a 101-day nationwide movement. As remarkable as the duration of the protest was its exuberant affirmation of inclusive nationalism and citizenship. The activists recited the national anthem at midnight on New Year's Eve, hoisted the tricolour on Republic Day and invited prime minister Narendra Modi to celebrate the festival of love together on Valentine's Day. Along with revolutionary speeches and readings of the Indian Constitution, protesters hosted performances by poets and musicians and decorated their tent with protest

---

* The title of our chapter draws on Nabiya Khan's poem 'Aayega Inquilab Pehenke Bindi Chudiyan Burqa Hijab' about the Shaheen Bagh protests. The empirical observations for this chapter draw on both secondary and primary sources. Amrita's observations are based on her visit to Shaheen Bagh in December 2019. Barkha Bhandari interviewed several students, activists and journalists in August 2020. Ghazala Khan interviewed members of the farmer's union, women's organizations and other activists in Malerkotla, Punjab, in July–August 2020. We refer to these as our (collective) interviews. We use pseudonyms for many of the people we interviewed. We are deeply grateful to Barkha, Ghazala and all the people who agreed to speak with them and with us. We thank Zoya Hasan, Tanika Sarkar, Joan Cocks, Elisabeth Wood, Martha Ackelsberg, Cynthia Enloe, Eileen McDonagh, Mary Katzenstein and Molly Shanley for their comments on this chapter. Thank you also to Adil Chhabra for invaluable feedback and editorial advice.

art. They forged community among people of different ages, faiths and social classes by sharing stories, reading, singing, painting, cooking and cleaning together. In Delhi's coldest winter in over 100 years, they knit each other shawls and sweaters and served hot tea to hundreds of supporters.

The women were protesting the government's passage of the Citizenship Amendment Act (CAA) and its calls for the creation of a National Register of Citizens (NRC), following recent police violence against student protesters at the nearby Jamia Millia Islamia University (hereafter Jamia). Within ten days, the sit-in grew to occupy half a mile of the highway, as it attracted thousands of supporters from across the city and later the country. The sit-in persisted, despite record-low temperatures, several court petitions seeking to evict the activists and false rumours that the Bharatiya Janata Party (BJP) spread, claiming that the protesters had been paid to resist the CAA and the NRC. The protesters remained peaceful and even distributed rose petals to their adversaries and the police, who ultimately evicted them and destroyed the protest site on 24 March 2020, when the government declared a lockdown to prevent the spread of Covid-19 (*The Wire* 2020a).

In this chapter we explore why Muslim women were at the forefront of the anti-CAA struggle and how their gendered experiences inform their affective relationship to citizenship. Before doing so, however, we provide some relevant background.

The CAA is the culmination of a series of steps the Modi-led BJP government has taken to establish Hindu domination and disenfranchise the Muslim community. It provides an accelerated path to citizenship for Hindu, Sikh, Buddhist, Jain, Parsi and Christian immigrants who arrived in India before 31 December 2014 from neighbouring Muslim-majority countries. It marks the first time that religion has been a criterion for granting Indian citizenship. The cabinet approved the creation of a National Population Register (NPR), which will document all Indian residents, citizens and non-citizens alike. By placing importance on the birthplaces of one's parents, it implies that Indian lineage is the basis for establishing citizenship. The legislation empowers government functionaries to profile Muslims by requiring that they verify their citizenship. The NRC, armed with the data furnished by the NPR, seeks to identify and deport non-citizens (Shankar 2020).

There is a clear link between the CAA and the government's adoption of the NRC in Assam in August 2019, which excluded the names of approximately two million people who have lived in India for decades (BBC News 2019). The CAA enables Bengali Hindu migrants in Assam whose names did not appear on the NRC to become citizens. If the BJP government adopts the NRC nationally, as it has repeatedly stated it plans to do (Chakravarty 2019), the government can revoke the citizenship of any person who lacks adequate documentation; most non-Muslims who cannot provide adequate documentation can gain Indian citizenship through the CAA, while Muslims cannot.

Movements demanding citizenship risk reproducing systems of exclusion, especially for minorities and women. As Giorgio Agamben (1998) argues, citizenship rights are inherently exclusionary because they are founded on the exclusion of the non-citizen. He argues that protests that employ what he terms 'constituent power' replace one exclusionary law with another. Universalist citizenship rights can also obscure or deepen biases towards minorities. As Irene Gedalof (2003) argues, and as we discuss later, liberal citizenship deepens the public–private divide and undermines women's rights in both spheres.

By contrast, the Shaheen Bagh protesters defied the logic of constituent power by challenging not only the CAA and the NRC but also broader power structures. For protesters, demands for citizenship became a fulcrum for addressing a multitude of societal problems and state policies, including the threat of violent displacement, discrimination against Muslims and Dalits, gender inequality, unemployment, poverty and the lack of civic amenities in poor neighbourhoods. Rather than simply relying on the state to fulfil their demands, they demonstrated civic responsibility and created an egalitarian community in which women played leading roles and men shared responsibilities for cooking and childcare. The activists upheld an inclusionary community-based model of citizenship which affirmed universalist principles while recognizing diversity.

The protesters upheld the Indian Constitution because it not only affirms civil and political rights but also, through directive principles, promotes social and economic rights. As historian and legal scholar Rohit De (2018) argues, and as we will discuss, there is a long history of subaltern groups invoking the Constitution to challenge the Indian state. Given the relatively recent adoption of the Constitution, older generations, like the women who led the Shaheen Bagh protests, remember its founding promises.

Two different aspects of the Constitution are especially relevant to understanding the Shaheen Bagh protests. On the one hand, the Constitution defines India as a 'sovereign socialist secular democratic republic' and accords citizenship rights on the basis of *jus soli* (birth within a territory), meaning that religion does not determine membership in the political community. Thus, as activists point out, by making religion or *jus sanguinis* (right of blood) the basis for citizenship, the CAA violates the Constitution and makes Muslims second-class citizens.

On the other hand, citizenship laws have always discriminated against Muslims. As we will describe, whereas the post-Independence Indian state considered Hindus and Sikhs natural citizens, it designed arbitrary tests to determine Muslims' loyalty to the Indian state. Vallabhbhai Patel, the first home minister and deputy prime minister of India, repeatedly questioned Muslim loyalty and their right to belong, while maintaining that 'the Hindus and Sikhs of Pakistan cannot be considered alien in India' (Zamindar 2007: 53). The CAA affirms Patel's vision of India as a homeland for Hindu and Sikh refugees from Muslim-majority countries.

For Muslims who were forced to leave their homes during Partition and have been subsequently displaced from their homes by Hindu–Muslim violence, the danger of losing citizenship and facing deportation is very real. The CAA and the NRC formalize Muslims' experiences of exclusion in everyday life. In the current political environment, Muslims' names, food, clothing and other markers of identity jeopardize their safety. Poet Aamir Aziz (2019) states: 'The name on my Aadhar card ... itself can cause me difficulties ... people have realised that your name has consequences. This [a Muslim name] is your name, be careful of what you say on the train.'

Muslim women's citizenship rights have always been especially tenuous. Post-Independence laws made their citizenship dependent on the domicile of their fathers and husbands. Conservative personal laws further increased their dependence on male heads of households. Muslim women have been caught within the cross hairs of conflicts between the state and spokespersons for Hindus and Muslims about their rights under personal law. In light of these exclusions, Muslim women have vigorously championed constitutional principles and broad-based citizenship rights.

We attribute the strengths of the Shaheen Bagh protest to women's leadership and gendered modalities of protest. We argue that Muslim women's unique experiences of displacement, dating back to Partition, influenced how protesters created and preserved community and belonging and thereby reclaimed civil society. Their strategic use of motherhood and femininity is a compelling rejoinder to the BJP's masculinist politics and Hindu nationalists' atavistic and exclusionary use of maternal symbolism. Women's decision to occupy public space through a sit-in reflected their experiences of poverty, displacement and gender-based exclusion. In their occupation of public space, creation of community and demand for equal citizenship, women at Shaheen Bagh not only opposed the BJP but also claimed visibility and political representation for women in the public sphere, implicitly championing feminist goals.

The first section of this chapter explores why the Shaheen Bagh protest prioritized constitutional rights; we then examine how the legacies of Partition, displacement and personal law mobilized Muslims, and particularly Muslim women. Following this, we analyse gendered modalities of protest and, finally, we show how the protesters linked demands for citizenship with attempts to refashion community and civil society. The conclusion explores how, despite its failure to achieve its demands, the Shaheen Bagh protest was successful in prefiguring an alternative model of the state and civil society to the one that the Rashtriya Swayamsevak Sangh (RSS) and its affiliates are promoting.

Constitutional Rights and Broad-based Citizenship

The Constitution was the most widely read text at Shaheen Bagh. Protesters read it aloud and displayed posters of its Dalit author B. R. Ambedkar (Fernando 2020). Shaheen Bagh activist Farida Ayub, who we interviewed, venerated the authors of the Constitution: 'People took their names with respect and pride. We knew we must follow in their footsteps.... In their memory, and through the example they set, we can build courage and strength, and move forward for truth and justice.'

The Indian Constitution, as Ambedkar recognized, is a living, breathing document. Compared to many other constitutions, it is easier to amend – and has been amended 104 times. Several of these amendments have been the subject of political contestation. De (2018) points out that numerous subaltern groups claim the Constitution as their own and have organized movements to demand constitutional rights. However, as De notes, most popular contestations around the Constitution in the post-Independence period have focused on particular aspects and clauses. By contrast, Shaheen Bagh and other concurrent protests against the CAA made demands based on broad constitutional principles.

The complex, amorphous, double-edged character of the Indian Constitution has given rise to many struggles around citizenship rights. On the one hand, the Constitution institutionalizes inclusion and promises to eradicate deep-seated hierarchies to create a community of civic equals. It affirms the equal legal status of citizens, the importance of not only equal civil and political rights, but also economic rights and the nesting of particular and diverse identities within a larger national-civic identity. On the other hand, the realization of citizenship rights has foundered as social democracy has given way to neoliberalism and secularism to Hindu nationalism.

The Constitution's promise, although far from being entirely fulfilled, has inspired anti-CAA protesters. The protesters cited Article 14, which guarantees all citizens equal protection before the law, and Article 15, which prohibits discrimination on grounds of religion, race, caste, sex and place of birth. They argued that the NRC violates Article 21 of the Constitution which guarantees the right to life and liberty (Meharban 2020). They questioned how the Parliament could pass the CAA that discriminates on the basis of religion when the Constitution describes India as a secular state. Muslim and non-Muslim protesters alike repeatedly stated that the protests represent the entire nation and not any one religious group. Farida Ayub told us: 'This is not just Muslims' fight; it is the Constitution's fight.' As Muslim women and underserved communities at Shaheen Bagh claimed a role as guardians of the Constitution, they commanded national attention and affirmed their belonging as equal citizens.

Those who are excluded from citizenship rights are often at the forefront of struggles to achieve them because, as Hannah Arendt (1973) argues, human rights are dependent on the state's provision and protection of citizenship rights. For the stateless, 'the fundamental deprivation of human rights is manifested first and above all in the deprivation of a place in the world which makes opinions significant and actions effective' (ibid.: 296). A loss of belonging renders the stateless invisible and their actions and thoughts meaningless because no law exists for them and no community claims them. The stateless face the loss of place and home and, more crucially, the 'impossibility of finding a new [home]' (ibid.: 293). With no place to belong to, they are displaced into internment camps, 'the only "country" the world [has] to offer [them]' (ibid.: 284).

In the following sections, we demonstrate that Muslim women's experiences of exclusion and displacement have defined their experience of citizenship since the nation's inception, informing not only their understanding of the material and psychic dangers of statelessness but also their ability to reimagine citizenship in ways that resist exclusion.

The Legacy of Partition: Linking Citizenship to Displacement and Exclusion

Narratives surrounding Partition and the creation of India and Pakistan are pivotal to understanding the importance that people attach to home and belonging. Even South Asians who did not experience it themselves have grown up hearing stories of its ravages. As Urvashi Butalia (1994) notes, people recall Partition in almost every instance of sectarian conflict in India. Gilad Hirschberger (2018) emphasizes the role of collective trauma in creating trans-generational memory and social identity, indicating how Partition trauma continues to impact identity in South Asia today.

The legacy of Partition is powerful not just because of the scale and brutality of the violence it unleashed but also because displacement at Partition influenced early citizenship laws and citizens' relationship to physical space, local belonging and national identity. Britain's hasty departure from India, as the British viceroy advanced the transfer of power from June 1948 to August

1947, exacerbated the displacement of new citizens. In the scramble to create the nation, the new Indian government was tasked with decisions about who belonged and how they belonged: 'The idea of the citizen in both India and Pakistan was put together hurriedly and subject to change, not least because the geopolitical shape of postcolonial South Asia itself was decided in a matter of weeks.' (Ansari and Gould 2019: 2) It was not until 1952, when the first Indian elections were held, that electoral politics and universal franchise determined citizenship.

Partition violence created a large population of displaced Muslims in India, and Sikh and Hindu refugees from Pakistan. Since much of the early political work of defining citizenship involved housing displaced people, national belonging became linked to property ownership. While the national government created broad citizenship policies, local administrators and bureaucrats made case-by-case decisions on allocating land and rehabilitating incoming refugees and internally displaced people. As Vazira Fazila-Yacoobali Zamindar (2007: 19) describes, this process pitted displaced Muslims and non-Muslims against each other:

> [For] it was in the hubbub of on-the-ground realities that the bureaucratic record began to give shape to the notion that there were two distinct sets of refugees, Hindu and Sikh refugees on the one hand and Muslim refugees on the other, and that the rehabilitation of one required the exodus of the other.

Sectarian violence amidst Partition displaced Muslims from their homes, as their property was destroyed or forcibly occupied by Hindu and Sikh refugees escaping similar violence in Pakistan. Others, fearing violence, abandoned their homes to seek safety in refugee camps, which came to be known as 'Muslim camps' (ibid.: 27–33).

The Indian state obscured Muslim displacement, creating foundational links between citizenship and Muslim exclusion. The state claimed that displaced Muslims no longer felt safe in 'mixed localities', and so rehabilitated them in 'Muslim zones' and only promised protection to Muslims living in segregated localities (ibid.: 29). An emergency committee to resettle refugees decided not to evict Hindu and Sikh refugees who had occupied Muslim homes unless they had other accommodation. Internally displaced

Muslims who had been forcibly evacuated or had left out of fear could not return to their homes. Bureaucrats referred to these homes as 'empty', 'vacant' and 'abandoned', to make them available to Hindu and Sikh refugees (ibid.: 31), and the executive rationalized Muslim displacement by prioritizing the rehabilitation of Hindu and Sikh refugees. Delhi Deputy Commissioner M. S. Randhawa claimed the 'general feeling amongst the public' was that Hindu and Sikh refugees had a right to occupy Muslim homes given the violence they had faced at the hands of Muslims in Pakistan (ibid.: 32). Vallabhbhai Patel warned 'that there was bound to be trouble if as a result of [internally displaced] Muslims not moving out [to Pakistan], it proved impossible to accommodate non-Muslim refugees coming in from the West' (ibid.: 39).

The legacies of Partition are starkly evident in uneven development and housing patterns in India today. Muslims who had already lost property and livelihood in Partition violence were housed in residentially segregated areas that municipal governments neglected. To date, sectarian violence forces many Muslims to leave their homes to live in predominantly Muslim areas where they feel safer. Shaheen Bagh is populated primarily by families who fled anti-Muslim violence in Ayodhya in 1992 and Gujarat in 2002 (Farooqi 2020). Displaced Muslims are forced to sell their property at low prices and buy new homes at inflated prices in localities where public services are meagre or non-existent. Shaheen Bagh, like many predominantly Muslim neighbourhoods, faces chronic shortages of key amenities, including potable water, and until recently, electricity and sewerage. This creates a cycle of poverty that makes Muslims among the poorest communities in India. Within this long history of repeated displacement, Muslims have strongly resisted the CAA and the NRC, which threaten to displace them once again and to formalize disenfranchisement and unequal citizenship.

Activists invoke Partition to caution against divisiveness and encourage the nation to learn from its past. They demonstrate Hirschberger's (2018) argument that collective trauma offers opportunities for affected communities to regain agency, self-worth and societal unity. Their recollections of Partition and related symbols stand in contrast to Hindu nationalists' divisive evocations of Partition. Hindu nationalists have engaged in an erasure of the trauma Muslims experienced, blamed Partition on Muslims and the Congress party (Dutta 2019), and said that Muslims should have been sent to Pakistan (Puniyani 2020). The BJP seeks to discredit anti-CAA protesters by claiming they are enacting a second Partition (*India Today* 2019). Modi has elevated Vallabhbhai Patel's legacy, ignoring his discriminatory views on Muslims, by commissioning the world's tallest statue (ironically termed the 'Statue of Unity') in his honour.

By contrast, anti-CAA protest art, which depicts the statue of Patel coming alive to walk with protesters (Pardiwalla 2019), subverts Hindu nationalist symbols to resist historical amnesia and past exclusion to create inclusivity. Activists have systematically challenged the government's view that the Shaheen Bagh protesters are separatist. Their slogans, posters and social media posts caution that the CAA and the NRC are preludes to a 'second partition'. Protesters in Malerkotla, Punjab, shout slogans like 'San santalis banne nahi denge' ('We won't let 1947 repeat itself') (Prabhu 2020). Farmers who travelled from Punjab to Shaheen Bagh held placards stating: 'Bhai se bhai ladne na paaye; phir se 47 [1947] banne na paaye' ('Let no brother fight a brother, don't let 47 [1947] recur') (A. Menon 2020).

Anti-CAA resistance was a powerful moment for activists to emphasize societal unity and Muslim belonging. A young woman at Shaheen Bagh highlighted the need to challenge narratives that depict all Muslims as having been secessionists at Independence and to remember Muslims' historical dedication to the nation:

> We have also shed blood for this country, [Modi] should think about this. Our families, our grandfathers have fought. Our sacrifices are also in this soil. Our struggles are being erased. Today we have to remind our children of our history, that we too have done something for this country. (NDTV 2020a)

Activists at Shaheen Bagh promote a critical and active engagement with history to raise social consciousness. Speaking of the police destruction of the Jamia library, Nur Haider, a Shaheen Bagh resident we interviewed, said: 'If you want to destroy a country, destroy the libraries. Burn the books. So that the coming generations don't know their own history.' Protesters created the Fatima Sheikh-Savitribai Phule Library at Shaheen Bagh to preserve history.

Protesters' subversive politics embodied what Michel Foucault (1982) calls the 'politics of refusal' to resist exclusionary citizenship. Gedalof (2003:

93) explicates a Foucauldian understanding of how a politics of refusal can resist coercive power through subversion:

> Power works by producing useful bodies and subjects. Resistance involves revisiting those useful bodies ... to refuse the ways in which their usefulness has been managed and constrained within prevailing deployments of power; it is from that refusal that new forms of subjectivity can emerge ... [and] ... create the possibility for new forms of collective belonging.

Protesters rejected the 'usefulness' Hindu nationalists assigned to symbols and official narratives of Muslim disloyalty. With this refusal, they accessed the social power embedded within these symbols and narrations to create new possibilities for inclusive belonging.

Agamben's (2014) theory of destituent power expands on a Foucauldian politics of refusal to describe how subversive politics can avoid the exclusionary dangers of constituent power, through what he terms 'inoperativity'. Agamben imagines inoperativity to be the way in which bodies can be opened to new use by 'rendering inoperative' the socioeconomic reasons and purposes that define human activity (ibid.: 70). Like Foucault's politics of refusal, Agamben's conception of inoperativity encourages the reuse of human potential, actions and identities to challenge pervasive systems of power and exclusion. Through inoperativity, destituent power transforms and deposes systems of power entirely:

> The difference between *veranlassen*, 'to induce, to provoke', and *vollziehn*, 'to accomplish, to realize', expresses the opposition between constituent power, which destroys and always recreates new forms of law, without ever completely destituting it, and destituent power, which, in deposing law once and for all, immediately inaugurates a new reality. (Ibid.: 71)

Central to Agamben's destituent power is the notion that an inclusive, emancipatory power remains 'in potential', rather than cementing new laws and thus new exclusions. Through gendered modalities of protest and demands for community-based citizenship that rejected explicit hierarchies of power, protesters embodied the inoperativity and potentiality of destituent power. As participants at the sit-in forged community bonds, through food, art and caring for children and each other, they demonstrated a destituent character that evokes what Agamben (ibid.: 69) argues is exemplified through the feast:

> [T]he feast is defined ... by the fact that what is done – which in itself is not unlike what one does every day – becomes undone, is rendered inoperative, liberated and suspended from its 'economy', from the reasons and purposes that define it during the weekdays.... If one eats, it is not done for the sake of being fed ... if one wakes up, it is not done for the sake of working ... if one exchanges objects, it is not done for the sake of selling or buying.

As we describe in the following section, even as the Shaheen Bagh model of citizenship employs destituent power, Muslim women, having experienced displacement and discrimination, also seek national belonging.

Women's Experiences of Partition Displacement and Early Citizenship

Virginia Woolf's (1938: 197) celebrated disavowals of nationalism, when she declared that 'as a woman I have no country. As a woman I want no country', do not capture the sentiments of those whom nation states threaten to exile or those who have been excluded from equal citizenship. Muslim women's affirmation of local and national belonging stems from their repeated and prolonged experiences of displacement and the fragmentation of family life during Partition.

Soon after Independence, India and Pakistan began efforts to 'recover' and 'rehabilitate' women on both sides of the border (Butalia 1998; Menon and Bhasin 1993). The two governments forced Muslim women who had married Hindu men and settled in India to return to Pakistan and Hindu women who had married Muslim men in Pakistan to return to India. The state forced many women who had already experienced dislocation as a result of Partition to relocate again. India's post-Independence government decided that women's citizenship should be determined by the religion of their families of origin. In 1949, it passed the Abducted Persons (Recovery and Restoration)

Act, which established a date after which women who had married men of different religions would be deemed forcibly abducted and returned to their families of origin. Ironically, despite its democratic proclamations, the Indian state denied women choices over where to live, whom to marry and how to raise their children. It ignored the protestations of Hindu women whose kin shunned them and who wanted to remain married to Muslim men in Pakistan. Niraja Jayal (2013: 76) writes: 'A powerful patriarchal nationalism informed such interpretations of the abducted woman's body as a metaphor for national purity, honor, and morality.'

Shaheen Bagh women's demands for citizenship should be located in the context of early citizenship laws which excluded Muslim women from independent citizenship. The first citizenship provisions in November 1949 were premised on the notion of 'domicile': men's domicile or residence in India was the basis of their citizenship, but women's citizenship was dependent on their father's or husband's residence.

While Muslim women's domicile was deemed irrelevant to their citizenship, it paradoxically determined whether their husbands were considered loyal citizens. In the aftermath of Partition, the Delhi administration determined that Muslim male employees with wives or children in Pakistan had to repatriate their families within a month or their employment would be terminated. Government documentation describes the loyalty of some Muslim government workers who could not repatriate their wives for financial and health-related reasons as 'doubtful' (Zamindar 2007: 106–119). These rulings established Muslim women's responsibility for their family's belonging. As the NPR, voicing long-standing suspicion over Muslim loyalty, characterizes without substantiation some people as 'doubtful' citizens (Mohanty 2019), Muslim women once again took on responsibility for protecting their family and community.

Today, even women who are national citizens are often unable to prove it. Sixty-nine per cent of the 1.9 million people in Assam who lacked citizenship papers when the NRC was updated in August 2019 were women (Bhowmick 2020). With lower literacy rates and fewer land titles in their names than men, most Indian women lack needed documentation, specifically education certificates and land titles. Women are likely to change their surnames and move from their place of birth upon marriage. Many women have only vague knowledge of where and when they were born and, even if they have documentation, do not travel with it. We interviewed Amandeep Kaur, general secretary of the women's group Stree Jagruti Manch, who participated in anti-CAA protests in Malerkotla. She commented that many women, especially Dalit women, are *pravasi* (expatriates). They lack documentation of their status and are often cast out by their in-laws after their husbands die. Domestic abuse may result in further displacement. Since under the NPR anyone can call on officials to question someone's citizenship, Kavita Krishnan, secretary of the All India Progressive Women's Association, warns that the NPR empowers abusive husbands to silence women, since by speaking up these women could lose citizenship (Bhowmick 2020).

Muslim women have experienced a long history of the state denying them citizenship rights and are mindful of the dangers associated with the BJP's attempt to render Muslims as outsiders. They have also borne inordinate responsibility for the well-being of their community because the Indian state has long suspected Muslim men of being disloyal, and within the current context, terrorists and Pakistani spies. Due to their prolonged and repeated experiences of displacement and their responsibility to recreate home thereafter, women are pivotal to creating community-based citizenship.

Personal Law: Women's Exclusion from Citizenship and the Public Sphere

Equal citizenship has been a normative ideal but a distant dream for Indian women. Although the Indian Constitution called for a Uniform Civil Code governing all citizens, the state was reluctant to offend religious communities by adopting it. It thus retained distinctive customary laws for members of the five major religious communities on matters related to the family. And in virtually all cases, these customary laws prescribed a subordinate status for women. Thus, from the start of the post-colonial period, women were treated as members of their religious communities rather than as rights-bearing individuals.

The most politically contentious issues concerned Muslim law. Whereas Hindu law was codified and reformed in the 1950s to provide more rights to women in marriage and divorce, Muslim succession and inheritance are still governed by the Muslim Personal Law (Shariat) Application Act, which the British government enacted in 1937 (Hasan 1998). The rights of Muslim women were sacrificed to the claim that Shariat law was a marker of Muslim community identity, as conservative Muslim clerics alleged when they opposed a 1986 Supreme Court decision which provided maintenance to Shah Bano after her husband divorced her (Bhargava 2004). They were also sacrificed to the political expedience of the Congress government that, fearing a loss of Muslim political support, passed the Muslim Women (Protection of Rights on Divorce) Act, 1986, which nullified the Supreme Court's decision. This Act increases women's financial dependence on their families and communities, stipulating that divorced Muslim women must be supported by relatives or *waqf* (charity) boards, 'anchor[ing] the dependency of women upon a male-dominated, hierarchical structure' (Benhabib 2002: 93). The BJP's attack on Muslim law as a means of deprecating the Muslim community further undermined Muslim women's abilities to defend their own interests (Hasan 1998).

Feminist theorists have argued that the public–private divide in liberal democracies confers full citizenship rights on men in the public sphere while relegating women to the subordinate, private domain (Pateman 1998). Thus, women must challenge private-sphere inequalities to achieve equal citizenship rights. However, for Muslim women to subscribe to liberal feminist ideals and oppose personal law risks disavowing their Muslim identity (Agnes 2018), Ghazala Jamil (2017: 98) writes:

> The common experience of communal discrimination along with violence (or the anticipation of violence) binds Muslim women and Muslim men together more strongly than the common experience of patriarchy binds Hindu women and Muslim women. The problem is that in the public sphere the Indian Muslim women's voice is merged, dissolved, and, thus, lost in the Muslim male voice, while the Muslim male voice is effectively silenced except when it is raised to curtail Muslim women's rights and freedom.

Gender-based discrimination through personal law and anti-Muslim violence force Muslim women to confront an agonizing dilemma: either demonstrating support for their beleaguered community or seeking to advance their individual rights. Gedalof (2003) emphasizes the importance of recognizing ethnic and communal bonds as being foundational to women's identities and experiences. She encourages an inclusive understanding of citizenship that recognizes the dynamic work that women do to form, maintain and rebuild community, thereby challenging the false dichotomy between mobile, public citizenship and static, private community.

Muslim women's experiences of unequal citizenship through personal law and their role in recreating home after displacement influenced their conceptions of citizenship. The politics of refusal (Gedalof 2003) was key to their resistance at Shaheen Bagh, as Muslim women refused to be located exclusively in the private sphere and rejected the false dichotomy between citizenship and community.

Like many other Muslim women activists, the Shaheen Bagh protesters rejected presumed incompatibilities between religious and secular goals. The All-India Muslim Women's Personal Law Board rejects patriarchal undertones of personal law without calling for a Uniform Civil Code, while the Mumbai-based non-governmental organization Aawaaz-e-Niswaan opposes triple *talaq* while promoting women's education, financial independence, and marital counselling (Vatuk 2008). For Muslim protesters, activism and faith were compatible. In our interview, journalist and author Ziya Us Salam recalled that women at the protest had said: 'If we do not do the right thing in this life, how will we stand before Allah? Allah is just, and to fight for justice is the calling of every human being.'

Shaheen Bagh activists have been inspired by a rich history of women's activism, as Amira Bashir, a Shaheen Bagh resident we interviewed, expressed: 'Lakshmibai and Begum Hazrat Mahal instigated the first fight for independence, and today women's voices have rung out across the world once again. This gives us pride and confidence.' They have been joined by women students at Jamia who have been active in protest movements for many years, starting with the 2012 movement against rape and continuing with the #MeToo campaign and the Pinjra Tod (Break the Cage) campaign against restrictive curfews on women students (Dixit 2019).

Gendered Modalities of Protest

Shaheen Bagh stands out from other anti-CAA protests for its duration, scale and the bonds it forged within and beyond the locality. We attribute these achievements to the protesters' use of gendered themes and images. We analyse three significant gendered modes of protest: the strategic use of motherhood, the feminization of politics and women's occupation of public space.

Motherhood

State violence is often a catalyst for women's activism. Women, highlighting their maternal roles, have mobilized against authoritarian states and demanded the reinstatement or strengthening of democracy in Israel, Russia, Argentina, Sri Lanka, the United States and Pakistan, among other places. Women who were not formerly politically active took to the streets to protect their husbands, sons and fathers in the Madres de la Plaza de Mayo in Argentina, the Mutual Support Group in Guatemala and the Association of Families of the Detained-Disappeared (Agrupacion) in Chile. The 'Wall of Moms' which emerged in Portland, Oregon, to oppose the Trump administration's deployment of federal troops in the city and police brutality against Black people has opened chapters in St Louis, New York, Chicago, Philadelphia, and Washington, DC (Lang 2020).

In India, mothers have been at the forefront of protests against the government's repressive actions in Kashmir, Assam and other northeastern states (Nepram 2017). In Kashmir, the women-led Association of the Parents of the Disappeared Persons in 1994 documented and resisted the disappearance of Muslim men (Osuri and Fatima 2020). The Mothers of Manipur protested against legislation that protected rapists in the Indian army. At Shaheen Bagh, mothers were the first to take to the streets in response to police violence against their children and other university students.

Through maternal and gendered frames, Muslim women can resist state violence when it would be counterproductive for men to do so because Hindu nationalists have demonized Muslim men as violent abductors of Hindu women and patriarchal oppressors of Muslim women. Zemlinskaya Yulia (2010) argues that mothers are successful in resisting oppressive and violent states because they are considered apolitical and less threatening than men. Strategic maternal framing enables them to peacefully resist police violence and state repression. A viral video clip of female students at Jamia protecting a male student from police violence offers an emotive depiction of gender framing (Kuchay 2019). In another instance of strategic maternalism, women in Bengaluru shielded male protesters from arrest in December 2019 (G. Menon 2019).

Protesters at Shaheen Bagh were politicized by witnessing police brutality against their children at universities. In our interview, Farida Ayub said: 'Only mothers know the depth of pain they feel ... mothers have a unique *junoon* [passion]; they were the only ones capable of this resistance.' Zaara Hashmi, a protester at Shaheen Bagh, told us: 'All the inappropriate comments on television motivated more women to come out onto the streets.... If you abuse her children she will become a lioness, a snake, Kali, Durga; she will become anything to protect her children, her future and her self-respect.'

Women who engage in grassroots activism often develop an expansive understanding of motherhood. As Pnina Werbner (1999: 221) argues, they anchor maternalism within democratic values and engage in active citizenship through 'political motherhood'. By denigrating certain mothers, repressive states inadvertently create the space for counter-mobilization by their female critics. Hindu nationalists depict Muslim women as subservient to male domination and lacking agency. While belittling Muslim mothers, they idealize Hindu mothers in telling stories, like those of Jijabai, who encouraged her son, the seventeenth-century Hindu leader Shivaji, to resist Muslim rule and fight for a Hindu nation (K. D. Menon 2010).

Activists denaturalize categories of identity when they employ them politically to achieve social transformation. Motherhood acquires entirely different connotations when it is a tactic for opposing a repressive, rights-denying state than when it idealizes women's domestic roles within the private domain. At Shaheen Bagh, women link their responsibilities as mothers to their responsibility for national well-being. They speak of their duty to prevent legislation and police brutality that threaten their children's right to live in India.

The protesters challenge Modi's claims to serve as father and protector of the nation. One woman criticized his 'Beti Bachao, Beti Padhao' ('Save the Daughter, Educate the Daughter') campaign for girls' welfare: 'You [Modi] say "beti bachao, beti padhao" – today your daughters are sitting on the streets in protest. It has been an entire month, have you not seen that your daughters are out on the streets and should be able to return to their homes?' (NDTV 2020b). While Modi argues that his lack of familial ties makes the nation his family, some protesters question the ability of childless BJP leaders to care for the nation (*Indian Express* 2020). Even as protesters criticized Modi, Shaheen Bagh *dadi* (grandmother) Asma Khatoon magnanimously said: 'We are [Modi's] mother; he is my child. He should not trouble us like this. If we curse him even once, he will burn to dust. But a mother's soul is such that she can never wish harm to her child' (Mojo Story 2020).

Shaheen Bagh women transformed traditional motherhood into political motherhood by demonstrating that they, rather than Modi, were protecting the nation. In doing so, they challenged traditional understandings of the public–private divide and state policy in both spheres.

Feminization of Politics

Feminine politics represents a powerful alternative to the masculinist, right-wing populist politics that Modi and the militaristic RSS and its affiliates champion. Even female Hindu nationalist leaders, like Sadhvi Rithambara, Uma Bharati and Pragya Singh Thakur, engage in aggressive, muscular displays of strength (Basu 1999). Sikata Banerjee (2005) argues that they must shed markers of femininity to engage in masculinized Hindutva politics. Even when Modi embodies feminine traits, his goals are majoritarian (Basu 2021). According to Karuna Nandy, a prominent lawyer who has spoken against CAA at multiple demonstrations:

[T]he rise of Hindutva has been powered in part by a toxic masculinity. A lot of the imagery and action around it is very macho, violent, explicitly supremacist and hostile to women.... What we are seeing in some women's leadership and at Shaheen Bagh is an energy that's gentler. It's happier, more nurturing and yet strong and determined.

And I think that is really speaking to the country as a counter to the toxic masculinity of Hindutva. (Ellis-Peterson and Rahman 2020)

The differences between feminine and masculine nationalisms are strikingly evident in the celebration of Republic Day at Shaheen Bagh. Three local elderly women, known as the Shaheen Bagh *dadi*s, hoisted the flag, projecting matriarchal authority. The gathering was joyous and festive. Street vendors sold balloons, toys and food (*The Wire* 2020b). Ziya Us Salam called the Republic Day celebration at Shaheen Bagh a 'heartwarming sight for democracy'. As he told us, 'We tend to equate our patriotism on Republic Day with only the prime minister and other government leaders – here it was just the common women of Shaheen Bagh who were hoisting the national flag'. Contrast this with the official 2020 Republic Day celebration, featuring Jair Bolsanaro as chief guest, which was grim, tightly rehearsed and heavily policed.

Darab Farooqui's protest poem, 'Naam Shaheen Bagh Hai' ('The Name is Shaheen Bagh'), describes feminine modalities of protest that imbue the movement with warmth, love and support. He reveres the women who 'sacrificed' their homes to make the sit-in their collective home and invites us to 'warm [our] hands with the warmth of [protesters'] hearts'. Farooqui uses inclusive feminine motifs, including the *hijab* and the *dupatta*, draws on the legacy of revolutionary women like Lakshmibai and likens women's perseverance and optimism to 'wounds break[ing] into a smile'. Women's patience through a prolonged sit-in contrasts sharply with confrontational, masculinist political engagement (*The Quint* 2020a).

Other protest poetry emphasizes non-confrontational, emotive protest. The widespread popularity of Faiz Ahmad Faiz's poem 'Hum Dekhenge' amongst anti-CAA protesters demonstrates transnational solidarity amongst women protesters: it was popularized when Iqbal Bano sang it in Lahore, Pakistan, in 1986, to protest Zia-ul-Haq's military regime (Singh 2019). The poem's revolutionary history refutes public perceptions of Muslim women's passivity.

Appeals to feminine principles may seem antithetical to feminism, which seeks to challenge women's sex-linked roles. However, activists who feminize the public sphere demonstrate a critical understanding of how the Modi government weaponizes masculinity. Their expressions of femininity mobilized support, created community and encouraged resilience at Shaheen Bagh.

Women's Occupation of Public Space

Globally, there are many instances of women staging sit-ins to peacefully protest militarization and state violence, including the Greenham Common Women's Peace Camp to protest the storage of cruise missiles in Berkshire, England (1981–2000) (Stead 2006), and weekly Women in Black protests, which Israeli women organized to oppose human rights violations by Israeli soldiers in the Occupied Territories (1988–1993).

The Shaheen Bagh protest is another chapter in India's long history of women's occupation of public space to resist displacement. Women were at the forefront of the Chipko movement against deforestation (Jain 1984), protests against the construction of the Narmada dam which threatened to submerge thousands of villages and displace their inhabitants (Huggler 2009) and opposition to the threatened demolition of shantytowns (Appadurai 2001).

Shaheen Bagh protesters linked their sit-in to their right to retain their homes, citizenship and nationality. As Lucy Jackson (2016: 5) theorizes, groups excluded from state-defined citizenry experience 'emotive citizenship', 'situated within their everyday intimate lives', and linked to physical belonging, rooted in the 'here' of home. Asma Khatoon refused to be removed from the protest site because she would not allow the BJP to tell her that India 'is not [her] home after 90 years' (Ellis-Peterson and Rahman 2020). Amira Bashir told us: 'The whole country is our home. We are in the homes of our ancestors; we don't know how many generations of our family have passed through this home. And now we are being asked: is this your home or not? It brings tears to my eyes.'

Women's sit-ins have important implications for women's visibility. Orna Sasson-Levy and Tamar Rappoport (2003: 399) describe the transformative nature of Women in Black's occupation of public space:

> By forcing the public sphere to take notice of what was supposed to remain hidden, the women asserted identities that were denied them. Thus, the women's mode of protest opened up the political discourse

by redefining who is a legitimate political participant and what is the legitimate manner of participation. This mode of protest blurs existing gender distinctions and enables women to transgress them.

The Shaheen Bagh protest created what Farida Ayub called *bedari* (an awakening) about women's public roles. She said: 'People have understood that when women raise their voices they strengthen and elevate communities.' Zaara Hashmi told us:

When we're in our homes, we can't be heard, but on the streets we can. Women were already aware, that is why they came out to protest. The movement made society realise that a woman's purpose is not just to have children and cook food. We can do a lot for this nation. We have capabilities that are suppressed, and [the protests] have created an atmosphere in which every woman can realize her potential.

Feminist themes emerged over the course of the sit-in. A poster at Shaheen Bagh read: 'Ab nari ke naron se inquilab ayega' ('Women's slogans will herald the uprising'). A frequently heard chant in Shaheen Bagh, 'Meri behne mange azaadi / Hai haq hamara, azaadi / Hum leke rahenge, azaadi' ('My sisters demand freedom / Freedom is our right / We will claim freedom, come what may'), has been a slogan of women's movements in South Asia for several decades. *Azaadi* refers to freedom from both patriarchal and state oppression (R. Menon 2020).

Reflecting on these chants, a Muslim woman activist commented:

Not only do we demand scrapping of the CAA, NRC and NPR, we are also looking at the larger picture. Women here are also voicing their demand for freedom to move freely and fearlessly, the liberty to study, freedom to pursue their vocation and profession of choice and even the freedom to choose whom to marry. (*Outlook* 2020)

The protests at Shaheen Bagh compel us to expand our understanding of feminism. Unlike many feminist movements, this one does not challenge women's domestic roles or seek women's autonomy from the family. To the contrary, women in Shaheen Bagh emphasize maternal roles in their resistance, challenging the false dichotomy between their private and public lives. Women's desires for national freedom give expression to their desire for freedom as women. The complementarity of these two goals is evident not just from activists' pronouncements but also from the performative and embodied character of the sit-in.

Linking Citizenship to Community and Civil Society

Contrary to Partha Chatterjee's (2004) view that civil society in the postcolonial world is characterized by elitist, statist values, whereas political society is the domain of subaltern politics, the Shaheen Bagh protesters tether what he terms political and civil society. They believe in the progressive potential of the courts and law but maintain that citizenship entails civic responsibility for community welfare. They lament public disregard for the lives of the poor and ask the government to improve living standards in their neighbourhood, emphasizing that 'enshrined alongside their right to life and citizenship, is the inalienable right to a life of dignity, and these seemingly smaller issues are also an indicator of how [they] are treated as lesser citizens' (Shaheen Bagh Official 2020a).

The protesters recognized that the CAA and the NRC formalize economic inequality through unequal citizenship. The new laws disproportionately impact poor people, who often lack the documentation needed to prove citizenship. Since income inequality is uneven across communities, these laws also target Dalits and Adivasis. As Ijaz Farooq, co-convener of 'Haa Da Naara Sangharsh Morcha', a collaboration of youth organizations in Punjab told us, poor communities are especially likely to lose documents in states like Orissa, Bihar and Assam, which experience frequent natural disasters. Amira Bashir argued that poor people would lose crucial working hours and employment if they spent time searching for documentation for the NRC.

Shaheen Bagh activists question the BJP's narrative of economic progress and call for improvements in public housing and civic amenities. As Amira Bashir told us, protesters criticize the government for investing millions of rupees in the NPR and the NRC rather than funding programmes for women and the poor: 'There is no budget for *tabdeeli* (progress or change), and poor people will suffer ... the government should use funds to support migrant workers, and rape and child abuse victims. They should improve rural healthcare; even today poor people are dying because there are no doctors in their villages.'

In highlighting the links between citizenship and the concerns of low-income, marginalized communities, the protesters showed that, far from being empty abstractions, citizenship rights are crucial to peoples' security and well-being. As Martha A. Acklesberg and Myrna Margulies Breitbart (1987–1988) argue, multifocal social movements that address broad socioeconomic concerns, especially 'quality of life' issues, often produce radical collective consciousness. Women, who often organize these movements, recognize and demystify the connections between oppression in the family, community and the nation. By refusing these separations, the Shaheen Bagh protest 'reduce[d] participants' distance from the facts of their lives, enabling them to recognise the significance of the larger social context in which their oppression takes place' (ibid.: 172).

Activists at Shaheen Bagh not only demanded welfare from the state but also made the community at the sit-in responsible for the care of all those who were present. The protesters thus engaged in what Acklesberg and Breitbart (ibid.: 173) term 'active participation in community institutions and in struggles to create alternative public spheres', which transformed common conceptions of citizenship, community and belonging.

The protesters provided shelter and food to the homeless. Sikhs created a *langar* at the protest site. (The *langar* is a community kitchen in Sikh temples which serves free meals to all visitors, regardless of their religion, caste, class and gender.) Protesters created a health centre at the sit-in, through the support of volunteer doctors and donations (*The Quint* 2020b). Concerned for their children's education, as student protester Maya Bhagat told us, some protesters spent their entire day in the 'children's corner' at Shaheen Bagh, teaching children to draw and read and telling them stories. As author and activist Farah Naqvi told us, responsibilities for cleaning, cooking and taking care of children were shared by men and women, rich and poor.

By emphasizing civic responsibility, the protesters affirmed what Paulina Ochoa Espejo (2016) identifies as place-specific duties, which are based solely on a person's presence in a particular place and, as Espejo argues, call for a 'right to stay' in a place, independent of citizenship rights. When protesters engaged in mutual care, they embodied belonging and a 'right to stay' that transcended citizenship on the basis of *jus soli* or *jus sanguinis*.

The protesters also subverted traditional gender, religious and class roles to create an egalitarian space. Ziya Us Salam and Uzma Ausaf (2020) observe that women from middle-class homes and their domestic workers sat together at the protest, creating cross-class solidarity. Jamia students and older Shaheen Bagh residents fostered cross-generational bonds, which deepened a collective political consciousness among protesters. As student protester Sunil Chatterjee told us: 'These [older residents] are the people with whom we have eaten and sat with; we've had discussions about Faiz, about Manto ... [about] Agha Shahid Ali, Ghalib. That is what binds us together.' The protesters recited scriptures from the Geeta, the Bible, the Quran and the Guru Granth Sahib, as well as poems by revolutionary poets such as Pash, Habib Jalib, Muhammad Iqbal and Ramdhari Singh Dinkar (*The Week* 2020). In her interview, Zaara Hashmi quoted lines from Iqbal's 'Tarana-e-Hindi' ('Anthem of the People of Hindustan'): 'Religion does not teach us to bear animosity among ourselves. We are of Hind, our homeland is Hindusthan.'

These acts of equality and inclusion forged a community that welcomed different identities, further extended the scope and concerns of the protest and broadened notions of belonging. The protesters embodied what Kenneth Plummer (2003: 72) describes as 'intimate citizenship', which does not 'imply one voice, one way, or one model. On the contrary, it ... designates an array of stories and a multiplicity of voices, in which different lives, different communities, and different politics dwell'. As Farah Naqvi told us, 'for those who participated it was a moment of absolute conviction that this was [their] fight too' and not simply solidarity with Muslims. Zaara Hashmi emphasized the empowering unity protesters experienced as they took a stand for the entire nation: 'Everyone fought their own fight. Nobody fought as *ehsaan* (a favour) for anyone else. Everyone came together.'

The destituent elements of the protest empowered participants to raise further concerns and acquire agency in calling for change. Sikh farmers who belonged to the Bharatiya Kisan Union and travelled from Punjab to attend the Shaheen Bagh protest encouraged Sikh–Muslim unity and criticized the BJP government for failing to address agrarian distress, such as indebtedness, which has led to farmers' suicides (A. Menon 2020). Trans activists joined the protest, using Shaheen Bagh's platform to raise awareness about transgender rights in opposition to both the CAA and the new Transgender Persons (Protection of Rights) Bill, 2019, which requires that people provide proof of gender confirmation surgery to be registered as transgender (Sarfaraz 2020). Even some BJP supporters, like Saksham Mishra from Kanpur, joined the protest because, in Mishra's words, they felt that the new laws were polarizing the country and were an 'assault on the cultural fabric of the nation' (Mishra 2020). Shaheen Bagh became not just a physical space but symbolic of a broader anti-CAA movement that identified citizenship with community and collective accountability.

As protesters forged community and civic responsibility outside the boundaries of the state and state-mediated civil space, they embodied key features of destituent power. Their calls for social change transcended single-issue demands that could be met through reform. Protesters refused to provide a platform for political parties, disavowed external financial support, and created their own, independent Citizens' Charter. It states: 'Our struggle has been for an inclusive and participatory form of citizenship based on values of mutual empathy, care, and dignity. Now that we are called upon to show our commitment to these values, we shall rise to the occasion' (India Legal 2020). As they circumvented constituent power by creating sociopolitical space outside the purview of the state, they demonstrated the possibility of non-exclusionary belonging.

Conclusion

In concluding we demonstrate how Shaheen Bagh provides a model for opposing the ideologies and practices that undergird right-wing populism and religious nationalism in India.

Whereas most protests remain confined to the distinctive cultural and political conditions in the localities where they emerge, Shaheen Bagh inspired similar protests across the country, in Gaya, Kolkata, Prayagraj, Mumbai, Bengaluru, Lucknow, Patna, Jaipur, Bhopal, Malerkotla and other places (*The Quint* 2020c). Maya Bhagat told us that those who could not visit Shaheen Bagh regularly staged sit-ins wherever they lived and thereby created 'local Shaheen Baghs'. Ziya Us Salam recounted a popular slogan: 'Har shehar Shaheen Bagh' ('Every city, Shaheen Bagh').

The protesters challenge exclusionary principles that some scholars consider intrinsic to nationalism. Political theorist George Kateb argues that nationalism and patriotism are premised on group particularism and hence hatred of national Others (Kateb 2006). Kateb captures the exclusionary character of right-wing populism and religious nationalism, which identify the nation with the beliefs and practices of the Hindu majority, but not the inclusionary nationalism of Shaheen Bagh.

Shaheen Bagh activists displayed the national flag, recited the national anthem and repeatedly expressed their national loyalties, while proudly affirming that they were both Muslim and secular. They contested Hindu nationalists' claims that their religious beliefs trumped their nationalist commitments, and as Hilal Ahmed (2020) argues, they broadened Indian nationalism to include Muslim identities:

> [Protesters'] creative re-articulating of symbolic nationalism takes us beyond the given imaginations of Muslim political identity. The Muslim community, which is often treated as religiously inward-looking and politically untrustworthy (or *siyasi*), is reasserting its Muslim-ness as an inseparable part of the Indian identity. And precisely for this reason, creating a binary between Islamic belief and patriotism of Muslims is a [sectarian], anti-national agenda.

The Shaheen Bagh protest prefigured an alternative model of the state and civil society to the one the RSS and its affiliates are promoting. These Hindu nationalist organizations provide preferential social service to Hindus, conjoin Hinduism and nationalism, and police people's diets, religious practices and sexual relations. Right-wing populism in India, as elsewhere, thrives on sowing fear and distrust of internal and external enemies.

Shaheen Bagh activists opposed the BJP's conflation of 'the people' with Hindus by demonstrating the shared values and interests of all people. They expressed their support for Kashmiri pandits (Brahmin Hindus) who were forced to migrate out of the state when they were targeted by militant groups in the 1990s. When BJP supporter and filmmaker Vivek Agnihotri claimed that the protesters of Shaheen Bagh would celebrate 'Kashmiri Hindu Genocide Day' on 19 January 2020, the protesters organized a meeting in which they observed a two-minute silence to express solidarity with the Kashmiri pandits. They invited two prominent Kashmiri pandits, performance artist Inder Salim and theatre personality M. K. Raina, to speak at the gathering (Ashraf 2020). As a rejoinder to Modi's claim that you can identify those who engage in violence 'by their clothes' (*The Quint* 2019), Sikh and Muslim protesters exchanged their turbans and skullcaps. In doing so, they disputed Modi's attempt to create identity-based dichotomies between lawful and unlawful citizens and demonstrated the fluidity and coexistence of different and equal identities.

The protesters called attention to the way the government diverts attention from domestic problems by heightening fears of terrorism and Pakistani aggression. By highlighting the government's neglect of the poor, they questioned its populist claims to serve the common person. By taking on the task of providing for the welfare of the local community, they challenged the discriminatory and opportunistic bases on which Hindu nationalists engage in the provision of social services.

The protesters' expansive understanding of belonging and community evokes Agamben's (2007) prefigurative vision for an inclusive community based on unconditional belonging that neither excludes particular identities nor ignores them in favour of an abstract, universal identity. Rather, it accepts and includes people exactly as they are, with all their particular identities and traits. Through unconditional belonging, the Shaheen Bagh protest holds prefigurative potential to contest the basis of statelessness upon which the CAA and the NRC rest. As 'humans co-belong without any representable condition of belonging' (ibid.: 86), they challenge the conditions the nation-state places on inclusion and reveal its refusal to protect the stateless. Agamben (ibid.) concludes: 'A being radically devoid of any representable identity would be absolutely irrelevant to the State. This is what, in our culture, the hypocritical dogma of the sacredness of human life and the vacuous declarations of human rights are meant to hide.'

The state prevented Shaheen Bagh protesters from meeting their immediate goals by destroying the protest site in March 2020, arresting several activists and preventing public gatherings there (Lama 2020). The Supreme Court deemed prolonged occupation of public space unlawful (Krishnan 2020). However, Shaheen Bagh remains a potential, replete with destituent possibilities and ideational value in India's political imaginary.

Zaara Hashmi emphasized the protest's power as a historic symbol of resistance:

> When our children ask us, 'Where were you all when this was happening?', we can say, 'We were sitting on the streets fighting for you.' In this, we were successful: that we can look the next generation in the eye without shame and know that with whatever life we had in us, we fought.

In considering alternatives to right-wing populism and religious nationalism, we are moved by the ability of inclusive, peaceful protest to empower its targets and to challenge the normalization of hatred and violence. The official Twitter page for the Shaheen Bagh protest says: 'To speak for sanity, peace, dignity, justice and equality should be normalised, not violence and targeting' (Shaheen Bagh Official 2020b). We conclude by celebrating the power of marshalling empathy and kindness to overcome fear and foster community across markers of difference.

Bibliography

Acklesberg, M. A., and M. M. Breitbart (1987–1988). 'Terrains of Protest: Striking City Women'. *Our Generation* 19, no. 1: 151–175.

Agamben, G. (1998). *Homo Sacer: Sovereign Power and Bare Life*. Stanford, CA: Stanford University Press.

———. (2007). *The Coming Community*. Minneapolis, MN: University of Minnesota Press.

———. (2014). 'What Is Destituent Power?' *Environment and Planning D: Society and Space* 32, no. 1: 65–74. DOI: https://doi.org/10.1068/d3201tra.

Agnes, F. (2018). 'The Politics Behind Criminalising Triple Talaq'. *Economics and Political Weekly* 53, no. 1: 12–14.

Ahmed, H. (2020). 'Who Represents India's Muslims? Thanks to CAA Protests, We Now Know the Answer'. *The Print*, 17 January. https://theprint.in/

opinion/who-represents-indias-muslims-thanks-to-caa-protests-we-now-know-the-answer/350709/. Accessed on 24 June 2021.

Ansari, S., and W. Gould (2019). *Boundaries of Belonging: Localities, Citizenship and Rights in India and Pakistan*. Cambridge: Cambridge University Press. DOI: https://doi.org/10.1017/9781108164511.

Appadurai, A. (2001). 'Deep Democracy: Urban Governmentality and the Horizon of Politics'. *Environment and Urbanization* 13, no. 2: 23–43.

Arendt, H. (1973). *The Origins of Totalitarianism*. New York: Harcourt Brace & Company.

Ashraf, A. (2020). 'Shaheen Bagh Protesters Express Solidarity with Kashmiri Pandits on Exodus Day'. *India Today*, 20 January. https://www.indiatoday.in/india/story/kashmiri-pandits-exodusday-migration-refugees-1638294-2020-01-19. Accessed on 24 June 2021.

Aziz, A. (2019). 'My Name Is Aamir Aziz, Ask Me About Myself'. Karwan e Mohabbat, YouTube video, 4:37. https://www.youtube.com/watch?v=gyfCt-8J2jA. Accessed on 24 June 2021.

Banerjee, S. (2005). *Make Me a Man! Masculinity, Hinduism, and Nationalism in India*. Albany: State University of New York Press.

Basu, A. (1999). 'Women's Activism and the Vicissitudes of Hindu Nationalism'. *Journal of Women's History*, 10, no. 4: 104–124.

———. (2021). 'Many Right-wing Populists Strut Their Manliness. Why Does India's Modi Stress His Softer Side?' *Washington Post*, 26 May. https://www.washingtonpost.com/politics/2021/05/26/many-right-wing-populists-strut-their-manliness-why-does-indias-modi-stress-his-softer-side/. Accessed on 24 June 2021.

BBC News (2019). 'India Puts 1.9m People at Risk of Statelessness'. 31 August. https://www.bbc.com/news/world-asia-india-49520593. Accessed on 24 June 2021.

Benhabib, S. (2002). *The Claims of Culture: Equality and Diversity in the Global Era*. Princeton: Princeton University Press.

Bhargava, R. (2004). 'The Majority–Minority Syndrome and Muslim Personal Law in India'. In *The Fate of the Nation-state*, edited by M. Seymour, 327–356. Montreal: McGill-Queen's University Press.

Bhowmick, N. (2020). 'India's New Laws Hurt Women Most of All'. *Foreign Policy*, 4 February. https://foreignpolicy.com/2020/02/04/india-citizenship-law-women/. Accessed on 24 June 2021.

Butalia, U. (1994). 'Community, State and Gender: Some Reflections on the Partition of India'. *Oxford Literary Review* 16, no. 1: 33–67. DOI: https://doi.org/10.3366/olr.1994.002.

---. (1998). *The Other Side of Silence: Voices from the Partition of India*. Navi Mumbai: Penguin Books India.

Chakravarty, I. (2019). 'The Daily Fix: The BJP Owes It to India to Honestly Explain Its Stand on a Nationwide NRC'. *Scroll.in*, 24 December. https://scroll.in/article/947715/the-daily-fix-the-bjp-owes-it-to-india-to-honestly-explain-its-stand-on-a-nationwide-nrc. Accessed on 24 June 2021.

Chatterjee, P. (2004). *The Politics of the Governed*. New York: Columbia University Press.

De, R. (2018). *A People's Constitution: The Everyday Life of Law in the Indian Republic*. Princeton: Princeton University Press.

Dixit, N. (2019). 'The Women at the Front Lines of India's Citizenship Law Protests'. *Al Jazeera*, 23 December. https://www.aljazeera.com/features/2019/12/23/the-women-at-the-front-lines-of-indias-citizenship-law-protests/?gb=true. Accessed on 24 June 2021.

Dutta, P. K. (2019). 'Jinnah or Congress, Who Partitioned India in BJP Book of History?' *India Today*, 10 December. https://www.indiatoday.in/news-analysis/story/jinnah-or-congress-who-partitioned-india-in-bjp-book-of-history-1627030-2019-12-10. Accessed on 24 June 2021.

Ellis-Petersen, H., and S. A. Rahman (2020). '"Modi Is Afraid": Women Take Lead in India's Citizenship Protests'. *The Guardian*, 21 January. https://www.theguardian.com/world/2020/jan/21/modi-is-afraid-women-take-lead-in-indias-citizenship-protests. Accessed on 24 June 2021.

Espejo, P. O. (2016). 'Taking Place Seriously: Territorial Presence and the Rights of Immigrants'. *Journal of Political Philosophy* 24, no. 1: 67–87.

Farooqi, F. (2020). 'To Better Understand the Shaheen Bagh Protest, We Must Understand the Locality Itself'. *The Caravan*, 20 January. https://caravanmagazine.in/politics/shaheen-bagh-locality-caa-protest. Accessed on 24 June 2021.

Fernando, B. (2020). 'Reading the Signs'. *Indian Express*, 5 January. https://indianexpress.com/article/express-sunday-eye/reading-the-signs-caa-nrc-jamia-ambedkar-constitution-india-narendra-modi-amit-shah-muslims-6196347/. Accessed on 24 June 2021.

Foucault, M. (1982). 'The Subject and Power'. Afterword in H. Dreyfus and P. Rabinow, *Michel Foucault: Beyond Structuralism and Hermeneutics*. London: Harvester Wheatsheaf.

Gedalof, I. (2003). 'Taking (a) Place: Female Embodiment and the Re-grounding of Community'. In *Uprootings/Regroundings: Questions of Home and Migration*, edited by S. Ahmed, C. Castaneda, A. M. Fortier and M. Sheller, 91–112. New York: Berg Publishers.

Hasan, Z. (1998). 'Gender Politics, Legal Reform, and the Muslim Community'. In *Appropriating Gender: Women's Activism and Politicized Religion in South Asia*, edited by P. Jeffery and A. Basu, 71–88. New York: Routledge.

Hirschberger, G. (2018). 'Collective Trauma and the Social Construction of Meaning'. *Frontiers in Psychology* 9, no. 1441. DOI: 10.3389/fpsyg.2018.01441.

Huggler, J. (2009). 'One-Woman Protest Helps Halt Huge Indian Dam Project'. *Independent*, 2 April. https://www.independent.co.uk/news/world/asia/one-woman-protest-helps-halt-huge-indian-dam-project-6103415.html. Accessed on 24 June 2021.

India Legal (2020). 'A Letter Addressed to the Judges of Supreme Court by "the People of Shaheen Bagh"'. 26 March. https://www.indialegallive.com/top-news-of-the-day/news/letter-addressed-judges-supreme-court-people-shaheen-bagh/. Accessed on 24 June 2021.

Indian Express (2020). 'Our Men Are with Us: Shaheen Bagh Women Respond to Yogi Adityanath'. YouTube video, 24 January, 3:36. https://www.youtube.com/watch?v=qhtiN76zuZA. Accessed on 24 June 2021.

India Today (2019). 'Time to Punish Tukde-Tukde Gang for Anti-CAA Violence in Delhi: Amit Shah'. 26 December. https://www.indiatoday.in/india/story/time-to-punish-tukde-tukde-gang-for-anti-caa-violence-in-delhi-amit-shah-1631655-2019-12-26. Accessed on 24 June 2021.

Jackson, L. (2016). 'Intimate Citizenship? Rethinking the Politics and Experience of Citizenship as Emotional in Wales and Singapore'. *Gender, Place and Culture* 23, no. 6: 817–833. DOI: https://doi.org/10.1080/0966369X.2015.1073695.

Jain, S. (1984). 'Women and People's Ecological Movement: A Case Study of Women's Role in the Chipko Movement in Uttar Pradesh'. *Economic and Political* Weekly 19, no. 41: 1788–1794.

Jamil, G. (2018). *Muslim Women Speak: Of Dreams and Shackles*. New Delhi: SAGE Publications India.

Jayal, N. G. (2013). *Citizenship and Its Discontents*. Cambridge (MA): Harvard University Press.

Kateb, G. (2006). *Patriotism and Other Mistakes*. New Haven (CT): Yale University Press.

Krishnan, M. (2020). 'Can't Occupy Indefinitely, Says Supreme Court on Shaheen Bagh'. *Hindustan Times*, 8 October. https://www.hindustantimes.com/india-news/can-t-occupy-indefinitely-says-supreme-court-on-shaheen-bagh/story-IIT5EU5GMn9CujGGX2ZoSL.html. Accessed on 24 June 2021.

Kuchay, B. (2019). 'Meet India's Jamia Women Who Took on Delhi Police in Viral Video'. *Al Jazeera*, 17 December. https://www.aljazeera.com/

news/2019/12/17/meet-indias-jamia-women-who-took-on-delhi-police-in-viral-video/. Accessed on 24 June 2021.

Lama, P. (2020). 'An Uneasy Calm in Shaheen Bagh, One Year After Protest'. *Hindustan Times*, 17 December. https://www.hindustantimes.com/india-news/an-uneasy-calm-in-shaheen-bagh-one-year-after-protest/story-ICbGQmdhTarXDLa8PbekiN.html. Accessed on 24 June 2021.

Lang, M. J. (2020). 'Wall of Moms' Groups, Inspired by Portland Protesters, Emerge in New York, Chicago and D.C.' *Washington Post*, 22 July. https://www.washingtonpost.com/nation/2020/07/22/portland-moms-protests/. Accessed on 24 June 2021.

Meharban, Md. (2020). 'Shoot the Traitors: Discrimination Against Muslims under India's New Citizenship Policy'. Human Rights Watch, 9 April. https://www.hrw.org/report/2020/04/09/shoot-traitors/discrimination-against-muslims-under-indias-new-citizenship-policy. Accessed on 24 June 2021.

Menon, A. (2020). 'United by Grief: Why Sikhs and Punjab Farmers Are at Shaheen Bagh'. *The Quint*, 20 February. https://www.thequint.com/news/politics/shaheen-bagh-sikh-farmers-punjab-langar-muslims-caa-nrc-protests. Accessed on 24 June 2021.

Menon, G. (2019). 'Bengaluru Women Form Human Chain to Shield Anti-CAA Protesters from Being Detained'. InUth, 23 December. https://www.inuth.com/india/bengaluru-women-form-human-chain-to-shield-anti-caa-protesters-from-getting-detained/. Accessed on 24 June 2021.

Menon, K. D. (2010). *Everyday Nationalism: Women of the Hindu Right in India*. Philadelphia: University of Pennsylvania Press.

Menon, R. (2020). 'Anti-CAA Protests by Muslim Women Are about Where, How and Why You Belong'. *Indian Express*, 4 February. https://indianexpress.com/article/opinion/columns/shaheen-bagh-anti-caa-protest-mother-india-6249503/. Accessed on 24 June 2021.

Menon, R., and K. Bhasin (1993). 'Recovery, Rupture, Resistance: Indian State and Abduction of Women during Partition'. *Economic and Political Weekly* 28, no. 17: WS2–11.

Mishra, S. (2020). 'I Am a BJP Supporter but I Oppose the CAA. And I'm Not Alone'. Arré, 16 January 2020. https://www.arre.co.in/pov/i-am-a-bjp-supporter-but-i-oppose-the-caa-nrc/. Accessed on 24 June 2021.

Mohanty, P. (2019). 'CAA & NRC III: Who Are "Doubtful" Citizens NPR Seeks to Identify?' *Business Today*, 24 December. https://www.businesstoday.in/current/economy-politics/caa-nrc-iii-who-are-doubtful-citizens-npr-seeks-to-identify/story/392587.html. Accessed on 24 June 2021.

Mojo Story (2020). 'Shaheen Bagh's Oldest Protester, Asma Khatoon Who Took Legal Action against Head of BJP IT Cell'. YouTube video, 20 January, 5:37. https://www.youtube.com/watch?v=KfKmqlFzTh0. Accessed on 24 June 2021.

NDTV (2020a). 'Ravish's Ground Report on the Unshakeable Women of Delhi's Shaheen Bagh'. NDTV, YouTube video, 9 January, 39:16. https://www.youtube.com/watch?v=TQm7nBa49WQ&ab_channel=NDTV. Accessed on 24 June 2021.

———. (2020b). 'Versus | Shaheen Bagh Protesters vs Residents Over Road Block'. NDTV, YouTube video, 13 January, 13:49. https://www.youtube.com/watch?v=bPjiH_X2unE&t=618s. Accessed on 24 June 2021.

Nepram, B. (2017). 'Indigenous Women of Northeast India at the Forefront of a Strong Non-Violent Peace Movement'. In *Indigenous Peoples' Rights and Unreported Struggles: Conflict and Peace*, edited by E. Stamatopoulou, 109–121. New York: Institute for the Study of Human Rights, Columbia University. DOI: https://doi.org/10.7916/D8QC1B36.

Osuri, G., and I. Fatima. (2020). 'A Provisional Biography of a Journey Towards Justice for the Enforced Disappeared'. Association of Parents of Disappeared Persons, Kashmir, 2 February. https://apdpkashmir.com/ebmedia/sitename_eb/wp-content/uploads/2020/02/APDP-biography-02-02-2020.pdf. Accessed on 24 June 2021.

Outlook (2020). 'A Shaheen Bagh in Kolkata's Park Circus'. 17 January. https://www.outlookindia.com/newsscroll/a-shaheen-bagh-in-kolkatas-park-circus/1711076. Accessed on 24 June 2021.

Pardiwalla, T. (2019). 'Anti-CAA Protests Have Inspired Some Creative and Powerful Artwork'. Mashable India, 23 December. https://in.mashable.com/culture/9738/anti-caa-protests-have-inspired-some-creative-and-powerful-artwork. Accessed on 24 June 2021.

Pateman, C. (1998). *The Sexual Contract*. Stanford (CA): Stanford University Press.

Plummer, K. (2003). *Intimate Citizenship: Private Decisions and Public Dialogues*. Seattle: University of Washington Press.

Prabhu, M. (2020). 'A Spirit of Protest: How Indians Are Uniting in Punjab'. *Al Jazeera*, 19 March. https://www.aljazeera.com/indepth/features/spirit-protest-indians-uniting-punjab-200310053308585.html. Accessed on 24 June 2021.

Puniyani, R. (2020). 'Go to Pakistan and Demonising Indian Muslims'. NewsClick, 4 January. https://www.newsclick.in/go-pakistan-demonising-indian-muslims. Accessed on 24 June 2021.

Salam, Z. U., and U. Ausaf (2020). *Shaheen Bagh: From a Protest to a Movement*. New Delhi: Bloomsbury India.

Sarfaraz, K. (2020). 'Transgender, Queer Groups March against CAA, NRC'. *Hindustan Times*, 4 January. https://www.hindustantimes.com/cities/transgender-queer-groups-march-against-caa-nrc/story-MU5PFAPVbhdLIUT4Q2y2lO.html. Accessed on 24 June 2021.

Sasson-Levy, O., and T. Rapoport (2003). 'Body, Gender, and Knowledge in Protest Movements: The Israeli Case'. *Gender and Society* 17, no. 3: 379–403.

Shaheen Bagh Official (@Shaheenbaghoff1) (2020a). 'The Shaheen Bagh Protest May Have Ended, but Our Movement Lives On'. Twitter, 24 March, 5:55 p.m. https://twitter.com/Shaheenbaghoff1/status/1242434958523760643. Accessed on 24 June 2021.

———. (2020b). 'Collective Statement from All the Shaheen Baghs of the Country'. Twitter, 27 March, 8:33 p.m. https://twitter.com/Shaheenbaghoff1/status/1243561815528943621. Accessed on 24 June 2021.

Shankar, S. (2020). 'India's Citizenship Law, in Tandem with National Registry, Could Make BJP's Discriminatory Targeting of Muslims Easier'. *The Intercept*, 30 January. https://theintercept.com/2020/01/30/india-citizenship-act-caa-nrc-assam/. Accessed on 24 June 2021.

Singh, S. (2019). 'The Story of Faiz's Hum Dekhenge: From Pakistan to India, Over 40 Years'. *Indian Express*, 27 December. https://indianexpress.com/article/explained/the-story-of-faizs-hum-dekhenge-from-pakistan-to-india-over-40-years-caa-protest-6186565/. Accessed on 24 June 2021.

Stead, J. (2006). 'The Greenham Common Peace Camp and Its Legacy', *The Guardian*, 5 September. https://www.theguardian.com/uk/2006/sep/05/greenham5. Accessed on 24 June 2021.

The Quint (2019). '"Those Creating Violence Can Be Identified by Their Clothes": PM Narendra Modi on CAA Protests', 15 December. https://www.thequint.com/news/india/can-be-identified-by-their-clothes-pm-narendra-modi-on-caa-protesters. Accessed on 24 June 2021.

———. (2020a). 'Naam Shaheen Bagh Hai: An Ode to Protesters Who Sparked a Movement'. 24 February. https://www.thequint.com/news/india/naam-shaheen-bagh-hai-an-ode-to-protesters-who-sparked-a-movement. Accessed on 24 June 2021.

———. (2020b). 'Behind Shaheen Bagh's Women, An Army of Students, Doctors and Locals'. YouTube video, 14 January, 7:02. https://www.youtube.com/watch?v=ih_yQxpSIwA. Accessed on 24 June 2021.

———. (2020c). 'How Shaheen Bagh Inspired Women-led Protests across the Country'. 22 January. https://www.thequint.com/videos/news-videos/how-shaheen-bagh-inspired-women-led-protests-across-the-country. Accessed on 24 June 2021.

The Week (2020). 'Anti-CAA Protest: Gita, Bible and Quran Recited at Shaheen Bagh, in Novel Inter-Faith Meet'. 12 January. https://www.theweek.in/news/india/2020/01/12/anti-caa-protest-gita-bible-quran-recited-shaheen-bagh-in-novel-inter-faith-meet.html. Accessed on 24 June 2021.

The Wire (2020a). 'After a 101-Day Sit-In, Shaheen Bagh Protest Cleared Due to Coronavirus Lockdown'. 24 March. https://thewire.in/rights/shaheen-bagh-cleared-coronavirus-lockdown. Accessed on 24 June 2021.

———. (2020b). 'In Photos: Republic Day at Shaheen Bagh'. 27 January. https://thewire.in/rights/in-photos-republic-day-at-shaheen-bagh. Accessed on 24 June 2021.

Vatuk, S. (2008). 'Islamic Feminism in India: Indian Muslim Women Activists and the Reform of Muslim Personal Law'. *Modern Asian Studies* 42, no. 2–3: 489–518. DOI: https://doi.org/10.1017/S0026749X07003228.

Werbner, P. (1999). 'Political Motherhood and the Feminization of Citizenship.' In *Women, Citizenship and Difference*, edited by N. Yuval-Davis and P. Werbner, 221–245. London: Zed Books.

Woolf, V. (1938). *Three Guineas*. London: Hogarth Press.

Yulia, Z. (2010). 'Social Movements through the Gender Lens'. *Sociology Compass* 4, no. 8: 628–641.

Zamindar, V. (2007). *The Long Partition and the Making of Modern South Asia: Refugees, Boundaries, Histories*. New York: Columbia University Press.

Glossary

aachaaram	ritual, ceremony
Ab nari ke naron se inquilab ayega	Women's slogans will herald the uprising
adivasi	indigenous people, tribal
agresar	junior RSS leader
aravani	transgender women in Tamil Nadu
azaadi	freedom
baal gana	children's group
Bal Sanskar Kendra	Child Education Centre, a non-governmental organization which seeks to impart Hindu values to children
Balika Shikshan	Education for Girls, a programme aimed at girls' education by Vidya Bharati, the educational wing of the RSS
band kar	close down
baudhik	intellectual
baudhik pramukh	intellectual head
bedari	awareness
Beti bachao, beti padhao	Save the daughter, educate the daughter
bhagwa dhwaj	saffron flag
Bhai se bhai ladne na paaye;	Let no brother fight a brother;

phir se 47 [1947] banne na paaye	don't let 47 [1947] recur
bhaisahib	honorific term for a brother
bhakti	devotion to a deity in Hinduism
bharatiya	Indian
bharatiya sanskriti	Indian culture
Bharatiyata	Indian-ness
bi	marker of respect for a woman
bindi	decorative mark women wear on their foreheads
brahmacharya	stage of life entailing celibacy
burqa	loose garment covering head and face
charcha	discussion
chaupar	board game played in India
chhaap	indelible mark
chuniri	wide scarf
*churidar*s	tightly fitting trousers
dadi	grandmother
Dalit	broken or oppressed, the lowest caste, characterized as 'untouchable'
dand	stick
Dandyudh	game played by boys in RSS *shakha*s
darshan	sighting of a deity
dasi	female slave or servant; a female devotee
dharma	religion
dharna	peaceful demonstration
didi	older sister; a marker of respect for an older woman
dupatta	scarf
Durga	Mother Goddess

Durga Vahini	Army of Durga, the women's wing of the VHP
ehsaan	favour
ekatrikaran	unification
gana	group
garbhadaanam	Hindu ceremony performed before insemination and conception
gatanayak	group leader
gau rakshak dal	cow protection vigilante group
geet	song
ghar wapsi	return to the flock
goonda	thug
gopuram	monumental tower at the entrance of a temple, especially found in southern India
gowraksha	cow protection
Haa Da Naara Sangharsh Morcha	Rallying Cry for Justice Organization, a coalition of youth organizations in Punjab, India
halala	pure and ritually correct procedure; the remarriage of a divorced woman
hazaar	thousand
hijra	transgender woman
Hindu *dharm aur samaj ki raksha*	protection of Hindu religion and society
Hindu *swaraj*	Hindu self-rule
Hindutva	Hindu nationalism
istriwallah	a person who irons clothes
janeu	a sacred thread worn by upper Hindu males
janma-bhedam	difference-by-birth, a socio-economic order
jihad	struggle or fight in Islam

jogappa	transgender women who devote their lives to a deity
jogta	transgender women who devote their lives to a deity
joota	shoe
junoon	passion
jus sanguinis	right of blood; a principle of nationality law by which citizenship is determined or acquired by the nationality or ethnicity of one or both parents
jus soli	right of the soil; a principle of nationality law by which citizenship is acquired by birth within the territory of the state
kabaddi	a contact team sport
kar seva	voluntary labour; used by Sikhs and Hindus to describe people who engage in religious and philanthropic endeavours
kar sevak	male volunteer
kar sevika	female volunteer
kartavya	duty
karyalaya	office
karyavah	supervisor
Kashmir Hamara Hai	Kashmir Is Ours, a game played by boys in RSS *shakha*s
Kashmir Kiska Hai?	Who Does Kashmir Belong To?, a game played by boys in RSS *shakha*s
katha	saying; a story or tale
kinnar	transgender woman
kirtan	devotional singing session for women
kshatra-virya	masculine prowess
kurta	long, loose shirt

Glossary

laingikabandham	intimacy; sex
langar	community kitchen in Sikh temples which serves free meals to all visitors
lathi	bamboo cudgel
lauha purush	iron man
madrassa	school for Islamic education
mahamantri	chief secretary
Mahila Morcha	women's organization, the women's wing of the BJP
Mahila Vibhag	women's wing, the women's wing of the VHP
Mahilayen tatha svavlamban	Women and self-reliance
matrutva	motherhood
maulvi	Muslim religious scholar
Main Shivaji	I Am Shivaji, a game played by boys in RSS *shakha*s
milan kendra	centre for informal get-togethers
Meri behne mange azaadi	My sisters demand freedom
Hai haq hamara, azaadi	Freedom is our right
Hum leke rahenge, azaadi	We will claim freedom, come what may
mukhyashikshak	chief instructor of a *shakha*
Naam Shaheen Bagh *hai*	The name is Shaheen Bagh
*namajapa ghoshayatra*s	prayer processions
namaskar	an Indian greeting
napunsaka	impotent
nari shakti	women's power
Nayudh	game played by boys in RSS *shakha*s
netrutva	leadership
nishastra yudh	unarmed combat
padri	priest

pav bhaji	Maharashtrian snack
Pinjra Tod	Break the Cage, a campaign against restrictive curfews on women students
prabhat pheri	morning processions
pracharak	full-time male RSS preacher
pracharika	full-time female RSS preacher
pramukh	chief
pratigya	oath
proudh gana	group for older men
puja	worship
Rakhi Bandhan	ceremony where sisters tie a thread on their brothers' wrists
Ram *padukas*	Ram's slippers
Ram Janambhoomi	Ram's birthplace in Ayodhya
Ramrajya	the kingdom of Ram; imagined political utopia for Hindu nationalists
rashtra	nation
Rashtra Jagran Abhiyan	National Awakening Movement, a nation-wide campaign launched by the BJP against the United Progressive Alliance (UPA) government in 2007
Rashtra Sevika Samiti	National Women Volunteers or Women Worshippers of the Nation, the women's wing of the RSS
rashtra dharma	national virtue
rashtra hit	national cause
Rashtriya Swayamsevak Sangh	Indian Hindu Nationalist Organization
rath yatra	chariot procession
#ReadyToWait	campaign created by Malayali women on social media in 2016 to preserve the custom of prohibiting the entry of women

Glossary

	of menstruating ages at the Sabarimala shrine in Kerala
sadhvi	woman ascetic
salwar kameez	women's clothing; a set of long, loose tunic and pants
samiti	committee, society or association
samiti kshetra karyavahika	*samiti* district head
sangathan	organization
San santalis banne nahi denge	We won't let 1947 repeat itself
Sangathan mein shakti hai	Strength lies in the organization
Sangh Parivar	Sangh Family, the RSS family of Hindu nationalist organizations
sangh	union
sanskaar	rite of passage; correct conduct
sanskriti	culture
sanyasi	ascetic
saree	garment draped around the body by South Asian women
sarsangchalak	the head of the RSS
sati	the practice of burning widows on the funeral pyres of their husbands
satsang	religious congregation
satyagraha	non-violent resistance
savarna	upper-caste Hindu
seva (also spelled *sewa*)	community service
*seva basti*s	community service in slums
seva vibhag	RSS community service department
shakha	branch, a daily session for physical and ideological training held by the RSS
shakti	the female principle of divine energy

Shariat	Muslim Personal Law
sharirik	physical; bodily
shastra pujan	the worship of weapons and instruments used by Hindu goddess Durga
sheel	modesty
shishu gana	group for infants and children
Shiv Shakti	masculine (Shiva) and feminine (Shakti) divine power
Shourya Prashikshan Varg	Bravery Training Division, the Durga Vahini training camp for self-defence
siyasi	political
Stree Jagruti Manch	Women's Awareness Forum, an organization of women domestic workers in Punjab
subhashit	virtuous and moral sayings
suraksha	security
swadeshi	self-sufficiency; a movement of boycotting foreign goods and encouraging the use of domestic products
swayam	self
swayamsevak	RSS volunteer
tabdeeli	progress; change
tantri	Vedic head priest of Hindu temples
Tarana-e-Hindi	Anthem of the People of Hindustan; the formal name of 'Saare Jahan se Accha', a patriotic song dedicated to India by poet Muhammad Iqbal
tarun gana	group for teenagers and young men
tejaswi Hindu *rashtra*	glorious Hindu nation
thirunangai	transgender woman

triple *talaq*	instant divorce under a misapplication of Muslim law
tritiya prakriti	third gender
vada pav	Maharashtrian snack
vidyarthi vistarak	student supervisor
veranlassen	to induce or provoke
Vijaya Dashmi	major Hindu festival, also known as Dussehra
vollziehn	to accomplish; to realize
vratam	ritual; vow
waqf	charity
yuwati	young woman

About the Contributors

Amrita Basu is the Domenic J. Paino 1955 Professor of Political Science and Sexuality, Women's and Gender Studies at Amherst College, Massachusetts, USA. Her scholarship explores women's activism, feminist movements and religious nationalism in South Asia. Her most recent monograph is *Violent Conjunctures in Democratic India* (2015). She is also the author of *Two Faces of Protest: Contrasting Modes of Women's Activism in India* (1992) and an editor or co-editor of seven books, including *Appropriating Gender: Women's Activism and Politicized Religion in South Asia* (1998).

Arpita Chakraborty is the Principal Investigator of a project on sexual violence at the Dublin City University, Ireland, funded by the Irish Research Council. Her writings have been published in the *Economic and Political Weekly*, the *International Feminist Journal of Politics*, the *Raidió Teilifís Éireann* and the *Indian Express*, among others. You may contact her at arpita.chakraborty3@mail.dcu.ie.

J. Devika is a feminist researcher, historian, translator and teacher at the Centre for Development Studies, Kerala, India. She has contributed to the understanding of the intertwined histories of gender, politics, culture and development in modern Kerala. She has also translated literature from Malayalam to English, and social science from English to Malayalam. She offers social commentary on the blog Kafila (www.kafila.online) and maintains the website Swatantryavaadini (www.swatantryavaadini.in).

About the Contributors

Namrata Ravichandra Ganneri teaches History at SNDT College of Arts & SCB College of Commerce and Science for Women, Mumbai, India. She is currently working on a monograph on post-independent India's smallpox eradication programme, which is an outcome of her Commonwealth Rutherford Fellowship (2018–2020) at the University of York, UK.

Manjari Katju is a professor of Political Science at the University of Hyderabad, India, where she teaches courses on Indian and Comparative Politics. She has researched and written on various facets of Hindu nationalism as well as state institutions in India. She has authored the books *Vishva Hindu Parishad and Indian Politics* (2003) and *Hinduising Democracy: The Vishva Hindu Parishad in Contemporary India* (2017). Her research writings can also be found in journals like the *Economic and Political Weekly*, *Studies in Indian Politics* and *Contemporary South Asia*.

Amna Pathan is a master's student at the University of Heidelberg, Germany, studying South Asian Politics and Anthropology. She received her BA in Political Science from Amherst College, Massachusetts, USA, in 2020, where she worked as a student researcher.

Anshu Saluja has recently completed PhD from the Centre for Historical Studies, Jawaharlal Nehru University, New Delhi, India. Her work maps competing histories of intercommunity engagement in South Asia, encompassing shared bonds, fraught divides and constrictive hostilities. It highlights everyday routinized forms of coexistence and patterns of mutual engagement by different communities, while also taking account of oppressive moments of violent conflict and confrontation.

Tanika Sarkar held the chair of Modern History at the Centre for Historical Studies, Jawaharlal Nehru University, Delhi, India, before she retired. She has written several monographs on political and cultural nationalism in colonial India. She has also authored, co-authored and co-edited a number of works on contemporary Hindu nationalism in India, including *Women and the Hindu Right* (1995) which she co-edited with Urvashi Butalia. Her recent publications include *Rebels, Wives, Saints: Designing Selves and*

Nations in Colonial Times (2009) and *Hindu Nationalism in India* (2021). Her forthcoming volume for the 'New Cambridge History of Modern India' series is titled *Gender in the Colony and Post Colony: India, Pakistan, Bangladesh*.

Aastha Tyagi is a doctoral student at the University of Göttingen, Germany. She has degrees in English Literature, Media and Culture Studies, and Sociology from the University of Delhi, India, and the Tata Institute of Social Sciences, Mumbai, India. Her research interests are the contemporary Hindu nationalist movement, gender, youth cultures, right-wing movements and student politics.

Jennifer Ung Loh is an independent researcher. They completed their doctoral research and MA from SOAS University of London, UK, and BA from the University of Oxford, UK. They have taught at SOAS University of London and De Monfort University, Leicester, UK. They are one of the organizers of the platform 'Queer' Asia, an editorial member of *Feminist Review* and a practising potter.

Lalit Vachani is a filmmaker. His films include *The Boy in the Branch* and *The Men in the Tree* (on the RSS and Hindu nationalism in India), *In Search of Gandhi* and *The Salt Stories* (following Gandhi's salt march in Narendra Modi's Gujarat, India) and *An Ordinary Election* (an in-depth study of an Indian election campaign). He teaches courses on documentary film, media and politics at the Centre for Modern Indian Studies, University of Göttingen, Germany.

Rina Verma Williams is Associate Professor of Political Science and Affiliate Faculty in Asian Studies and Women's, Gender and Sexuality Studies at the University of Cincinnati, USA. She earned her PhD from Harvard University, USA, and BA and BS from the University of California, Irvine, USA. Her research and teaching interests include comparative Indian and South Asian politics; religion, law and nationalism; and gender and identity politics with a focus on the state and democracy. Her current book (forthcoming) traces women's participation in Hindu nationalist politics over time.

Index

aachaaram, 16
 #ReadyToWait women and the defence of, 273–277
 in twentieth-century Malayali society, 269–272
Aawaaz-e-Niswaan, 316
Abducted Persons (Recovery and Restoration) Act (1949), 312–313
abductions of women, 35
Abhyankar, C. P., 37
'Ab nari ke naron se inquilab ayega', 322
Abrahamic religions, 17
Adityanath, Yogi, 15, 205
 Hindu Yuva Vahini, 208
*adivasi*s, 3, 105, 119n52, 225, 233, 323
Advani, L. K., 91
 rath yatra, 79
Agamben, Giorgio, 303
 destituent power, 311
Agarwal, Purushottam, 92, 97
Agnes, Flavia, 154
Akhand Bharat (Undivided India), 204
Akhila Bharatha Ayappa Seva Sangham, 288n1
Akhil Bharat Hindu Mahasabha (ABHM), 27
Akhil Bharatiya Itihaas Sankalan Yojana (ABISY), 135

Akhil Bharatiya Sant Samiti, 224
Akhil Bharatiya Vidyarthi Parishad (ABVP), 117n38
Akhlaq, Mohammad, 208
All India Dalit Women's Conference, 32
All India Hindu Grand-Assembly, 27
All India Hindu Mahasabha (AIHM), 28–30, 31, 33
All India Hindu Mahasabha Papers (AIHMP), 43n11
All India Hindu Mahila Mahasabha, 30–35, 34
All India Hindu Women's Conference, 31, 33
All-India Muslim Women's Personal Law Board, 316
All India Progressive Women's Association, 314
All India Women's Conference (AIWC), 4, 32, 44n13, 45n19
All Manipur Nubi Manbi Association, 244
'All Powerful Hindu Religion,' 90
Alter, Joseph, 199
Ambedkar, B. R., 31
 in Indian Constitution, 306
 Jayanti celebrations, 178, 189n15

in movements with Dalit women and
anti-caste feminists, 4
in Shaheen Bagh protest, 305
in threat to convert out of Hinduism, 31
Amrit Bindu, 37, 45*n*30
Amrithanandamayi, Mata, 272
Anagol, Padma, 42, 44*n*12
androgyny, 15, 199
Antarrashtriya Hindu Parishad, 288*n*1
anti-Romeo squads, 207
anti-Sikh riots (1984), 128
Apte, Saraswati, 41
Apte, Vinayakrao, 41
Arendt, Hannah, 307
Article 370, of Indian Constitution, 66
abrogation of, 134
Arun, Shoba, 286
Arya Samaj, 44*n*15, 118*n*46, 216*n*14
ascetic masculinity, 15
communalized anxiety, 196
in Indian politics, 209
integral characteristics of, 209
and violence in post-2014 Indian politics, 204–212
in the works of Vivekananda, 195
*asthi kalash yatra*s, 116*n*34
Ayodhya
anti-Muslim violence in, 309
Babri Mosque, destruction of, 53, 58, 111*n*4
judgment of November 2019, 209
Ayub, Farida, 305–306, 318, 322
Ayyappan, Lord, 16
Aziz, Aamir, 304

Baal Bodh Kathayen (1992, 2008), 90
*baal swayamsevak*s, 90
Babri Mosque
demolition of (6 December 1992), 53, 58, 111*n*4
October 1990 assault on, 91
verdict, 206
Bacchetta, Paola, 59, 266

Bajaj, Jamnalal, 37
Bajaj, Jankidevi, 37
Bajrang Dal, 107, 118*n*44, 150, 155, 157, 159, 207
Balika Shikshan (Education for Girls), 138
Balilla organizations, 82
bal sanskar kendra, 158
Banerjee, Sikata, 41
Banu, Grace, 233
Basu, Amrita, 9, 17, 59
communalism, 67
*sadhvi*s of Sangh Parivar, 34
Basu, Manisha, 53
Begum, Hamida, 41
Bengalee, The (newspaper), 44*n*15
Berlant, Lauren, 268
'Beti Bachao, Beti Padhao' campaign, 319
bhagini mandal, 38
Bhagwat, Mohan, 79–80, 83, 84, 86
Akhil Bharatiya Sharirik Pramukh, 113*n*15
speech on 26 April 2020, 210
Bharati, Uma, 8, 58
Bharati, Vidya, 127
Bharatiya Jana Sangh (BJS), 56
foundation in 1951, 35
Bharatiya Janata Party (BJP), 1
in the 1990s, 56–61
case of *sati*, 58
dominated coalition in 2004, 11
founding of, 56
leaders in 2010s, 62
led National Democratic Alliance (NDA) government, 12
Mahila Morcha, 11, 69*n*14, 108, 288*n*1
policy goals, 66
women in the 2010s, 61–65
Bharatiya Janata Yuva Morcha, 288*n*1
Bharat Mata, 85, 95, 213
Bhatt, Chetan, 39
Bhima–Koregaon arrests (2019), 117*n*38
Bhonsala Military School, 40
Bhonsle, Jijabai, 131

Index

Bhonsle, Shivaji, 131
Bhopal riots (1992), 169
Bhopatkar, L. B., 33, 43*n*10
Bhopatkar, Sundaratai, 30
Bodas, Veena, 40
Bombay Hindu Mahasabha, 43n5
boudhik (intellectual training), 89–92
Boy in the Branch, The (1993), 77, 82, 85, 104, 113*n*13
brahmacharya, 197–200
Brahmanical Hindutva ideology, 209
Bunch of Thoughts (1966), 137

'Call to Motherhood', 5, 6
caste, in Hindu nation, 135–137
celibacy, 199
 in married relationships, 199–200
 swayamsevak, 200–204
celibate and the mother, tension between, 196–200
Chakraborty, Arpita, 14
 with Vivekananda and Golwalkar, 203
Chakraborty, Chandrima, 23*n*8
Chakravati, Uma, 287
Channel 4 radio programme, 78
Chatterjee, Partha, 323
'Chhatrapati' Shivaji, 131
Chipko movement, against deforestation, 321
Cholkar, M. R., 37
'Christianity in danger' slogan, 285
citizenship, 9, 17, 21, 28, 203, 246, 279, 286, 301–316, 318, 321, 323
Citizenship Act, 206
Citizenship Amendment Act (CAA, 2019), 17, 247*n*6, 302
 Modi-led BJP government, 302
 Patel's vision of India, 304
civil marriages, 20
communal holocaust (1946–1947), 14
communal riots, in January 2020, 128
 campaigns for, 12

Communist Party of India (CPM), 4, 265
constituent power, 303, 311, 326
Constitutional Rights, 232, 305, 306
 and broad-based citizenship, 305–307
cultural vigilantism, 159–161

Dalit, 4, 7, 31–32, 45*n*23, 189*n*14, 226, 244, 253, 267, 284, 305, 314
Dalit Mahila Federation, 32
Dandyudh (game played by boys in RSS *shakha*s), 86, 88, 95, 108
darshan, 16
Date, S. R., 30
Datta, P. K., 29
Datta, Pradip, 40
 on Women's Protection League formation, 40
Deepjyotirnamohstute, 37, 46n40
Deoras, Balasaheb, 103
Deshseva Nibandhmala, 42
Devika, J., 9, 16
Devkule, Bakul, 40
 attended political meetings, 41
Devkule, Bakultai, 47*n*46
dharma, 155, 177, 200, 202, 224, 273
dharna, 18
'Dilli Humari Hai' (Delhi Is Ours), 113*n*18
District Screening Committee, 237, 251*n*26, 252*n*34
Dongre, Sulochanabai, 32
Doordarshan, 205
Dravid, Appaji, 37
Dravid, Laxmibai, 42
Durga Vahini (Army of Durga), 13, 14, 127, 149
 in the 2010s, 155–156
 and the BJP government, 161–162
 cultural vigilantism, 159–161
 pamphlet circulating in 1997, 154
 street warriors and activists, 156–159
 lathi play, 157
 uniform of, 157

Facebook
 campaign against 'love jihad,' 208
Fadnavis, Devendra, 105
Fatima Sheikh-Savitribai Phule Library, 310
female 'chastity,' 36
Film and Television Institute of India (FTII), 102
Foucault, Michel, 310
frenemies with feminism, 280–284

Gandhi, Indira, 8
Gandhi, Mahatma, 92
 definition of *brahmachari*, 197–198
 lecture on Sita, 36
 shooting an effigy of, 27
Gandhi, Sonia, 8
Ganneri, Namrata Ravichandra, 10
 on Hindutva women's militarism, 10
Gau Raksha committees, 197
*gau-rakshak dal*s (cow-protection vigilante groups), 208
gay marriage, 12, 240
Gedalof, Irene, 303
Gehlot, Thawar Chand, 232
gendered Hindutva, making of, 135, 137–138
 Hindu nation, 135–137
gendered modalities of protest
 feminization of politics, 319–321
 motherhood, 317–319
 women's occupation of public space, 321–323
Gender Justice Murder Day, 251*n*27
George, Anjali, 284
Ghai, Dhawal, 83
ghar wapsi, 149, 163*n*1, 183
Godse, Gopal, 43*n*10
Godse, Nathuram, 23*n*9, 43*n*10, 195
Godse, Sindhu Gopal, 30
Golwalkar, M. S., 5, 29, 82, 137
 on children's education, 7
 imprisonment in Gandhi's murder case, 206
 on Sangh values, 7
 on 'Swadeshi' beliefs, 6
Gore, Sumatibai, 33
Government of India (GOI) Act (1935), 32
Goyal, D. R., 92, 97
Greenham Common Women's Peace Camp, 321
Gudi Padwa, 173, 189*n*10
Gujarat carnage (2002), 210
Gupta, Charu, 43*n*6

Haa Da Naara Sangharsh Morcha, 323
halala, 158, 164*n*8
'Har shehar Shaheen Bagh' slogan, 327
Hedgewar, Keshav Baliram, 29, 36
hegemonic masculinity, 196, 209–213
hijra/transgender, 12, 234
 defined, 236–237
 NALSA judgment and restrictive meanings, 234–235
Hilsum, Lindsey, 78
Hindu Aikya Vedi, 288*n*1
'Hindu in peril,' 286
'Hindu ki jeet, Hindu ki jeet!' slogan, 85
Hindu Mahasabha, 23*n*9
 founding of, 29
Hindu Mahila Sabha, 30, 43*n*11
Hindu–Muslim relations, 56
Hindu nation, dissonance and engagement with stories, 139–142
Hindu numbers, fear of declining, 31
Hindu Rashtra, 3, 29, 127, 130, 186, 187*n*1, 204, 240
Hindus: A Dying Race (1909), 44*n*15
Hindu Sangathan: Saviour of the Dying Race (1926), 44*n*15
Hindu *swaraj* (self-rule), 84
Hindu Swayamsevak Sangh (HSS), 99, 113*n*18, 119*n*53

Index

Hindutva and history
   fictionalizing history, 134–135
   threat of the non-Hindu, 128–134
Hindutva, women's involvement and militancy within, 169
   activist K. D., 170–171
   activist R. S., 170–171
   communication networks, 171–174
   campaign of 'Love Jihad,' 182–185
   caste question, 177–179
   centrality of violence, 176–177
   Hindutva: Who Is a Hindu? (1923), 28
   limits of agency, 179–182
   misplaced rage, mistaken target, 174–176
   role of women in, 58
Hindu Women's Conference, 31, 38
Hindu Women's Organization, 32
Hindu Yuva Vahini, 207–208
Hirlekar, Yamunabai, 38
Hirschberger, Gilad, 307
homonationalism (queer Hindu nationalism), 13, 228, 248*n*9
Hosabole, Dattatreya, 12, 240
'Hum Dekhenge' (Faiz Ahmad Faiz's poem), 320
'Hum Hinduon ke liye bhi to koi hona mangta hai,' 40

'inclusion-moderation' thesis, 65
Indian Council of Historical Research (ICHR), 135
Indian Medical Service (IMS), 44*n*15
Indian Penal Code (*Mohd. Ahmed Khan v. Shah Bano Begum*, AIR 1985 SC 945), 57
indigenous feminist movement, 281
Indo-Aryan race, 44*n*15
instant divorce (triple *talaq*), 67
institutionalisation of homosexuality, 240
internally displaced people, 308
International Women's Day, 280

intimate digital public, 17
'iron man' image, 15, 203, 212

Jaffrelot, Christophe, 46*n*35, 84
Jagirdar, Sammera, 233
Jamaat-e-Islami, 41
Jamia Millia Islamia University, 302
Jammu and Kashmir Study Centre (JKSC), 134
janma-bhedam order, 269, 287
Jaripatkanagar *shakha*, 80, 82–85, 95, 114*n*25
Jinnah, Muhammad Ali, 131
Jodhani, Rajesh, 82
Joshi, Jankibai, 30, 32, 33, 34, 43*n*11
   All India Hindu Mahasabha, 33
   All India Hindu Women's Conference, 31
   contested 1946 elections, 33
   letter to Dr. Khare, 45*n*24
   of Mahila Mahasabha, 10
   on women's self-defence training, 10
jus sanguinis (right of blood), 304
jus soli (birth within a territory), 304

Kaalapani Prison (Andamans), 90
Kafur, Malik, 91
Kale, Anasuyabai, 38
*kar sevak*s, 66, 91, 104, 106, 111*n*4,
*kar sevika*s, 151
'Kashmir Hamara Hai' (Kashmir Is Ours), 84, 85
Kashmiri Hindu Genocide Day (19 January 2020), 328
Katju, Manjari, 13
'Kattar Hindu Ekta,' 119*n*47
Kelkar, Girijabai, 31, 44*n*12
Kelkar, Lakshmibai, 5, 126, 138
   founder of Rashtra Sevika Samiti, 10, 35
   married to Brahmin *malguzar* in Wardha, 35
   meeting with K. B. Hedgewar, 36

visit to Gandhi's *ashram* in Wardha, 35
on women self-defence, 10
Kelkar, Yashwant, 38
'Kerala Model,' 266
Kesari, 37
Khare, Baburao, 38
Khare, N. B., 34, 37
Khurai, Santa, 244
#KidsForSabarimala, 273
Kinnar Akhada, 12
demand for construction of Ram temple, 224
kinnar battalion, 243
Kumar, Radha, 45*n*22

Left Democratic Front government, 286
lesbian, gay, bisexual (LGB), 13
LGBT+ groups, 225
LGBTQ+ rights, 229
Liberhan Commission, 111
Lodh community, 79
Lok Sabha, 67, 240, 251*n*25
BJP-led national government, 161
elections in 2019, 170
Lok Sabha Bill (2016), 236
Transgender Persons (Protection of Rights) Act (2019), 232
on transgender self-determination, 12
love jihad, 13, 19, 20
in 2009, 118*n*44
campaign, 182–185
incidents of, 99–100

Mahajan, Susheela, 37, 46*n*40
biography, 37
Maharaj, Sakshi, 205
Maharashtra Hindu Sabha, 30
Maharashtra Provincial Hindu Mahasabha Papers, 43*n*11
Maharashtra Vidyalaya, 38
Maharashtrian Chitpavin Brahmin community, 108
Maharashtriya Mandal of Poona, 48*n*47

Mahasabha Constitution, 33
Mahila Mahasabha conference, 10, 32
political fortunes, 35
mahila mandal (women's association), 45*n*23
Mahila Morcha (MM), 11, 69*n*14, 288*n*1
Mahila Sabhas, 33
Mahila Vibhag (Women's Wing), 13, 149, 150
Mahilayen Tatha Svavlamban (1932), 38
Mahishikal (daughters of Mahishi), 284
'Main Shivaji' game, 83–84
Malaviya, Madan Mohan, 31
Malayali Hinduism, 17, 274, 277, 280
'masculine Hinduism,' 29, 249*n*13
Masurkar Ashram, 47*n*47
Masurkar, Vinayak, 47*n*47
Meghwanshi, Bhanwar, 7
Men in Dark Times (1968), 144
Men in the Tree, The (2002), 77, 84, 95, 97, 119*n*53
#MeToo campaign, 316
*milan kendra*s, 14, 172
establishing of, 172
Ministry of Social Justice and Empowerment (MSJE), 229, 249*n*15
Modi, Narendra, 111*n*4, 112*n*5, 114*n*20, 197, 205, 301
in 2019 election, 22*n*4
as *brahmachari*, *lauha purush* (iron man), 203
cabinet in 2014, 62
charisma of, 3
election campaigns of 2014 and 2019, 97
as 'modern, development hero,' 212
Modi magic, 3
as most followed politician on Twitter, 211
revoked Article 370, 113*n*19
RSS–BJP under, 77
as RSS *pracharak*, 15
silence on Golwalkar, 206

Montague–Chelmsford Reforms (1919), 32
Mookerjee, S. P., 34
Mudraboyina, Rachana, 232
Mukherji, U. N., 44*n*15
mukhya shikshak, of Jaripatkanagar *shakha*, 84
Muslim camps, 308
Muslim disloyalty, narratives of, 311
Muslim homes, right to occupy, 309
Muslim law in India, validity of, 67
Muslim League, 32
Muslim Personal Law (Shariat) Application Act, 315
Muslim women, 2, 3, 9, 17, 18, 21, 57, 99, 100, 101, 158, 183, 184, 185, 305–307, 312–318, 320
　in anti-CAA struggle, 302
　anti-Muslim violence force, 315
　citizenship rights, 304
　protests in Delhi against discriminatory Citizenship Law, 9
　and Shariat law, 315
　sub-committee in 1938, 32
Muslim Women (Protection of Rights on Divorce) Act (1986), 315
Muslim Women (Protection of Rights on Marriage) Bill, 101

'Naam Shaheen Bagh Hai' poem, 320
Nagel, Joane, 42
Nagpur Congress, 38
Nair Service Society (NSS), 265, 285
National Legal Services Authority (NALSA)/NALSA judgment, 12, 23*n*10, 225–227, 229, 231–240, 245, 246, 247*n*5, 249*n*15, 249*n*16, 249*n*17, 251*n*26, 252*n*28, 252*n*34, 253*n*36, 254*n*39, 245*n*44
　National Legal Services Authority (NALSA) v. Union of India and Others (2014), 12, 225
*namajapa ghoshayatra*s, 278

'Nari shakti ka apman band karo' slogan, 160
National Federation of Indian Women, 4
National Population Register (NPR), 17, 302, 313, 314, 322, 323
National Register of Citizens (NRC), 247*n*6, 302–304, 306, 309, 310, 313, 322, 323, 328
Nawaz, Begum Shah, 32
Nehru, Jawaharlal, 92
neo-*savarna* (upper caste), 16, 265, 267, 268, 271–274, 277, 280, 285–288, 290*n*8,
　social formation, 267
New Education Policy (2019), 141
new female mission, 13
'new woman' mission, 13
nishastra yudh (unarmed combat), 86
'no criminalisation, no glorification' approach, towards gay marriage, 12, 240
non-Hindu faiths, 210
Nuremberg Laws (1935), 21
　Protection of German Blood and Honour, 21

Officers' Training Camps (OTC), 106
Other Backward Classes (OBC), 128, 272

pagan diversity, 275–276
Paik, Shailaja, 45*n*23
'Pakistan' movement, 32
Pandey, Gorakh, 144
Pandey, Pooja Shakun, 27
Parliamentary Standing Committee, 232, 251*n*25
partition of India (1947), 2
　legacy of, 307–312
　violence during, 97, 308
　women's experiences of, 312–314
Patel, Sardar Vallabhbhai, 304
Pathan, Amna, 9, 17

Pathey, Shilpa, 108
Peto, Andrea, 27
Pillai, C. V. Raman, 270
Pillai, Padma
    accusation of, 284
    statement on BJP, 284
Pinjra Tod (Break the Cage) campaign, 316
pinkwashing, 13
Plummer, Kenneth, 325
polygamy, among Indian Muslims, 5, 185
*prabhat pheri*s (morning processions), 162
pracharak, 15, 86, 104, 106, 114*n*22, 188, 196, 205–206, 216*n*12
*pracharika*s, 8, 188*n*8
Prachi, Sadhvi, 157
    boycott of Bollywood, 161
Prakash, Indra, 43*n*9
pramukh sanghchalika, 41
Prayagraj Kumbh Mela, 242
Purushance Band (Men's Rebellion), 44*n*12

queer communities, 12, 225

Ramakrishna Missions, 15, 214*n*1, 215*n*2, 216*n*14
Ramaswamy Naicker, E. V., 4
Ram Janmabhoomi movement, 47*n*55, 78, 108, 111*n*4
Ram temple, in Ayodhya, 12, 67
    construction of, 66
Rao, Pursushottam, 46*n*42
Rappoport, Tamar, 321
Rashtra Jagran Abhiyan (National Awakening Movement), 97
Rashtra Sevika Samiti, 5, 126–127
    in 1936, 30
    founding of, 35–39
Rashtriya Swayamsevak Sangh (RSS), 3, 29, 149
    and All India Hindu Mahasabha, 28–30
    baal gana, 80

bauddhik pramukh of, 204
boudhik (intellectual training), 89–92
campaigns for *ghar wapsi*, 'love jihad' and 'cow protection', 149
camp in 2013, 130
charcha session in the Delhi camp in 2017, 141
created in pre-Independence days, 214*n*2
daily routine, 81
relief distribution during Covid-19, 210
establishment of, 79
filming in 1992, 77
founded in 1925, 22*n*3, 96
Friends of RSS, 117*n*38
gatanayak (group leader), 94
home and the world
    family, 107–109
    incipient yearnings and social control, 101–104
    professional networks, 104–107
in 1992, 77
led Sangh Parivar, 149
mukhya shikshak of, 85
'non-political', 29
number of *shakha*s in, 201
on physical training for Hindu men, 10
proudh gana, 80
and Rashtra Sevika Samiti, 126
secrets of, 86
seva vibhag of, 204
*shakha*s, 5, 9, 79–81, 93
    adaptation, 98–99
    dissemination and mobilization, 96–98
    expansion, 95–96
    internal threats and external enemies, 99–101
    retention, 94–95
sharirik (physical training), 81–89
shishu gana, 80
tarun gana, 80
women's wing of, 28–30, 126

Index

rath yatra (chariot procession), 79, 91, 111*n*4, 116*n*34
Raut, Vilas, 88
#ReadyToWait (RTW), 16
    and female individuation, 280–284
    Sabarimala conflict and, 281
    women and the defence of *aachaaram*, 273–277
    women extolled Hindu pluralism, 17
    women's agency and, 277–280
Reception Committees of Ahmedabad, 32
refugees, rehabilitating of, 308
refusal, politics of, 310–311
Reich Citizenship Law, 21
relationship between citizenship, community and civil society, 323–326
Religious nationalism, 21, 42, 266, 326, 327, 329
religious personal laws, elimination of, 67
'rescue homes', founding of, 43*n*5
Rights of Transgender Persons Bill, 2014, 232, 250*n*23
Right wing populism, 326, 327, 329
right-wing women's mobilization, 27–28
    All India Hindu Mahasabha, 28–30
    All India Hindu Mahila Mahasabha, 30–35
    Rashtra Sevika Samiti founding of, 35–39
    Rashtriya Swayamsevak Sangh and their women's fronts, 28–30
    self-protection, promise of, 39–41
    *shakha*s, physical training in, 39–41
Rithambara, Saddhvi, 8, 58, 154

Sabarimala temple
    Dalit women who tried to enter, 284
    pilgrimage controversies, 16
    Supreme Court judgment on, 16
sadachar (moral education), 138

*sadhvi*s, 8, 34, 150–152, 161
saffronizing trans, 238
    selective histories, 238–239
    trans for the 'nation', 239–242
Sahasrabudhe, Umabai, 32
Sakaal, 38
Saluja, Anshu, 19
    case studies of VHP women, 13
    intercommunity relationships with hatred, 14
'Samiti ka Janam Vritant', 45*n*30, 46*n*30
Sampoorna Working Group, 233
'Sangathan Mein Shakti Hai' (The Organization Has Strength), 85
'Bharat Mata ki jai' (Victory to Mother India), 85
Sangh Parivar, 27
'San santalis banne nahi denge' (We won't let 1947 repeat itself), 310
*sanskaar/sanskara*s, 7, 13, 82–83, 94, 108, 127, 150–151, 153, 162, 187
sanskarsheel women, 151–153
sanyasi, 201
Saraswati, Swami Dayanand, 40
Sargacchi Ashram, 215*n*2
Sarkar, Tanika, 43*n*6
    physical training regime of *shakha*, 40
Sasson-Levy, Orna, 321
*satsang*s (religious congregations), 162
satyagraha, 37
Savarkar, Vinayak Damodar, 3, 28, 33, 90
    and AIHM, 29
    at Kaalapani Prison, 90–91
    mastermind of Rashtriya Swayamsevak Sangh, 3
savarna, 270–272, 277, 287
Sawant, Gauri, 245
Scindia, Vijaya Raje, 58–59
self-protection, promise of, 39–41
Semmalar, Gee Imaan, 231, 233
Sengupta, Shuddhabratha, 119*n*48

Servants of India Society, 37
*seva basti*s, 158
Sewa Bharati, 145*n*3
sex reassignment surgery (SRS), 253*n*36
sexual and moral codes, 184
Shah, Amit, 62
Shah Bano controversy (1984–1986), 57, 58, 67, 315
Shaheen Bagh
 on 14th December 2019, 18, 301
 anti-CAA protests, 317
 broad-based citizenship, 305
 'children's corner' at, 324
 and Constitution, 304
 dadis, 320
 farmers from Punjab to, 310
 Fatima Sheikh-Savitribai Phule Library at, 310
 Jamia students in, 325
 'Kashmiri Hindu Genocide Day', 328
 mothers in, 317
 population of, 309
 protesters, 303
 protest movement in, 17
 protests against the CAA, 306
 Republic Day celebration at, 320
 sit-in by local Muslim women, young and old, 18
 strengths of, 305
 women's demands for citizenship, 313
*shakha*s, physical training in, 39–41
Shankar, Sri Sri Ravi, 205
Shariat Protection Committee, 69*n*7
sharirik (physical training), 81–89
shastra pujan (weapon worship) ceremonies, 176
Shayara Bano v. Union of India, 67
shishu (infant) category, 83
Shourie, Arun, 96, 116*n*35
Shourya Prashikshan Varg (Groups for Training in Bravery), 157
Shraddhanand Anath Mahila Ashram, 43*n*5

Shraddhanand, Swami, 44*n*15
Shriram Janma Mukti Andolan, 155
Singh, Bhagat, 130
Singh, Kalyan, 79
Singh, Rajnath, 62, 240
social-media-savvy operation, 62
social opprobrium, 21
somatic conceptualization, of sexuality, 199
Soviet Bloc, 28
spermatic economy, 201, 203
Striyancha Swaraga (Women's Paradise), 44*n*12
Sudarshan, K. S., 83, 88, 114*n*23
sudras, 16, 259, 270–271, 285
Sunandan, K. N., 269, 289*n*7
Supreme Court (SC)
 judgment on *NALSA v Union of India*, 232
 limit NALSA beneficiaries, 232
 on prohibition of women of menstruating ages in Sabarimala temple, 265
swadeshi, 6, 31, 205
swayamsevak, 37, 80–81, 83, 90, 95, 99, 103–104, 108, 115

Tarana-e-Hindi (Anthem of the People of Hindustan), 325
tejaswi Hindu *rashtra* (glorious Hindu nation), 127
Telangana Hijra Intersex Transgender Samiti, 232–233
Telecomnagar *shakha*, 80, 96, 98, 104
Thakur, Pragya Singh, 170
Thiranagama, Sharika, 272
third gender, 230–235, 249*n*17, 253*n*36
Thomas, Sonja, 285
Tilak, Bal Gangadhar, 37
tit-for-tat strategy, 96
Transgender Day of Remembrance, 232
Transgender Persons (Protection of Rights) Act, 232, 251*n*24, 326

transgenders
  guise of belonging, 242–245
  state definitions of, 230
    in state policy, 230–231
    through the state, 231–234
trans-groups, 12
trans rights, support for, 225, 227–229, 232, 240, 243
Tripathi, Laxmi Narayan, 224, 242–244, 249n17
triple *talaaq*, 5, 316
  adoption of Hinduism for protection against, 158
  as criminal offence, 67
  in Muslim law, 67
  passing of bill on, 101
  practice of, 67, 164n8
  Shah Bano case, 67

Ung Loh, Jennifer, 12
UN Human Rights Council, 240
uniform civil code, 55, 56
  establishment of, 56, 67
  progressive advocacy groups on, 57
'Unity against Left', 117n38
upper-caste Hindu woman, duty of, 135
Uttar Pradesh Prohibition of Unlawful Conversion of Religion Ordinance (2020), 20

Vachani, Lalit, 9
  in Asha Sadan *karyalaya*, 101–102
  on RSS family, 107–109
  RSS revisit in 2016, 85
  on women's roles in RSS family, 9–10
Vajpayee, Atal Bihari
  as *brahmachari*s, 205
  NDA coalition government, 77
Valiani, Arafat, 88
Valmiki Jayanti, 178, 189n14
Vanvasi Kalyan Ashram (VKA), 107
Vidarbha women's conference, 38
Vidya Bharati, 127, 134, 138

Vidya, Living Smile, 244, 252n33
vigilantism, 13
violence
  centrality of, 176–177
  communal violence, 183
virile masculinity, 197, 203, 211
Vishnu temple, of Guruvayur, 285
Vishva Hindu Parishad (VHP), 8, 22n5, 68n1, 111n4, 127, 149, 155, 157, 158, 162, 170, 187n3, 288n1
  Durga Vahini, 155–156
    and the BJP government, 161–162
    cultural vigilantism, 159–161
    street warriors and activists, 156–159
  founded in 1964, 149
  launches women organizations, 150–151
  Muslim 'other', 153–155
  sanskarsheel women, 151–153
  temple construction project, in Nagpur, 105
Vivekananda, Swami, 15
  on ascetic masculinity, 207
  birth of, 214n1
  on BJP, 207
  founding of Ramakrishna Mission, 214n1

WhatsApp
  anti-Muslim violence by Hindutva groups, 116n38
  campaign against 'love jihad', 118n47, 119, 208
  Friends of RSS, 117
  shakha as a closed group on, 98
  Unity against Left, 117
Williams, Rina Verma, 11, 34
  on BJP women's roles, 11, 52, 53, 61
  interviewed K. R. Malkani, 56
  interviewed Sikander Bakht, 56
women. *See also* Muslim women
  agency and RTW campaign, 277–280
  and BJP (1990s to 2010s), 52–56
  exclusion from citizenship, 314–316

experiences of partition displacement and early citizenship, 312–314
of Hindu nationalist movement, 126–127
in Hindutva politics, 8
Women of Ku Klux Klan (WKKK), 188*n*8

Women's Protection League, 40
World Parliament of Religions, 214*n*1

Young Indian Lawyers' Association, 288*n*2

Zamindar, Vazira Fazila-Yacoobali, 308